D1234265

THE BOOK THAT CHANGED EUROPE

THE BOOK
THAT
CHANGED
EUROPE

PICART & BERNARD'S

Religious Ceremonies of the World

LYNN HUNT

MARGARET C. JACOB

WIJNAND MIJNHARDT

THE BELKNAP PRESS OF
HARVARD UNIVERSITY PRESS
Cambridge, Massachusetts
London, England
2010

Library of Congress Cataloging-in-Publication Data
Hunt, Lynn Avery.
The book that changed Europe : Picart and Bernard's Religious ceremonies of the world /
Lynn Hunt, Margaret Jacob, Wijnand Mijnhardt.
p. cm.
Includes bibliographical references and index.
ISBN 978-0-674-04928-4 (alk. paper)
1. Cérémonies et coutumes religieuses de tous les peuples du monde.
2. Religions—Early works to 1800. 3. Rites and ceremonies—Early works to 1800.
4. Picart, Bernard, 1673–1733. 5. Bernard, Jean Frédéric, d. 1752. I. Jacob,
Margaret C., 1943– II. Mijnhardt, W. W., 1950– III. Title.
BL80.3.H86 2010
203′.8—dc22   2009048372

To David Brafman

Contents

Contents

Illustrations

THE BOOK THAT CHANGED EUROPE

Introduction

One Book, Two Men, and a
New Attitude toward Religion

The book came in seven weighty folio volumes with more than 3,000 pages and 250 plates of engravings covering all the religions known to Europeans in the early 1700s. It was called *Cérémonies et coutumes religieuses de tous les peuples du monde* [Religious ceremonies and customs of all the peoples of the world; hereafter *Religious Ceremonies of the World*]. Published between 1723 and 1737, all its volumes bore the name of Bernard Picart, the most famous engraver of the eighteenth century after Hogarth, on whom Picart in fact had a direct influence. *Religious Ceremonies of the World* was published by Jean Frederic Bernard, who was also the unsung compiler, editor, and author of this pioneering work on the world's religions. The volumes began with Judaism and Catholicism, moved on to the Americas and India, then to Asia and Africa, only to return to the familiar, to the many forms of Protestantism, before finally tackling Islam (see Appendix A). No other work before then had ever attempted, in word and image, such a grand sweep of human religions.[1]

Religious Ceremonies of the World marked a major turning point in European attitudes toward religious belief and hence the sacred. It sowed the radical idea that religions could be compared on equal terms, and therefore that all religions were equally worthy of respect—and criticism. It turned belief in one unique, absolute, and God-given truth into "religion," that is, into individual ceremonies and customs that reflected the truths relative to each people and culture. This global survey of religious practices effectively disaggregated and delimited the sacred, making it specific to time, place, and institutions. Once labeled in time and place, religion became not an unchanging system of beliefs but a discrete entity concerned everywhere with the gods or the heavenly. The earthly, secular sphere where bookmen, like other mortals, plied their trade could no longer so easily be engulfed by religious demands and sacred edicts, potential obstacles blocking critical thinking or tolerant behavior.[2]

Ironically, however, the move to cast a "profane" or secular light onto every form of worship, everywhere, had sacred and theologically inspired antecedents. Obsessed with Catholic practices they considered idolatrous, devout Protestant scholars of the seventeenth century had sought the ammunition of analogy in Jewish and New World idolatries. They delighted in showing that Catholic practices such as the veneration of images of saints, displays of relics from saints' bodies, and the cult of the Virgin Mary had idolatrous counterparts in other times and places.[3]

These pious examinations of non-Christian idolatry generally served the theological polemics of the age. Still, as John Calvin and his followers believed, backsliding into idolatry threatened Protestants, too. Even as devout Protestants scrutinized the nature of idolatry so as to protect themselves better from its allure, their labors inspired some to take a further, more dangerous step: if the origin of idolatry could be traced to the quotidian imagination of the human brain, might not the notion of the sacred itself and its many manifestations be so linked? By the late seventeenth century dutiful Protestant antiquarians, like the English clergyman John Spencer, had come to see idolatry not simply as imaginary but as functional, as securing benefits from, or appeasing, the gods. Some deists then went further and embraced the impious notion that religion itself concerned not the eternally and verifiably sacred, not absolute truth versus error, but rather specific customs, practices, belief systems, and values. In other words, culture and social organization determined the boundary between the profane and the sacred, between matters concerning this world and those relegated to the supernatural place reserved for the gods or God. The stakes of studying the religious ceremonies by which peoples constituted and elevated the sacred were not small. Bernard and Picart had embarked upon an intellectual adventure that flirted with danger on all sides, that could offend pious Christians and arouse the wrath of their clerical protectors.[4]

The endeavor had commercial motivations, too. Bernard aimed to capitalize on recent innovations in the book trade, raising money, for example, by advertising to potential subscribers in newspapers. He integrated a scrupulously footnoted text, far from routine at the time, with a huge number of engravings worthy of a fine art collection. By doing so, the publisher-turned-author essentially created a new genre that broke the confines of encyclopedias, dictionaries, or collections of engravings. The gamble paid off. Celebrated in its time, the work was immediately translated into Dutch, then English and German, and reprinted, plagiarized, and pirated in multiple editions and languages for generations afterward (see Appendix B).

Yet twentieth-century scholars largely neglected *Religious Ceremonies of the World.* Given Bernard's innovations in publishing, his undeniable originality as a thinker and as an author, and Picart's fame, why is their great work so often overlooked? The lack of attention follows from some longstanding assumptions about who authored the European Enlightenment (usually Montesquieu, Voltaire, Rousseau, Smith, Hume, Kant, and the like). In this respect, studies of the Enlightenment would benefit from a consideration of recent works on the other great intellectual and cultural movement of the early modern period, the Scientific Revolution. As these works have shown, advances in the world of learning cannot be uniquely attributed to a small elite of intellectuals and scholars whose ideas then slowly percolate from the top to the bottom of the social pyramid. Discovery, whether in science, naval exploration, or humanistic investigation, required (as it still requires) an enormous army of personnel, not only astronomers, mathematicians, ship captains, or scholars, for example, but also instrument makers and apothecaries, merchants and traders, sailors and artisans, engravers, publishers, and printers. Just as important, these contributors to new learning traveled or corresponded, often crossing national boundaries as they went along. But Anglo-American, German, and French scholars writing under the spell of national history often lost track of those who crossed borders. When Bernard and Picart fled from France to the Dutch Republic to seek religious and intellectual freedom, they made, as it were, an inadvertent but momentous historical mistake. They left one of the "great" nations and thus consigned themselves in scholarship to barely the status of a footnote.[5]

Religious Ceremonies of the World fits perfectly into this new vision of the artisanal and cosmopolitan circulation of knowledge. Bernard was neither a professional scholar nor an intellectual attempting to live exclusively from his pen. He was a highly educated artisan without a formal higher education. He apprenticed at a young age in the publishing trade. He was also intensely engaged in that other emerging enterprise of the period: the study of humankind, society, and religion, inspired by the discoveries of new peoples and new religions. The work of artisans like Picart and Bernard in creating the Enlightenment has fallen victim to the same myopia that has eliminated the artisan from the emergence of the natural sciences.

The comparison to the Scientific Revolution is particularly salient because Bernard and Picart eagerly followed the new science. Bernard helped foster the ongoing disintegration of the Aristotelian world picture, taking as his lodestars Francis Bacon and especially René Descartes. Picart used microscopes to better depict precious gems and did a number of engravings on scientific themes. As first articulated by Descartes, Hobbes, and Newton in the seventeenth century, two principles remain central to modern science: the uniformity and regularity of nature. They were crucial to Bernard's and Picart's reconstruction of the development of the religions of the world. They made it possible for the two men to postulate a universal human nature as the root of religiosity. One of the leading Newtonians of the early eighteenth century, Willem Jacob s'Gravesande, it should be noted, belonged to the circle around Bernard Picart and his close friend and fellow French refugee Prosper Marchand. Indeed, during the second decade of the eighteenth century a French-language journal that Marchand coedited with s'Gravesande served as an early forum for the dissemination of Newton's science onto the Continent.[6]

Still, Bernard's and Picart's fascination with religion sprang not from a single-minded and mechanistic Cartesianism nor from a crudely deductive rationalism, such as that found in the outrageously heretical *Treatise of the Three Impostors* (the three were Jesus, Moses, and Muhammad). True to their artisanal backgrounds, Bernard and Picart had a more empirical enterprise in mind. It would prove much more subtle and persuasive and, in the end, much more threatening than other approaches. They wanted to show how, as Bernard put it, "[in the course of history] humankind began to lose the True Idea of the divine being and took upon itself to attribute corporeal qualities and human frailties to [that being]. Man added superstition to his worship, served God under corporeal notions, and, being no longer capable of contemplating him in spirit, whether through pride, fear, or weakness, he was pleased to represent him by images and statues." As will become clear, such statements could be interpreted in more than one fashion. Was this the austere Protestantism of Bernard's youth that loathed any scent of idolatry? Was it the ecumenical religion of the spirit that he had found among some small sects in Holland that refused identification with any orthodox confession? Was it an esoteric belief in a universal natural religion with links to deism? Would Bernard be willing to walk the path taken in the nineteenth century by the philosopher Ludwig Feuerbach, who argued that God was a projection of the human mind, or conclude with the sociologist Emile Durkheim later still that the sacred was society's way of worshipping itself?[7]

The only available sources to document this complicated historical process by which humans lost the True Idea of the divine being were found in the ancient texts of the Greeks and Romans and the travel reports on the religious customs and ceremonies of peoples around the globe. As witnessed by their personal libraries, both Bernard and Picart read widely among the ancient classics and modern travelogues. Travel accounts and studies based on those sources had flooded the European book markets since the early 1500s. In that century European presses produced 456 books on travel; in the seventeenth century, 1,566; and in the eighteenth century, 3,540. Though Bernard might miss an occasional title, the selection of sources used in *Religious Ceremonies of the World* constitutes a representative sample of what was available in the first decades of the eighteenth century.[8]

Picart's engravings in *Religious Ceremonies of the World* are often clearly linked to the text, but they are not just auxiliaries to it. They offer a separate, highly condensed commentary on the meaning and value of the different religious practices found around the globe. Unlike most of his predecessors, who quickly seized upon the strange and violent aspects of other cultures, Picart tried to depict the kaleidoscope of the world's religious activities from the inside, from the point of view of the religious tradition in question, however difficult that might have been.

I.I Picart's depiction of a Passover Seder. Picart most likely made this oil painting as a gift for the Curiel family depicted here. After four years of seeking permission to sketch Jewish rituals firsthand, he produced several engravings that many consider to be the finest in *Religious Ceremonies of the World* (for the original engraving on which this painting is based, see Figure 7.4). The painting was last sold at Sotheby's Tel Aviv in 1996. (Courtesy Perry Collection; photograph by Miri Greenshpon)

This desire for authenticity took several forms. He sketched the Dutch Jewish and Protestant rituals while participating in them or just afterward based on his fresh memories of the proceedings. For the Roman Catholic ceremonies, he relied not only on personal memory from his youth in Paris but also on illustrations in official Catholic sources, such as the *Roman Pontifical*. Even when casting a negative light on a practice, as in the depictions of the Spanish and Portuguese Inquisitions at the end of volume two, Picart drew from recent authors offering firsthand knowledge of the events.[9]

Although indigenous images of foreign lands proved harder to find, Picart sought them out with determination. In this way, his visual approach paralleled the textual approach of Bernard, who argued explicitly, and with prescience, that Europeans could not judge other religious systems without "better comprehension of their languages and being able to read their books." Bernard raised doubts about the common European practice of taking extracts out of context, arguing that such snippets do not "suffice to judge the opinion of a Nation [India] whose religion and philosophy are hidden beneath enigmas and allegorical fictions." For his part, Picart tried to penetrate those enigmas by finding native visual sources. Thus, alongside adaptations of available Western images of Hindu deities in volume three, the reader finds a series of engravings that look very much like Mughal miniatures. Both Bernard's text and Picart's images must be "read" to understand this artisanal contribution to making enlightened judgments about humanity's religious impulse.[10]

By offering a global and culturally relative depiction of religious diversity, Picart and Bernard's book supported those voices arguing for religious toleration. They themselves had grown up in a world in which religious belief was very much a life and death matter. James II of England had lost his throne in 1688 because his Protestant subjects feared he would reintroduce Catholicism. They had reason aplenty to worry because in 1685 the French king Louis XIV had revoked toleration for Calvinists. Protestants were purged from all schools and state academies; Protestant churches were torn down; and Protestant children were sometimes taken from their parents, rebaptized, and sent to live with Catholics. Despite the barriers in their way, some 150,000 people fled illegally to nearby Protestant countries. Among those escaping was the child Jean Frederic Bernard, whose father was a Calvinist pastor in the south of France. More than twenty years later, in 1709–1710, Picart followed in Bernard's footsteps. He left behind his established career in Paris and his Catholic identity to make his way north to Holland as a convert to some sort of Protestantism. *Religious Ceremonies of the World* cannot be understood apart from Bernard and Picart's own experience of religious intolerance and persecution.

Not surprisingly, then, the work encapsulates the religious ferment leading up to the early Enlightenment. Toleration was far from the only issue. The educated public, in both Protestant and Catholic Europe, avidly followed theological debates about the existence of devils, angels, the doctrines of anti-Trinitarians (those who denied that God, Jesus, and the Holy Spirit were manifestations of one Divinity), and free will. After Columbus's discovery of the Americas, scholarly and public discussion of religious difference had taken on a new urgency. After all, neither the Bible nor any ancient author ever mentioned the peoples of the New World. Once Europeans decided that the indigenous peoples were humans like them, they had to make sense of native beliefs. Predictably, perhaps, travelers and missionaries first concluded that indigenous peoples had no notion of the divine, only fables and superstitions.

In the sixteenth century a few Spanish priests, appalled by the treatment of the natives, recoiled from the cruelty shown by the conquerors and portrayed it as counterproductive for the purposes of conversion. They refuted the no-religion thesis but also depicted the peoples of Mexico and the Caribbean as simple souls, harmless and weak. Needless to say, the damning accounts of Spanish brutality written by the conquerors' own clergy immediately fed into Protestant propaganda against the Spanish and the Catholic Church. The search to understand the "idolatry" of natives led other commentators to compare their practices to those of the ancient Greeks and Romans. Late in the sixteenth century the Spanish Jesuit José de Acosta traveled extensively in Mexico and Peru and described in great detail the weather, plants, soil, gold, and silver to be found there. Despite his belief that "the prince of darkness is the teacher of all the heathen," de Acosta's widely read account further described the objects of their worship, the sacrifices they made to their idols "to obtain good growing seasons or health, or to deliver them from dangers and evils." His description also dwelt at length on the human sacrifices, "the vassalage that [these wretched people] paid to the devil."

From the inspired curiosity of de Acosta Europeans received vivid accounts of religious customs and rituals practiced by the Indians as well as multiple comparisons to ancient practices.[11]

Bernard and Picart aimed to move beyond these increasingly common comparisons among heathen idolators to a truly global analysis in which the beliefs and practices of Catholics, Protestants, Jews, Muslims, Chinese, "Canadians" (Hurons), and others were all juxtaposed to one another. Rather than attribute New World customs and rituals to the power of the devil's seduction, as de Acosta had, for example, they sought out the different ideas and practices concerning devils around the world. Were not all the religions of the world in some fundamental ways alike?

The idea of comparing dispassionately the religions of the world is hardly surprising today, much less shocking, even if we do it too infrequently or with too little willingness to suspend our own beliefs. As late as the early eighteenth century, however, most Western writings about religion either laid out the true doctrine (that of the author) or focused on debunking the competitors: Catholics and Protestants wrote against each other; the various Protestant sects justified their separate understandings of religious truth; and Christians wrote against Islam and Judaism, the other monotheistic religions. The customs of the rest of the world's religions were lumped together as pagan idolatry. Interest in them was pursued, when at all, mainly as a way of facilitating Christian missionary efforts. The hefty five-volume *Atlas geographus,* for example, printed in London between 1711 and 1717, repeated the common European view of the origins of Buddhism in China: "A 2d Sect sprung up about 32 Years after Christ's Death, and introduced the Worship of an Idol called *Foe* [Buddha]. This filled the Empire with Idolatry, Atheism, Superstition and Fables."[12]

About the same time, more radical thinkers, also interested in comparing religions, imagined that they spied the spirit of Spinoza's philosophy in Buddhism and Confucianism, an erroneous but understandable view that made its way into Picart and Bernard's thinking. Bernard was careful to offer such comparisons gingerly and to note without endorsement the considerable similarity between Spinoza's pantheism and the metaphysics of Chinese intellectuals; both appeared to identify the Supreme Being with nature itself. He then left the matter at that. Atheism was the great bugbear of the time, and religious and political leaders saw little difference between atheism and pantheism (or, for that matter, deism).[13]

A contemporary of Picart and Bernard's, the French Jesuit Joseph-François Lafitau, spent many years in Canada studying the religiosity of the natives, which he then wrote about to prove the atheists wrong. European atheists, he claimed, try to persuade us that "the barbarian peoples have themselves no religious sentiment and the origin of the divine cult must be the result of the hard work of Legislators." Lafitau may well have had *The Treatise of the Three Impostors* in mind, since it had argued that religion had been cynically foisted upon a credulous people by their rulers. While believing that God was the author of all human religion, and dispensing with much talk about the devil, Lafitau saw the sincere religiosity of the natives as dimly reflective of that initial divine spark, and he undertook something like ethnographic fieldwork to nail down his point. It is hardly irrelevant that *The Treatise of the Three Impostors* itself came out of a circle with close ties to Picart and his friend Marchand.[14]

Given that virtually no one in Europe at the time countenanced full religious toleration, especially for atheists, Bernard and Picart had to watch their step. It was commonplace in freethinking circles to speak about exoteric knowledge, fit for public display, and esoteric beliefs, best kept to one's self and one's close friends. Bernard and Picart balanced on a tightrope between the two poles, wanting to make previously esoteric beliefs more widely available but not wishing to risk explicitly advocating those heretical beliefs. So they chose their sources very carefully; they gave voice and view to esoteric positions but claimed that the voices and views were not theirs. In the text Bernard reproduced the most recent and trustworthy accounts he could find that explicated positions he wanted to put forward, yet when he ventured into dangerous territory, such as atheism or pantheism, his own prose turned oblique.

Similarly, Picart drew either from firsthand observation or from the most reliable sources he could find. Nevertheless, he also wanted to stamp the work with the obvious marks of his originality. He chose the scenes to illustrate from among the thousands upon thousands of descriptions available to him, and he lavished his attention on certain of them, such as the Jewish ceremonies. Picart's astounding frontispiece provides a kind of treasure map to the men's approach. The lengthy caption draws attention to common criticisms of Roman Catholicism and seems to present the Protestant Reformers, in contrast, in a very positive light. A knowledgeable contemporary would have discerned several more subtle messages as well. Picart is clearly favorable to some Catholics, in particular the Jansenists condemned by the Papal Bull Unigenitus of 1713. He presents the Protestant Reformers as a group without choosing sides among Lutherans, Calvinists, Anglicans, Mennonites, or Quakers, even though within Protestant countries these groups fought bitterly against each other and the majority rarely tolerated the minorities. Unlike most Christian artists, Picart does not depict Judaism or Islam negatively. Indeed, Islam is especially prominent in the very front of the tableau, and Shia Islam gets pride of place with the depiction of Ali, the central figure for Shiites. Finally, the tableau underlines above all else the multiplicity of religions in the world rather than the inherent superiority of one of them. Among the Europeans displayed most conspicuously, virtually all appear completely absorbed by actions in their own sphere. Picart and Bernard would elaborate these points in detail in the engravings and text that followed.[15]

Despite a pronounced hostility to Roman Catholicism, on the whole Bernard and Picart tread lightly, in part because their underlying message was much more challenging than the usual Protestant critique of Catholicism. They were delivering messages about religion in general; if Catholicism had faults, they were the defects found in any religion that had degenerated with the passage of time, as all religions seemed to do. Bernard and Picart preferred to let readers draw their own conclusions from firsthand accounts, comparative essays, and ethnographic perspectives on the various religions found around the world. They would provide some guidance along the way, especially in the explosive preface and introductory essay, but they did not insist on a single point of view. Instead, they invited readers to distance themselves from their own beliefs and customs and to think about religious practices around the globe. This distance marked a crucial first step toward toleration.

Bernard and Picart could get a hearing for these ideas because they had gone to live and work in the most tolerant country in Europe, where commerce brought Jews and Christians of all descriptions together and ensured a steady influx of new information about a far-flung world. The Dutch had embraced the principle of freedom of conscience in 1579 amid their struggle for independence as Calvinists from Catho-

B. Picart direxit et fecit 1723.

TABLEAU DES PRINCIPALES RELIGIONS DU MONDE.

En premier lieu, on voit la RELIGION CHRESTIENNE au pied d'un grand Arbre, qui represente la BIBLE ouverte, qui en Moyse François, qui a esté choisi de former d'une main, en montrant de l'autre le Livre où est écrit CONCI
LES & TRADITIONS, sur lequel L'EGLISE ROMAINE est appuyée. Elle est representée la Tiare en tête, tenant d'une main le SACREMENT, et de Livre un Rameau d'Olivier 3. Symbole de Paix, qu'elle semble presenter
à toutes les autres Religions, qui se vont d'en entrer dans son Sein. L'EMPIRE ROMAIN sur les débris duquel elle s'est élevée, paroît abatu sous ses pieds, tenant encore le Globe marqué de l'autorité impériale, que la Superstition leur enleve pour se revêtir le PONTIFE ROMAIN, a a assisté, on voit les Magistrats et les Austerités. Un peu plus haut un Jésuite presente la BULLE UNIGENITUS à un Evêque, qui par son action semble la refuser. Le Cardinal qui est à côté de lui paroît en balance : l'accepteras l'entre des deux derniers paroît l'Evêque de Sebaste. Un Rabin renversé tenant le PENTATEUQUE cité, foulé aux pieds par
l'Eglise Romaine. Le Patriarche des Grecs qui est devant elle, semble reconnoître son autorité. 5. Derriere eux on voit des Evêques, et des Moines de tous Ordres, entre lesquels on distingue un Dominiquain : tenant l'Etendard de l'Inquisition. LA REFORMATION, montrant d'une main la BIBLE, tenant de l'autre une Serpette et embrassant l'Arbre 3, s'elait elle a emondé les Branches inutiles, a aattré d'elle tous les
Reformateurs. 6. Au bas sur le devant du Tableau ALI Successeur de MAHOMET explique L'ALCORAN aux divers Peuples, qui ont embrassé la Religion Mahometane. 7. Adroite de lointain represente les
Peuples, et les Dieux des Indes Orientales et à gauche ceux des Indes Occidentales. Dans le plus profond éloignement on voit quelques Idoles des Sçavans, &c.

1. L'Eglise Romaine vous prie, qu'après avoir entierement en matiere de foi.
2. L'Eglise Romaine dit d'avoir sur ses maximes parce qu'en montent une sur laquelle il faut Achever et ôter dans le concernant absolute montagnes en evité la Purgatoire.
3. Une petite illustre au peu vient Serpent dans le Romain, le la chaine qui cristal, lient con-
contre qui se élevaient apparente mille toujours quelque verité, et qui l'enlevage est
tout ce qui en en doit déduire.

4. Son marque enfin un avant mille, qui fait voir qu'il n'a qu'a l'attent qui l'empe-
ce a est hommage ivrée.
5. Cette represente la Religion chrestienne, dont la Reformation a retranché les Cérémonies
et les idées Superieux sur les branches nouvelles.
6. Savoir Luther Calvin, Melancthon, Zan, Mer. Ecclesi. Pierre, Marie-au-Marie, Dean. A
droite de la Religion chrestienne on voit Notre Dite, et à sa gauche Erasme, Auteurs de

la Reformation, L'Inquisiteur, Sermons Cadres Armeniens, et plus bas un Ecuador son
Anglicans et de tête à son Ocean fermes lointains on Adulte : l'act le Chef des Minovant
qu'on assenne par elus Anabaptistes.
7. Savoir Turc, Japonais, Morte, Tartares, Arabes, Persans. Le Persan tient une table
sur laquelle sont les Articles fondamentaux de la Religion Mahometane, on voit
derriere lui le Sacrement, qu'ils sacrifient tous les Ans.

Apud Chéreau, la Boutique du Château.

I.2   Frontispiece for *Religious Ceremonies of the World*. First prepared for the Dutch translation but clearly intended to be bound with every edition, Picart's frontispiece, "Tableau of the Principal Religions of the World," underestimates the actual importance of "idolatrous peoples" in the work and gives priority to the criticism of Roman Catholicism. The caption reads: "In the first place one sees [the female figure for] CHRISTIAN RELIGION at the foot of a great tree holding open the BIBLE, which a **Franciscan Monk** is trying to close with one hand while pointing with the other to the book on which is written COUNCILS and TRADITIONS (1) on which leans the ROMAN CHURCH. She is shown tiara on head (2) holding in one hand the BLESSED SACRAMENT and in the other an olive branch (3), symbol of peace that she seems to be offering to all the other religions that wish to return to her bosom. The ROMAN EMPIRE, on whose debris she [Roman Church] has been built, appears knocked down under her feet, still holding the globe that signals Imperial Authority, which [the figure of] Superstition is taking from him in order to hand it over to the ROMAN PONTIFF. Behind her [Superstition] one sees forms of penance. A little higher a **Jesuit** presents the [papal] BULL UNIGENITUS to a bishop, who by his action seems to refuse it. The cardinal at his side appears undecided as to whether he will accept it. Between the last two appears the bishop of Sébaste [Saint Blaise, a fourth-century martyr for the faith]. A **Rabbi** who has been knocked down holding the PENTATEUCH is trampled by the **Roman Church;** the **Patriarch of the Greeks** facing her seems to recognize her authority (4). Behind them one sees the bishops, and the **Monks** of every **Order**, among whom one can distinguish a **Dominican** holding the standard of the **Inquisition**. The REFORMATION, pointing with one hand to the BIBLE, holding in the other a pruning knife and embracing the **Tree** (5) from which she has pruned the unnecessary branches, has around her all the **Reformers** (6). At the bottom front of the Tableau ALI successor to MAHOMET explains the KORAN to the diverse peoples who have embraced the **Mahometan Religion** (7). In the distance on the right are **Pagodas** and **Gods** of the East Indies, and on the left those of the West Indies. Farthest away one sees some of the **Idols** of the Lapps, etc. (1) The Roman Church wants everyone to refer to these entirely in matters of faith. (2) The Roman Church is placed on a protuberance in relation to the seven mountains on which the city of Rome is built. Beneath these mountains one sees Purgatory. (3) A little serpent that one sees snaking in the branch, and the chain hanging from it, make known that her [Roman Church] apparent mildness always hides some venom and that slavery is all that one should expect from her. (4) His mask hides a cunning smile which shows that self-interest alone gets him to make this forced homage. (5) The tree represents the Christian Religion, from which the Reformation has cut back the ceremonies and abuses depicted by the dead branches. (6) That is, Luther, Calvin, Melancthon, John Hus, Zwingli, Peter Martyr, and Martin Bucer. To the right of Christian Religion one sees Henry VIII and on his left Cranmer, authors of the Reformation in *(continued)*

(continued) England. Behind Calvin is Arminius, and lower down [is] a Quaker with his hat on his head who is next to Menno Simons baptizing an adult. Simons is the head of the Mennonites, who are derisively called Anabaptists. (7) That is, Turks, Algerians, Moors, Tartars, Arabs, and Persians. The Persian holds a tablet with the fundamental articles of the Mahometan Religion. One sees behind him the camel that they sacrifice every year. See Chardin for the sacrifice of the camel. B. Picart inventit et fecit 1727." (Research Library, The Getty Research Institute, Los Angeles, California)

lic Spain. After years of armed struggle in which Dutch Catholics often fought side by side with Calvinists, the newly sovereign Dutch Republic displayed a revulsion against outright religious persecution. Still, Dutch toleration offered scant acceptance for the public practice of Catholicism; Catholics held their services in private, in churches made to look like ordinary houses or barns. Toleration had other limits. Though not an official state religion, the Dutch Reformed Church often acted like one. Membership in a church was not required, but every important official post in the cities and the central state was held by a Calvinist. Until the 1630s Jews had to bury their dead twenty-five miles away from Amsterdam, and they were forbidden to worship in public or to employ female Christian servants.

Despite these shortcomings, religious tolerance in Holland surpassed that of any other place in Europe (with the possible exception of London itself). Little wonder, then, that religious minorities began to make their way to Dutch towns and cities, starting with Jews who had been persecuted in Spain and Portugal. Bernard and Picart were but two among thousands of French Calvinists who sought refuge in Dutch cities. Small Protestant sects, now extinct and known only from seventeenth-century sources, arrived as well, or sprang up as homegrown versions of Dutch Protestantism: Anabaptists, Socinians (anti-Trinitarians), Collegiants (pious Dutch who worshiped as a group without any priests or ministers), English Brownists (a breakaway movement within English Calvinism), and Puritans, who went to Holland first before they set sail for the American colonies. Even Catholics went to Holland. Calvinist ministers likened Amsterdam to a "whore" because it "serves Pope and heathen, Moor and Turk, [and] it bothers neither about God nor the fatherland." If the multitudes of European clerical and political enemies of toleration had their way, there would be no Amsterdams to be found anywhere.[16]

The first internationally acclaimed arguments for religious toleration came not from the Dutch themselves but rather from those who benefited from Dutch openness, such as Pierre Bayle, who fled the repression of Louis XIV, and John Locke, who went to Amsterdam to hide from the agents of James II. The tide began to turn in favor of toleration on both sides of the English Channel at about the same time. From the mid-1600s onward Jewish students were admitted to Dutch universities to study medicine (though not theology). Celebrating this new tolerance, in 1675 Portuguese Jews in Amsterdam opened the most magnificent synagogue ever seen in Europe, an event commemorated in one of the engravings of *Religious Ceremonies of the World.* In most other European cities the Jews had to keep a low profile, and in many places they were forced to live in ghettos. After the English revolution of 1688–1689 that deposed James II, Parliament established religious toleration for all Protestants (except anti-Trinitarians), and Locke published his plea for toleration that would resonate across Europe. Cracks began to appear in the ancient structure of religious intolerance.[17]

Yet even in post-1689 England, Catholics, Jews, and non-Anglican Protestants were barred from public office and university positions, and across Europe Catholic authorities still denounced "tolerationism" as undermining the true religion. After the crackdown on Calvinists in his kingdom, Louis XIV spent most of his remaining years persecuting Catholic dissidents such as the Jansenists, who wanted a more austere practice, and the Quietists, who favored a more mystical religion. In this atmosphere, the isolated examples of limited official toleration could hardly produce a new consciousness. Everyday attitudes had to change for religious tolerance to take root. People had to understand and to some extent sympathize with different religious practices they had been taught to think of as profane and deviant, if not monstrous.

Bernard and Picart aimed to produce just this kind of understanding. The title of Bernard's opening essay (signed only * * * * *) made this clear. "Dissertation sur le culte religieux" [Dissertation on religious worship] implied that every kind of worship fit under one all-encompassing rubric of religion. In his first sentence, he set the tone for what was to come: "Most men would not know there is a God, if the worship that one renders him was not accompanied by some exterior signs." Bernard began not with the revelation of God's word but rather with human weakness. He did not distinguish between true and false religion, between Christians and non-Christians, or even between religion and idolatry. He referred instead to "men" or "all men" and presented a subtle psychological analysis of the origins of religion, which he in effect attributed to an innate sense of guilt. Marshaling an astonishing array of examples from around the world as well as from ancient history, he showed the universality of such ceremonial practices as music, dance, purification rites, and the ritual kiss.[18]

Although two of the volumes bore the title *Religious Ceremonies and Customs of the Idolatrous Peoples,* Bernard made clear in the preface and opening essay to volume one that he considered many forms of Christianity, in particular Catholicism, to be just as idolatrous in their practices as any heathen cult, and conversely, many heathen practices as meaningful as those of Christians. Everywhere a sense of sin led to prayer, which led in turn to temples, which inevitably resulted in priestly castes. If priests found the secret for getting men to consult them on everything, if they intrigued with rulers to protect their positions, "such has always been the authority of ecclesiastics in all the religions." This kind of universalizing argument would be credible only if Bernard and Picart could show the underlying similarities even in the strangest and most unlikely places. Consequently, the two volumes on the idolatrous peoples are the longest and most copiously illustrated in the set. They contain one-third of the total text and a whopping 43 percent of the images, in part because Picart died in 1733 as volume five was being published, but also in part because he and Bernard clearly found much to ponder in the idolatrous religions.[19]

Bernard and Picart could have fled to another Protestant country such as England, Sweden, or Prussia, but the Dutch Republic (of which Holland was the richest and most populous province) offered important advantages, among them a very large Francophone community. The Dutch book trade, moreover, presented them with an unrivaled opportunity. Dutch publishers printed half of all the books in Europe in an astonishing variety of languages. Just at this moment, the first great classics of the European Enlightenment began to appear in Holland. Montesquieu's *Persian Letters,* for example, was published anonymously and under a false imprint in Amsterdam in 1721. It could never have been published in Paris. In its pages, fictional Persian visitors to Paris provided a humorous ethnographic view of European social customs, including an occasional jibe at the influence of priests and in particular of the pope. Its tongue-in-cheek satire, not to mention its racy account of life in a Persian harem, took Europe by storm. Montesquieu had used an earlier work by Bernard as his model; it, too, featured Persian visitors, but Bernard's Persians dissected life in Amsterdam, not Paris.[20]

Although this link between the famous Montesquieu and the little-known Bernard is intriguing, we have no intention of tracing the entire Enlightenment to Bernard and Picart (nor to any single author or co-terie of authors). Montesquieu made fun of European religious intol-erance and resisted ridiculing the Persians, but he made no concrete argument for toleration and provided little information about Persian religion or ways of life. Persians were only a foil for him, a largely fic-tionalized grab bag of telling contrasts with Louis XIV's France. Ber-nard and Picart had their reasons to criticize Louis XIV, too, but they followed a very different method from that of Montesquieu, compiling, adapting, and synthesizing the best information available about reli-gious practices around the globe. Theirs was not a short and pithy book nor a titillating read, despite some juicy bits here and there, especially on the subject of courtship and marriage. They got in their digs at "Ro-man Catholicism" (a term chosen to link the Inquisition, for example, with Rome and not necessarily with Catholicism elsewhere), but for the most part they aimed even higher: at religion itself. They wanted to show that the religious search for the sacred was a universal impulse and as such suffered from universal forms of corruption. To make this point, however, they first had to provide credible information about ev-ery religion ever encountered by Europeans.

Could one book, even a large one with great intellectual and artis-tic ambitions, possibly make a crucial difference? *Religious Ceremonies of the World* did not change attitudes singlehandedly, yet it did add up to an enormous stride forward. It channeled various streams of knowl-edge and criticism in one direction, summing up what was known about the world's religions and giving that knowledge a new significance. This was the right book published at the right time in the right place. With no author's name on the title page—the entire work appears in every library catalogue under the name of Picart, the engraver—it could be viewed as an unbiased compendium of the most up-to-date writings, especially since many of the writers cited were Catholics. It offered readers the chance to learn about other religions, wherever possible from an insider's or at least an eyewitness's perspective. In both text and images, readers were learning to see other religions from a radically new perspective. By its very structure, then, the work encouraged readers to see the logic of other religions and to take more distance from their own beliefs.

Given that this work was a large-format, heavily illustrated set of volumes, it is hardly surprising that its expense put it beyond the means of workers, artisans, or ordinary shopkeepers even in wealthy Dutch cities. Originally planned as a four-volume work offered to subscribers at 50 florins (guilders) for the less expensive version, it ended up fetching 150–200 florins a set as prices rose steadily over time. Even relatively prosperous artisans and shopkeepers made only about 1,000 florins a year, so it was out of reach for all but rich merchants, professionals, clergy, and gentry. Picart and Bernard, but not their workshop assistants, could have afforded it.[21]

The English translation also commanded a high price. The *Monthly Chronicle* published in London in April 1731 gave a price for subscribers of 5 guineas (1 guinea is equal to 1 pound sterling plus 1 shilling) for unbound sheets in folio format. When the set actually began to appear in 1733 it sold for slightly more, but the bookseller assured prospective buyers that the plates alone would sell anywhere else for 3 guineas. At the time London craftsmen made £25–35 a year and shopkeepers £100–200 a year. The bookseller insisted that "this work does not contain a dry Narrative of Customs and Ceremonies, but is every where intersper'd with the most agreeable Particulars, which make the whole equally Entertaining and Instructive." As with the French original, the English translation appeared in installments. Buyers could either purchase the unbound sheets and the separate engravings and arrange for the binding themselves with the help of tables signaling the placement of the engravings, or they could buy sets that were already bound.[22]

Its price notwithstanding, the Catholic Church found the work so threatening that it put the volumes on the Index of Forbidden Books in 1738 and renewed its proscription in 1757. The secret report to Rome on the book focused in particular on the opening preface: "This Preface breathes the spirit of heresy, not only because of its dogma *concerning spiritual religion* . . . but also because of its position concerning the

Vicar of Christ [the pope], holy intercession, sacrifice, and many other things." Protestants would not have minded an attack on Catholicism, but the general preface clearly concerned them as well, and the English translation published between 1733 and 1739 simply dropped the opening remarks altogether. In those pages, Bernard had brashly suggested the superfluity of most organized religion: "If all men could agree to only regard God as a very simple Being, sovereignly perfect in his Essence, his virtues, and his immense capacity," then they could suppress all intercessors and "go directly to God." They would then eliminate the unnecessary trappings of worship and rely only on their love of virtue.[23]

Despite the official condemnation and the association of Picart and Bernard with Huguenot circles of publishers in Holland, the book was received warmly in Catholic France, too. It ranked among the top ninety books owned by prosperous Parisians in the 1750s, putting it in the same category as Bishop Bossuet's influential *Discours sur l'histoire universelle* [Discourse on universal history] of 1681 and the early volumes of Denis Diderot's famous *Encyclopédie* (1751–1772). Only three years after the book made its way onto the Index, two French clergymen began publishing a bowdlerized version in Paris. They kept all the engravings and even reproduced the section on the Catholic Inquisition, which Bernard had compiled from writings by French Catholics critical of a practice associated in particular with Rome, Portugal, and Spain. French booksellers simply could not resist the commercial opportunity created by the papal condemnation.[24]

The book had an astonishing afterlife. It helped create the field of the comparative history of religion, and to this day its engravings still appear in museum exhibits as documentation for religious customs. The experience of the English Romantic poet Robert Southey may not be typical, but it is telling. He first saw the engravings reprinted in a Christian magazine and immediately sought out their source. "I got at Picart when I was about fifteen," he recounted in a letter written in November 1812, "and soon became as well acquainted with the gods of Asia and America as with those of ancient Greece and Rome." Just one word—Picart—was enough to identify the work for his correspondent. Southey cherished "Picart" as one of his favorite books, and it prompted him to write a long narrative poem. Yet as the Paris edition already suggested and our conclusion demonstrates, "Picart" was so well known that it was virtually inevitable that the work would be diluted and reframed in ways unrecognizable to its creators. Readers of these adulterated versions saw some of the same pictures, but all the sharp edges of the original message had been sandblasted away.[25]

We have divided our chapters into two main parts, one on the intersecting journeys of the two main protagonists and the other on the major sections of their big book. The first part uncovers the ups and downs in the lives of these two exceptionally ambitious men who lived and worked on the border between artisanal labor and the higher reaches of artistic and intellectual life. They shared this originally precarious, but ultimately richly rewarded, life with a cosmopolitan network of French, Dutch, German, and English friends in The Hague and Amsterdam. Among those friends were some of the most important publishers and booksellers in Europe, members of the families in the book trade who brought the Enlightenment to the rest of the world.

In constant communication with one another and with writers elsewhere, the circle around Picart and Bernard began to think and write about religion in new and sometimes irreverent ways. They held it out for examination, turned it over, and pried into its inner workings. For them, religion ceased being a given defined by one's relationship to a divinely inspired sacred text and a church built on its absolute truths. It became instead a set of historically conditioned beliefs and ritual practices that offered insight into human nature in general. Bernard and Picart took this central idea and ran with it. By using the best recent scholarship and their own original interpretations of it, they helped transform attitudes toward Judaism and Islam, not to mention Confucianism, Hinduism, and the indigenous practices of the Americas, north and south. Throughout, they maintained a tension between recounting differences and underlining similarities in the religions of the world. Similarity gained its significance from a full appreciation of the differences in beliefs and customs found across the globe.

Traditional religious polemics held little interest for Bernard, Picart, and their friends. True, they could hardly claim to be religiously neutral, especially about Catholicism. Yet more important even than their distance from Catholicism was the perspective they had gained on all claims to religious truth. If Catholicism had corrupted primitive Christianity, then it simply provided an especially dramatic example of the degeneration that threatened every religion. The priestly keepers of orthodoxy—and orthodoxy could be found everywhere—tried to suppress the dissidents in order to keep their own power intact. Religious toleration, therefore, was an essential tool in the search for religious truth. All views had to be made freely available. If knowledge of other religions could be more widely disseminated, then Europeans would see that everyone believed equally fervently in the truth of their own religion, even the supposedly savage peoples of the Americas. To feel respect for other people's religions, one first had to know something about them, such as why they believed what they believed and why they did what they did. Bernard and Picart invited readers to join them on an armchair voyage of discovery and to think about the significance of what they discovered.

We refuse to reduce Bernard and Picart's work to one predetermined religious program. Neither man can be pigeonholed as a Huguenot, a Dutch Calvinist, a deist, a pantheist, or an atheist, though there is evidence for each of these. As men once persecuted for their religion, they cherished religious freedom. Toleration, in their view, did not lead ineluctably to disbelief; rather, it opened the door to uncensored knowledge, to deeper reflection on the significance of the religious impulse, and to a sense of kinship rather than hostility to other people's beliefs and practices. If any one belief characterized their position it was that religious ceremonies and customs embodied contradictory meanings. Such rites expressed universal fears and aspirations, but over time they also inevitably distorted and perverted those original underlying feelings. The goal was not to dismiss religion as a mirage but to discern within religious diversity itself the truths one could honestly live by and cherish. In a time of seemingly unending religious conflict, Bernard and Picart asked readers to sit down, sift through their newly purchased pages, admire the engravings, savor an account of a religion they did not know or perhaps even loathed, and come back again and again to read, look, wonder, imagine, and ponder. It's an adventure and a quest that we hope to recapture.

I

THE WORLD
OF THE BOOK

I

A Marketplace for Religious Ideas

O N NOVEMBER 24, 1710, Bernard Picart joined a group of friends
in The Hague for a meeting of what they called the general chapter of the Knights of Jubilation. At first glance, we appear to have stum-
bled upon an early eighteenth-century version of a stag party. Gathering around a table "laden with a huge sirloin," amid the merriment of
drinking large quantities of wine, the "brothers" considered whether to
expel one of their members for an infraction against "our most gallant
and joyous *constitutions* . . . the *statutes* and *regulations* of our order." Apparently Brother Jean, instead of following the rules "to be always merry,
high-spirited and happy," had fallen in love, "the complete opposite of
all joy," and was planning to get married, even though marriage was "the
grave of all laughter and fun." The Grand Master asked the assembled
brothers to decide if they should condemn the young man. His brother
by birth rose to his defense, reminding those assembled that no woman
could resist such a handsome face. Jean got off with a small fine.[1]

The knights, however jubilant, would have disappeared from history if the record of this meeting had not been preserved in the papers
of the notorious English freethinker John Toland. In 1710 he had been
living in The Hague for two years. He may have been present at the
meeting, raising his glass and chatting in French, which he knew quite
well. The Toland connection and the early trappings of freemasonry—a

movement only just emerging in Scotland and England and not yet implanted on the Continent—suggest that this was no ordinary gathering. Who were these "brothers" so enamored of their "constitutions"? The account in Toland's papers came from the pen of the knights' secretary, Prosper Marchand, Picart's close friend and fellow Protestant exile who had within the year come with him from France to start a new life. In the nascent Republic of Letters Marchand acted as a jack-of-all-trades: he edited, published, and wrote books, including the first history of printing; he worked as a journalist; he bought and sold books; and he acted as a literary agent, matching writers and their projects to publishers and sorting out their contractual disputes. Marchand loved to be involved in slightly risky, even *risqué*, publishing ventures but usually without putting his name to the project. He circulated forbidden books and manuscripts but somehow managed to avoid legal trouble.[2]

A closer look at those present at the meeting reveals an international network of publishers who had gathered in the relative freedom of Dutch cities. The Grand Master was Gaspar Fritsch, who together with fellow German and "cupbearer of the order" Michael Böhm, owned a publishing company in Rotterdam. Back in Germany the Fritsch family, in conjunction with the Gleditsch clan, had developed one of the most important publishing houses in the book capital of Leipzig. Gottlieb Gleditsch was treasurer of the knights that evening in The Hague, and it was he who defended his older brother Jean Frederic (or Johann Friedrich) when it became known that he planned to marry. Picart served as graffiti master and "illuminator" of the order; by July 1710 his engravings were already listed for sale by Fritsch and Böhm in Rotterdam, Marchand in The Hague, and J. L. de Lorme in Amsterdam, the last being one of the Dutch Republic's biggest publishers. Less known as a publisher at the time was Charles Levier, the anointed buffoon of the knights, who was without question the most daring of the bunch. Yet another French Protestant refugee, Levier would publish in 1719 what must count as the single most infamous book of the eighteenth century, a work he called *La Vie et l'esprit de Spinosa* [The life and spirit of Spinoza]. Two years later Michael Böhm republished the same text under the title for which it would evermore be known, *Le Traité des trois imposteurs* [The treatise of the three impostors].[3]

Are we hearing echoes here of an ordinary stag party or of a subversive conventicle of freemasons and atheists? There were no doubt elements of both but also of something else. The chilly November evening brought together men in the book trade who would thrive in a new marketplace of religious ideas. They were not just in it for the money that could be made, though that was hardly irrelevant. They met to celebrate and encourage one another in their common quest for knowledge, especially knowledge about religion. Their ways of socializing were resolutely secular, and in the end their books often had a subversive impact, not because they were explicitly atheistic, but because they encouraged readers to distance themselves from religious orthodoxy of all kinds. Religious belief and practice became an object of study for these men rather than an unquestioned way of life. They wanted to put on the table all the possible opinions about religion. They published to foster an open and critical discussion about religion. But they did not necessarily reject it. *The Treatise of the Three Impostors* would not appear for another nine years (although Levier had it in hand as early as 1711), and it is not at all evident that it represents the common thinking of these men in the book business. What they surely believed was that even the most notoriously atheistic ideas should be available to the reader, who should be free to form his own opinion of them. Bernard and Picart's *Religious Ceremonies of the World* explicitly put forward these same premises, which would prove so crucial to the Enlightenment in the decades that followed. Immanuel Kant provided the enduring motto for the Enlightenment in his 1784 essay "What Is Enlightenment?": *sapere aude!* [Dare to know!]. By 1784 this ideal was widely shared among the educated classes; sixty or sixty-five years earlier, when Bernard and Picart prepared their great work, it had a much sharper cutting edge.

Jean Frederic Bernard may or may not have been present among the Knights of Jubilation, but his path had certainly begun to cross with those of Picart and the other knights. In 1709 he corresponded with Marchand, still in Paris, concerning his book brokerage. The exact circumstances of Picart's first meeting and decision to collaborate with Bernard are unknown, but by 1712 Picart had moved to Amsterdam, where Bernard also lived. In that same year Picart married Anne Vincent, the daughter of a paper merchant. His first wife had died in France in 1708. Picart and his new wife set up shop on the busy Kalverstraat, known as the center of the book trade as well as of money transactions and prostitution. Bernard lived and worked there from 1707. Born in southern France, he had fled with his family to Amsterdam as a child.

In 1704 he had gone to Geneva, another Protestant stronghold, to set himself up as a broker between the Genevan guild of booksellers and their counterparts in Amsterdam. In 1711 Bernard anonymously published under a false imprint his *Reflexions morales satiriques & comiques, sur les Moeurs de nôtre siécle* [Moral satirical and comic reflections on the mores of our century; hereafter *Moral Reflections*], which used a Persian philosopher to criticize religious fanaticism in Europe and provided a prototype for Montesquieu's *Persian Letters* a decade later. Did Picart already know *Moral Reflections* or its author? We cannot be certain, but Jean Frederic was mentioned by name in a letter written by Picart's father-in-law, Ysbrand Vincent, in January 1713. In that year Picart enrolled in the same Amsterdam booksellers guild that Bernard had joined two years earlier. By then, they no doubt knew each other.[4]

A new literary society set up in The Hague in 1711 was typical of the intellectual aspirations of this circle. Did the group grow out of that evening in The Hague the previous year? The ubiquitous Marchand recorded its minutes from 1711 until 1717, and just like the knights, the society maintained an air of secrecy and its members appear to have called one another "brother." It included leading Dutch intellectuals alongside the usual cast of French refugees and other foreigners. In 1713 the club began publishing in French a *Journal Littéraire* [Literary journal] that specialized in discussions of new literature, religious issues, and Newtonian science. In the more anodyne form required by regular periodical publication (as opposed to anonymous publications under false imprints), the new journal capitalized on the public's growing demand for new approaches, especially in matters religious. Its first pages announced that the journal was the work of "several persons from different countries, who have formed a kind of society, whose unique goal is public utility and instruction."[5]

The Hague literary society may also have consciously imitated a circle in Rotterdam centered around the English Quaker merchant Benjamin Furly, who was a friend to many of the men in the new club. Furly's circle included the famous skeptic Pierre Bayle; the notorious English republican Algernon Sidney; the republican and moralist Anthony Ashley Cooper, the third earl of Shaftesbury; John Locke; William Penn, the founder of Pennsylvania; and Charles Levier, among others. Furly had held meetings in his home of this literary and philosophical society known as The Lantern. Its name, possibly indebted to the

1.1 Bernard Picart as a young man. This self-portrait in red chalk is very similar to the mezzotint portrait of Picart produced by Nicolaas Janz. Verkolje in 1715 after a 1709 painting by Jean Marc Nattier (see Figure 6.2). In 1709 Picart was thirty-six years old. (Rijksmuseum, Prentenkabinet M. RP-T 1965)

Quaker notion of "the inner light," also suggests its role in propagating early Enlightenment ideas. The Furly circle was in many ways the epicenter of the first generation of the European Enlightenment. Before his death in 1714 Furly had established contact with many of the aspiring young intellectuals and bookmen who will become part of our story.[6]

Readers of the new *Journal Littéraire,* the editor recounted, had for some time bemoaned the lack of a publication to explain the intellectual stakes of new books. And what were these books? Many refuted atheism—and thus intentionally or unintentionally gave atheism a kind of audience—and others were among the best-known supporters of greater latitude in questions of religion, works by men like John Tillotson and Samuel Clarke in England. The editors explicitly supported freedom of conscience ("a good granted by God himself") but carefully insisted that they would offer no public positions on matters of theology or philosophical subjects directly pertaining to religion. Instead they would give faithful extracts of the works under review and would "offer the different opinions to public scrutiny." A decade later Bernard and Picart would emulate this same strategy in *Religious Ceremonies of the World.* Picart himself owned the works of Tillotson and Clarke. Bernard went a step further and republished them time and again during his life.[7]

The rationale the journal editors gave for their position tells much about the tenor of religious debate at the time, even in the relatively tolerant Dutch Republic: "Everyone believes himself orthodox in his sentiments, and everything outside of the sphere of his opinions appears to him far removed from Holy Doctrine. Thus, no matter what position we take, we would never be able to avoid the odious label of heretics, with which one is so prodigal in our century." They drew the line at atheism, however. Silence could not rule when it came to those who "declare themselves against all religion in general," and so they persistently returned to this theme, prompting the reader to wonder if they were not protesting just a bit too much. The journal also provided lively commentaries on intellectual life in Paris, focusing in particular on the quarrel between Jesuits and Jansenists that was erupting at just that moment. The editors clearly favored the Jansenists against the "slavish bishops of the Society of Jesus [Jesuits]," but even the Jansenists came under fire for being "opinionated." *Religious Ceremonies of the World* would express similar positions: a preference for Jansenism over orthodox Catholicism, an underlying tension about atheism (explicitly rejected but not negatively portrayed), and an insistence on the right of the reader to decide for himself in religious matters. This emphasis on choosing for oneself was inherently heretical for many of the world's religions.[8]

As the proliferation of French-language publications like the *Journal Littéraire* shows, the Dutch Republic had been profoundly affected by the arrival of Protestant refugees from France. Although Huguenots had fled to Switzerland, Prussia, England, and even the American colonies, the greatest number had sought safe haven in the Dutch Republic. Of the estimated 150,000 Protestants who left France, some 50,000–70,000 found new homes among the Dutch. In Amsterdam the influx transformed the character of the city. After 1685 almost one-fifth of its population was of French-language origin. Popping up across the city were French quarters, French shops, schools, watering holes, notaries and lawyers, even French-language churches. The attraction of the Dutch Republic is not difficult to explain. Francophone communities had already taken root during the first half of the seventeenth century, when Protestants fled northward from the southern Netherlands as Catholic armies recaptured territory lost in the uprising against Spanish rule. Once the Spanish had been forced to officially recognize Dutch independence in 1648, the Dutch Republic served as headquarters of the international Protestant resistance against the imperial aspirations of the French king Louis XIV. Dutch city councils eased guild and citizenship regulations and offered subsidies to the newcomers. In addition, no law mandated church membership or the baptism of children, and no tithe favoring a single faith was levied on believers and unbelievers alike. Some French refugees were horrified by such freedom, but others must have found it liberating.[9]

Publishing offered young Huguenot intellectuals like Bernard and Picart an unusual opportunity. Printing of books and pamphlets had played a crucial role in the development of Protestantism from its beginnings. Without the printing press, Luther's break from Rome would have remained a tempest in a teapot. Print fed polemics between Protestants and Catholics and among the various Protestant sects as well as different Catholic factions. It could also on occasion threaten the very foundations of Christianity. In 1685 two Dutch presses printed copies of a book in French censored by the French authorities, Richard Simon's *Critical History of the Old Testament.* A Catholic priest, Simon brought together the best available biblical criticism to show that the text of the Old Testament had been repeatedly altered over time by Jewish authorities. If the Bible was a historical document, could it still be considered a sacred instrument of revelation? Controversy raged all over Europe, even among Protestants who saw Simon as carrying forward the efforts of Hobbes and Spinoza to question Moses's authorship of the Pentateuch. The intellectual circle around Furly took a special interest in discussing Simon's many books that effectively historicized the Bible, even though Simon believed himself to be a devout Catholic.[10]

Despite or even because of these controversies, the book trade had its allure, especially for Huguenot intellectuals with nonconformist religious ideas who enjoyed few other career options. Positions in the Dutch church and universities were strictly limited to those subscribing to orthodox Reformed theology. Skeptics and seekers need not apply. Even Protestant clergy who held liberal theological positions faced harassment from the consistory of the Calvinist Church. Moreover, the presence of what everyone called "the French colony" produced a strong local demand for all kinds of French texts: schoolbooks, hymns, Bibles, sermons, and almanacs—works that comprised the profitable core of any publishing business. French-language publishers had excellent connections with France and the other Huguenot communities, and shipping books proved relatively easy owing to the extended network of Dutch merchants, not to mention the favorable disposition of some customs officials. Still, French censors could make selling books to France a hazardous and extremely costly enterprise.[11]

The influence of Huguenot writers and publishers on European culture and politics proved to be remarkably deep and long-lasting. Their first standard-bearer was Pierre Bayle, a philosophy professor forced to leave France for Rotterdam when Louis XIV shut down the Protestant university in eastern France where he held his position. As his brother lay dying in a French prison in 1684, Bayle helped to establish a more critical and international public of readers by putting out a journal called *News from the Republic of Letters*. It paved the way for Bayle's real bombshell, the *Historical and Critical Dictionary* of 1697.

Every major Enlightenment writer of the eighteenth century found inspiration and encouragement in the pages of Bayle's *Dictionary*. Simon had applied historical criticism to the Bible in the hope of providing a more accurate text for Christians and showing the necessity of an authoritative ecclesiastical interpreter of its meaning. By contrast, Bayle embraced uncertainty and cast its net of doubt more widely, subjecting all philosophical and religious positions to witheringly skeptical scrutiny, often saving his most acerbic comments for his extensive footnotes.

He included a startlingly forthright discussion of Spinoza and atheism and criticized fantastic Christian tales about Muhammad. To this day critics differ heatedly about Bayle's own religious position: he has been labeled everything from an atheist to a conservative Calvinist to a secret Jew or even a covert follower of Spinoza.

Bayle opened the floodgates of religious discussion, not just of Protestant criticism of Louis XIV's Catholic dogmatism, but of religious intolerance more generally. He showed how a brash encyclopedic approach—rather than a focus on a central controversy such as that about transubstantiation—could stimulate a nascent public hunger for participation in philosophical and religious discussions that previously had been limited to clerical or professorial circles. This unemployed professor-turned-journalist offered an encyclopedic tool for managing new information and for sifting through the polemics. Moreover, Bayle offered the reader a spicy brew of reasoned analysis and satirical dismantling of superstition, credulity, and fanaticism. He liked to tweak his readers' expectations, suggesting, for instance, that atheists might be more moral in some circumstances than Christian believers. Since the Dutch Republic rarely exercised the kind of national censorship that rulers wielded in the other continental countries, publishers could try out new formulas for presenting controversial issues, such as atheism, to the public. New publishing ventures such as the *Journal Litéraire* or, another decade later, *Religious Ceremonies of the World* built upon Bayle's breakthroughs.

When Picart and Marchand arrived in the Dutch Republic in very late 1709 or early 1710, four years after Bayle's death, they immediately threw themselves into the debates provoked by Simon and Bayle. Bernard, too, shared the enthusiasm; he had even served as book buyer for Bayle in Geneva. Bernard and Picart both owned the original 1685 edition of Simon's critical study of the Old Testament as well as many of his other works. Their personal libraries also included multiple copies of Bayle's works. The opening volume of *Religious Ceremonies of the World* would feature Simon's translation of Leon Modena's book on the ceremonies and customs of the Jews as well as Simon's attempt to compare Jewish practices to those of Catholicism. *Religious Ceremonies of the World* would also make repeated references to Bayle's most inflammatory dictionary entries. In 1720 Michael Böhm published Marchand's edition of Bayle's *Dictionary;* this third edition became the definitive one. It included an engraving by Picart, not of Bayle but of the duke of Orleans, regent upon the death of Louis XIV and potential agent of change in official French policies. Many exiled French Protestants still dreamed of returning to France, and they hoped, futilely it turned out, that the regent might lift the ban against them.[12]

In cities such as The Hague, Amsterdam, and Rotterdam Huguenot writers, engravers, and publishers consorted with an international mix of like-minded men, not only German publishers such as Böhm, Fritsch, and Gleditsch, but also the English freethinkers John Toland and his friend Anthony Collins. Toland was in many ways the original freethinker; he may well have been the first writer labeled as such. A "freethinker" in the early eighteenth century was someone who refused to submit to ecclesiastical authority in matters of doctrine, and many people considered the term a synonym for "atheist" and "libertine," that is, for someone who rejected Christianity and lived a loose moral life as a result. In 1713 Collins published *A Discourse of Free-thinking*, in which he embraced the pejorative label and tried to turn it into a positive value. He attacked the authority of priests and prelates and argued that free-thinking was an inherent right that offered the only way of gaining true knowledge. Because Marchand saved their letters, we know that Collins corresponded with Levier, the publisher of the *Three Impostors*. In their letters they discussed English politics and possible book projects about the science of Newton and his followers, who were after all their contemporaries. Bernard and Picart each owned the French translation of Collins's defense of freethinking.[13]

Were Collins's and Toland's unorthodox ideas about religion also those of the knights and their circles? In 1709, just before the arrival of Picart and Marchand from Paris, Toland published in The Hague a book in Latin, *Adeisidaemon* [Free from superstition]. He used a thinly disguised examination of the Roman author Livy to argue that super-stition threatened civil society much more than did atheism. Toland claimed to be seeking a middle ground between atheism and priestly imposture. He made no bones about his rejection of the Trinity, and in his later Latin tract *Pantheisticon* (1720) he offered a pantheistic ritual in praise of nature and reason to be performed by his "brotherhood" as a kind of substitute for religion. Toland claimed to have followers in London and many Dutch cities, and French translations of this work did circulate in manuscript in this period.[14]

Pantheism, a term given currency by Toland, could take many forms. Most contemporaries assumed it to be atheism *tout court.* Often traced to the influence of the philosophy of Spinoza, pantheism, it was said, equated God with nature. When Bernard explicated Spinoza's idea of God, he came to the conclusion (taken up by others only much later in the century) that Spinoza had meant what he said when he spoke of God as creator of nature and embodied in it. While open to many meanings, pantheism, or what some called Spinozism, possessed one stable characteristic: God was not a being separate from nature and creation; rather, he was in some way a part of them.[15]

Bernard had *Pantheisticon* in his library, and in *Religious Ceremonies of the World* he, too, frequently lashed out against the evils of superstition. Moreover, in volume six he quoted directly from two works by Toland, *Christianity not Mysterious* (1696) and *Adeisidaemon.* Although Bernard claimed to reject Toland's more extreme positions as tending toward atheism, he gave them extensive coverage. Even in 1736, when Bernard published volume six, Toland's ideas remained controversial. An Italian follower of Toland was arrested in London after publishing a pantheist work in 1732. He fled to The Hague when released on bail. The English writer Daniel Defoe, who shared Toland's support for the post-1689 English political order, nonetheless loathed his views on religion, complaining that Toland "poisons souls with his infected Breath."[16]

In the face of possible accusations of atheism, the knights and their associates, like Toland himself, avoided putting their names to works that were frankly hostile to organized religion. As good businessmen they printed what the market wanted, which included publications of every description: periodicals, travel accounts, satires, encyclopedias, histories, and sermons. Still, their philosophically inclined books invariably took the side of, indeed promoted, the emerging Enlightenment. They generally praised the new learning of the day, popularized science, pushed the envelope of religious skepticism, satirized the prevailing social and sexual mores, and cast a cold eye on clergy and dogmas. Artisans of the book trade like the knights were the intellectual and mercantile foot soldiers for progressive thought. Their journals kept up the pressure against absolutism and the Catholic Church, and for the most part, they got their books into France under the radar of the censors. Without them the Enlightenment would have been a few brave critics of the status quo like Voltaire or major philosophers like Hume or Kant, but never a cultural movement. Their social networks stretched from Amsterdam and The Hague to London, Geneva, Berlin, and even the Dutch colony of Surinam. Along the tracks that they laid, ideas like pantheism, gossip about kings and courts, and news rattled through the growing Republic of Letters.

Writing in 1706 from the safety provided by an imagined Republic of Letters, the third earl of Shaftesbury, one of Toland's acquaintances, wrote enthusiastically to a friend in Holland, "There is a mighty Light which spreads itself in those two free Nations of England and Holland." Both countries offered an exceptional degree of religious toleration and relative freedom of the press. By 1700 the prepublication censorship of books no longer existed in either place. Books were still occasionally burned, as happened to Toland's *Christianity not Mysterious* in the late 1690s, and the Blasphemy Act of 1697 made it a criminal offense in England to preach or write against the Trinity or to deny the divine authority of the Bible. In Holland, writers or publishers could still be thrown in prison, for Spinozism for example, and languish there conceivably until death, though the number of such cases could be counted on the fingers of one hand. In both countries, then, heterodox religious views had to be expressed cautiously, and ideas about atheism, if published, had to be done so anonymously.[17]

Although the precise religious beliefs of Bernard, Picart, and their overlapping circles of friends are difficult to pin down, the affiliation with Bayle and Toland suggests at the very least a healthy appetite for skepticism about religious orthodoxies. Bernard's anonymously published book *Moral Reflections* confirms this tendency. It begins as an inquiry into the origins of religion: "Our parents take care to give us an idea of a Being of whom they know little . . . we serve God in many different ways, but there is only one cult that can please him, and this cult, rendered very equivocal and very obscure by men, is called *Religion*. In religion each person has his visible gods; (because the sovereign is invisible) these gods have different names; they change names according to the different projects of man." Already in this early work Bernard seems to be sketching the existence of some sort of universal religiosity that simply gets expressed in different forms, and its origins appear to be entirely human.[18]

Pious Protestants believed that God embedded belief in Himself in the human heart, not that men created their own "obscure" and "equivocal" cults. It is no wonder, then, that for his first publication on religion, Bernard chose an anonymous nonexistent publisher, "Pierre Marteau, Cologne." Under the cover of anonymity, Bernard's Persian philosopher could make any manner of iconoclastic remark about European practices: "These barbarians view people from other parts of the world with disdain. They treat them almost as savages, especially those who obey the precepts of the Koran. To call a man a Turk, a Moor, an Arab is to designate a scoundrel. We have the same right, dear friend. If we encounter an unjust or vindictive man, a knave or a traitor, we should call him a Christian." Bernard trains a skeptical eye on religion, yet he is clearly fascinated by what it says about the human condition. In matters religious, he is far from indifferent.[19]

In such issues, moreover, he grew bolder over time. Did the coming of peace in 1713 after more than ten years of war against Louis XIV's armies create a greater sense of security in the Dutch cities? In that year Bernard reissued and slightly altered *Moral Reflections,* and for the first time he put his name on it as publisher. He added a poem identifying the speaker as a merchant and revealing that he knew quite a bit about Dutch religious and theological quarrels of the day. He now drew attention to the growing impact of Dutch cafés; the knights may well have met in one. The visiting Persian enters a café to find "a kind of Altar stocked with liquors." In such establishments, the Persian continues, men often consume a warm dark beverage [coffee] or smoke. These rituals seem to constitute the "principal point of the ceremonies they practice in these places," though the customers also engage in animated conversation while passing printed sheets known as gazettes from hand to hand. They decide on the interests of the state, the conduct of armies, on war and peace. They dethrone kings and cut off the heads of princes; in short, the atmosphere of the café exudes "a spirit of sedition and discord . . . an anarchy of libertine discourse."[20]

In a third edition of 1716, Bernard grew yet more audacious. He attached a "key" to all the principal characters to aid readers in recognizing the previously unidentified figures. They are entirely contemporary to the events of the time, from leading political figures in the Dutch Republic and England to specific Protestant ministers. Bernard now makes clear that the city being described from the second edition onward is Amsterdam: "in this great city, rich and peopled by men of trade . . . we are charmed by the beauty of its streets, by the cleanliness of its homes. Its inhabitants enjoy a full liberty and live with abundance. They have few cares of the spirit; their unique occupation is to amass a great livelihood." Bernard no doubt hoped to make his fortune as a book merchant, too, but he would do so by publishing works about just such "cares of the spirit." With his Persian observer, Bernard was already opening up a kind of ethnographic perspective by turning the tables on the Dutch themselves. Bernard had little patience for those who considered religious questions exclusively from their own point of view.[21]

Picart, for his part, had acquired enough of a reputation as a religious maverick that Anne Vincent's father, Ysbrand, initially opposed the marriage, writing to a family friend, the Antwerp publisher Balthazar Moretus, that no child should marry someone "with no belief or religion." The original Dutch was emphatic: "geen geloof of religie." Moretus had helped Ysbrand Vincent, a Dutch Protestant married to a French Huguenot wife, get two of their children out of France after the revocation of the Edict of Nantes in 1685. Because of Louis XIV's determination to convert French Calvinists to Catholicism, by force if necessary, getting the children out took years. Vincent in turn regularly traded in paper with Moretus, who had become one of his closest friends. Now in 1712 Vincent wrote from Amsterdam asking Moretus to ascertain the circumstances under which Picart had left Paris in the first place. Vincent sulked for months about the marriage, even though his wife favored the couple's plans. In the end he attended the wedding and thereafter provided much practical help, working with Picart to find a suitable press to print his engravings. In return Picart produced engravings for the many Dutch plays that Vincent had printed and then performed in Amsterdam.[22]

Clues about the religious and philosophical leanings of Bernard and Picart can also be gleaned from the catalogues of their personal libraries. They each had about 2,000 titles in French, Latin, Dutch, English, and Italian—large libraries for the time, even for men involved in the book trade. Like most men of the eighteenth century, they owned many histories, religious polemics, especially liberal Protestant sermonizing, and works of ancient and modern literature, including *Robinson Crusoe,* which appeared in French translation in Amsterdam in 1720 with a frontispiece by Picart. Not surprisingly, their collections of travel books were even more complete than those of most educated men; such books provided the essential textual and visual sources for *Religious Ceremonies of the World*. Even more striking is their taste for what people of the time called natural philosophy—Galileo, Descartes, Newton—and for the generally heterodox. Picart owned not only many volumes by or about Hobbes, one of the most maligned thinkers of the time, and six extremely rare works by Giordano Bruno, who was burnt at the stake in Rome in 1600 as a heretic, but also the writings of early seventeenth-century "libertine philosophers" such as Gabriel Naudé and Giulio-Cesare Vanini. Bernard possessed the complete works of Spinoza.[23]

The libertines were among the first partisans of freethinking in that they refused to hold orthodox religious views just because they were traditional. The Toulouse authorities burnt Vanini at the stake in 1619 for sodomy and "atheism," though he professed to believe in God. Rather like Giordano Bruno, Vanini infused matter with spirit, making nature into a force. Although the word had not yet been invented, we may describe him as an early pantheist. In 1714 Bernard affiliated himself with the libertine tradition in a public fashion by publishing a reworking in French of Adriaan Beverland's treatise on original sin (1678). Beverland maintained that sexual desire was the original sin, an argument that justified the inclusion of countless passages of erotica and condemnations of moral conformity. In place of the name of a publisher and place of publication, Bernard offered only the untraceable phrase "printed in the world." Near the end of his life, in one of the supplements to *Religious Ceremonies of the World*, Bernard reproduced pornographic engravings of sexual orgies said to have occurred among the ancients. Picart, too, demonstrated an interest in the erotic, especially in engravings done in his Paris period.[24]

One omission from the published catalogues of Picart's and Bernard's personal libraries calls out for some commentary: *The Treatise of the Three Impostors*, the most outrageous book published in a century that specialized in them. The men surely knew the work, as Bernard makes clear in volume six of *Religious Ceremonies of the World*, if indeed they were not directly involved in its dissemination. Bernard gave a very exact citation to it in that volume. In 1719 the joker of the Knights of Jubilation, Charles Levier, was the first to print it. Twenty years later, one of the knights, Gaspar Fritsch, wrote a letter to Marchand in which he recalled that in 1711 Levier had hurriedly copied the treatise from a manuscript found in Furly's private library in Rotterdam. Furly's library

1.2 An erotic print from Picart's Paris period, signed "Drawn and engraved by B. Picart 1705." The legend reads, "If your Claudine rebels / Don't let her first refusal put you off / The time will come when the most cruel woman / Will make a false step while fleeing." (Rijksmuseum, Prentenkabinet P 1938-1724.00)

of some 4,400 books was one of the largest in Holland; the knights Fritsch and Böhm published a sale catalogue of it when Furly died in 1714. Furly had close political ties to Adriaan Vroese, a former mayor of Rotterdam and the father of Jan Vroese, whom some see as having a major role in producing *The Treatise of the Three Impostors*. In any case, Furly's circle was dedicated to complete intellectual freedom, religious toleration, and, in Furly's words, "the liberty of the whole world."[25]

Levier's book, published with the title *La Vie et l'esprit de Spinosa*, had two parts. The first reproduced an anonymous but perfectly respectable biographical sketch of the philosopher that is usually attributed to one of Spinoza's disciples, Jean Maximilien Lucas. Bernard quoted freely from it in volume six in the section on deism. The second was explosive: it combined a portion of Spinoza's *Ethics*, previously untranslated into French, with citations and paraphrases of Hobbes, Naudé, and Vanini, and added to them a new, full-barreled barrage against the three great impostors Moses, Jesus, and Muhammad. The work claimed that the three charlatans had manipulated the credulity and fears of ordinary people to set up systems of deceit that, in addition, subverted long-standing forms of republican government. Neither Levier's nor Böhm's edition two years later (now with the three impostors title) made its way to the market. The Dutch authorities, who usually cared little about French books that could be read only by the better-educated minority, absolutely forbade its circulation. When Levier died, Marchand burned the remaining copies of the 1719 edition, or so he said. Marchand complained that Levier was "completely infatuated with the philosophy of Spinoza," and even Bayle had described Spinoza in his *Dictionary* as a "Jew by birth, and then deserter from Judaism, and finally atheist . . . systematic atheist." A handful of remaining copies of the 1719 edition have only recently been rediscovered.[26]

Jean Frederic Bernard also did his part to spread the ideas found in *The Treatise of the Three Impostors*. With financial backing from another Huguenot refugee, Henri du Sauzet, Bernard operated behind the scenes as an intellectual impresario for a weekly journal, *Nouvelles Littéraires* [Literary news]. Bernard persuaded the otherwise timid Sauzet to print in the journal, in the same year that Levier tried to publish the book, its first part, Lucas's laudatory biography of Spinoza. It was too dangerous to print the second part about the three impostors. Such a step would have brought the authorities to Sauzet's doorstep and risked the future of the entire journal, not to mention the very freedom of Sauzet and Bernard themselves. Although short-lived, *Nouvelles Littéraires* became one of the most sought-after publications among the many journals of the period. Information about Spinoza attracted attention, even sales. Sauzet was shocked by the stir resulting from his publication of Lucas's piece.[27]

As with Voltaire's God, if *The Treatise of the Three Impostors* had not existed, someone would have had to invent it. An oral tradition in several languages had repeatedly surfaced with the charges that Moses, Jesus, and Muhammad were not the holy men acclaimed by their followers, but rather deceptive scoundrels. Medieval scholastics claimed that the twelfth-century Andalusian-Arab philosopher Averroes had written a work on the subject, and Pope Gregory IX accused Holy Roman Emperor Frederick II of embracing the view in the early thirteenth century. The charge came up repeatedly thereafter. In the London suburbs in 1672, for example, a man was arraigned for announcing that "Jesus Christ, Moyses and Mahomet were three greate rogues." It seems all but inevitable that someone with access to a printing press would eventually oblige by actually printing such a book, if only because there might be money to be made. We now know that men connected to the Knights of Jubilation were involved in compiling the text as well as in publishing it. Although we do not know exactly who did what, there is no question that some of the knights and their friends had a part in it. In 1716, three years before Levier published the book, Jean Rousset de Missy, another Huguenot refugee, anonymously published an article in which he gave a very precise description of the contents of the book. Rousset went on to become the leader of Amsterdam freemasonry and an intimate friend and correspondent of Marchand's, writing openly on freemasonry and the possible triumph of pantheism.[28]

The Treatise of the Three Impostors has the air of a work written by committee. A bricolage of contemporary radical and heretical ideas, its various sections seem clumsily juxtaposed rather than artfully stitched together. The writing is aimed at a very general audience, and the ideas are punched out rather than philosophically reasoned. Speaking of the fear that prompts humans to project the existence of gods, for example, the treatise exclaims that "ever since men have got it into their heads that there were invisible Angels which were the cause of their good or bad fortune, they have renounced good sense & reason, & they have taken their chimeras for so many Divinities which were in charge of their conduct." It seems quite likely, too, that Toland had a hand in developing the argument, if not the book itself. He had written essays claiming that Moses was basically a pantheist, and he left behind in his papers a manuscript that called Jesus a magician.[29]

Even if it did not circulate above board to a wide audience, *The Treatise of the Three Impostors* haunted "freethinking" throughout the century. Freethinking, many authorities argued, led ineluctably to views like pantheism and ultimately atheism. *The Treatise* seemed to prove these officials right as it moved effortlessly from the idea that God is only a projection of the anxieties found in the human psyche to the notion that "God . . . [is] but nature, or, if one wishes, the assemblage of all beings, of all properties, & of all energies." From this pantheist position, the book then took the next step and argued that the great monotheistic religions were based on superstitions and lies and that priests and their images were nothing more than means to hide the truth from ordinary people.[30]

Despite censorship, these ideas seeped gradually into the European intellectual water table. In 1717, just before Levier's printing, the Huguenot pastor David Durand published a life of Vanini in which he claimed that the Italian libertine philosopher had been charged with bringing to light a book called "Of the Three Impostors." In the 1730s Bernard repeated some of its ideas about God in his discussion of deism in *Religious Ceremonies of the World.* At the very end of the eighteenth century in his utopian work *Sketch for a Historical Picture of the Progress of the Human Mind,* Jean-Antoine-Nicolas de Caritat, marquis de Condorcet, referred to the "imaginary" book about the three impostors. He nonetheless went on to insist that "the title alone announced the existence of an opinion that followed naturally from the examination of the three beliefs [Judaism, Christianity, Islam]. Born from the same source, these were only the corruption of a purer cult rendered by more ancient peoples to the universal soul of the world."[31]

Picart and Bernard may have subscribed to a similar position at one time or another, and they certainly knew of the arguments firsthand. Indeed, it is not too farfetched to suggest that they developed their own ideas about religion in part in reaction to what they either knew or had heard of *The Treatise of the Three Impostors.* We must emphasize, moreover, that Bernard was not the only one of the collaborators with intellectual aspirations. In 1762, nearly three decades after the death of Picart, Willem Bentinck, a leading Dutch diplomat and acquaintance of Rousseau, sent a copy of *Religious Ceremonies of the World* to his young friend the prince of Orange, who was to become William V, stadholder of the Dutch Republic, in 1766. Bentinck told of Picart's leading him into a deep philosophical discussion that would interest his highness as much as the collection itself.[32]

Picart moved in the same circles as Rousset de Missy, the author of numerous works on diplomatic and military history, international law, education, and even the history of Russia, in addition to his involvement with *The Treatise of the Three Impostors.* Picart and Rousset were both close friends of Marchand, and they shared an additional connection through one of Rousset's intimates, Lambert Ignace Douxfils, a postal commissioner in Brussels. When customs officials seized a packet of Picart's engravings as it entered France in 1712, Anne and Bernard Picart appealed to "our friend" Douxfils to help them with the authorities, which he promptly did. Rousset always addressed Douxfils as *mon frère*, and Douxfils sent him poems with masonic themes. What other services might Douxfils have performed for booksellers eager and ready to ship illicit and blasphemous books into France? We know that a few such books got through because the French police arrested people who had them in their possession. Douxfils ultimately lost his job.[33]

Separately at first and then later in collaboration, Picart and Bernard learned to maintain a precarious balance between their leanings toward the radical and heretical and the decorum required by their family ties, membership in the local Huguenot congregation, and business affairs. As Protestant exiles from France, they embraced the mission of criticizing the absolutism and Catholic dogmatism of Louis XIV's France. They relied on their Huguenot friends in pursuing that mission, and in company with some of them, they translated that criticism into analyses that challenged more than French absolutism. But they did not wish to jeopardize their hard-won successes in their new country, so they did not advertise opinions that might prove problematic to either the authorities or even their families. Never once did *Religious Ceremonies of the World* use the phrase "three impostors," though "charlatans," "impostors," and "imposture" more generally appear repeatedly.

We have seen the kinds of friends and associates whom Picart sought once he arrived in the relative safety of the Dutch Republic. But how did he come to leave France and the Catholicism into which he had been born and raised? Why would a highly successful artist throw over his bright prospects and guaranteed sources of patronage for the life of exile and a very different intellectual and artistic world, a world like that of the Knights of Jubilation? To understand his choices, we need to retrace his steps back to Paris and the world he left behind.

2

Bernard Picart

Religious and Artistic Journeys

U NLIKE Jean Frederic Bernard, who left France with his family as a young child, Bernard Picart grew up in Paris as the son and successor of a prosperous Catholic engraver, Etienne Picart. After he arrived in Amsterdam, Bernard Picart married Anne Vincent and with her raised their three daughters in the Walloon Reformed Church. But he had also been married in Paris as a younger man, to Claudine Prost, a fellow Catholic with close ties to the Cramoisy family, which specialized in Catholic, even Jesuit, publications. None of the children from his first marriage survived, and when his first wife died in 1708, the prospect opened of finally making the life-altering move that he had been mulling over for years. In late 1709 or early 1710 Picart abandoned his life as a good Catholic engraver in Paris and moved northward with his close friend Prosper Marchand.[1]

Something about Picart's life journey troubled his future father-in-law, and it is not hard to imagine why. If Picart had been a Protestant for some time, why did he leave Paris only at age thirty-seven? If he was a more recent convert, how did he come to embrace Protestantism in a country where it had been illegal since he was twelve years old? Perhaps a clue can be found in the fact that his father, a member of the prestigious Royal Academy of Painting and Sculpture, went with him to Amsterdam and lived out the rest of his days there, too. Etienne Picart had stood by as the Royal Academy, which had admitted him in 1664, began to purge suspected Protestants in 1681, even before the revocation of the Edict of Nantes.[2]

Other factors might also have been at work. The Picarts may have sympathized with Jansenists who wanted a more austere—some said more Calvinist—form of Catholicism, as did many intellectuals, artists, judges in the royal courts, and even clergymen. Louis XIV forced leading Jansenists into exile (some went to the Dutch Republic) and in 1710 razed the convent of Port-Royal when its nuns refused to retract their Jansenist views. Protestants shared with Jansenists the experience of being persecuted for their religious views, and both groups viewed with horror the growing rapprochement among Louis XIV, the Jesuits, and the pope. In the first decade of the new century Prosper Marchand, Picart's very close friend, kept both Protestant and Jansenist versions of the New Testament in his private library.[3]

Signs of discontent appeared relatively early in Bernard Picart's life. In 1696–1697, he spent a few months in Antwerp and the better part of a year in the Dutch Republic. He may already have been contemplating a permanent move, but he returned to Paris when he got word of his mother's death and the serious illness of his father. Yet young Picart could hardly complain about lacking advantages in the Parisian art world. He learned the techniques of engraving and etching from his father at age ten or eleven and signed his first work at age twelve. Although the signature on the engraving of a now lost painting by Jean Jouvenet is open to discussion, it is clear that Etienne had jump-started his son's career. At age sixteen Bernard began study at the Royal Academy with leading artists and soon won a prize, attracting the favorable attention of the academy's celebrated leader, the painter Charles Le Brun. Within a year or two Picart had already embarked on his lifelong career of engraving famous paintings, which would include many by Le Brun himself. He also began to produce fashion engravings, which commanded an important market in Paris, and prints of stock figures in the wildly popular *commedia dell'arte,* an improvisational theater. By the mid-1690s Picart had established enough of a reputation that a representative of the Swedish court tried to lure him there.[4]

Lack of success, then, did not prompt Picart to go to Catholic Antwerp in 1696. Religion might have played a role, though evidence for this motive is only circumstantial. Some of the most prominent

2.1 The father or the son? This 1685 engraving titled "Healing of the Paralytic" after a painting by Jean Jouvenet is clearly signed "B. Picart romanus," but Bernard was only twelve at the time, and his father more commonly signed himself "romanus" ("le romain," because he had studied in Rome). (Research Library, The Getty Research Institute, Los Angeles, California, 2003.PR.48)

leaders of French Jansenism had taken refuge in the Spanish Netherlands, including Pasquier Quesnel, the son of a Parisian bookseller who had joined the congregation of the Oratory or Oratorians and written one of the most influential Jansenist works, *Moral Reflections on the New Testament*, which appeared for the first time in 1671. No educated French person could have ignored the furor surrounding Quesnel's book, especially not someone like Picart, who moved in much the same circles of booksellers and printers. Under increasing pressure, Quesnel fled to Brussels in 1685 and published expanded versions of his book in 1693, 1695, and 1699, just about the time Picart went to nearby Antwerp.

2.2.   Detail from bottom left corner of "Healing of the Paralytic" (see Figure 2.1). The "B" has given rise to much discussion. Many commentators believe that the original "E" has been altered. (Research Library, The Getty Research Institute, Los Angeles, California, 2003 PR.48)

In this period, Belgian cities became important centers for the publication of Jansenist works.

Quesnel argued that salvation depended on the grace freely given by God; grace could not be earned, and those who received it were predestined to do so. In addition, he recommended the reading of the Bible, criticized the Catholic Church's stifling of dissent, and urged greater lay participation in Church governance, without, however, advocating a break with Catholicism altogether. In 1703 Louis XIV got the Spanish king to arrange Quesnel's arrest, but the author's brother, also a priest, helped him escape, and Quesnel eventually made his way to Amsterdam. In 1713 the papal bull Unigenitus declared Quesnel's main positions seditious, blasphemous, and heretical and forbade Catholics to read his work on pain of excommunication. Picart himself owned an edition of the book, and his frontispiece to *Religious Ceremonies of the World* highlights the controversy and clearly favors the Jansenists. Picart no doubt found some Jansenist doctrines congenial, but he also shared with them common enemies in the Jesuits and the pope.

Other, more mundane motives might have drawn Picart to Antwerp, where he won a prize for drawing offered by the Antwerp Academy of Fine Arts. Was he dissatisfied with the status of engravers in Paris? Although his father, Etienne, was a member of the elite Royal Academy, as an engraver he ranked below the painters and sculptors, who were considered the true creators. The French Royal Academy deemed engravers useful because they could make copies of the masterpieces produced by the more highly regarded painters. Engravers in the academy had to defend tenaciously their special privileges against the master printer-engravers of Paris, who were granted the right to form their own guild in 1692. The master printer-engravers insisted on the right to print any engraving that the academy engravers had not themselves incised in the copperplate. A dispute between three academy engravers, including Etienne Picart, and the master printer-engravers made it all the way to the royal council in 1703 before it was resolved in favor of the academy engravers.[5]

In Antwerp, the young Bernard found an artistic scene very different from the one he had known in Paris. The Antwerp Academy got its name in the 1660s when the Spanish king, ruler of the southern Netherlands, allowed the city authorities to elevate the craftsmen's guild of St. Lucas so that it might compete for prestige with the academies in Rome and Paris. The Dutch-speaking guild of St. Lucas included not only painters but also engravers, booksellers and binders, printers, decorative box makers, and glass makers—in short, a wide variety of creative men (and a few women) who worked with their hands and met together as equal members.

In Paris, by contrast, booksellers, painters and sculptors, and printers of engravings all had their own separate guilds, while engraving itself was in theory open to anyone. Yet hierarchy imbued every aspect of printmaking in Paris: a workshop of engravers under the control of the king's favorite painter enjoyed a virtual monopoly on royal commissions; others got the right to live in the Louvre palace; and those who gained a royal privilege for their work had their engravings automatically entered in the royal library and were thereby guaranteed a kind of early copyright. At the top of the system sat the engravers in the Royal Academy. While the French Academy was the creation of the king and completely dependent on his good will, the guild of St. Lucas owed allegiance first and foremost to the city of Antwerp, which continued to supervise its activities.[6]

By the time Picart arrived in Antwerp, the academy's glory days,

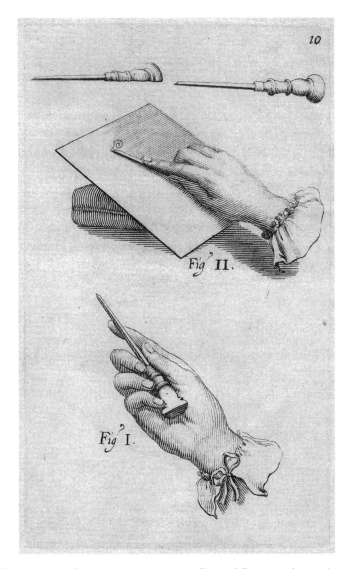

2.3   The burin used for copperplate engraving. Bernard Picart used a combination of etching and engraving in his work. In this etching the engraver's hand is using a burin to work a copperplate that has been set on a leather, sand-filled engraver's cushion, which enables the artist to move the plate in different directions. These techniques were described in a widely used French manual, Abraham Bosse, *Traicté des manieres de grauer en taille douce sur l'airin: par le moyen des eaux fortes, & des vernix durs & mols: ensemble de la façon d'en imprimer les planches & d'en construire la presse, & autres choses concernans les-dits arts* (Paris: Bosse, 1645), from which this is plate 10. (Research Library, The Getty Research Institute, Los Angeles, California)

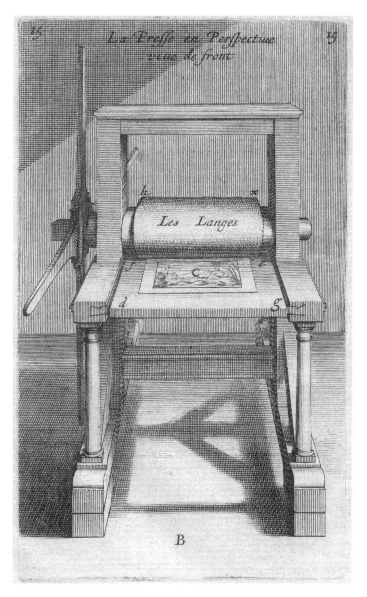

2.4 Printing from copperplate. The copperplate printer used a roller press. The plate was covered with a dampened piece of paper that literally soaked up the ink from the lines on the metal once it was run under the press. The press consisted of a heavy wooden roller, turned by a four-handed wheel. It both forced the weight of the roller onto the surfaces of the paper and plate and moved the paper-covered carriage forward under the roller. Plate 15 from Bosse, *Traicté des manieres de grauer en taille douce sur l'airin.* (Research Library, The Getty Research Institute, Los Angeles, California)

associated with Peter Paul Rubens (d. 1640) and Anthony Van Dyck (d. 1641), had passed, but it was still a lively place. The descendants of Pieter Bruegel the Elder (d. 1569) all belonged to the Antwerp guild, then academy, well into the eighteenth century. The academy's most important painter after 1660, David Teniers (d. 1690), had pioneered the production of what would become the modern art book. Working from his own painted copies of famous originals in Brussels owned by Archduke Leopold Wilhelm, the governor of the Spanish Netherlands, in 1660 Teniers published *The Theatre of Painting*, a collection of prints that reproduced the paintings in exquisite detail. The prints made the archduke's collection famous, and the book inspired other depictions of prized collections. When Picart returned to Paris, he collaborated on a similar project: he engraved some of the Rubens paintings in the Luxembourg Palace that were printed in a famous collection published in 1710. At the end of his life he prepared his own collection of "innocent impostures" of the famous masters. The Antwerp interlude was short but rich in lessons about both artistic and religious questions.[7]

Less is known about Picart's sojourn in Holland, though he clearly made some important contacts in 1696–1697, for he produced or assisted in a great number of prints for Dutch publications that appeared during or just after his visit. Among them were a few engravings for the French Huguenot Isaac de Larrey's history of England (1697) and no less than fifty engravings for the Mortier Bible, an illustrated history of the Old and New Testaments that appeared simultaneously in Antwerp and Amsterdam in 1700. An entirely pious work with a decidedly Protestant cast, it aimed "to instruct the people in the word of God." One of the other engravers with the project, Matthys Pool, turns up twelve years later as the keeper of letters sent from Antwerp by Balthasar Moretus to Ysbrand Vincent, Picart's father-in-law. Pool executed one of the engravings that Picart designed for the Mortier Bible.[8]

Even more important in the long run was the relationship Picart cemented with the biggest publisher in Amsterdam, Jean Louis de Lorme. Picart contributed engravings to at least five De Lorme publications in 1697–1698, including all seven plates for *The Ancient and Modern Religion of the Muscovites* (1698), a kind of prototype for *Religious Ceremonies of the World*. De Lorme also undertook a joint publication with Picart's father in 1698 of Le Brun's famous lecture on human expressions; it was illustrated by Bernard Picart. Picart continued to work for De Lorme

2.5 The Mortier Bible. Picart produced many pious biblical scenes, this one to illustrate Ezekiel chapter 3, verse 1, which he designed for David Martin, *Histoire du vieux et du nouveau testament: enrichie de plus de quatre cens figures* (Amsterdam: Pierre Mortier, 1700), p. 239. (Research Library, The Getty Research Institute, Los Angeles, California)

even after he returned to Paris; his engravings appeared in several works published by De Lorme between 1699 and 1709, and a few extant letters from 1708 show a lively commercial exchange between the two over prices to be paid, engravings to be shipped, orders to be checked on, and the like. De Lorme was always in a hurry, telling Picart on several occasions that if he could not complete a particular project within three months, he would drop the idea altogether. He also tried to bargain with Picart about the prices he paid him. How could each drawing of a medal cost five sous, he asked? When Picart held firm, he relented, but only if Picart really did them himself: "I will not contemplate paying you for those you do not draw yourself. It would not be fair." De Lorme collected payments from other Dutch booksellers for Picart, but he refused to sell Picart's engravings on commission. He wanted to buy them in lots and resell them himself.[9]

As might be expected, most of Picart's contacts in Amsterdam, De Lorme included, were Protestants. Had Picart already become a Protestant or was he simply pursuing the best business opportunities? De Larrey, for one, had vehemently criticized the French king Louis XIV in his history, and the French police threw a Parisian bookseller in the Bastille in 1705 for purveying his book, which was forbidden in France. Yet while in Holland Picart did not hesitate to produce engravings that celebrated Louis's greatest enemy, William III, stadholder of the Dutch Republic and king of England, including his victory over the French king at Namur.[10]

Still, once he returned to France, Picart immediately reverted to engraving the paintings of Louis XIV's favorite artist, Le Brun; medals of Louis himself; a vignette of the archbishop of Paris; as well as the Rubens cycle of paintings of Marie de Medici in the Luxembourg Palace. In Paris he still enjoyed the patronage of many leading artists, publishers, and courtiers, including the duke of Orleans, the nephew of Louis XIV who would become regent in 1715 when Louis XIV died, leaving his five-year-old great grandson as heir to the throne. Among Picart's supporters were Antoine Coypel, one of the eventual leaders of the Royal Academy who was named First Painter of the King in 1716; Jean-Marc Nattier, who did the drawings of the Rubens paintings in the Luxembourg Palace and also an early portrait of Picart; Antoine Watteau, who may have developed his famous gallant scenes of aristocratic life from models first drawn and engraved by Picart upon his re-

2.6   Picart's mentor, Roger de Piles. The portrait of the art theorist and champion of engraving was executed by Picart in 1704 on the occasion of De Piles's death. (Rijksmuseum Prentenkabinet P OB-51.041)

turn to Paris; and Roger de Piles, the day's most influential theoretician of art. Picart did not lack for friends in high places.

In these years in Paris, 1698–1710, Picart tried his hand at virtually every genre of printmaking in the market and soon developed an international reputation, thanks in part to help from his friends in Amsterdam. Even while vaulting from success to success, whether in fashion prints, snuff boxes, culs-de-lampe (decorative vignettes), reproductions of famous paintings, historical scenes, portraits, or moralizing allegories, Picart was also developing more subversive contacts. He made friends with Marchand, a publisher with a much coveted license to sell books, in a shop ideally placed on rue St. Jacques just steps from the Sorbonne. Picart engraved various images and decorations for Marchand, even designing the logo for Marchand's bookshop. Sales catalogues of the contents of that shop reveal a deep interest in religion and philosophy, as well as travel literature and multiple editions, by both Catholic and Jansenist editors, of the New Testament. Marchand also penned a trea-

2.7 Logo for Marchand's bookshop. Among the last pieces produced by Picart while still in Paris, this engraving served as the logo for Marchand's bookshop on rue St. Jacques and admonishes the viewer, "What you would not wish done to yourself, do not to another." Although hard to see, the date is 1709. (Rijksmuseum Prentenkabinet 11471.1709)

tise on geography that indicated a wide knowledge of the globe as it was then understood.[11]

A particular book item does not appear on the published list of the contents of Marchand's shop. Indeed it would never have withstood the gaze of the French censors. One of Marchand's earliest publications, on the sixteenth-century freethinker and skeptic Bonaventure Des Périers, included a letter Marchand had written to Picart in 1706 when they were still in Paris. Both book and letter were published only in 1711, when they reached the safe haven of the Dutch Republic. Marchand's letter to Picart argued for the merits of Des Périers, noting how unfair it seemed to compare his book to that of "the famous *de tribus impostoribus* [three impostors], if it ever existed." As we saw, a few years later the friends of Picart and Marchand would bring that very book into existence. Marchand left a private note in which he described the letter he eventually published as "vindicating this work [Des Périers]" against the charges of atheism and impiety. The published letter confirms that Marchand and Picart enjoyed an intellectual camaraderie, an interest not just in books but in their contents. When they sat and talked in Marchand's shop they had to hand a large number of books about theology and philosophy, from Catholic, Jansenist, and even Protestant sources, as well as writings about almost every place then known in the world.[12]

Marchand shared Picart's enthusiasm for the "moderns" in the quarrel that raged in Paris in the 1690s and early 1700s between adherents of the ancients and proponents of the moderns in literature, art, and science. For centuries in the West the writers of Greek and Roman Antiquity had been touted as the font of all wisdom, superior in learning to all who came after them. Late in the seventeenth century a new boldness appeared. Could it not be that the advances in learning, particularly in the study of nature, had turned the tables, and modern knowledge had come to exceed what even Plato and Aristotle had known? That was the burning question of the day.

The hero of the moderns was Descartes, the philosopher who first articulated their mechanical philosophy, whereas the ancients looked to Aristotle and his followers. In the seventeenth century the Aristotelians were known as the schoolmen, and their philosophy, based on Thomas Aquinas's interpretation of Aristotle, formed the core of the curriculum in every institution of higher learning in Catholic Europe. The moderns championed the new natural philosophy which argued that nature was composed of tiny corpuscles—called atoms by Newton—that moved as the result of contact action between bodies. Aristotle held that heavy bodies fall because it was in their nature to do so; the new philosophers insisted, in opposition, that they fell when struck by another body, and that their acceleration, if unchecked by another body, increased according to mathematically knowable laws.

Much more was involved than a dispute about school curricula. The quarrel between the ancients and the moderns went to the heart of how human and physical nature should be understood. Descartes claimed that true learning depended upon following a rigorous method anchored in clear and distinct ideas located in one's own mind. Truth was founded on the thinking self, not on dogmas taught, doctrines memorized, or principles put in place in the first instance to promote eternal salvation. Many who sided with the ancients thought, not without reason, that this new learning might ultimately undermine Christian orthodoxy, whether Catholic or Protestant. Although born a Catholic, Descartes found favor first in the schools of Protestant Europe, not least in Holland, where he lived for many years before his death in 1650.

Picart left no doubt as to the side he took in the quarrel between the ancients and the moderns. In 1707 he produced an engraving in praise of Descartes for the frontispiece of an academic thesis. Marchand wrote the legend explaining its meaning. In the print Minerva crushes ignorance after sending off an old man who represents closed-mindedness. Moreover, among the earliest of Picart's engravings were two on Descartes, since lost, including one from 1690, when Picart was seventeen, entitled "Justice and Truth, a Vignette for the Life of Descartes." Picart's 1707 portrayal of Descartes offended the Catholic university authorities because it featured the modern philosopher and made no reference to the need for faith. Truth depended entirely on secular learning. Usually the frontispieces of university theses provided occasions for the expression of piety, since the clergy dominated university teaching, and the genre was especially beloved by the Jesuits. Picart's father, Etienne, had been known for his thesis frontispieces. The Jesuits and many other clerics did not much like the actual thesis, either, as it was a thinly disguised exegesis of the philosophy of Descartes. Marchand wrote a letter to a French Huguenot journal in Amsterdam about the furor created by

2.8   Picart in praise of Descartes. In "The Truth Sought by the Philosophers," a thesis frontispiece produced by Picart in 1707, Descartes is shown just to the right of the female figure, who represents philosophy. According to the caption, she leads the philosophers to truth, which is triumphing in a dramatic allegorical scene. (Courtesy Leiden University Library, PK-P-106.523)

2.9   The retraction. According to Marchand, Picart was forced to publish a kind of visual retraction of his thesis frontispiece, titled "The accord of religion with philosophy, or reason with faith." (Courtesy Leiden University Library, PK-P-106.524)

Picart's engraving and later reported that Picart had been forced to do a retraction in the form of another engraving about the "accord of religion and philosophy."[13]

The number of scientific books in Picart's personal library, from Descartes's works to Newton's *Principia*, confirms the artist's dedication to the modern science of his day. Science did not inhabit a separate domain in Picart's time. The French schoolmen who followed Aristotle were Catholic clergymen, and their philosophical arguments provided crucial support for Church doctrines such as transubstantiation. Without Aristotelianism, transubstantiation—the transformation of the bread and wine of the Eucharist into the actual body and blood of Christ—became more difficult to maintain as doctrine. Siding with the moderns and the Cartesians might have inclined Picart toward Calvinism, for Calvinists rejected transubstantiation. An early nineteenth-century collection of Picart's engravings bundled together for sale includes a set of engravings on chemistry, engineering, botany, and the arts and sciences. Moreover, when Picart engraved a famous collection of gems he used a microscope to achieve a greater degree of verisimilitude. This artist was also a man of science.[14]

Although Picart took his enthusiasm for the moderns further than most artists in Paris, he could have drawn support from the art theorist Roger de Piles, who stood as godfather to Picart's son born in 1703. One of Picart's self-portraits showed him surrounded with books by De Piles, and Picart engraved a portrait of De Piles in 1704. Well known as a writer on art and artists, De Piles was elected an honorary member of the Royal Academy in 1699 at the advanced age of sixty-four. He was the first such nonartist member to be known for his theoretical writings and lectures on art theory. De Piles distinguished himself as an ardent defender of the moderns in painting, preferring the color brush stroke of Rubens to the classical emphasis on design in the work of the French painter Nicolas Poussin. In taking the side of the "Rubenists," De Piles had been influenced by Descartes, who sought to liberate the human passions by treating them as natural and involuntary movements of the soul. When applied to art or literature Cartesianism valorized the ability of the work of art to arouse the emotions. Rubens used color and movement to elicit an emotional response from the viewer. His figures run riot on the canvas as the saved ascend to heaven at the last judgment, or lions devour their human prey, or the damned tumble into hell.[15]

The defenders of the ancients were led by the academician André Félibien, who held up Poussin (d. 1665) as the greatest painter of the century. Félibien and the "Poussinists" subscribed to Poussin's belief that painting is an expression of reason and understanding, whose emotional impact flows from the coherence and unity of its composition, imposed by the stern intelligence of the artist. The Poussinists allied themselves with Aristotle and the ancients in part because Aristotle's *Poetics* had provided the justification for viewing painting as an independent form of intellectual creativity rather than as a mere imitation. Himself a pupil of Poussin, Le Brun ensured the official dominance of Poussinist views in the Royal Academy, but he was not entirely unsympathetic to the other side. On the one hand, Le Brun produced monumental paintings that valorized the military triumphs of Alexander the Great, for example, an apt subject for the young and increasingly bellicose Louis XIV. On the other hand, Le Brun's influential lecture on the passions illustrated by engravings of Le Brun's own drawings by Picart's teacher Sébastien Leclerc and then by Picart himself showed the impact of Cartesian notions about the expression of emotions. In Le Brun's view the passions of the soul produced bodily effects; "the soul receives the impressions of the passions in the brain and feels their effects in the heart."[16]

Since Le Brun died in 1690 when Picart was still an adolescent learning his trade, De Piles ultimately exerted the greater influence, especially when De Piles publicly championed engraving as the first truly modern art, an invention more or less contemporaneous with the advent of print. Because De Piles believed that the goal of art was "the simple and faithful imitation of the motions which express nature," printmaking held a special place. Prints are essential, he argued, for "philosophers . . . [and] the increase of their knowledge of Natural Things." Engraving and etching went hand in hand with the new science because they could display what is seen by microscopes, illustrate the invisible, such as the motion of corpuscles, or depict complex machinery and its operation. Indeed by 1700 most scientific writers followed Descartes in employing etchings or engravings to explicate their message. The three scientific treatises that accompanied Descartes's *Discourse on Method* in 1637 included more than 150 illustrations. If the sixteenth century saw the liberation of painting from the status of mere handicraft, then the late seventeenth and early eighteenth century witnessed a comparable attempt at the elevation of printmaking.[17]

Picart could only have found De Piles's writing on the virtues of engraving, first published in 1699, immensely heartening. Although Picart continued to engrave paintings by Le Brun, one of his earliest patrons, De Piles's praise of Rubens must have made Picart especially excited about his work on the Rubens cycle of paintings of Marie de Medici in the Luxembourg Palace. De Piles even connected art to religion, a linkage increasingly important to Picart. Sculptors and painters had originally depicted the false divinities, "which gave rise to fables," and had set those images before "the eyes of the Egyptians for their adoration." Art thereby laid the foundation for religion, and by implication it now merited the right to investigate those same fables. Just as science benefited from the art of engraving, so too could religion. Toward the end of his own life Picart took up some of De Piles's themes again in a short treatise on the value of engraving, its artistic merits, and the originality or "spirit" that the engraver brings to his copper plates even when he is "copying" a painting. From at least the 1690s, when he first met De Piles, until his death in Amsterdam in 1733, Picart lived by De Piles's artistic principles, that is, by a body of thought and practice first learned and applied in Paris. The visit to Antwerp and Amsterdam may have opened his eyes to new business opportunities and, in the case of Amsterdam, religious options too, but before leaving Paris he had further honed his skills and participated in one of the most significant quarrels in what would come to be seen as the first stirring of the Enlightenment in France.[18]

He had also, in conversation and growing friendship with Marchand, undertaken an inward journey toward Protestantism. While in Holland in 1697, according to Marchand's account, Picart had read a book by a leading Protestant apologist, Jean Claude, a French Huguenot pastor forced to flee to The Hague at the time of the revocation in 1685 (he died there two years later). In 1678, before Louis XIV outlawed Calvinism in France, Claude had publicly debated the leading Catholic theologian Bishop Jacques Bénigne Bossuet, arguing for the superiority of Protestantism over Catholicism. The most fatal flaw of Catholicism, according to Claude, was its emphasis on externalities: "they [the Catholics] imagined that the entire essence of the Church consisted in an externality, and that just as to be a true member of civil society it sufficed to observe the laws by one's external behavior, so too making a public profession of faith and religion would suffice to make one a true member of the Church without interior virtues such as faith, charity and hope being absolutely necessary." In 1685 the French authorities confiscated every copy of Claude's works that they could get their hands on. His reproach against Catholicism, which became a standard feature of French Huguenot criticism, would resonate throughout the pages of *Religious Ceremonies of the World.* Not only did Bernard and Picart focus on this aspect of Catholicism, but they also extended the critique globally in an attempt to weed out the superficial from the essential core of all religions in the world.[19]

The particular book by Claude that set Picart to rethinking his religion would hardly seem likely to cause a crisis of faith. *Response to the Book of Mr. Arnaud Titled Defense of the Perpetuity of the Faith of the Catholic Church concerning the Eucharist* ran to more than 900 dense pages of debate on the central doctrine separating Catholics and Protestants, transubstantiation. Claude had published the book as part of an ongoing polemic more than twenty years earlier, in 1670 (Picart owned a 1671 edition from the same publisher in Rouen). At the time, leading Jansenists like Antoine Arnauld had turned their energies to rebutting the principal positions of the Protestants. Claude appealed to the senses in his attack on transubstantiation. Just ask yourself, he urged, what you see when you look at the bread and wine before and then after the priest has said the words of consecration. Have they really changed? The appeal to the senses became central to enlightened as well as to scientific reasoning.

Most helpful for understanding Picart's future interests is the manner in which the Calvinist Claude developed his overall argument. In addition to arguing that the Catholic position had in fact changed over time (the belief in transubstantiation was an innovation and therefore unnecessary to true faith), Claude also placed great emphasis on the beliefs of other Christians considered schismatics by the Roman Catholics, such as the Greek Orthodox, the Russian Orthodox, the Armenians, the Maronites, and the Copts. According to Claude, none of them supported the doctrine of transubstantiation, and he cited among other sources the travel literature available at the time. In this way, the Catholic-Calvinist disputes over theological doctrine opened a crack of historical and cultural relativism that Picart and his collaborator Bernard would later widen beyond anything imaginable to Claude himself.[20]

Picart did not change his religious views overnight, however. Once back in Paris he began discussions and reasoned debates with various acquaintances on the relative merits of Protestantism versus Catholicism, a very risky topic in Paris at the turn of the century. The records of the Bastille prison are filled with the names of some sixty suspected Protestants arrested, interrogated, and jailed between 1698 and 1710. Over at the Hôtel Dieu, French and foreign-born Protestants lined up to "abjure their heresy," prompted by a theologian from the Sorbonne who imposed a penance and then absolution. Some of those arrested, if they were lucky, were released from the Bastille after a few months, but only if they promised to take Catholic instruction. The unlucky ones like Jansenists, who were susceptible to arrest and imprisonment even before Unigenitus, remained under lock and key for years or died in prison. Officials reserved especially harsh treatment for those Protestants who were accused of spying for the Protestant powers allied against France (England and the Dutch Republic); one Protestant medical student charged with espionage on behalf of the Dutch remained in the Bastille for fourteen years. Such traumatic events help to explain the low profile that Marchand and Picart maintained in Paris.[21]

It is perhaps not surprising, then, that Marchand's description of Picart's conversion in his brief biography written after his friend's death would be highly melodramatic and also secretive about Marchand's own role. An architect suspected of Protestantism was arrested in 1701, for example, for plotting with a woman friend to escape to a foreign country. According to Marchand, Picart befriended a bookseller of similar persuasion—no doubt Marchand himself—who lent him books and discussed religion with him at great length. Together they decided to leave France, which became possible when Picart's Catholic wife and children died and his eighty-year-old father decided to convert to Protestantism too. Since the Swedes had long held out the prospect of a pension, Picart asked the Swedish ambassador to officially request a passport that would allow him to leave France for Sweden.

On the very day the passport was to be delivered disaster struck. Having been informed that Picart wanted to leave because he had converted to Protestantism, the chief of police in Paris put off the Swedish ambassador and summoned Picart to his office: "The king forbids you to leave." When Picart demanded to know the reason, explaining that he was leaving only because he lacked commissions in Paris, the police chief responded, "The king does not have to explain his reasons." Picart insisted, at which point the chief exploded, "Do you want me to put you away for good [in the Bastille]?" No, Picart responded, as meekly as he could. He must have known all too well that people were arrested just for having relationships with Protestants who had fled to England or Holland. Only a couple of months before this meeting, a postal worker had been sent to the Bastille for mailing a handwritten newsletter to Holland. Softening his tone in response to Picart's sudden deference, the chief of police then promised that he would help him find work. Picart protested that he had already sold all his furniture and rented his house.[22]

The next day Picart dutifully returned with samples of his work, which the police chief found enchanting: "I had no idea you were so talented. This is perfectly gorgeous! And you want to leave us? You would prefer to go to Sweden? Oh, no! You must stay with us. I will take care of you." Having discovered the real reason behind the passport refusal, Picart then set out to prove his Catholic credentials to the police. He returned with a thick dossier that included his and his father's Catholic baptismal certificates, an indulgence good for three generations from Pope Alexander VII that his father had brought back from Rome, a silver medal personally given by the same pope to his father, and various other attestations, none of them in fact very relevant to Bernard Picart's own convictions. Relenting nonetheless, the police chief sent his case on to the secretary of state, who first tried to arrange a major commission for Picart to make staying more attractive. Picart agreed to remain only if he was given a state pension, lodging at Versailles itself, and the permission of Louis XIV to engrave all the paintings in his personal collection. Whether or not Picart knew he would be refused, he was, and after various other official offers had been parried as well, he finally was allowed to leave, though permission to do so would expire in a week's time. He immediately bought two tickets in the coach for Brussels leaving the next day. (Were these for him and his father? Had Marchand already left separately? Or did he and Marchand travel together, with his father following shortly thereafter?) After passing through Antwerp, they arrived eventually in Rotterdam. Rather than continue on to Sweden, they moved to The Hague, which had no doubt been the plan all along.[23]

Although Picart left no firsthand account of his religious views, Marchand wrote about his own, and given the evidence of their lifelong intimate friendship, it is probably safe to extrapolate from Marchand's personal letters. In 1713, early in the years of their exile, Marchand explained his position in the draft of a letter to an unnamed Catholic correspondent. In the letter, he angrily refuses to return in a "blind" or "absurd" fashion to the fold of a church that arrogates its authority "so haughtily and unjustly." He explains that a book by Jean Claude (yet another one, published in 1683) in defense of Protestantism against Jansenist attacks was one of those that "contributed the most to disabusing me of the opinions of Rome." Marchand does not rest there. He insists that everything required for sound doctrine can be found in the New Testament and among the primitive Christians. In a particularly provocative aside, he calls to his defense the work of the Catholic cleric Nicolas Malebranche, whose 1674 book *Search for Truth* tried to reconcile Cartesianism and Catholicism. Malebranche's efforts produced furious reactions from Bossuet and the Jansenist Arnauld, both sworn enemies of the Protestants as well. It hardly seems accidental that the title of Malebranche's book was the one chosen by Picart, and explicated in the legend below it by Marchand, for his controversial 1707 engraving in praise of Descartes.

Near the end of the letter Marchand drops a bombshell, noting that since he himself is not "Lutheran, Calvinist, Arminian, Socinian, Anabaptist, or Quaker," anything charged against these Reformers and their various sects fails to concern him in the least. Writing privately from the relative safety of the Dutch Republic, Marchand can say that he belongs to no particular religion. Since anyone reasonable, he insists, will conclude that the Roman Catholic Church has fallen into "the most gross and contemptible idolatry," it is time to return to the New Testament and circumvent "all the superstitions and criminal innovations" introduced in the last 1,700 years. It was views such as these that no doubt motivated Picart's father-in-law to announce that his prospective son-in-law was a man of "no religion." What kind of religion was it that required no organized church and no official doctrine?

Still, Marchand appears to believe firmly that Jesus is "the Son of God." He wants to return to a "pure and simple doctrine" based on Scripture and to avoid the "infinity of bizarre cults and ceremonies" introduced by Roman Catholicism. In the same year, 1713, Marchand wrote a preface to a new collection of the chief Protestant works refuting transubstantiation that was published by Fritsch and Böhm in Rotterdam. Taking pride of place among them were works by Claude. Did this concern with refuting the central doctrines of Catholicism lead Marchand—and Picart and Bernard—toward what the age came to call "natural religion" and which some viewed as tantamount to deism, even atheism? At this moment, Picart and Marchand were clearly committed to a Protestant identity of some sort, but their intellectual and religious journey was just beginning. It would come to bear a remarkable similarly to the intellectual odyssey undertaken by an English refugee of the previous generation, Benjamin Furly, who began life as a devout Quaker and ended up increasingly enamored of intellectual freedom and at odds with those who had once been his coreligionists. Perhaps it was inevitable that Marchand and his friends, the knights, would quickly fall into Furly's circle.[24]

Although religion clearly played a major role in Marchand and Picart's decision to emigrate, commercial prospects also weighed in the balance. Picart may well have been telling the truth when he complained to the chief of police that business was bad. The war against the coalition led by the English and Dutch had not been going well for the French, and royal patronage began to decline. Royal commissions had been lucrative for a handful of engravers in 1708, but they apparently fell to nothing in 1709. Payments for paintings at Versailles fell precipitously between 1706 and 1708, stabilized a bit in 1709, but took off again only in 1710–1711. Moreover, the general economic situation was nothing short of disastrous. The year 1709 proved to be the coldest in memory, with a particularly long and hard freeze in January. Virtually every major French river froze over. All the olive and orange trees in the south died, as did most of the vines. What remained was carried away in spring floods. By the summer food prices had skyrocketed, and the poor began to starve amid widespread rioting. More than 600,000 people died. Picart's decision to leave therefore coincided with a very low point in French affairs in general.[25]

It is perhaps not so surprising, then, that some of Picart's most prom-

inent Parisian students, such as Henri Simon Thomassin and Louis Surugue, came to Holland at the same time and spent a few years working
in Picart's new workshop. Their religious convictions seem not to have
entered into their decision to move, for both Thomassin and Surugue
returned to Paris, Thomassin in 1713, Surugue in 1715, and both were
eventually elected to the French Royal Academy. Surugue ultimately
became one of the richest engravers in Paris.[26]

Picart himself continued to turn out pro-Jansenist and sometimes
highly satirical anti-Jesuit engravings and etchings right into the 1720s.
He even produced the frontispiece for a collection of satirical Jansenist
poems and songs, *Poésies sur la constitution Unigenitus,* that appeared
under a false imprint in 1724. The work ridiculed the Jesuits for foment-
ing the attack on Quesnel and contributed to the ongoing controversy
over the papal bull that erupted three years after Picart's departure from
Paris. So worried were the French authorities by the possible diffusion of another of Picart's pro-Jansenist prints in 1727 that they asked
the Estates General of Holland to forbid its publication and, that failing, tried to bribe the Dutch publisher into suppressing it. The print
showed the evil Jesuits manipulating French bishops like puppets on a
string, an even stronger statement than the one Picart made the same
year in his frontispiece to *Religious Ceremonies of the World.* Collectors,
even those in Paris, did not hesitate to include these prints in their collections when they could. Marchand and his circle commissioned Picart
to do a frontispiece for the *Journal Littéraire,* and in it Picart exalted
modern learning and the union of the arts with science. Yet he also did
a few orthodox Catholic engravings intended for the Paris market. It
is evident, then, that a mixture of motives propelled him when he undertook an engraving, ranging from contributing to the opposition to
French absolutist policies to making money. Picart knew his market.[27]

In retrospect, the move to Holland might appear foreordained. Despite glimpses of the Enlightenment to come in the quarrel between
the ancients and the moderns, Paris was still gripped by religious persecution, the tensions of international war, and strict censorship. London,
Geneva, and Berlin offered refuge to French Protestants but not the
same commercial opportunities as Holland. Picart might have chosen
Antwerp, a city he knew well, but by 1710 it sat uncomfortably near the
front lines of war between France and the Dutch Republic and was
in any case still ruled by Catholic Spain. Censorship there invariably

worked in favor of Catholic orthodoxy; indeed, the city became famous for its Catholic publishing houses. Protestants might visit, but settling in the southern Netherlands meant trading in one form of legalized persecution for another kind of official intolerance. The Dutch Republic beckoned. It would turn out to be a wise choice.[28]

3

Why Holland?

W HEN Picart and his friend Marchand made their way to Holland, they were seeking to escape from an increasingly repressive French regime. They were also choosing to reside in a country that had been at war with France on and off for nearly forty years. The stakes were high, especially for men who hoped that they had not yet burned all their bridges. After all, Louis XIV was old—seventy-two in 1710—and his successor might well change course, or not. The bloodiest battle of the current conflict, the War of the Spanish Succession, had taken place in September 1709, only a few weeks before Picart and Marchand left Paris. Nearly 40,000 soldiers were either wounded or killed at Malplaquet, on the border between northern France and the southern Netherlands. A coalition of British, Dutch, Austrian, and Prussian armies ultimately forced Louis XIV's men to withdraw, but not before the French left the allied troops in tatters. Peace remained a distant glimmer.

From its inception in a revolt against Spanish Catholic rule in the 1560s, the Dutch Republic had served as a Protestant refuge from Catholic persecution. The Dutch Republic gained official independence from Spain only in 1648, but even before then it had begun to attract Protestants from the southern Netherlands (now Belgium), which remained Catholic and Spanish. Over the years, thousands upon thousands of French and Flemish Protestants had sought safety in the newly created republic. French-speaking Protestant, or Walloon, churches could be found in various Dutch cities, and unlike many other Protestant sects, they gained official recognition. After 1685, in particular, French Protestants found the Dutch Republic attractive as a launching pad for a crusade against Louis XIV; from the relative safety of the republic they could plot their eventual return to France. Many such refugees saw their new Dutch home as a temporary way station; few imagined a permanent exile. Picart, Marchand, and perhaps even Bernard shared this optimism about the future.

The Dutch authorities did not need French Protestants to remind them of the threat posed by Louis XIV. Louis and his prime minister, Jean-Baptiste Colbert, wanted to expand French territory in Europe and develop colonial possessions that would rival those of the English and the Dutch. The Dutch posed an obstacle on both counts. Colbert employed humanists, historians, and antiquarians to develop a case for the French king's right to lands in the Spanish Netherlands on the French border, which Louis invaded and conquered in 1667. As the French inched closer, Dutch publishers let loose a flood of books in both French and Dutch that aimed to alert all of Europe to the potential danger of Louis's expansionism. Describing Holland as "a heap of mud created by French rivers," Louis invaded the Dutch Republic itself in 1672. His soldiers made examples of two small Dutch towns, Bodegraven and Zwammerdam. After raping the women, they herded the inhabitants into their wooden houses, which they then burned down, killing 2,000 people. Such atrocities only strengthened Dutch resolve, however, and in the popular imagination the Spanish tyranny of the previous century came to be replaced by the cruelty of the French. More than fifty years later Picart supervised the engraving of a print retelling the horrors of 1672. Although eventually forced to give up the Dutch lands he conquered, the French king nibbled away at more territory in the Spanish Netherlands. Throughout the 1670s Dutch presses poured out lampoons, satirical journals, mocking poems, and erotic novels targeting Louis. These works were so successful in mobilizing public opinion that Louis complained bitterly to his courtiers about the damage inflicted by Dutch publishers.[1]

Events that took place in 1685 brought the Dutch new partners in

Cruautez de l'Armée Françoise contre les Habitans des Villages de Bodegrave et de Swammerdam en 1672.

3.1 The slaughter at Bodegraven and Swammerdam in 1672. Romeyn de Hooghe, a famous Dutch engraver of the previous generation, first published this image of the atrocities committed by the French army. Picart honored the image by doing his own version of it. (Courtesy Teylers Museum, Haarlem, KG 12582, The Netherlands)

holding the line against Louis XIV's ambitions: the English. Since 1660 the English kings had actually embraced Louis as their role model and ally because they hoped to introduce Catholicism and perhaps also absolutism in England. The English joined the French in declaring war on the Dutch Republic in 1672; they had previously fought the Dutch in two brief and inconclusive naval wars in the 1650s and 1660s. Like the French, the English resented the upstart nation's success in overseas commerce and especially colonial competition. In 1685, however, the tide turned when James II, known to be a Catholic, became king of England. English Protestant leaders looked for help to the Dutch stadholder, William of Orange, who had married James's Protestant daughter Mary. The ensuing Revolution of 1688–1689—sometimes called Glorious—brought William and Mary to the throne of England and cemented a Protestant alliance between the English and the Dutch that lasted into the 1750s.

English Protestant leaders must have been galvanized as well by events taking place in France, for in 1685 Louis dealt a great blow to the Calvinists in his realm. That year he officially revoked the Edict of Nantes, which had granted toleration to French Protestants in 1598. A systematic campaign of intimidation, incarceration, and forced conversion ensued. Ministers who would not convert were ordered to leave the country within two weeks but were not allowed to take any children over the age of seven with them. Ordinary parishioners were forbidden to leave; if caught fleeing they would be sent to the galleys and their property confiscated. A subsequent edict ordered that all children of Protestant families between the ages of five and sixteen be removed and placed in Catholic homes. Troops were garrisoned in the towns of recalcitrant congregations; they used all manner of harassment, pillage, and sometimes torture and death to convince the obstinate to convert. In Paris alone hundreds of Protestants were arrested and jailed for the "crime" of professing "la religion Protestante." Jean Frederic Bernard's father, who was a Calvinist pastor in Provence, led his family into exile; fortunately Jean Frederic was allowed to leave with his parents because he had not yet turned five years old. Within months his father's church in Velaux had been reconsecrated by the local Catholic bishop; there were no Calvinists left. Before the revocation about 5 percent of the French population had been Huguenots. In response to government pressure, perhaps as many as 700,000 Protestants converted to Catholicism, but 150,000, like the Bernards, chose to flee rather than submit. Among the 50,000–70,000 who went to the Dutch Republic were scores of writers, artists, and publishers who would channel their anguish and fury into a public relations war against France.

Louis's revocation had been prepared by a meticulous strategy. For years his chief minister, Colbert, had been developing a vast system of information-gathering and secret surveillance. Louis wanted to know everything in order to anticipate any problems and to extend his control, especially over all forms of print. One of the areas most important to him was religion. He never believed in religious toleration and rejected any form of dissent even from within the Catholic fold. He spent years planning to eliminate the toleration that his grandfather, Henry

IV, had granted to the Calvinists. He moved quickly after 1679, demolishing Protestant chapels; eliminating special courts to hear Protestant cases; refusing to allow Protestants to hold synods without royal permission; denying Protestants the right to practice certain professions, from midwifery to lower court positions and the law; and legally prohibiting mixed marriages as well as conversion from Catholicism to Protestantism. The revocation represented the culmination of a long-term strategy.[2]

Colbert's campaign of surveillance and control extended far beyond the Protestants; he suppressed any clandestine or foreign literature as "scandalous doctrines." The import of Dutch-produced French-language books posed the greatest threat, especially when aided and abetted by customs officials willing to look the other way. Booksellers caught with banned books on Protestantism and Jansenism were sent to the galleys. Richard Simon's books came in for particular scrutiny. At the urging of Bishop Bossuet, Simon's critical history of the Old Testament was vetted by the king's ministers, and all the copies originally printed in France were seized by the police. It was harder to keep out the editions then printed in Holland. As French presses were shut down and the contents of bookstores subjected to regular searches, the relative freedom of publication in Dutch cities could only enrage French authorities. No one pricked them more painfully than the French Calvinist refugee Pierre Bayle, who began publishing his *News from the Republic of Letters* in Amsterdam in 1684. Bayle praised the freedom of the press available in Holland while deriding the religious intolerance of Louis XIV's government. Even before the official revocation of toleration, Louis's ministers considered Bayle "dangerous": "The esteem he enjoys from the Prince of Orange and the fact that his father and brother are ministers of the so-called reformed religion in France render his actions suspect." A few months before the revocation, the French authorities arrested Bayle's brother Jacob and threw him in prison because they could not get at Pierre himself. Colbert and his minions managed to silence many members of the French Republic of Letters or coopt them to work for the regime, but they turned the Calvinist refugees into sworn enemies. Holland gave them refuge and access to publishers eager to broadcast works like those of Simon and Bayle.[3]

The new wave of French refugees resulting from the revocation of the Edict of Nantes must have found the religious diversity of the

Dutch Republic nothing short of dizzying. French Calvinists jostled Italian freethinkers, defrocked French priests, English deists and spies, Quakers, Moravians, breakaway sects from Dutch Calvinism including one known as the Hebrews, Dutch Calvinist ministers who denied the existence of the devil and hence the possibility of witchcraft, Socinians (anti-Trinitarians), and a multitude of homegrown Spinozists, including a self-taught Spinozist basket maker named Willem Deurhoff. Picart engraved Deurhoff's portrait. Religious intolerance had compelled French, German, and English immigrants to seek refuge in Holland, but what they found there gave them new food for thought. The very multiplicity of confessions raised questions about faith, fostering support, for example, for anticonfessionalism, that is, for the idea that faith depended on something more spiritual than a narrowly defined creed or theological doctrine enforced by a church and its ministers. Louis XIV and Colbert detested this kind of Dutch freedom, but many others embraced it and even pushed it in new directions.

When Picart and Marchand arrived in The Hague in late 1709 or early 1710, the opponents of Louis XIV had cause to feel optimistic. In coalition with the Austrian Habsburgs, longstanding rivals of the French kings, and various German Protestant states, the English and Dutch armies were successfully challenging the French juggernaut. A second major war was now winding down. In the first, lasting from 1689 to 1697, the coalition fought the French to a stalemate. Armies clashed in Western Europe, the West Indies, and the French and English colonies in northern America. The second conflict, the War of the Spanish Succession, had erupted just four years later, in 1701, when Louis XIV arranged to put one of his grandsons on the Spanish throne. This time fighting raged from Vienna to the southern Netherlands and from Gibraltar to Nova Scotia. The final peace treaties would be signed only in 1713 and 1714, but Louis XIV's forces had been checked and his treasury was now exhausted. Louis's grandson would keep the Spanish throne, but in exchange the new king had to hand over the Spanish Netherlands to the Austrians and renounce any future claim to the French throne.

Although we have no direct testimony as to why Picart and Marchand chose wartime Holland rather than French-speaking Calvinist Geneva or somewhere else in Protestant Europe, it is likely that the vibrant Dutch book trade counted for a great deal, especially since they

3.2   The Spinozist William Deurhoff, a self-taught basket maker. Deurhoff died in 1717, and Picart presumably did this engraved portrait of him before then. The portrait shows Picart's interest in Spinozism. (Courtesy Gemeente Amsterdam Stadsarchief, Inv. no. 010097008369)

both already enjoyed multiple connections to it. Unlike the English, who also had a relatively free press by then, the Dutch had ready access to the French- and German-language markets, not to mention other language markets even further afield on the Continent. Thus, in addition to offering religious toleration and incredible religious diversity as well as longstanding opposition to the French, the Dutch cities offered the means to put writings and engravings about all these subjects into the widest possible circulation.

Cities were the obvious places to build a business around publishing, and the Dutch were the most urbanized people in Europe. Holland, which included Amsterdam, Rotterdam, The Hague, and Leiden, was the most urbanized province of the seven that made up the Dutch Republic, and that density fueled a market for consumption in all manner of goods, including books and engravings. An astounding number of immigrants fed the growth of Holland's cities. In the seventeenth and early eighteenth centuries more than 1.5 million people flocked to the western seaboard towns of the Dutch Republic, and only one-third of them came from the Dutch countryside. More than a million immigrated from foreign lands. The influx produced not only religious diversity of a sort never before seen in Europe but also remarkable social, cultural, and linguistic heterogeneity. Although many immigrants arrived from Calvinist territories, the majority were actually Lutherans and Catholics, and many Jews and members of other persecuted sects also made their way to the republic. Religious diversity combined with the urban division of labor in complex ways. Men dependent upon one another in commerce might have vastly different religious identities or nationalities. Such divided loyalties made the imposition of uniform standards of behavior nearly impossible. Dutch cities consequently fostered an atmosphere conducive to change, innovation, and flexibility. They held out a standing invitation to question conventional social mores, just the kind of orientation that would appeal to men such as Bernard and Picart and their friends.

The wartime alliance of the Dutch and the English encouraged travel of another kind. John Toland, for example, had close ties to the British Whigs, the party most committed to the Anglo-Dutch alliance. He may well have come to The Hague in the first instance to establish secret contact with Eugene of Savoy, a leader of the allied forces. The Whigs had lost control of Parliament to the Tories, and as a result, the English commitment to the war and the alliance began to falter. Yet as the minutes in Toland's papers show, when the Knights of Jubilation met on November 24, 1710, they were in an ebullient mood. They may well have been celebrating in part because two weeks earlier a coalition

PROCESSION des PALMES chez les JUIFS PORTUGAIS.

3.3 Portuguese Jews carrying palms for Sukkot, or the feast of tabernacles. Residents of Amsterdam were much more likely to see Jews in their midst than were denizens of Paris or London, much less smaller cities and towns in Europe. Picart's title, "Procession of Palms of the Portuguese Jews," demonstrates his interest in drawing comparisons (in this case, to Palm Sunday among Christians), and his signature (B. Picart delineavit 1724) signaled that he had drawn it himself. *Cérémonies et coutumes religieuses* (hereafter CC), vol. I (Amsterdam: J. F. Bernard, 1723), between pp. 122 and 123, top half of the plate.

of English, Dutch, and German armies had retaken the town of Aire in Flanders, which had been conquered and annexed by the French in 1678. In October 1711 a preliminary agreement was signed between Britain and France, and general peace negotiations opened in Utrecht in January 1712.

Even during this time of turmoil, newly arrived French Protestant refugees like Picart and Marchand found a very receptive environment. Public funds supported the pastors in the Walloon churches just as they did the *predikanten* of the Dutch Reformed Church. The world-renowned universities of Leiden and Utrecht had a decidedly Protestant cast. Professors taught Newton's science already in the 1690s, before anyone else in continental Europe. Leiden still enjoyed a reputation as the finest medical school in Europe, and it attracted many students from abroad, especially from Protestant countries. As might be expected, the city also supported a thriving group of book dealers and publishers, of whom the most famous was the Elzevier family. Around 1660 they introduced the fictitious imprint "Pierre Marteau, Cologne," found afterward on countless publications thought too risky to claim as one's own. The imprint served as cover for the earliest attacks on Louis XIV, his court, and the French church. In 1711 Bernard used it for his first book. Separated from The Hague, Leiden, or Utrecht by only a few hours barge travel, Holland's commercial center of Amsterdam possessed a thriving stock exchange, with bookshops built into its outer walls, and the largest public building in Europe, its famous *stadhuis,* or

3.4 The Amsterdam stock exchange with bookshops. The heart of Amsterdam's commercial life, the stock exchange, or Bourse, also hosted many bookstores. From Phillips von Zesen, *Beschreibung der Stadt Amsterdam* (Amsterdam: Joachim Noschen, 1664), pp. 232–233. (Research Library, The Getty Research Institute, Los Angeles, California)

city hall. It and the local Portuguese synagogue were "must-see" stops on any grand tour of the Continent (see Figure 7.2).[4]

The intellectual attractions of Dutch cities had long been recognized, even by non-Calvinists. The French philosopher René Descartes had moved to the Dutch Republic in 1628, learned to read and speak Dutch, and immersed himself in local intellectual life and, in particular, medical studies. His famous *Discourse on Method* was published in Leiden in 1637. Writing just before the wealth and power of the republic became the talk of Europe, Descartes had this praise to offer for his newfound home: I have come "to this country in which the long duration of the war [against Spain] has led to the establishment of such discipline . . . and where in the midst of a great crowd actively engaged in business, and more careful of their own affairs than curious about those of others, I have been able to live without being deprived of any of the conveniences to be had in the most populous cities, and yet as solitary and retired as in the most remote deserts." In self-imposed exile among the Dutch, the ostensibly Catholic Descartes had found himself tolerated, offered the freedom and solitude to think and write, and left to pursue his studies amid the bustle of urban commercial life. Perhaps the example of Descartes had inspired Picart, who was a great admirer of the French philosopher.[5]

Dutch radicals quickly became Descartes's first European disciples, embracing the idiosyncratic Cartesianism taught freely at the Dutch universities beginning in the 1640s. Pamphlets helped bring the new ideas even to the man in the street. A generation later the ideas of the philosopher Spinoza began to filter down through the same channels. Like Descartes, Spinoza developed his startling new understanding of nature in the Dutch Republic and in conversation with local Dutch intellectuals. Descartes and Spinoza considered themselves first and foremost philosophers, but their Dutch followers hoped that the new ideas might help them find solutions to the more mundane problems of the young republic: among these were the proper alignment of the republican political system, the relationship between state and church, and even the interpretation of the Bible, which had become intensely politicized.[6]

Dutch intellectuals hoped to establish a new scientific basis for Christian concord. The Reformation had destroyed the unity of medieval Christendom, but most other European states had succeeded in imposing new forms of religious conformity. In the republic religious strife continued, albeit in debates and pamphlet wars rather than in armed battles. In their quest for Christian reconciliation Dutch intellectuals followed in the footsteps of sixteenth-century Dutch humanist scholars like Erasmus, who had struggled to find a new religious understanding capable of superseding dogmatic differences. By the early eighteenth century, however, these intellectuals, now inspired by Cartesianism and Spinozism, shifted the debate to a new level. They attempted to achieve the impossible: a secular, rational foundation for religious unity. Their ideas resonated amid the religious confusion and conflicts of the republic. Many nonconformists had yet to decide which, if any, church to join. Not surprisingly, many orthodox Calvinists interpreted their efforts as an attack on religion itself.

In Latin or in translation, this new rationalist religious vocabulary soon found a cosmopolitan audience in the German states, England, France, and Scandinavia. Simon's critical histories of the Bible and Bayle's attacks on superstition fed into the same channels. These debates over religion helped lay the foundation for the radical phase of the early European Enlightenment, in which Toland, Collins, Marchand, and Bernard all played important roles. Religion was not just a private matter of individual choice; it had important implications for the state and for international relations, too. When Picart and Marchand arrived in Holland, Dutch Calvinist and French Huguenot ministers were still actively preaching and publishing against the religious nonconformists, perhaps all the more vigorously because so many French Huguenots had joined their ranks. Taking the side of nonconformity would not be without risk, but these were men who felt compelled to examine every alternative in the light of reason, no matter what the consequences. Some of them, like Bayle, or men of the next generation, like Jean Rousset de Missy, Marchand's great friend, examined religion while their relatives languished in French prisons.[7]

Although complete tolerance remained impossible because the orthodox Calvinists who had a decisive share in both local and national governments would never have allowed it, a kind of "live and let live" ethos promoted a specifically Dutch version of religious toleration. Decades of war against Spain, waves of immigration, the density of urban life, and not least high literacy gave the Dutch impressively self-regulating habits of discipline and social control. Different religious groups could coexist because control was exercised more by social custom and self-censorship than by official decrees and policing. Conspicuous consumption, for instance, was deemed unacceptable, and most people stayed comfortably within the bounds of the acceptable. Official intolerance, with the elevation of Calvinism to the status of established or state church, proved as impossible to effect as complete toleration. In the end, practical politics shaped the Dutch brand of toleration, which took different forms even from one town to the next. Dutch law forbade public worship by Catholics, for example, but did not rule out private services. Supposedly, "secret" Catholic churches could be found in nearly every city. Though they were discreetly hidden in townhouses or behind store fronts, everyone knew their location, and Catholic worshippers heard their masses in peace.[8]

Booksellers quickly learned to profit from this ambiguous regime. They remained watchful, however, because repressive censorship did not entirely disappear. Threats to public order or complaints from foreign ambassadors could prompt the authorities to act swiftly and harshly, as the publishers of the treatise on the three impostors learned for themselves. In 1711 a pseudonymous pamphlet dared to support the French cause against the Anglo-Dutch alliance. An English diplomat observed that "the fellow who printed the pamphlet . . . has been condemned by the Court of Justice to shut up his shop & never more to deal in this country." Political censorship on behalf of the interests of the Dutch state was real enough.[9]

In contrast, religious censorship almost never worked effectively, even though the Calvinist clergy continually pestered the authorities with requests to suppress offensive writings. Right into the 1770s officials considered instituting preventive censorship, that is, vetting of books before publication, but the town regents never agreed, and they had the final say. On occasion, the Walloon (French Huguenot) churches took action against publishers who belonged to their congregations. In the late 1740s, for example, the council of the Walloon Church in Leiden reported the publisher Elias Luzac to the authorities. Luzac had published a materialist work by a doctor trained at the medical school of Leiden University. Pious Huguenot that he was, Luzac worried so much about his fate that he wrote an entire tract to refute the very book he had published. Reputations and, consequently, businesses could easily be ruined by the taint of materialism; the Leiden officials described Luzac as "a scandalous and unholy follower of Spinoza."[10]

Defenders of the freedom of opinion contended that the Dutch Republic had always recognized the ancient rights of the Romans and that within its borders "nobody is punished for speaking freely or reading a forbidden book." Yet no Dutch writer—unlike Milton in England—ever put pen to paper to offer a philosophical defense of freedom of the press. As with the freedom to practice one's chosen religion, it held in practice more than in theory; governments could not enforce censorship or religious orthodoxy even if they wished to do so. This informal and sometimes contradictory system of control seemed to work reasonably well for most people.[11]

The Hague held obvious attractions for newly arrived French Protestants such as Picart and Marchand. Among the 35,000 residents of this international and cosmopolitan city could be found 1,000 French Huguenots, a receptive local community for two men looking for new opportunities. Early in the eighteenth century (as now) stately mansions lined the elegant Lange Voorhout, the grand boulevard running through the heart of the city. There ambassadors of the many countries involved in the War of the Spanish Succession conducted the negotiations vital to keeping the anti-French coalition intact and then to the eventual peace settlement. Yet war was not the only topic of conversation. Ambassadors and the inevitable spies rode carriages down the same streets as Dutch representatives to the republic's Estates General, actresses from the local Comédie française, not to mention the Dutch, French, and German booksellers who plied their trade in books of many languages.

The Hague's publishers and bookshops counted among the best stocked in Europe. They catered to an international audience, especially one that could read French, the *lingua franca* of elite audiences all over Europe. French could be heard on the Lange Voorhout nearly as frequently as Dutch. By comparison to Amsterdam, which was bursting with 200,000 people, The Hague seemed a relatively small world where businessmen rubbed shoulders with ambassadors and statesmen. Yet in this period three out of four households in The Hague with disposable property owned books, on religion to be sure, but also covering philosophy, literature, history, law, and the applied sciences. A study

3.5   Street scene in The Hague from the early 1700s. The Korte Voorhout is seen from
the Tournooiveld; on the west side is a short portion of the Lange Voorhout, and to the
right is the Lange Houtstraat. Pen in gray and black; pencil in gray by Daniel Marot, Jr.
(ca. 1694–1769), son of a French Huguenot refugee to Holland. (Courtesy Gemeentearchief,
Den Haag, no. 5256.01)

of publishing in the 1740s has shown that booksellers offered no fewer
than 100,000 titles in just that one decade. As the political center of the
rich Dutch Republic, The Hague exuded confidence and sophistica-
tion even as its citizens experienced wartime tensions and worried that
only complete victory would preserve Dutch independence and Protestantism.[12]

Although Marchand and Picart quickly made friends and contacts in
The Hague, Amsterdam offered many more opportunities, for it was
home to most Dutch publishing firms. There Picart would marry for a
second time, develop a lucrative business as an artist and engraver, and
meet Jean Frederic Bernard, his collaborator on *Religious Ceremonies of
the World.* As the indisputable capital of the Dutch book industry, Am-

sterdam played a decisive role in the creation of European print culture. Already by the 1660s the Dutch Republic had 781 printers and booksellers. In the period from 1650 to 1725 the Dutch published almost half of all the books printed in Europe, and the book trade became one of the pillars of the Dutch export industry. Amsterdam publishers produced twice the number of books churned out by the publishing machine to the south, The Hague.

Amsterdamers could typeset just about any European language: not only Dutch, French, German, Italian, English, and Latin but also Hebrew, Greek, Russian, Yiddish, Hungarian, and Armenian. Some book dealers specialized in just one of those languages and regularly shipped to the countries where it was read and spoken. The international book trade, however, was risky. Even in its commercial heyday, it could not survive without large profits from the home market for books. Still, Bernard launched his own publishing business from this base, and Picart found a ready market for the talent and skills he had cultivated in Paris. In 1710 Picart signed a contract—at very favorable terms—to engrave illustrations for yet another Protestant Bible (see Figure 2.5).[13]

An intense burst of urbanization in the 1600s provided the basis for this huge Dutch market for books. By 1675 half of the Dutch Republic's population of two million was living in cities, a level that even industrialized England would reach only in the 1840s. Dutch cities were rarely very large, with Amsterdam the notable exception, but they dotted the landscape everywhere. Wherever one lived, a town or two could be found on the horizon. Their general prosperity can be illustrated by the possessions enjoyed by the good burgers of Delft. By the middle of the seventeenth century as many as two-thirds of the Delft population of around 30,000 people owned paintings. That means as many as 40,000–50,000 paintings hung on the walls of approximately 4,000 houses.[14]

Private collections of books varied greatly in size, but some people amassed substantial libraries. Furly's personal library of 4,400 books was unusual, as were even Bernard's 1,700 and Picart's 2,000 titles. English thinkers like John Locke, who owned more than 3,000 books, routinely looked to Dutch booksellers for the works they coveted. The third earl of Shaftesbury, living in London, sent a proxy to attend Dutch book auctions for him. Anthony Collins, the English freethinker, possessed no fewer than 7,000 books, including many French-language journals purchased in Holland as well as the first Levier edition of *The Treatise of the Three Impostors.* Dutch book dealers traveled throughout Europe, selling wherever they could, and publishers frequently advertised themselves as printing in more than one city. Books appeared explaining how to build up a worthwhile library. Needless to say, most ordinary personal libraries were much smaller than those of leading intellectuals or book fanciers. Indeed, only about 2 percent of households in The Hague owned more than 150 books. Still, there was no more attractive place in Europe—or perhaps the world—to pursue the book business.[15]

Although Amsterdam was the capital of Dutch publishing, bookshops could be found everywhere in the republic, and competition between them created a network of information that drew in all towns of more than 2,500 inhabitants. The result was the most vibrant literary culture in Europe. Dutch readers snapped up large quantities of Bibles, broadsheets, cheap novels, almanacs, and songbooks. Many were addicted to pamphlets covering domestic politics, foreign affairs, and religious disputes, often garnished with biting political commentary. The most popular genre of all was the *Schuitpraatje,* or barge talk. Writer upon writer set his arguments in dialogues that took place during the canal journeys that were so critical to transportation between towns. One such pamphlet even alluded to the importance of a free press. Barges were frequent, reliable, and relatively inexpensive, but they were also slow, and as such provided ample opportunity for the discussion of politics, philosophy, and religion. Religious exiles with even the slightest command of Dutch could partake in barge banter. Many of our Knights of Jubilation must have understood the basics of the language. Picart's new father-in-law used Dutch as his first language, and given the early tensions between them, we doubt that Picart could have avoided addressing him in it.[16]

When Picart and Bernard began to publish the volumes of their great collaborative work in the 1720s, they participated in an Enlightenment that was only just gathering steam. Its greatest continental thinkers were on the horizon and only beginning to write: Voltaire and Montesquieu in the 1720s, Diderot in the 1740s, and Rousseau in the 1750s and 1760s. Based in Paris, every one of them relied on Dutch publishers because the French censors would not permit them to publish their works. All of them also traveled to the Dutch Republic, if only to oversee their publications. Voltaire, for instance, visited Holland in 1713, 1722, 1737,

1740, and 1743. During the 1722 visit he made contact with some of the Knights of Jubilation and even tried to engage Picart as engraver for his long poem in praise of Henry IV, who granted toleration to the Protestants in 1598. This did not stop Jean Frederic from publishing a pirated edition of the poem shortly afterward. Holland did not lose its allure as a haven for intellectual freedom until the end of the eighteenth century. Indeed we might well ask if there would have been a French Enlightenment in print without the Dutch publishers.

Visiting the bookshops of Amsterdam must have been a remarkable experience, one shared by many of the leading intellectuals in Europe. In the 1730s and 1740s almost every street in the city center supported a bookshop. The Kalverstraat, where both Bernard and Picart made their homes and installed their businesses, was the absolute epicenter of the book trade. It housed at least eighteen booksellers in possession of income sufficient to be considered taxable. By going to Holland, these two immigrants had clearly landed on their feet. With the depth and breadth of its publishing businesses, the range of its seaborne trade, and the variety of its religious persuasions, Holland proved to be the best place in the world from which to articulate and promote a new understanding of the religions of all the peoples of the world.[17]

4

Jean Frederic Bernard

The Tumultuous Life of a Refugee Publisher

T HE LIFE of Jean Frederic Bernard may seem elusive, but aspects of
it peek through the mists of time and religious exile. Most information concerns his years in Amsterdam's publishing district, where
Jean sought his fortune. But his family experience, especially given the
Bernards' flight from France, must have been critically important in
shaping his life choices. Jean was born in 1680 in the small French town
of Velaux, situated in the hills of Provence, some twenty miles from
Marseilles. He was baptized on December 9, 1680, by his father, Barthélemy Bernard (1645–1694), a Huguenot pastor who served the congregation of Velaux from 1669 until 1685, when the revocation of the Edict
of Nantes ended the French phase of his career.[1]

The Bernards were a family of Huguenot pastors of long standing.
Barthélemy's father, Jean Bernard (1597–1679), had been a pastor like his
father before him. A nephew, also called Jean (1625–1706), was a pastor
in the town of Manosque, about fifty miles from Velaux. He was a well-
known theologian and would earn some notoriety during the Huguenot diaspora. When forced to leave France in 1685, he became a leader
of the Huguenots in exile in Lausanne. From there he was sent on a
fund-raising mission through Europe, ending in The Hague in 1688,
where he preached before Mary Stuart, the wife of the stadholder William III, imploring her to come to the rescue of the exiled Huguenots.

Bernard would end his career as a minister in the Walloon Church of Amsterdam.[2]

Jean Frederic's mother, Catherine Guib, also came from a family of pastors and professors. She was the daughter of Jean Frederic Guib, a scholar of Scottish descent who had traveled widely, received a degree in medicine from the renowned University of Valence, and ended up as a provost and a professor of rhetoric at the Collège d'Orange, which was located in the city of the same name. He enjoyed an international reputation as a scholar and as an educator. Athanasius Kircher, the Jesuit expert on Egypt and China, was his friend, and he was well known to Henri Basnage de Beauval, the Huguenot journalist and historian who would spend most of his life in the Dutch Republic. Guib, who acted as Jean Frederic's godfather, had three children of his own. The eldest, a son called Henri (1654–1712), was trained as a lawyer and succeeded his father as provost and professor at the Collège d'Orange. Henri's son, also called Jean Frederic and our Bernard's first cousin, became a lawyer in Orange. He was something of a scholar as well, publishing a much-reprinted study of the town of Orange in Roman times. In the 1720s Jean Frederic Bernard would publish extracts of the work in the journals he owned. In short, Jean Frederic came from an intellectually gifted family with a long tradition of scholarship and religious study.[3]

The Bernard family's roots in Velaux put them at the center of a vast Huguenot network. In one of the articles of the Edict of Nantes of 1598, the Huguenot ministry of the town had been assigned the spiritual care of all Protestant traders and merchants of the port of Marseilles. As a result, Velaux's Protestant community reached outward to much of Protestant Europe. Swiss and Dutch merchants had their marriages concluded in the town and their children baptized there. A Swiss merchant became the chief sponsor of the Huguenot temple built in Velaux in the 1620s. Another merchant, the Dutch consul-general at Marseilles, Nicolaas Ruts, originally from Amsterdam, became a close personal friend of the Bernard family.[4]

The family's connections with the Dutch Republic only began there and were reinforced from Jean Frederic's mother's side. Her father, Jean Frederic Guib, enjoyed a friendship with the personal secretary to the Dutch stadholder, the great Dutch poet and father of the famous physicist Christiaan Huygens, Constantijn, lord of Zuylichem. They became acquainted when Zuylichem spent a few years in the south of France, in Orange, a principality then owned by William III. Zuylichem represented William in the province. Both Zuylichem and Guib were passionately interested in poetry and above all in Petrarch.

The Calvinist college of Orange at which both Jean Frederic Guib and his son Henri served enjoyed the personal patronage of William III. In the protracted series of wars between the Dutch and the French from 1660 to 1715, Orange changed hands often, as Louis XIV, the French king, considered the principality to be originally French. Henry Guib had to flee his job as provost and professor regularly, staying often in Amsterdam, where he made a living as a lawyer. In 1711 French sovereignty over the principality was finally accepted, to be confirmed two years later at the Treaty of Utrecht.

Buffeted by treaties and revocations, the Bernard family made the best they could out of their religious identity and blended into a cosmopolitan network. They were well connected in the European world of learning; they had their contacts in high places in the Dutch Republic; and they were well acquainted with Amsterdam and Swiss merchant dynasties engaged in international trade. Reaching out to foreign friends may have come from the growing realization that their circumstances in France were only becoming more and more precarious. From the 1660s the erosion of their privileges and freedoms had become increasingly obvious. At first Catholic officials sent missionaries to try to convince Huguenots to give up their faith. When that failed, Louis XIV and the French clergy devised new, more punitive measures. Local rights to worship were first questioned, then abolished. Churches were closed and Protestants ejected from the local guilds and parliaments. The next step were the so-called dragonnades, the billeting of famished and riotous troops on Protestant families and the placement of their children in Catholic homes. According to the undisputed leader of the Huguenots, Jean Claude (1619–1687), if these measures were not successful, the French authorities

> strung up their victims, men and women, by their hair or by their feet, to the rafters in the roof, or the hooks in the chimney, and then set fire to bundles of moldy hay heaped up beneath them. . . . They flung them into huge fires which they lit for the purpose, and left them there till they were half-roasted. They fastened ropes un-

derneath their arms and lowered them into wells, pulling them up and down till they promised to change their religion.

The Edict of Fontainebleau of October 18, 1685, which repealed the Edict of Nantes, was merely the culmination of the king's anti-Huguenot policies. Four-fifths of the French Huguenots seem to have converted, while the rest fled to Switzerland, Germany, England, the Dutch Republic, and even the Americas. Protestants became a rare commodity in France.[5]

The town of Velaux, too, was cleansed of Huguenots. From 1680 onward military violence, legal intimidation, and endless harassment, aimed especially at the Bernard family, became routine. In the weeks after the revocation Catholic pressure was so forceful that between October 23 and November 12, 1685, more than 100 former Huguenots visited the local notary public to have their conversion to Catholicism officially recorded. Already on October 24, the royal intendant for the region could write to Paris that the arrival of the dragoons had produced such an intimidating effect that almost everybody had converted. The region would be free of Protestants within a week, he smugly concluded. In the next few days the last Huguenots, including the Bernards, who according to article 4 of the Fontainebleau edict had to leave France before November 15, were driven from the town. Within six weeks of the revocation, on December 3, 1685, the archbishop of Arles consecrated the former Huguenot temple where Barthélemy Bernard and his father had served their flock for decades. Thus ended a history of heresies against the Church that in the case of Velaux extended back to the middle ages, when the town had been a stronghold of the Waldensians. They will figure prominently when in the next chapter we attempt to reconstruct the mental universe of Jean Frederic Bernard.[6]

In the late autumn of 1685 the Bernard family slowly made their way through the Alps to Geneva. The group consisted of Barthélemy Bernard; his wife, Catherine, who was pregnant; his mother, Anne Asquel, aged fifty-eight; and their young sons, Jean Frederic, who was almost five, and Barthélemy, who was only two. The family first took refuge in Geneva, where the elder Barthélemy had completed his theological studies some years before, and then wandered to Frankfurt in Germany. Seven months later the Bernards ended their escape from absolutist France in Holland. The long flight saw the deaths, first of Anne Asquel, and then of young Barthélemy. Another son, Henri, was born in the early months of 1686. The family settled in Amsterdam, where through long cultivation they had acquired many friends, not to mention relatives.

The social networking of the Bernards paid off. Barthélemy quickly found a position as pastor in the fast-growing French-speaking reformed church of Amsterdam. Without friends in high places, securing such a post would have been extremely difficult. Of the roughly 600 Huguenot pastors who fled France, about 360 tried to make a living in the Dutch Republic, and the Walloon Church had room for only a few dozen. The fact that Bernard's credentials were impeccably orthodox might have helped as well. On May 29, 1686, he registered as a member of the Walloon Church. The next day he was made an Amsterdam citizen, something that normally took much longer and would have cost him a considerable amount of money. Shortly thereafter he obtained an Amsterdam ministry at the Runstraat Church. Because of ill health, however, he had to retire. Thanks to his friends he received a decent allowance of 400 florins a year before his death in 1694. His wife had already died a few years before. His will was witnessed by his old friend from Marseilles Nicolaas Ruts. His relatives in Amsterdam, Henry Guib and Jean Bernard, now acted as guardians for Jean Frederic, only fourteen, and his younger siblings, Elisabeth (born in 1689) and Henri.[7]

Everything in Jean Frederic's background suggested that he would go to university and become a Protestant *predikant* in his adopted land, or possibly a tutor or teacher. But he broke with family tradition. In 1704 he went back to Geneva, not as a student of theology, but to make a living in trade. In Amsterdam he had been apprenticed to a Huguenot dynasty of publishers, family relations of his future friend Pierre Humbert. In Geneva, with the help of his Swiss relations, his Amsterdam contacts, and their international network, he set up a brokerage business. Books formed an important part of the business, but soon Bernard became active in other markets as well. An ideal profession for those who had little capital but an extensive set of connections, brokerage meant long-distance trade. Such trade was a matter of trust that only well-connected brokers could supply. Before long Jean Frederic established an important clientele, in books and other commodities. Even Pierre Bayle made use of his services. In 1707 Bernard returned to Am-

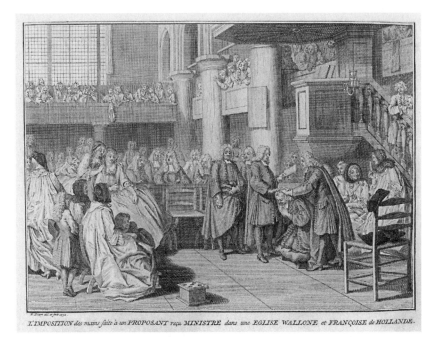

L'IMPOSITION des mains faite à un PROPOSANT reçu MINISTRE dans une EGLISE WALLONE et FRANÇOISE de HOLLANDE.

4.1 The installation of a new minister in a French Walloon (Huguenot) church in Amsterdam. Picart's signature on this engraving from 1732 clearly indicates his personal interest: "B. Picart del. et fecit 1732" means that Picart drew and engraved it in 1732, that is, he both designed and engraved the plate himself. CC, vol. V, facing p. 388.

sterdam to continue the brokerage business. He lived in rented rooms and rented a separate warehouse from which he ran his firm. In 1711 he decided that he had enough capital to become both a full-scale member of the booksellers' guild and a publisher.[8]

Though Jean Frederic possessed good business acumen, books for him were more than just a business. He quickly became a highly selective publisher with a small catalogue dominated by free-spirited theological inquiry and travel literature. The distance he had strayed from the pious path of his fathers is evident from the first book he published in 1711, authored by himself and entitled *Moral Reflections*. It critically analyzed and even ridiculed many religious customs and practices. To Bernard the problems caused by religion arose from its public and highly politicized nature. Writing in 1711 amid a raging European religious war, he claimed that if religion were to become a citizen's private business, then people could live peacefully together. Public religion de-

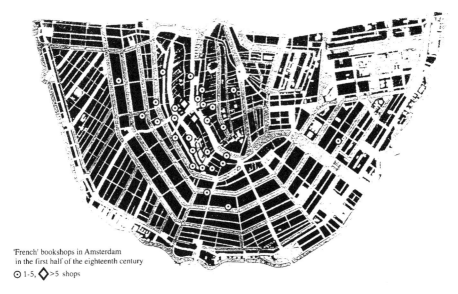

'French' bookshops in Amsterdam
in the first half of the eighteenth century
⊙ 1-5, ◇ >5 shops

4.2. Amsterdam booksellers. From Edwin van Meerkerk, *Achter de schermen van het boekbedrijf. Henri du Sauzet (1687–1754) in de wereld van de uitgeverij en de boekhandel in de Republiek.* (Amsterdam/Utrecht: APA-Holland Universiteitspers, 2001), p. 1 verso.

stroyed the fabric of society: as soon as kings and priests publish religious manifestos, people who have been living together in peace and friendship for ages begin to betray, hate, and kill one another. Religion in its political manifestation, Bernard concluded, is a sugar-coated drug that serves as a narcotic, robbing people of good sense. Public humiliation, persecution, flight, and the exile and death of much of his family, all because of religion, had laid the basis for a lifelong doubt about the value of established religion, and a quest for religion's underlying essence. Entering the book trade provided him with a living, and it also supplied the opportunity to promote the ideas supporting that quest.[9]

In his first years as a publisher not much distinguished Jean Frederic from the average newcomer. Between 1711 and 1715 he published a few political pamphlets and only nine books, among which were two he wrote himself: *Moral Reflections* (1711) and *Etat de l'homme dans le peché originel* [State of man in original sin] (1714). Both were radical tracts that could hardly have solidified his reputation as a publisher. Slow beginnings suggest that brokerage had not supplied him with enough capital to put his publishing firm on a course of quick expansion.

One can only conclude, therefore, that the very short marriage he contracted in 1715 with Jeanne Chartier proved crucial. The young woman from a French Huguenot refugee family died at the age of twenty-six, after less than two months of marriage. In their few weeks together, Jean Frederic took his seriously ill wife on a series of almost frenetic visits to Amsterdam notaries to finalize their financial arrangements. Chartier was a rich woman living on her own in a large mansion on the Keizersgracht, then and now one of the most expensive canals in Amsterdam, and Bernard was the sole beneficiary of her estate. Her death seriously accelerated his publishing activity. It made possible the beginning of his crucial publishing ventures, a series of travel accounts entitled *Voyages au Nord,* the first volume of which appeared in 1715. In 1718 he succeeded in marrying another rich wife. Marie Sophie Lacoste was the daughter of a well-to-do Huguenot family of velvet manufacturers, originally from Montauban in France.[10]

Jean Frederic needed all the financial help he could muster. While immensely lucrative for some, the Amsterdam book trade could be treacherous for the hapless or the naive. Consider the case of Henri du Sauzet (1687–1754), vilified by Voltaire in 1738 as "a rogue apostate Jesuit." Trained at the Jesuit Collège Royal in Toulouse, Du Sauzet turned Protestant, like Picart, well after the revocation of the Edict of Nantes. Naturally he fled to the Dutch Republic, where lapsed monks such as himself were in no short supply. In 1715 he established a shop in The Hague, moving it a few years later to Amsterdam. Du Sauzet joined with Bernard in 1719 to publish the *Mémoires du Cardinal de Retz,* one of the chief instigators of the seventeenth-century Fronde rebellion in France and perhaps the most accomplished political intriguer of his time. They also ventured into the market for learned journals, collaborating on the *Nouvelles Littéraires* and the *Bibliothèque Françoise.* Yet with neither financial backers nor family, Du Sauzet spent much of his working life on the verge of insolvency. Forced to sell his soul to more ruthless and less-educated competitors such as the powerful Wetstein family of publishers, he rarely benefited financially from such associations. In 1747 bankruptcy finally overtook him and he died a few years later, almost destitute.[11]

The commercial practices of the book trade exacerbated the struggle to survive. Very rarely were book sales concluded in cash. In both the national and the international trade bartering of printed sheets or full books was customary. Accounts were settled once a year, and even then payment in actual money was generally avoided. This system favored big publishers who offered more interesting book titles for exchange. Newcomers with a limited number of titles of their own needed cash to acquire the books to stock their shops, but their accounts were filled with promissory notes rather than with cash. When pressed to settle their accounts in cash, booksellers often had to organize auctions of at least a portion of their stocks, thus further diminishing their supplies. The system proved generally effective but fragile. If a relatively big publisher faced financial trouble and needed to cash in his promissory notes, he might take many smaller firms with him in a collapsing house of cards. Du Sauzet's career ended in precisely this fashion.[12]

The fate of Pierre Humbert (ca. 1680–1758), another business associate and lifelong friend of Jean Frederic, shows how these principles of either having cash or being seen as creditworthy worked in practice. The son of a Protestant lawyer, Humbert was born and educated in Geneva, where he presumably met Jean Frederic. In 1705 Humbert migrated to Amsterdam to seek his publishing fortune. He rarely managed to publish more than a few new titles a year, yet whereas Du Sauzet foundered Humbert survived, thanks to his friends and family. Jean Frederic himself acted as a guarantor after 1720. Even more significant, Humbert's mother had links to a powerful Huguenot dynasty of publishers, which allowed Humbert to acquire a small but profitable share in the lucrative partnerships being forged by the big publishing houses.[13]

Humbert and Bernard shared a skeptical, and even libertine, perspective. Early in their partnership they issued a new edition of a notorious work by the seventeenth-century French libertine Gabriel Naudé, *Apology for the Great Men Suspected of Magical Practices.* Humbert also published the more unorthodox works of Jean Barbeyrac, a famous law professor of Huguenot background who rejected the Calvinist doctrine of predestination. Barbeyrac's formidable international reputation and his willingness to maintain a relatively low religious profile were all that kept him from constant trouble. Together with Bernard, Humbert put out the sermons of England's most famous liberal theologian and eloquent preacher, John Tillotson; Barbeyrac had translated the sermons.

Even Humbert's private life proved controversial. The Amsterdam Walloon Church excluded him from communion because he cohabited with his mistress, who was also his maid.[14]

A final cautionary tale about life in the Amsterdam book business concerns a mutual friend of Bernard and Humbert, the Huguenot refugee Thomas Lombrail (1667–1711). Lombrail started out as a bookbinder and became a publisher in 1700 at the age of thirty-three. In his short career he succeeded in getting about a dozen books on the market. He aimed at building a serious, up-market reputation, publishing, for example, Greek classics by Menander. The well-known Huguenot intellectual and philologist Jean Le Clerc served as translator. Lombrail also published a French translation of Robert Beverley's best-selling book *History and Present State of Virginia* (1707). Still heavily in debt and only forty-four years old, Lombrail died. Humbert and Bernard liquidated his estate. His widow, who had brought the sizeable sum of 2,000 florins to the business, found herself penniless. She survived only by selling home remedies to supplement her meager welfare allowance of 125 florins a year granted by the Walloon Church. Stories such as hers must have been fresh in the mind of Bernard when he launched his business. They also remind us that church membership, regardless of personal beliefs, was crucial.[15]

An analysis of Bernard's publishing record in these first years shows him reprinting large quantities of successful French titles, which he sold all over Europe. Bernard operated on the high end of the reprint market. He specialized in easy-to-ship paperback-size reprints of bestselling authors such as the French storyteller Jean de la Fontaine, the Huguenot female novelist Anne de la Roche Guilhen, the study of François Hédelin on theater practices, and François Fénelon's work on rhetoric and poetics. He used the revenues from these reprints, plus the income from the estates of his wives, to finance ventures requiring more capital, such as the multivolume series of the voyages to the north. He could not expect to see large returns from his own writings or from unusual titles by Gabriel Naudé or the skeptical novels of the sixteenth-century humanist Bonaventure Des Périers.

Bernard paid little attention to copyrights when publishing his reprints. Piracy flourished in the early modern book trade, both in the Dutch Republic and elsewhere, and the implicit rules governing the publishing market virtually forced newcomers to be on the look-out for quick profits. At the low end of the market, small-time booksellers tried to sell large numbers of unauthorized books cobbled together from many sources. Publishers might even use pirating as a means to bankrupt competitors or to pursue personal vendettas. At the high end, unauthorized reproduction was just as common. Until 1795 legal authorities in the Dutch Republic refused to act against firms that reissued books originally printed by foreign publishers. The authorities prosecuted for piracy only when a title enjoyed the protection of an official privilege granted by the Provincial Estates. In the view of the authorities, then, protectionism vied with a firm belief in the mechanics of a free market. Copyrights made books unnecessarily expensive, and only costly publishing adventures deserved protection.[16]

Bernard turned out to be an expert pirate, and he reprinted many foreign, especially French, titles and resold them on the European market. About 70 percent of his total book production consisted of previously published titles marketed under his own name. In the 1720s he became part of a consortium of booksellers, called the Company of the Fourteen, devoted to large-scale piracy. The group had been founded in 1711 and remained in operation until 1738. It published great quantities of reprints from mostly French originals, including bestsellers such as the continuation of Jonathan Swift's *Gulliver's Travels* in French translation, Voltaire's *Histoire du Charles XII, roi de Suède,* and Charles Rollin's *De la manière d'étudier les belles lettres,* a manual for the humanities in use all over Europe. Jean Frederic became a member of the consortium around 1727 and eventually copublished about twenty-five of the company's titles. The Company of the Fourteen even endeavored to protect their own pirated imprints once published. In 1734, for example, the company brought out the *Provincial Letters* of the famous seventeenth-century French philosopher Blaise Pascal. The following year Bernard wanted to republish the set under his own name, but first he had to buy the copyright from the consortium. Other consortium members were subjected to the same treatment.[17]

Bernard rarely took the precaution of using false imprints as a cover for his pirated French editions, since the Dutch authorities hardly ever prosecuted for pirating. False imprints served other uses: they misled the censors and protected authors and publishers of radical or impious writings from persecution by political and religious authorities. With notoriously false imprints such as "Pierre Marteau, Cologne," the Dutch led all Europe in publishing clandestine writings. Bernard put false imprints on his own radical books *Moral Reflections* and *Original Sin.* The former appeared with the Marteau imprint and the latter with the even more mysterious phrase "printed in the world." In the early years of his career Bernard wanted to attract as little attention as possible from potential censors. He must have quickly discovered, however, that almost anything could be printed in the Dutch Republic. When the authorities took measures they were mostly on behalf of foreign powers whose ambassadors had lodged complaints.

Consequently, Bernard published the second and third editions of *Moral Reflections* (1713 and 1716) under his own imprint. *Original Sin* remained the only book among more than 170 titles published by Bernard that received special treatment: every edition carried the imprint "printed in the world." Bernard demonstrated his confidence in the relative freedom of the Dutch press by putting his name to later imprints of his essays, including *Dialogues critiques et philosophiques* [Critical and philosophical dialogues] (1730) and *Dissertations mêlées, sur divers sujets importans et curieux* [Various essays on different important and curious subjects] (1740). These collections contained not only essays written by Bernard but also treatises that since 1700 had circulated as clandestine manuscripts. The *Various Essays,* for instance, included the first version of an essay by Jean Baptiste Mirabaud which maintained that the ancients did not have a conception of the immortality of the soul.[18]

Although he was not very secretive about his activities as a publisher, as an author Jean Frederic never once revealed his identity. None of his edited or authored books came out under his own name, not even his magnum opus, *Religious Ceremonies of the World.* As a result, the book began its triumphant tour around the literary world under the name of Bernard Picart. Fear of the censors could not have inspired this prudence. If apprehension about the authorities motivated his behavior, Bernard would have organized his publishing activities very differently, and he certainly would not have set up a good friend like Picart to be an easy target of legal censure.

Bernard may have thought it bad for business to disclose his identity as author given that the combination author-publisher was even rarer then than today. Did modesty play a role as well? Jean Frederic never showed much admiration for the university-educated, whom he often derided for their pomposity. Yet he had great respect for knowledge and tended to downplay his own contributions. He unpretentiously presented his books as *quelques remarques* [some remarks] or referred to them in some other similarly disparaging terms. But we should not travel too far down this road. In the eighteenth century many journal articles and reviews were unsigned, and many books were published anonymously. Most women, but also many men, chose anonymity. Women authors were considered inherently immodest and therefore of suspect morals. Many male authors identified themselves only by their initials. The authorial persona was only just beginning to emerge.[19]

Bernard appears to have reveled in the cloak-and-dagger anonymity of eighteenth-century publishing. He took the trouble to invent elaborate pseudonyms and complicated disguises all through his life, but he also relished revealing them. In his first book, *Moral Reflections,* he used initials and pseudonyms when discussing contemporaries in Holland, and then a few years later, in the third edition, he added a key to the central figures in the volume. In the 1733 edition he announced that the first three letters of the alphabet, when added to the thirteenth, signaled his place of residence, his name, his religion, and his birthplace: Amsterdam Bernard of the Calvinist religion born near Marseilles. As late as 1740 he introduced himself in the preface of *Various Essays* as "an author who until now has never disclosed his full name to the public and has contented himself with giving them only his initials."[20]

Yet Bernard could not resist planting clues. At the end of the 1741 edition of *Original Sin* he included a Latin poem intended for anyone who wanted to know the author's name. It read, "The letter B reveals the index of my name, Gaul is my birthplace and a damp country keeps me as an exile while fate is denying me my return." In the 1735 edition of *Critical and Philosophical Dialogues* he adopted the pseudonym Monsieur l'Abbé de Charte-Livry and offered another of his teasers: the book was signed D.C.L.F.D.B.B.A.M.E.P.M.R.E.H, a riddle of initials none of us has managed to solve. Although the book had been published five years earlier under his imprint in Amsterdam, Bernard now pretended that this new edition was published in London, *chez Morphée,* that is, the God of dreams. In view of all these charades it seems highly likely that even the 1733 Liège edition of *Moral Reflections* contained another of his name games; the supposed Liège publisher J. F. Broncard, who was well known as a publisher of forbidden books, had the same initials as Jean Frederic.[21]

Although these deliberate obfuscations encouraged some false attri-
butions to the pen of Bernard, most notoriously *Praise of Hell* (1759),
still incorrectly listed under his name in catalogues more than 200 years
later, in general they have resulted in a serious neglect of his influence as
a writer and a publisher. Since an authoritative list of his publications
and authored books has never been established, his place in intellectual
history has been overlooked. He was a major contributor to the ferment
about religion in the formative period of the Enlightenment. Even early
in his career when he lacked capital and sufficient credit, Bernard
printed only what he deemed intellectually worthwhile. Throughout his
career he focused on certain subjects: liberal theology and freethinking,
histories and memoirs critical of the French absolutist regime, travel
narratives, and sexual politics as displayed in his collections of titillating
stories and of course in his book on original sin. Bernard was at heart a
free spirit and a nonconformist. Unlike his colleagues who published
surefire sellers, Bernard published only books, even if reprints, that fit
into his broader intellectual agenda.[22]

Jean Frederic may have dreamed of a place in the Parisian literary
world. Even at the high point of the wars against France, Huguenot
exiles still saw themselves as part of French literary culture. They used
their freedom of expression in their countries of choice to publish in
their native tongue what French censorship would not permit. After the
Peace of Utrecht, and two years later the death of Louis XIV in 1715,
many Huguenots expected a speedy return to the motherland. They
thought that the regent would soften the laws against the French Protestants and even encourage their return to France. Bernard tried to facilitate a potential publishing career in France by dedicating his books
to key figures in the Parisian literary scene such as Abbé Bignon, the
president of the Academy of Sciences and a member of the Académie
Française.[23]

Bernard's contemporaries must have been surprised when in 1720 he
announced the launch of a gargantuan project. The seven folio volumes
of *Religious Ceremonies of the World* required huge capital outlays; they
included hundreds of illustrations to be produced on fine paper by the
best-paid engravers of Europe. Bernard was an average publisher who
put quality above profit and whom one would not expect to launch such
a major enterprise. To reduce costs, he employed a novel marketing
technique, selling by subscription. English publishers had originated

the idea early in the seventeenth century, and then after 1700 Dutch publishers refined the practice. By advertising for subscribers through a prospectus announcing the work, publishers could gauge the number of prospective buyers. More important, they could collect as much advance money as possible to finance the project. Subscribers would receive the books at a reduced price, but in exchange they had to make an advance payment. For some people in the trade, subscription fraud proved irresistible. Occasionally publishers never completed the books they advertised or simply did not publish the works at all. But Bernard never disappointed his customers.[24]

Although the subscription system limited financial exposure, no entrepreneur in his right mind—not even the biggest, most dominant family firms such as Wetstein, Leers, Fritsch, or Böhm—would dream of embarking on such a venture singlehandedly. To minimize the risks, even the big publishers went "en compagnie," as it was called, using carefully drafted notarial deeds to divide shares and profits in advance. The large dictionary and encyclopedia projects of the time, such as those of Bayle, Louis Moreri, or Antoine Furetière, were all published by teams of prosperous and experienced publishers who acquired privileges from the political authorities in order to make copying illegal. Only one contemporary publisher took the chance of publishing a large illustrated work completely on his own. In 1729 Pieter van der Aa began printing a collection of twenty-seven volumes (with 3,000 engravings of maps, views, and costumes from all over the globe) called *La Galerie agréable du monde* [The agreeable gallery of the world]. His exception proves the rule. He already owned the copperplates of the engravings and did not have to commission new work. Moreover, he embarked on the project in order to close down his publishing business and turn his ongoing rights into a kind of pension fund. Bernard's experience with the Dutch translation of *Religious Ceremonies of the World* was more typical; it took shape only after five larger firms agreed to finance the venture, despite the fact that a few hundred subscriptions existed to reduce the risks involved.[25]

Publishing, writing, and compiling the many illustrated volumes of *Religious Ceremonies of the World* marked a turning point in Bernard's career. Before the summer of 1720, Jean Frederic was an intellectually interesting and financially solvent publisher, respected by his Dutch colleagues. From 1720 onward Bernard established himself as a capitalist entrepreneur, a pillar of the Amsterdam industry, and perhaps most surprisingly, an erudite savant. The size of his output would remain relatively small over the course of his career, but it stood out for its quality and its innovative character.

Everything seemed to come together at once. In 1722 Bernard started a new journal, *Mémoires historiques et critiques,* in collaboration with the highly regarded journalist Denis Camusat and the prolific historian and geographer Antoine Augustin Bruzen de la Martinière. Camusat took the intellectual lead while Bruzen produced most of the book summaries and reviews. Like *Nouvelles Littéraires,* which Bernard had undertaken with Du Sauzet a few years before, the new journal failed, but the association with Camusat and De la Martinière proved lasting. Camusat signed up as the leading journalist on Bernard's next journal project, the *Bibliothèque Françoise.* Aimed like its predecessor at the French market, *Bibliothèque* took an intellectually aggressive and defiantly Jansenist line and soon proved central to French learned debate. Published at the same time Bernard was working on *Religious Ceremonies of the World,* it remained for years to come a journal of wide influence.[26]

The success of *Bibliothèque Françoise* rested on the collaboration between Camusat and Bernard. Camusat had begun his career by researching and writing the first history of journalism; its preface appeared when he was only nineteen. However brilliant, Camusat consistently overspent and had to keep one step ahead of his creditors, rushing from Amsterdam to Paris and back again. This back and forth did not deter him from editing for Bernard various historical memoirs and collections of libertine poetry. They were kindred spirits. They shared a fascination with heresies of all kinds and outrageous varieties of free thought. They also shared distinctive views on the role of learned journals and an intellectual style of journalism.[27]

In both *Mémoires historiques et critiques* and *Bibliothèque Françoise* Bernard and Camusat delivered a devastating critique of the quality of contemporary journalism. They saw most journals as simply venues for advertising on behalf of owner-publishers. They detested the hard-nosed self-interest demonstrated by publishers such as Wetstein who refused to print in their journals subscription prospectuses of rival publishers. To counter the superficial opinions found in most contemporary journal writing, the two men aimed to produce honest, critical, and historically grounded assessments of genuinely new scholarship. Bernard's ideal of the independent publisher thus found its counterpart in Camusat's aspiration to become the independent journalist who would live by his own pen rather than depend on patrons. While Camusat continued to pursue this critical project until his death in 1732, Bernard seemed to lose interest once the new formula was successfully established in the *Bibliothèque.* He sold it to Du Sauzet, who published it until 1746, though under the new regime it soon lost its Jansenist and intellectual cutting edge. After Camusat's death, Bernard took upon himself the completion of his collaborator's still unfinished masterwork, *Histoire critique des journaux* [Critical history of newspapers], which remains today the single most important source on the subject.[28]

Even while pursuing these new ventures in journal publishing and gearing up to produce *Religious Ceremonies of the World,* Bernard also pushed ahead with *Voyages au Nord.* Its title derived from the central theme of the series, the quest for a northwest passage and a study of the territories one came across on that route. The stories written by missionaries and other explorers had ignited a string of controversies about the meaning of cultural, and especially religious, differences. Bernard set out to provide his readers with access to as many unfiltered eyewitness narratives as possible. In *Voyages au Nord* Bernard for the first time tried his hand at the technique he would bring to perfection in *Religious Ceremonies of the World:* compiling, translating, and editing existing texts to which he would add memoranda and dissertations of his own hand. He assembled a wide array of lesser-known but—in his eyes—reliable travel accounts that could help his readers draw their own conclusions. His ten volumes appeared in small (duodecimo) format and were cheaply priced, in part because they included hardly any illustrations other than a few essential maps and charts. The strategy worked, and the series proved highly successful, going through at least three full reprints in less than fifteen years. Bernard enthusiastically urged continuing exploration overseas on the ground that it would benefit indigenous peoples as much as it did the Europeans. Since he rather optimistically believed that the merchant companies played a positive role in this process of mutual improvement, he also reprinted seven volumes of accounts about the colonial successes of the Dutch East India Company.[29]

Given his experiences as a Huguenot refugee, it is perhaps not surprising that Bernard also published French memoirs that might help explain how the policy of religious freedom and toleration developed by King Henry IV in 1598 could have been steadily undermined during the reigns of his successors Louis XIII and Louis XIV. How and why had things gone wrong in France? Could the policy of intolerance be reversed, thus enabling the many thousands of Protestant refugees to return to France? Bernard's historical memoirs met with the same success as his travel narratives. Many of them were reprinted and remain key sources for seventeenth-century French history.

Nothing excited Bernard's interest more, however, than theology and religion. At first glance, his publications seem eclectic and without unifying theme. Included among them were the medieval monk Ratramnus on the supposed presence of the historic body of Christ in the Eucharist, Naudé's and Le Brun's writings on magical practices, and the sermons of Tillotson. Binding them together was Bernard's quest for religious truth uncorrupted by superstition, bigotry, and the machinations of priestcraft. As Bernard reiterated time and again in his own publications, priests and theologians built their systems on religious ignorance. They intended to rob believers of their rational faculties and lead them into a web of superstitions from which it would be impossible to escape.

Bernard set himself the task of providing his readers with the information necessary to find their way out of the labyrinth of delusions and begin to decide religious matters for themselves. In one of the dialogues in his *Critical and Philosophical Dialogues* of 1730 he satirizes a bookseller who is in the business only for the money. True to his family heritage of scholarship, Bernard believed that the goal for men like himself should be to "dispense lessons of wisdom." Bernard's didactic mission implied that he did not need to endorse every work he printed. His publication of Mirabaud's criticism of traditional views on ancient learning in *Various Essays* was a service to the public because its circulation in manuscript form was very limited. His philosophy of impartiality when informing the public is best illustrated by his publication in 1717 of a French translation of Samuel Clarke's *Demonstration of the Being and Attributes of God* (1705). Clarke was a well-known defender of the Christian religion, but when Bernard had the reprint of that translation reviewed in his own *Bibliothèque Françoise* in 1728 he did not shrink from including a summary of the ideas of Spinoza, one of Clarke's detested targets.[30]

These defining intellectual and religious interests set Bernard apart from most of his fellow publishers and booksellers; they also drew the attention of visitors. Charles Etienne Jordan, a leader of the Berlin Academy of Sciences and a notable bibliographer, wrote in his journal, "Mr. Bernard is a bookseller with intelligence and learning; he may like studying too much for the good of his business." Despite his various connections with colleagues in the trade, Bernard remained at heart a loner, and at times he paid the price in friendships lost. Du Sauzet, for example, eventually came to hate him, calling him a "beast" in his letters and accusing him of shady business dealings. Professional jealousy was always lurking beneath the surface; Du Sauzet lashed out at the moment he faced bankruptcy and Bernard began to flourish.[31]

The turning point in Jean Frederic's career occurred in 1720, the year of one of the greatest stock market bubbles in history. Bernard made a killing from it. The bubble was a kind of poisoned peace dividend. When the Peace of Utrecht of 1713 finally put an end to the wars of Louis XIV, financiers began to seek new business opportunities. The governments of England and France needed to find ways to consolidate their wartime debts. The conjunction of the two interests proved fruitful at first. After the death of Louis XIV, the French regent, the duke of Orleans, put the Scottish economist and speculator John Law in charge of French finances. Law set up a state-backed central bank to issue paper money for the first time and a new trading company, the Mississippi Company, to exploit the supposed riches of the river delta in Louisiana. When the company failed to satisfy potential investors, he merged the other trading companies with it and gave it a monopoly on foreign trade. The company also exchanged shares for notes on the government debt, thus dramatically reducing the debt. Shares that went begging at 150 livres in 1717 sold for more than 10,000 in January 1720.

England already had a state bank, yet even here the allure of quick fixes proved irresistible to government and investors alike. Like the Mississippi Company, the South Sea Company, a slave-trading enterprise, offered to convert a portion of the long-term national debt into company shares. The value of the shares would supposedly increase at a faster rate than government interest on bonds. In exchange, the government paid the company lower interest than the going rate. Dutch as well as English money flowed into the company, as share prices shot up tenfold over a year. Dutch companies, too, tried to get a piece of the action. In the summer of 1720 confidence began to falter on both sides of the Channel, and in the autumn the bubbles burst, leaving many stockholders across Europe with worthless paper. The paper money issued by the new state bank in France collapsed as well, dooming the very idea for generations. Law himself fled France.[32]

Whereas many people lost everything, others, like Bernard, gained spectacularly by turning their shares or French paper money into specie in the nick of time. Although records of his transactions do not survive, other evidence indicates that in the summer of 1720 Bernard began investing large sums of money in Dutch as well as French merchant companies. The total, as far as we can determine, reaches almost 100,000 Dutch guilders, a small fortune at the time. Bernard did not lose the money as so many others did, and in the next year he was still raking in the profits. Even in the absence of any final balance sheet, it is beyond doubt that his gambling on the first European stock market boom offered Bernard the prospect of true intellectual freedom. In the case of *Religious Ceremonies of the World* freedom meant the opportunity to write whatever he wished without having a consortium of publishers looking over his shoulder and limiting his options for commercial reasons.[33]

Bernard did more than invest in the speculative frenzy: he helped fuel it with his series of travel accounts. It is probably not coincidental that he started *Voyages au Nord* in the year of Louis XIV's death, and it seems even less accidental that he published a volume on Louisiana and Mississippi in 1720 itself. Did he think that the Law experiments in opening up the economy might eventually encourage new religious policies as well? The duke of Orleans, regent on behalf of Louis's five-year-old great-grandson, had a reputation for libertinism in morals; might he be something of a freethinker in religion, too? Would he open the way to the return of the Huguenots? We cannot know for sure just how religion, travel literature, and the profit motive came together in Bernard's mind at this moment, but there is no question that he saw the merchant companies as engines of change driving a new order. He intended to do everything in his power to convince his readers to become investors in colonial trade like himself.

Bernard laid out his general views on exploration and commerce in a lengthy introduction to the first volume of *Voyages*. It reads like a white paper for commercially oriented world travel, summarizing recently gained knowledge and listing all the unknown parts of the world that still needed to be explored, while stressing the opportunities for a rejuvenated France. The volume on the Louisiana-Mississippi region, in particular, is pointedly directed at potential investors, as the title makes clear: *Travel Accounts of Louisiana and the Mississippi River in which one sees the State of this Great Country and the Advantages that It Can Offer, etc.* At the same time, Bernard published all the official documents concerning the establishment of the Mississippi Company that might interest potential investors. It is hardly surprising, therefore, that *Travel Accounts of Louisiana* opens with a glowing description of John Law as the savior of France and of his mercantile projects as the most important contributions to the future of the French monarchy. Bernard knew on which side his bread was buttered. Ironically, his profits in the speculative boom would now allow him to launch his remarkable career as publisher and author of one of the most radical books of the early Enlightenment on the subject of religion.[34]

All these different streams—profit, travel literature, expectations of change in post–Louis XIV France, the desire for high-level journalism, and, above all, the search for religious truth—flowed into *Religious Ceremonies of the World.* In December 1720 and January 1721 Bernard published the subscription prospectuses. The event was carefully orchestrated; potential clients could sign up for the new series in Paris, London, Berlin, Hamburg, or Geneva. Only in Amsterdam, however, were sample sheets of the engravings and the text available for perusal. Bernard must have been thinking of such a project for some time. Little is known about the financial or production agreements concluded between Bernard and Picart; no notarial documents have been found. Presumably, Bernard paid for the paper, which alone accounted for at least half of the production cost, and the printing itself, and Picart contributed the publishing rights to his engravings while retaining the copperplates for himself. The revenues from the sale of the books would therefore end up in the pocket of Bernard, but Picart would be able to reprint the engravings and sell them separately in his shop. The quality of the engravings and the text indicates that both men invested much time and energy in research. Each of them amassed extensive libraries in which all the relevant travel accounts and philosophical debates about religion could be found. It seems likely, moreover, that they had discussed the possibility of such a project for some time. They lived in close proximity, and Bernard attended Picart's weekly evening presentations of his work. They had many mutual friends and relatives. They acted as godfathers to each other's children, and both had close relations with Picart's in-laws, the Vincent family, the producers of the paper so central to their businesses.[35]

Producing *Religious Ceremonies of the World* would dominate Bernard's career as a publisher. When he died at the age of sixty-one in 1744, eleven years after Picart, he had published the final supplement to *Religious Ceremonies of the World* only the year before. His influence on the Enlightenment is to be found not only in his books but also in his legacy. He died a relatively wealthy man. In 1742 his yearly income was evaluated at 2,000 guilders, and it probably was much higher, given that most taxpayers shielded part of their income from the inspectors. The tax registers categorized his business as semi-capitalist, a status only very few Amsterdam booksellers had acquired. Three years after his death his second daughter, Elisabeth, married Marc Michel Rey, a colleague of her father's who had helped sell off the Bernard book business. The Bernard fortune, combined with the business acumen of Elisabeth, enabled Rey to become one of the most important publishers of the Enlightenment. He published all the major names: Voltaire, Rousseau, and d'Holbach, not to mention the piles of once-clandestine manuscripts that he turned into anonymous books. His competitors considered him a business shark, and even his friends admonished him about all the heterodoxy that poured off his press. But like his father-in-law, he, too, remained a member of the Walloon Church, despite the odor of impiety given off by his publishing escapades. Rey even seems to have had a hand in helping to get Diderot's great *Encyclopedia* printed once the Parisian censors had closed it down. In December 1754 Rey offered to send Marchand a copy of its fifth volume—eleven months before it was actually published![36]

Wandering into Rey's shop on Amsterdam's Bloemmarkt, the aspiring philosophe would still sense something of the spirit of Bernard and Picart. Rey's impeccable eye for spotting what would appeal and therefore sell undoubtedly owed something to the knowledge acquired by his wife as she watched her father, Jean Frederic, and his good friend Picart struggle and then succeed in their adopted land. Jean Frederic not only left the world a crucially important new genre with his multivolume illustrated encyclopedia of the world's religions; he also founded a dynasty of gentleman-publishers that gave the world much of the radical Enlightenment. Knowing the contours of his business life gives texture to the early decades of the eighteenth century, when the market for books fueled the secularly inspired dismantling of Christian orthodoxy.

5

A Writer's Mental Universe

I will be thought a bit daring in this book;
But it is necessary to overcome the lie with courage,
And seek the truth as much as one can find it in this my world.

Epigraph to *State of Man in Original Sin,*
by Jean Frederic Bernard (1741)

DESPITE his audacious search for truth, Jean Frederic Bernard was a secretive man. No portrait or engraving of him has ever surfaced. As it is hard to imagine that his friend Picart never offered to make even a simple drawing of his face, we can only assume that Jean Frederic was determined not to reveal anything about his person. In the preface to the last volume of essays he published, *Various Essays* (1740), he even mocks himself for his supposed timidity. Bernard's decision to refrain from displaying his authorship on the title page of his magnum opus, *Religious Ceremonies of the World,* may not have fooled knowledgeable contemporaries. Nonetheless, the extensive introduction he authored was covered once again by that familiar disguise, the use of asterisks instead of his name. As a result, all intellectual (and bibliographical) credit went to his friend Picart. In turn the histories of enlightened thought for the most part lost track of Bernard.

There is no doubt, however, that Bernard was the central figure behind the text. In the preface to the supplementary eighth volume published in 1743, he made it perfectly clear that he alone was responsible for its content. He also left an important clue about one of the most formative influences on his outlook. In the course of excoriating the pirated and bowdlerized 1741 edition by two French clergymen, he cited among their many failings their use of Catholic attacks on generations

CEREMONIES

ET

COUTUMES

RELIGIEUSES

DE TOUS LES

PEUPLES DU MONDE

*Reprefentées par des Figures deffinées de
la main de*

BERNARD PICARD:

Avec une Explication Hiftorique, & quelques
Differtations curieufes.

TOME PREMIER,

*Qui contient les Ceremonies des Juifs & des Chrétiens
Catholiques.*

A AMSTERDAM,

Chez *J. F. BERNARD,*

M, DCCXXIII.

5.1   Title page from the first volume of *Religious Ceremonies of the World.* Although the spelling of Picart's name is corrected in the next volume, the visual highlighting of his contribution and the absence of any mention of Bernard's authorship remain constant throughout. (Research Library, The Getty Research Institute, Los Angeles, California)

of Waldensians, in French, the *Vaudois*. This reference might have escaped the unsuspecting reader, but as we shall see, it was deeply meaningful to Bernard himself.[1]

Bernard and Picart came to their mature thinking about religion from very different experiences. Picart left devout Catholicism and made his way to Protestantism by a circuitous route that included contact with Jansenism and enthusiasm for the new science. Like his friend Marchand, he probably moved from distaste for Catholic doctrines such as transubstantiation toward a nonconfessional or churchless religious identity.[2]

Jean Frederic's religious journey, in contrast, began in the Huguenot community of Provence, which had its own distinctive history among French Protestant groups. In Provence Protestantism originated in the medieval heretical movement of the Waldensians. Its founder, the twelfth-century Lyon merchant Vaudès, preached the principles of early Christianity, stressing the virtue of poverty and the role of lay preaching. Though harshly persecuted, his followers survived in small communities in the remote Alpine regions of France and Italy. In the late 1400s the noble and clerical lords of Provence whose territories had been devastated by war, disease, and famine had invited Alpine Waldensians to come repopulate their lands. As a result, in the fertile region northeast of Marseilles villages such as Merindol, Lourmarin, Cabernières, Manosque, and the Bernards' home town, Velaux, became markedly Waldensian.[3]

The Waldensians preserved their faith by means of an effective secret network of wandering preachers and by accommodating, wherever necessary, to their Catholic religious surroundings. They bonded together as "brothers" (Bernard tells us that only the followers of Jan Hus and the Freemasons also describe one another as *frères*). Their ministers, called *Barbes*, disguised themselves as gentle uncles when dispensing pastoral care and admonition. In volume five of *Religious Ceremonies of the World* Bernard devotes an entire essay to the history of the Waldensians and, perhaps even more significantly, cites them no fewer than 107 times in that volume, often comparing them with other Protestant sects. His account, while maintaining his usual stance of detached objectivity, nonetheless displays an intimate knowledge of the Waldensian catechism and illustrates the belief that the Waldensians lie at the root of European Protestantism.[4]

The coming of the Reformation changed everything. The Waldensians, previously labeled heretics, now faced two alternatives: they could either migrate to Protestant lands or strive for legal recognition. Before the 1540s the Protestants in Provence were alternately tolerated and murdered, but in 1545 more than 3,000 Waldensian Protestants either lost their lives or were forced to flee, often to Geneva, the capital of French Calvinist Protestantism.

In the 1560s they managed to rebuild their church organization, and in Provence a particular form of Protestantism, buttressed by Waldensian ideas, took root. Under the provisions of the Edict of Nantes of 1598, they would be tolerated again, and a new phase of peaceful cohabitation of Catholics and Waldensian Huguenots began in Provence. In the early 1660s Louis XIV, whose concept of absolutism allowed for only one religion, launched a new offensive against the French Protestants. The revocation in 1685 led to the almost complete obliteration of Waldensian Protestantism in the south of France.

The Bernard family had been supplying pastors to this community for more than a hundred years. Their university training made them intellectual leaders of the Waldensian Huguenots, serving their congregations in towns like Velaux, which became the internationally oriented center of the movement. The Bernards experienced every phase of its tragic history, and eventually all would be chased from the region. Bernard's secrecy about his person and his caution about publicizing his name had their roots, at least in part, in this turbulent history. Clandestinity accompanied by distrust of authorities inevitably characterized the behavior of Bernard's family members, as well as their friends and relatives, for centuries.[5]

Pre-Reformation Waldensian theology laid overwhelming emphasis on morality, on the vices to be avoided and the virtues to be relentlessly pursued. In Waldensian belief Christianity consisted first and foremost in the law of God. However, the medieval Church had presented the sacraments, the intervention of saints, and the offices of pope and clergy as essential instruments of God's forgiveness. Waldensian religious literature simply passed over the sacramental assistance of the Church. Only God had power over mortal sin; church rituals were meaningless. They were, as Bernard described the practices of all the religious cults in his general preface to volume one of *Religious Ceremonies of the World*, a "strange bizarreness."[6]

Although some elements of traditional Waldensian belief, especially the emphasis on good works, gave Protestants great discomfort, the Waldensian heritage resonated with many of their core convictions. In order to buttress their claim to represent the True Church of early Christianity, the Reformers made a sharp distinction between the visible hierarchy of Rome with its priests and ornate ceremonies and the primitive Christianity of the True Church. Rome had introduced one error after another: canon law, papal primacy, transubstantiation, and purgatory, in short, what Bernard labels "the disorders of this Church." The Waldensian heresy could be seen as the sole remnant of what had once been the True Church, now overshadowed by ages of popish darkness. A legion of Protestant theologians extolled the sufferings and martyrdom of the Alpine heretics, culminating in James Ussher's *Historical Exposition of the Unbroken Succession and State of the Christian Church* (1613) and Jean Léger's *General History of the Evangelical Churches of the Piedmont or Waldensian Valleys* (1669). Bernard cited Léger's work extensively in his essay on the Waldensians. All over Protestant Europe the idea of Waldensianism as the repository of original Christianity had an enormous appeal.[7]

The Bernard family must have regarded themselves as the heirs of that tradition and would certainly have made it a central element in Jean Frederic's religious education. In the absence of private papers, however, we have to rely on his books and essays, his publishing record, and the introductions, notes, and commentaries he prepared for some of his editions to document his beliefs. They reveal a distinct affinity with this idea of an original or primitive True Church. The introductory essay of *Religious Ceremonies of the World*, which deals with religious worship, for example, argues that man "has lost the true idea of the Divinity," and that out of that loss come all "the extraordinary ceremonies and many extravagant devotions." This central notion appears again and again in the book.[8]

The search for the True Church some 1,700 years after Jesus was by definition an impossible task. Yet the search itself made Bernard sympathetic to a great variety of radical ideas. Over time he amalgamated traditional religious beliefs with new scientific concepts and eventually tested them both against the evidence he gathered in his grand survey of all the world's religions. The Waldensian heresies learned in his youth set Bernard off on a path toward encounters with deism, pantheism, and possibly even a form of atheism. But he did not know the outcome of his journey at the start, and we should not read too much retrospectively from *Religious Ceremonies of the World*. Our scrutiny of his work will show that Bernard always maintained his secretive and even quixotic qualities, refusing all the known categories, valuing the provocative and his freedom to be so above all else.

Bernard's first book, *Moral Reflections*, already hints at the Waldensian influence even while it builds on the French tradition of moralizing founded by Montaigne and Pascal. It includes, for instance, a chapter on devotion that describes the first Christians as patient and gentle compared with later Christians, who are false, cruel, vindictive, and full of pride. He could be even more forthright than this, however. In 1717 he reprinted a book by the French Protestant minister Jonas Porrée (d. 1646) that had originally been published in 1629 in The Hague. Bernard gave it a new title that fit better with his own ideas: *A History of the Superstitions and Ceremonies Introduced into the Church*. Porrée's book was a French Protestant classic that was added to the papal Index of Forbidden Books in 1669. An English translation of 1668 had been dedicated to the English king, Charles II, as an admonition not to succumb to Catholic ideas and practices. The German translation after the revocation of the Edict of Nantes in 1685 served as a reminder of the true character of the French Roman Catholic Church.[9]

Porrée's account of the degeneration of early Christian practices into superstitions matched the established Waldensian chronology of the decline of the True Church. It began with "the thick shadows of the papacy" in the twelfth century and lasted until the arrival of Martin Luther. Bernard dedicated his edition of Porrée's work to the prince of Wales, later George II, perhaps as a playful reminder of the ineffective previous dedication to Charles II. The introduction by Bernard reveals his commitment to the notion of the True Church: "In this book one observes how the darkness of error slowly obscured the enlightened days of early Christianity and how bigotry and the spirit of arrogance have replaced the devotion and humility of the apostles."[10]

As an appendix to Porrée's classic, Bernard published a new edition of the treatise of the ninth-century monk Ratramnus written against the newly emerging doctrine of transubstantiation. Ratramnus in his time failed to find acceptance for his views, and his treatise was condemned as heresy. However, it re-emerged later to convince famous protagonists of the English Reformation such as Thomas Cranmer that transubstantiation was irreconcilable with reason. Bernard's campaign against such "superstitions" continued throughout his career and culminated in the publication in two large folio volumes of *Ancient and Modern Superstitions* (1733–1736), a collection of famous studies in the field. Though *Religious Ceremonies of the World* was published separately and as part of a different enterprise, readers of that work often saw the two volumes of *Ancient and Modern Superstitions* as its supplements. They frequently had them bound as volumes ten and eleven of the set.[11]

Superstition was a burning issue in the early 1700s, in both Protestant and Catholic circles. In 1691 the liberal Dutch Calvinist philosopher Balthasar Bekker set off a firestorm of controversy across Europe when he roundly denounced belief in pacts with the devil, witches' Sabbaths, demonic possession, and the like in his four volumes of *The World Bewitched*. Spinoza in his *Tractatus Theologico-Politicus* (1670) and Pierre Bayle in his *Thoughts on the Comet,* his *Philosophical Commentary,* and many articles in his *Dictionary* (1697) offered even more radical propositions. Bayle followed philosophical arguments to their logical conclusion and emphasized that the idea of superstition was a double-edged sword. Since Protestants and Catholics alike used the term "superstition" for the false beliefs of the other, superstition might turn out to be entirely relative, if not devoid of meaning.

The effort to cleanse the church of superstitious practices was an ongoing project open to well-meaning Catholics as well as Protestants. *Ancient and Modern Superstitions* consisted of the tracts of two moderate Catholic priests with Jansenist leanings, Jean Baptiste Thiers and Pierre Lebrun. They aimed at purifying the Catholic Church of abuses and superstitious practices. Bernard's reprinting of Jansenist writings suggests that religion itself was not his ultimate target, only its accretions and corruptions. *Ancient and Modern Superstitions* left out more radical perspectives such as those of the Neapolitan jurist and historian Pietro Giannone, or the French village priest Jean Meslier, who in the 1720s had identified Christianity itself as a blasphemy and as an economic exploitation of the poor.[12]

Bernard's deployment of Jansenist Catholics in the battle against superstition shows that he was prepared to depart from conventional Protestant polemics. His heretical background had made him intrinsically suspicious of the clergy, their established religious institutions, and ideological faultlines. In *Moral Reflections* he uses arguments that closely resemble those of renowned deists and atheists such as Charles Blount, John Toland, and Henri de Boulainvilliers. Just like them he makes a sharp distinction between those who had founded religions (Jesus, Moses) and those who exploit those religions for their own benefit. Priests, clergymen, and theologians fill the heads of their congregations with belief in demons, wonders, and prophecies to impose their will, and instead of explaining religion, their sermons are full of unintelligible phrases that leave their flock dumbfounded. According to Bernard, "superstition is the illness of an empty soul." Only common sense and a serious reflection on the nature of religion would remedy that sickness.[13]

Religious ceremonies also serve to disguise the real goal of religion. For most people religion is limited to the outward observance of customs and ceremonies, and they could not care less about the morality and spirituality that are, according to Bernard, the core of real religion. In the 1735 edition of his *Critical and Philosophical Dialogues* Bernard includes a hilarious conversation between Jupiter and Muhammad on the best strategies to achieve a large following. Muhammad makes fun of Jupiter, asserting that nobody fears his streaks of lightning anymore, and then extols the qualities of his own mullahs, who are so much better at enslaving their flock. At the end Muhammad offers Jupiter a secret alliance: together they will rule the world. Christianity, however, is even worse. For Bernard its behavior can best be summarized in the work of a subtle Florentine philosopher called Machiavelli. Christian clergy flatter the corruption of the monarchs, punish the innocent, and ruin society by feeding suspicion among its members.[14]

Bernard's Machiavellian loathing of the anti-intellectual priesthood and his abhorrence of superstition seep from the pages of *Moral Reflections*. The book mirrors Gabriel Naudé's *Apology for Great Men Suspected of Magic* (Paris, 1625), which Bernard reprinted almost simultaneously. Naudé denounced the priesthood's penchant for mobilizing the illiterate masses against dissident scholars and humanistic thinkers and portrayed them as a danger to society. Jean Frederic stressed Naudé's qualities as a critic of witchcraft and sorcery who emphasized the continuity of belief in magical practices between pagan and Christian cultures. He praised Naudé's rationalist method, which rejected everything unless it could be validated as just and reasonable. This principle eventually would lead Naudé to assert in his Machiavellian political tract of 1639 that rulers subordinated religion to politics, and that in the end all historical religions were inventions of the ancient Lawgivers, a proposition that would be expanded in *The Treatise of the Three Impostors*.[15]

Naudé was only one of Bernard's intellectual heroes among the humanists and libertines. Early on Bernard had reprinted the free-spirited novel of Bonaventure Des Périers, and he also published the best eighteenth-century edition of the collected works of François Rabelais. Rabelais, like Des Périers, had been a member of the circle around Marguerite of Navarre (1492–1549), the sister of the French king Francis I and a champion of religious liberty and reform. Both Des Périers and Rabelais were suspected of atheism. A correspondent of John Calvin, Marguerite tried to mediate between the early reformers and the Catholic Church. Not surprisingly this inquisitive world of learning and the tolerant royal policies that made it possible coincided with the early successes of the Waldensian reformation in southern France. Its demise in the last days of Francis I, a period that also brought Des Périers and Rabelais under suspicion, led to the great massacre of Waldensian Protestants in 1545.[16]

Another major source of inspiration for Bernard among these early sixteenth-century humanists was Guillaume Postel, the father of Arabic studies in Europe. Postel learned Arabic when he accompanied a French ambassador to the court of the Turkish sultan. Like many French humanists he believed that the Catholic Church needed reform and that French intellectuals were destined to accomplish that task. In 1544 he published *Concerning the Harmony of the Earth*, in which he prophesied a universal religion. Postel argued that Jews, Muslims, and even the heathens could be converted to Christianity once it became clear that all the religions of the world had common foundations. Although he believed that Christianity best represented those foundations, he was also fascinated by Hermes Trismegistus, supposedly an Egyptian sage who was the fount of all secret knowledge, such as alchemy and astrology. Since some version of Hermes could be found in various Christian, Jewish, and Muslim sects, it was only a short step to believing that all religions might be traced back to him as a kind of original source.

The so-called *Corpus Hermeticum*, actually an amalgam of neo-Platonic and neo-Pythagorean texts probably written in the first to

third centuries, had influenced Renaissance humanism since its redis-
covery in the fifteenth century. Some humanists at the time of the Reformation believed that a restoration of the true religion could be accomplished by drawing upon this hermetic tradition. Bernard seems to
have been intrigued by the idea. In 1714 he republished a famous treatise on Pythagorean theology, and in *Religious Ceremonies of the World*
Pythagoreanism (and the accompanying doctrine of metempsychosis)
pops up in many different places. Picart, too, was a hermetic aficionado.
He possessed a great number of books on the subject, including a rare
copy of Postel's *De cosmographica disciplina et signorum coelestium vera
configuratione* [Cosmography and celestial signs], which tried to incorporate Arabic astrology and Greek hermetic philosophy into a truly
cosmic religion under the authority of the pope.[17]

Two issues shaped Bernard's religious interests: the quest for a virtuous life and the degeneration of early Christianity. In his *State of Man
in Original Sin* he comes close to resolving them. The book is a complete reworking of *On Original Sin* (1678), a notorious treatise by the
Dutch humanist Adrianus van Beverland. A scholar of the classics who
was particularly fascinated by authors of erotica such as Martial, Juve-
nal, and Petronius, Beverland insisted that the biblical account of Adam
and Eve's fall from grace had been misinterpreted for more than a thousand years. The story should be read as an allegory for the discovery
of sexual intercourse. Hence sexual desire drove the human quest for
knowledge, a theory he supported with a host of references not only
to classical authors but also to Hobbes and Spinoza. Materialist statements such as "out of dead matter comes forth life" could only have
further alarmed the Dutch authorities. The book was immediately forbidden and Beverland went for some time to the prison for students
maintained by Leiden University. Because he was unwilling to recant,
he was forced to spend the rest of his life in exile. He died penniless in
London.[18]

Sexual politics fascinated Bernard from the beginning of his career.
His reworked version of Beverland, published in 1714, had been preceded in 1712 by a new edition of the *Stories* of Poggio Bracciolini. The
extensive commentary Bernard had added to that edition already contained many of the ideas he would expand in his *State of Man in Original Sin.* Bernard's version of Beverland was reprinted six times in Jean
Frederic's lifetime. It is difficult to determine whether this success was

due to the notoriety of the Beverland original, which was extremely rare and available only in Latin, or to Bernard's own unusual views. Bernard wholeheartedly adopts Beverland's arguments that the sexual drive is the essence of original sin, that mankind is universally susceptible to sexual urges, and that suppression of them is counterproductive. Beverland then went on to plead for the full enjoyment of sexual intercourse, including masturbation, female as well as male orgasm, within or outside marriage. Bernard turns instead to rehabilitating the fundamental premise for a religious argument, albeit a radical one at odds with both Calvinist and Catholic doctrine. He maintains that Christ's death on the cross redeemed all the sins that followed from the original one. God's grace is consequently available to anyone who tries to live a virtuous life. The sexual drive, and its accompanying guilt, are a burden humankind has to shoulder as best it can, aided by reason, preferably within the bounds of marriage, but that failing, outside of it.

Bernard's choice of Beverland is certainly a curious one, designed to tweak the noses of religious authorities. He uses the notorious humanist to denounce established churches, especially the Roman Catholic Church, and their officials, who for time out of mind have threatened believers with eternal damnation for an urge they are unable to suppress. The church yokes humankind with a convoluted system of ceremonies that are fundamentally superfluous because the death of Christ has already earned all of humankind God's grace. The consequences of the relentless crusade against sexuality in the name of religion are dramatic: a perverted church whose officials do not shrink away from exploiting brothels themselves, a lascivious society, an abundance of superstition, the prevalence of external devotion rather than inner conviction, and a distressing record of persecution that has lasted more than a thousand years.

Humankind, however, need not follow these misguided regulations. As Bernard stipulated time and again, thanks to the grace of God we are born free. Our rational faculties will help us to unravel the conspiracy of the church and lead us away from the thorns and thistles of misleading theological debate. Reason enables us to reconstruct the unadulterated ideas of the apostles and prophets of early Christianity. For Bernard prime examples of this reason were the biblical criticism of Simon and Bekker and Bayle's attack on the extravagant beliefs about the devil. Though Bernard acknowledges Satan's role in the seduction of

Eve, in his view Satan's function ended there. If anything, the perverted church had taken over the devil's despicable work.

Clearly, Bernard's quest for a satisfactory solution to his heretically inspired religious dilemmas pushed him far from the beliefs and convictions of even the most liberal variety of Protestantism. Although he preserved many notions and terms of Protestant discourse, he took them in a new direction toward a much more universalist message. *State of Man in Original Sin* considered both traditional topics such as the parallels between Roman Catholic and pagan ritual and new themes such as the comparative role of ablutions in religious rites. In this work Bernard explicitly tied the rituals of purification found in many religions to the feelings of shame and remorse about the sexual act induced by religious teaching itself. Most significantly, he had come to believe that God's grace and hence the knowledge of the true principles of religion were not limited to Jews or Christians. Grace and knowledge might have come to them first, but in the end God's grace embraced all the great sages of paganism, too. God was present in all the religions of the world, and everyone who struggled to avoid vice and to steadfastly pursue virtue was fulfilling God's law.

In *Religious Ceremonies of the World* Bernard develops the insight taken from *State of Man in Original Sin* in a different way. His opening essay on religious worship discusses not original sin but the fact that a sense of having sinned pervades the world. Now he argues that consciousness and anxiety, guilt and shame (he is assuming over sexual urges) actually predate the repression transmitted by religion. Now, indeed, a sense of guilt rather than fear of the unknown is the universal source of the religious impulse. Wherever one has found "the signs of a religious cult, one has found . . . the ceremony of penance." Ablutions and rituals of purification are also ubiquitous for the same reason. Bernard has concluded that the universal experience of sexual arousal also triggers the impulse to purify the body, to cover it in white, to ask the gods for a primordial act of forgiveness because human urges are by definition too powerful to resist. The resulting shame breeds the necessity for religious ceremony. Both Christians and pagans have recourse to water, what Christians call "holy water," so that all might be cleansed of impurities. Once sexually conscious, human beings seek ceremonial purity, and once invented, religions are then enclosed in their rural temples, where worship can continue peacefully. With the temples come statues and other paraphernalia; then, as people settle in towns, the temples become inhabited by priests.[19]

What may have begun as a search for an original true religion has sent Bernard into an examination of every religion known to his age. It is clear from the opening essay that he has been canvassing the historical and travel literature looking for commonalities. In the end Bernard has found not a universal religion but a universal psychological impulse, an anxiety born out of human sexuality. He has gotten past the simplistic notion that the church and the priests have invented religion to repress humankind. In the first instance human nature invented religiosity as witnessed among the Jews, Christians, Muslims, Persians, Greeks, Indians, Amerindians, and the peoples of Africa. The Waldensians sought out a primitive Christianity; now in his flight from orthodoxy Bernard channeled the search in the direction of a universal natural religion.

We cannot be sure that at the moment he completed *State of Man in Original Sin* Bernard was already considering the daunting task of researching his claims with an analysis of all the religions of the world, but such an undertaking must have been an obvious next step. As highly educated artisans with contacts throughout the world of books, both Bernard and Picart were well equipped for that mission. Moreover, Bernard knew where he stood in the tradition of brutal religious persecution lasting more than 150 years. Even though he enjoyed an unparalleled degree of religious freedom in the Dutch Republic, he must have been desperately looking for a more stable and principled basis for toleration. Waldensian Protestantism compounded by a vast knowledge of European radical religious literature had set him on the road toward historical and cultural relativism. Sometime in the 1710s he came to share a vision with Bernard Picart, who was also looking for a way to use his talents in the service of principled religious toleration. In their magnum opus they would widen that relativist perspective beyond anything then imaginable in the European intellectual tradition. Their quest began in religious heresies against the Catholic Church and ended in psychology, ethnography, and comparative religion.

In the 1720s offering an account of other religions could hardly be described as new. From the sixteenth century onward the discovery of new worlds had compelled early modern society to come to terms with much greater religious and cultural variety. Historians, cosmographers, and moralists had risen to the task, and the first great work to inform a

European audience of the new diversity was Johannes Boemus's *Fardle of Facions Containing the Aunciente Maners, Customes and Lawes of the Peoples Enhabiting the two Partes of the Earth* (London, 1555, original Latin edition, 1539). Boemus primarily intended to provide knowledge, but he also struggled with the issue of how to reconcile the classical idea of the growth of civilization with the accepted Christian idea of degeneration from a primitive monotheism into idolatry.[20]

In the early seventeenth century the British writer Samuel Purchas would solve that problem by boldly putting European Christianity center stage. In *Purchas, his Pilgrimage; or, Relations of the World and the Religions observed in all Ages,* he took the classical division of the religions, established by the sixteenth-century French universal scholar Jean Bodin, as his point of departure. He carved up the world into four categories of rather unequal size and stature: Jews, Christians, Mohammedans, and the rest, who could be termed alternatively idolatrous peoples, superstitious heathens, or pagans. Purchas's *Pilgrimage* soon found competitors, the most famous of which was Alexander Ross (1590–1654) and his *Pansebeia, or View of all the Religions in the World* (London, 1652). Ross was a prolific writer and a former chaplain to Charles I, as well as a close collaborator of Archbishop Laud. His *Pansebeia* was reprinted often and translated into Dutch and German. Ross produced the first translation of the Koran into English, but his approach to the subject hardly differed from that of Purchas. His chief aim was to invigorate his readership's opposition to idolatry and atheism at the same time. According to Ross, people needed to understand all the different religions so as to see "the deformity" of their ideas. He noted that men otherwise "barbarous" had embraced a religion, a fact he used to highlight the impudence of modern atheists. Purchas and Ross confidently endorsed their categories and polemics despite the fact that neither had ever set foot out of England.[21]

At the end of the seventeenth century the spectacular growth of knowledge created the modern encyclopedia, which found an ever-expanding readership. Louis Moreri's *Grand Dictionary* of 1674 was the first example of the new genre. Europe was soon awash in dictionaries and their reprints, the most famous being Pierre Bayle's *Historical and Critical Dictionary.* Specialization was inevitable, and the early eighteenth century saw the emergence of dictionaries devoted to separate disciplines such as religion or geography. In 1704 in London the first *Dictionary of All Religions* was published, presumably edited by Daniel

Defoe, and the geographical dictionary of Bernard's collaborator De la Martinière constituted the most important lexicon of the sort found in the early eighteenth century. Encyclopedias and dictionaries did not offer uncontested, stable knowledge; on the contrary, dictionaries constituted a battlefield. Many new versions or editions were launched only because their predecessors were too Protestant, too Catholic, too Dutch, too French, or too English, and in the learned periodicals almost every new edition of one of the famous dictionaries was responsible for a wave of serious polemics.[22]

Bernard and Picart's *Religious Ceremonies of the World* did not fit into the procrustean bed laid down by most dictionaries and encyclopedias. Though many buyers must have acquired a copy precisely because of its encyclopedic character, Bernard and Picart had a completely different objective from the authors of such volumes. They wanted to confront their audience with a radically new religious education that would turn the traditional religious surveys—from Boemus to Defoe—upside down: they wanted to show the public that acquired religious ceremonies and customs had obscured the universality of religion. They aimed at transforming prejudice into inquisitiveness, because they were certain that knowledge would lead to the acceptance of deviant religious teachings and practices.

Another novelty was their deliberate employment of the illustration. The late sixteenth century had witnessed the first illustrated travel accounts, but until Diderot and d'Alembert's *Encyclopédie* of 1751–1772, the new encyclopedias did not contain engravings. Neither Purchas nor Ross nor Defoe was illustrated. The first illustrated encyclopedic accounts date from the last quarter of the seventeenth century and include, for instance, Louis de Gaya's *Matrimonial Customs; or, The Various Ceremonies, and Divers Ways of Celebrating Weddings, Practised amongst all the Nations, in the whole World* (London, 1687), first published in 1680 in Paris. The Parisian atelier of Picart turned out engravings for works of a similar nature in great numbers, and it is very likely that Bernard and Picart wanted to tap into this bestselling market for illustrated volumes with their original book project.

One of the first attempts to completely integrate text and visual material for scholarly purposes was *Antiquity Explained* by the Benedictine monk Bernard de Montfaucon, volume one of which appeared in Paris in 1719. De Montfaucon aimed to present the first amalgamated view of

Maniere dont les FEMMES se BRULENT aux INDES apres la Mort de leurs EPOUX.

5.2 Widow burning in India. In most European engravings of sati, or widow burning, in India, the widow, in conformity with European expectations, was more or less naked. Picart deliberately dressed her in rich European clothes, thus hindering the customary reaction of condescension toward primitive peoples with barbaric rituals. Readers might even be induced to imagine the central figure to be a highly placed widow of European stock and thus be encouraged to ponder the superstitious rituals of their own culture. CC, vol. IV, 26 (top half of the plate). (Research Library, The Getty Research Institute, Los Angeles, California)

fragments found in antiquarians' scholarship on Roman antiquity. Bernard and Picart each owned a copy, but it seems unlikely that their project received its initial inspiration from his work. They definitely had a scholarly project in mind, but they intended to do something much more elaborate than *Antiquity Explained.* They did not simply plan an integration of text and engravings. They also wanted each of these media to tell a story of its own.[23]

Given his contributions to innovations in publishing and his undeniable originality as a thinker, Bernard may be considered one of the founders of the European Enlightenment. His work dispels a long-standing assumption about early modern knowledge production. As recent research on the Scientific Revolution has clearly demonstrated, knowledge production is a circulating process, involving a great many people from a great variety of professions, high and low. Bernard did not see himself as a scholar, even though he came from a family of pastors and professors. He never received a formal higher education, but he was intensely engaged in that other emerging enterprise of the period: the study of humankind, society, and religion, inspired by the discoveries of new continents, peoples, and religions. Just like Picart, Bernard was a disciple of the new science. Both Bacon and Descartes were his idols. René Descartes inculcated two principles that remain central to modern science, the uniformity and regularity of nature. With them it became possible for Bernard to postulate a universal human nature as the root of religiosity. Bacon helped him to build on the traditional humanist method of scholarship and to apply his empiricist ideals to the study of religion. Travel reports, toward the publication of which Bernard had contributed so much, supplied him with the sources for this grand enterprise[24]

Bernard's method in tackling these sources is best characterized as eclectic. He adopted research techniques from all the new scholarly worlds, from the realm of books and reading, from the humanist's domain, and from the field of science and medicine. Already in his first books Jean Frederic had come to appreciate comparison, a method that had its origins in circles of humanist philologists and biblical scholars, and which he adapted to his own goals. In *Moral Reflections* (1711) he included eleven letters of a Persian traveler with acute observations of European politics, religion, and society.[25]

Bernard's approach was most deeply influenced by Simon, the great French Bible critic. Simon's commentary on *Ceremonies and Customs Observed Today among the Jews,* written by the Venetian rabbi Leon Modena, could be found in both Bernard's and Picart's libraries. It served as a model for their *Religious Ceremonies of the World,* starting with its title. Bernard followed Simon in using comparisons between what could be found in the present and what lay in the past, and he used both to illuminate contemporary practices. Simon had used contemporary Jewish rituals to illuminate Jewish rites in biblical times, and he cited biblical Jewish rituals as a way to better understand contemporary Catholic issues. By comparing the functions of the Jewish Sanhedrin with those of the Papal Councils, for example, he hoped to find a recipe for settling the great European theological debates of his time. Simon was a disciple of modern philosophy, too, and his work rested on the Cartesian principles of uniformity and regularity.[26]

Simon had limited his comparisons to the Jews and Christians. In 1681 one of Simon's epigones, the French church historian Claude Fleury, embarked on a comparison of Jewish practices with Chinese, Turkish, and Indian ceremonies and customs. The epitome of the young comparative tradition was the English scholar of Hebrew John Spencer, who in 1685 for the first time compared Jewish and Egyptian ritual and ceremony. Bernard would use both Spencer and Fleury in *Religious Ceremonies of the World,* but he would expand their model until it included all the religions of the world. Only by seeking to survey the whole of humankind could he test his hypothesis about the presence of universal principles at the heart of true religious behavior.[27]

The comparative method hardly exhausted Bernard's scholarly arsenal. The seven volumes of *Religious Ceremonies of the World* are organized in a unique fashion. They do not contain a running argument that continues throughout the 3,500 pages but rather offer a carefully selected menu of reprints of existing treatises, extracts from other books, and original essays by Bernard himself, bringing together evidence from many sources. Readers were expected to draw their own conclusions from this material. This invitation to readers to make up their own minds—a practice Bernard also favored in his editorial policies—echoes the religious practice of one group of his contemporaries. Among the large group of Christians without a church who could be found in the Dutch Republic, a small congregation that called themselves Collegiants caught the imagination.

The Collegiants did not present themselves as a church community, though many of their visitors came from Mennonite or Arminian backgrounds. They convened in "Colleges," hence their name. Characteristic of their meetings was that every man had the right to speak or to put subjects on the agenda. No topic, however radical, was excluded from discussion. Spinoza in his time was associated with the group. The Collegiants saw the early communities of Christians as their examples. They refused to appoint ministers and they abhorred every form of doctrinal authority because clergy and dogmas were the chief cause of the ever-growing dissension in Christendom. The Collegiants supplied a tolerant platform for everyone who, without any interference of religious or secular authorities, was searching for the core of religion. As far as records go, neither Bernard Picart nor Jean Frederic Bernard belonged to this loose confederation of seekers. However, from the beginning they felt an affinity with these groups and admired their tolerance. In volume six of *Religious Ceremonies of the World* Jean Frederic devoted a chapter to their meetings and extolled the custom of free speech and abhorrence of dogmatic authority.[28]

Bernard sought to apply his own variety of empiricism to the study of religion. The carefully selected excerpts from the best authors available provided the raw material for the study of the universal laws underlying the religious behavior of humankind, a practice that can be seen as a response to Bacon's plea for a systematic collection of medical case histories. Bacon believed that a careful analysis of those histories would produce an evidence-based pathology, which in turn would result in general principles of treatment. Among the champions of Baconian medicine were the English physician Thomas Sydenham and the Leiden professor Herman Boerhaave. The debate on medical casuistry revived interest in older books in the genre, such as the diagnostic survey by the Dutch physician Jodocus Lommius, *Medicinalium observationum libri tres.* Medical books were a marginal category in his publishing catalogue, but Bernard produced three reprints of Lommius's book and reprinted Boerhaave's nosologic textbooks as well. Not surprisingly, Jean Frederic also shared Bacon's interest in the *prisca theologia,* the idea that Neoplatonic and Hermetic writings might hold the key to the original true religion.[29]

Bacon did not view evidence dispassionately, and neither did Bernard. Bacon sought knowledge as a way of battering down the orthodoxies of Aristotle and of Roman Catholicism. Bernard shared those goals, but he had another aim that would have been foreign to Bacon's time: a radical religious tolerance. The gap between Bernard and Picart and many of their contemporaries becomes quickly apparent when their views are compared with those commonly expressed at the time. The Huguenot diaspora had put the issue of religious toleration high on the agenda again, especially in England, France, and the Dutch Republic. Yet most Huguenots abhorred the idea of religious toleration. The leading theologian of the Huguenots in exile, for instance, the Rotterdam-based pastor Pierre Jurieu, who saw himself as the successor of John Calvin, denounced toleration as the worst possible sin that ought to be punished by the magistrates.[30]

Philosophers and theologians on all sides considered religion not a private but a public activity. The advocates of intolerance consequently associated any departure from the true religion with sedition, treason, libertinism, and even sodomy. Most defenders of toleration likewise started from the necessity of "the preservation of public tranquillity." A plea for toleration became possible only if they had successfully eliminated the supposed dangers for political society of the religion or sect involved. Thus John Locke refused to tolerate Catholics for reasons of state, and his Dutch Arminian friend Petrus van Limborch was prepared to tolerate the Mennonites only after having ascertained that they could be trusted not to upset the social and political order. Very few authors, the most notorious of whom was Pierre Bayle, were ready to argue that toleration was the logical consequence of the impossibility of finding absolute truth in any religious position.[31]

Debates about religion or scriptural interpretation in England, the Dutch Republic, and France—even those inspired by Cartesianism and varieties of Spinozism—almost never aimed at the propagation of libertinism or even atheism. They should be interpreted first as attempts to educate and inform, and second as efforts to establish an intellectual basis for religious unity and consequently to end the permanent state of religious conflict. In the Dutch Republic, in particular, these ideas had a social basis in the many dissenting groups without strict church affiliations and in circles of liberal Mennonites, with whom Bernard and Picart were intimately familiar.[32]

In the French Huguenot community similar pacifying ventures were tried by theologians such as Isaac d'Huisseau, who in 1670 in his tract *Reunion of Christianity* had urged all Christians to subscribe to a simplified creed with distinct latitudinarian leanings. His work was immediately translated from French into Dutch and fiercely debated. Bernard himself would endorse the principles of the Cartesian mystic Pierre Poiret, who in *The Peace of Souls in Every Part of Christianity* (1687) urged Christians to concentrate on the principles that would bring them together.[33]

In the early eighteenth century, however, reuniting Christianity was only part of the conundrum facing religious thinkers. Ever since the discovery of the new worlds many new religions and numerous unfamiliar religious practices had been brought to light. The travel narratives documenting these religions raised fundamental questions about their relationship with monotheism and the Judeo-Christian tradition. The Americas were considered especially alien. The strangeness and diversity of their people even compelled the confirmed heretic of the 1590s Giordano Bruno to conclude that the American Indians had been the product of spontaneous generation, thus compromising the unity of the human race. Such theories produced passionate debates among Catholic and Protestant theologians alike, and they raised the issue of whether all these religions had a genealogical relationship with the original true faith and had merely gone through a process of corruption over time.[34]

Incorporating all religions into one system with a single origin might be imaginable, but including all of them in one single regime of religious toleration was beyond anyone's imagination. A small number of European theologians and intellectuals were prepared to accept some toleration for Jews and Muslims, though in the 1670s only the Dutch allowed the Jews to practice their religion in public. Since the Crusades Muslims had received uniformly bad press. The principle of the freedom of conscience observed by the Turkish regimes nevertheless would slowly earn Islam the reputation of being a tolerant religion. Yet an intellectual abyss separated the monotheistic Muslims and Jews from the heathen tribes found in Africa and the new world. In European eyes the latter's only hope for salvation lay in renouncing their repulsive and barbarous religious practices and embracing a full conversion.

That impossible task—uniting all world religions in one single regime of religious toleration—was exactly the project that Picart and Bernard had assigned themselves. The magnificent frontispiece Picart devised in 1727 to be bound with the first volume of *Religious Ceremonies of the World* (see Figure I.2) is a beautiful illustration of their mission. It represents all religions with something approaching even-handedness, a quality that would permeate all seven volumes. The so-called idolatrous peoples are relegated to the background in the print, but they are not derided, and they occupy a very prominent place in the text that follows. Even more important is the subtext. The frontispiece's most important figure is the modest female on the left, who points to the Bible and embraces the tree of original Christianity and the True Religion, whose useless branches she has cut away. She is surrounded by all the leading figures of the Protestant Reformation. The Reformers initiated the process of removing superfluous ceremonies and superstitions; Picart's and Bernard's *Religious Ceremonies of the World* would continue that pruning, aiming at a universal and natural religion.

A few decades later this view of religion would be celebrated in Rousseau's tale of the Savoyard vicar in *Emile* (1762): knowledge of God, said Rousseau, is found in the observation of the natural order and one's place in it; any organized religion that correctly identifies God as the creator and preaches virtue and morality is therefore true. Rousseau's vicar criticizes the ceremonies of the church, vows humility in the face of the complexity of nature, and endorses the writings of the English Newtonian Samuel Clarke. As we shall see in Chapter 11, Bernard also had a special place in his heart for Clarke, whose works he published three times. Almost universally Rousseau was denounced as a deist, if not worse. But his vicar abandons skepticism and even the fashionable materialism of the age and finds his religiosity not in ceremonies or doctrines but in the beauty of nature and in his own inner light. In effect Rousseau invents a new heretic of the spirit, worthy of the Quakers or the Collegiants. Rousseau had probably never heard of the Collegiants, as they were extinct by the 1760s, when he frequented the Amsterdam publishing houses. But groups like the Collegiants would have understood what the Savoyard vicar was trying to say.

Most of Rousseau's books were published by the Amsterdam publisher Marc Michel Rey, who had succeeded in establishing his boutique thanks to his marriage to Bernard's wealthy daughter Elisabeth. She carried on an intimate correspondence with Rousseau. It is hardly accidental, then, that in Rousseau's words, aspects of Bernard's mission would obtain canonical status. We can only ponder what influence, if any, *Religious Ceremonies of the World* might have had on making possible the profession of faith offered by Rousseau's vicar. Had he been alive, Bernard would have understood what Rousseau was trying to say even if he did not agree with the vicar's rather saccharine piety. Out of the crisis of the European mind on the matter of true religion, Bernard and Picart found a solution that would reverberate throughout the eighteenth century and beyond. They read among the ancients and the moderns, they surveyed religious practices globally, and they found what humankind placed in the category of the sacred. Confronted by vast differences in religious expression, author and engraver described and represented as accurately as they could the myriad ceremonies and customs they believed could only be understood through a combination of curiosity and tolerance.[35]

6

Picart's Visual Politics

THE PRINTING press made it possible for book makers to combine words and illustrations in new ways for an ever-expanding readership. Medieval manuscripts had glistened with gold, silver, ultramarine, saffron, and vermilion, but their delights remained restricted to the monks who made them and later the artists or the wealthy patrons who commissioned them. Textbooks on Aristotle prepared by Renaissance scholastics seldom made use of any graphics except the occasional table of logical relations. In contrast, woodcuts, engravings, and etchings, though usually available only in black and white, could be bound with the pages that flew off the new printing presses, and they were used to great effect by naturalists, from the doctor Andreas Vesalius to the mechanist René Descartes. These printed images illustrated the human body or explained the swirling vortices that held the planets in orbit; they also provided faithful copies of works of art that an ordinary person would never be able to visit. Engravings offered firsthand depictions of people and products seen, sometimes for the first time by Europeans, in the farthest corners of the globe. Illustrated books served the functions that are now divided among books, television, film, video, and the Internet.[1]

Religious Ceremonies of the World relied on fine art engravings to give a living sense of the different religious practices found across the continents. Although Picart died while some of the last volumes were still in press, he had a hand in producing the lion's share of the illustrations in the work. Because the entire project rested in the first instance on his artistic reputation, his active participation had to be evident. The signatures in the lower left- and right-hand corners of the prints make Picart's role explicit by signaling whether he drew the print from his own observation or imagination, engraved the print himself, provided the drawing and supervised the engraving, or just oversaw the work of his assistants.[2]

Picart and Bernard must have consulted frequently because the engravings are often closely linked to the text. Though the engravings were printed separately (except for vignettes found on text pages) and bound with the text only after it was printed, Bernard's text often refers to specific plates. Moreover, footnotes sometimes refer to a plate facing or following a specific page. Yet on occasion the image and the text seem, if not exactly at odds with each other, then at least to point in different directions. Long sections of text go unillustrated—sometimes more than 100 pages, save the decorative vignettes at the beginning and ending of sections—and then all of a sudden several engravings appear in the space of a few pages.

Picart and Bernard no doubt agreed on the general lines of their approach, yet they had to work independently if only because the copperplates had to be printed separately. Moreover, the two men no doubt labored in a frenzied atmosphere because they both had so many other projects under way at the same time. Picart had already designed and printed nineteen plates for *Religious Ceremonies of the World* in 1721, two years before the first volume appeared, and in that same year he finished two portraits as well as various book frontispieces, freestanding fine art reproductions, vignettes, and printer's flowers, all printed either by himself or by other publishers, not Bernard. Similarly, while hurriedly preparing the text of *Religious Ceremonies of the World,* Bernard also had his publishing and bookselling business to run. As publisher, he eventually provided buyers of the work with the list of engravings for each volume and their correct placement, so that the buyer could have the plates and text sheets bound together into the actual book.[3]

As far as we know, Picart did not document his plans for the visual program of *Religious Ceremonies of the World,* but he clearly believed that engraving should be considered a major art. Near the end of his life, he

BERNARD PICART
LE ROMAIN,
DESSINATEUR ET GRAVEUR,
Né à Paris le 11 Juin 1673. Mort à Amsterdam le 8 Mai 1733.

L'HISTOIRE, tenant negligeamment un Livre fermé, & tristement accoudée sur une Table auprès de sa Plume qu'elle a comme abbandonnée, paroît inconsolable de ce que les plus beaux de ses Monumens ne seront plus consacrez au Temple de Mémoire par cet illustre Dessinateur. Le Génie du Dessein, pénétré de Douleur, déplore amèrement sa Perte, & celui de la Gravure tâche de le consoler en lui faisant voir la Couronne de l'Immortalité que les beaux Ouvrages de ce grand Maître lui ont si légitimement acquise.

6.1   Portrait of Picart in *Impostures innocentes* (frontispiece). In this posthumous representation of Picart's life and work, *Religious Ceremonies of the World* lies on its side in the lower right-hand corner of the print, thus signaling its importance in Picart's life work. The engraving was executed in 1734 by one of Picart's pupils, Jacob van der Schley, probably from a pre-existing portrait. (Research Library, The Getty Research Institute, Los Angeles, California)

penned "Discourse on the Prejudices of Certain Collectors [*Curieux*] Concerning Engraving," a brief piece in which he defended engraving, especially modern copies of great paintings. The "Discourse" appeared alongside the unsigned biography of Picart and a catalogue of his works in *Impostures innocentes,* a volume organized by his widow to advertise Picart's reputation far and wide. The engraved portrait of Picart at the front of the book registers the importance of *Religious Ceremonies of the World;* a big volume labeled *Ceremonies* sits in the right corner below the bust of Picart. It is one of the few works represented by name in the print, which is meant to sum up his major contributions.

Picart must have written "Discourse ... Concerning Engraving" with an eye to his posthumous reputation. He had clearly learned from his mentor, Roger de Piles, about the importance of engraving in the modern world. De Piles insisted that "there is no one of whatever status and profession who would not get great utility" from engravings. They offer diversion in the same manner as the other visual arts but also have more pragmatic uses. They instruct more forcefully and promptly than mere words and provide an efficient way of recalling one's reading. Prints allow the viewer to study several things at once because they take up so little space compared with paintings and can represent such a diversity of objects. Finally, according to De Piles, engravings teach good taste by introducing the fine arts, something no respectable person can ignore.[4]

Picart wanted to go even further than De Piles, who was after all an art theorist rather than an engraver himself. Picart rejected the view of some self-proclaimed connoisseurs that modern engravings could not hope to capture an old master as well as prints done by the master's contemporaries. He tells the story of Hendrik Goltzius, the leading Dutch print maker of the late sixteenth century, who engraved a print in the manner of Albrecht Dürer, burnt off the area where the signature should have been, and smoked the print to make it look older. Collectors in Rome, Venice, and Amsterdam paid exorbitant sums for what they considered a previously unknown work by Dürer and were enraged when Goltzius revealed the hoax. Picart's point is that expert modern engravers such as himself could use a burin to carve or a needle to etch a design on copperplate that would magically give the impression of freehand drawing, depth and roundness of lines, and above all chiaroscuro (bold contrasts of light and dark). They could thus capture ele-

NEC VETERA ASPERNERE, NEC INVIDEAS HODIERNIS

BERNARDUS PICARTUS, Delineator & Sculptor, Stephani Picarti, cui Romano cognomen, Filius, natus Lutetiæ 11. Junii anni MDCLXXIII. *à J. Marc Natter pictus anno* MDCCIX. *& à N. Verkolje in ære expressus Amstelodami* MDCCXV

6.2   Engraved portrait of Picart from 1715. This mezzotint by Verkolje was based on a 1709 painting of Picart by his Paris friend Jean Marc Nattier (see Figure 1.1). Picart points to his art as engraver but he is also surrounded by books, including many he had illustrated. (Graphic Arts Division, Department of Rare Books and Special Collections, Princeton University Library)

ments in great painting that had previously been lost or deformed. Modern engravings were simply superior to those of the old masters.[5]

Since his purpose in writing the "Discourse . . . Concerning Engraving" was to elevate the status of fine art prints and thus promote the value of his own work, Picart did not mention the torrent of engravings and etchings that accompanied political and religious polemics from the 1720s onward. While preparing his illustrations for *Religious Ceremonies of the World,* he also designed prints that fed into those controversies both in Holland and back in France. He satirized the nearly simultaneous bursting of speculative bubbles in 1720 in France, England, and Holland and produced, often for false imprints, pro-Jansenist and anti-Jesuit engravings that appeared during the 1720s in France (see Figure 7.7). In 1721 police sent four French engravers to the Bastille prison in Paris for producing Jansenist prints, and four others faced the same fate in 1732; the authorities considered such prints too inflammatory to ignore. Picart could contribute his influential two cents from his safe haven up north.[6]

It seems entirely possible, if not likely, that Picart personally took the lead in blurring genres in this period; it became increasingly difficult for collectors to distinguish among engravings that were meant to be portraits, satires, allegories, or scenes of everyday life. Picart's "Monument Consecrated to Posterity in Memory of the Incredible Folly of the Twentieth Year of the Eighteenth Century" (Figure 7.6) crossed precisely those lines, and in so doing, it helped prepare the way for the century's greatest print maker, William Hogarth, who himself found direct inspiration in Picart's work. One of the double plate engravings in volume 6 by Picart's student Jacob van der Schley was based on a design by Hogarth, and it may well be that another was produced after a drawing sent to Picart by Hogarth himself.[7]

When preparing the engravings for *Religious Ceremonies of the World,* Picart had to maintain a delicate balance between aesthetics and accuracy. More was involved than the faithful replication of well-known paintings by masters such as Rubens and Raphael or the humorous satire of contemporary mores. As the "Discourse . . . Concerning Engraving" showed, Picart wanted to be known as a great creative artist. His renditions of scenes, whether based on earlier prototypes or drawn for the first time by himself, had to be beautiful, as understood in terms of the quality of the design, the depth and roundness of the lines, and the use of chiaroscuro, elements that can be seen in each and every engraving he did for *Religious Ceremonies of the World*. Yet in this work covering every known religion of the world, he also strove for recognition as a kind of scientific researcher, just as De Piles had said an engraver could. If the volumes were to accomplish their broader purpose of enabling comparisons among religions across the globe, the engravings had to be accurate, authentic, and true to the religion in question.

Picart's efforts at guaranteeing the authenticity of his depictions in *Religious Ceremonies of the World* are highlighted in Marchand's "eulogy" (really a short biography) included in *Impostures innocentes*. There Marchand recounts that Picart's work on the project took place for the most part in the 1720s but continued for some volumes right up to his death in 1733. Wherever possible, Picart aimed to draw "after nature," that is, from real-life models, and as a consequence, he carried his sketchbook with him everywhere he went. His "exactitude" when depicting fellow Protestants was so striking, claimed Marchand, that many viewers felt they could identify the people portrayed (see Figure 4.1 for an example). Picart closely supervised the engravings of Catholic ceremonies, sometimes correcting the drawings made by others, but in the case of non-European religious practices, he had to rely on books and prints previously published. Even here, however, Picart left no stone unturned, as the catalogue of his personal library demonstrates. He owned scores of travel books, in several languages, and Marchand maintained that he studied his sources intently, often having assistants read to him while they worked together. He even owned a book written in Chinese characters, and one of the engravings of China does prominently feature Chinese characters.[8]

Picart's obsession with real-life models comes through most strikingly in the prints of Jewish rituals, most of which he drew himself and many of which he also personally engraved. He did not finish all the Jewish engravings by 1723, when the text was first published, because he could not get permission to attend a Passover Seder. Every time he thought he had succeeded, he found himself rebuffed at the last moment. After four years of frustration, Alvaro Nuñes da Costa (he used the name Nathan Curiel in Dutch), the commercial representative of the Portuguese government in Amsterdam, finally intervened on Picart's behalf, invited him to his home for the ceremony, and described the particulars of the rituals to him in great detail.

The result was one of the most interesting plates in the entire work, according to Marchand (see Figure I.1 as an oil painting; Figure 7.4 as an engraving). Everyone, Jew and Christian alike, was "charmed" by the meticulous attention Picart paid to furniture, dress, and ritual objects in these engravings. No one had ever seen anything quite like it. Picart's preoccupation with the Seder scene led him to produce a sizeable oil painting of it, too. The painting reproduces many of the elements of the engraving but eliminates the large cabinet in the background and concentrates the light on the faces of the observants at the table, making the scene even more intimate than in the engraving. Has Picart depicted himself as one of those present? Some argue that he is the man without a hat on the far left, which seems most likely given the figure's resemblance to his self-portrait (see Figure 1.1), yet others insist that he must be the one with the three-corner hat on the right. If only he had told us himself![9]

When he could not gain personal access to the ceremonies, Picart drew from the store of images available in firsthand accounts, whether in books prescribing ceremonial practices, as in the case of Roman Catholicism, or in books by travelers who had witnessed, or claimed to have witnessed, rituals themselves. Dutch prominence in the book trade made such images more accessible in Dutch cities like Amsterdam than anywhere else in the world. In many instances, Picart copied the illustrations directly from books he owned himself. His engravings of the procedures that were followed in the election of a new pope, for instance, reproduce the etchings available in a history of papal conclaves found in his library. The thirty-five scenes showing the different stages in the celebration of an ordinary Catholic mass are based on engravings by his Paris teacher Leclerc, and the rendition of rituals such as the ordination of priests comes from the official books of Catholic ceremony in his collection, for example, the *Roman Pontifical,* the *Roman Processional,* and the *Ceremonial of Bishops.* In addition to these manuals of official Catholic ceremony, Picart owned various histories of saints and popes and assorted illustrated books about the traditional dress of the different Catholic orders. He may have broken with Catholicism himself and disliked many of its practices, but he aimed to depict them accurately. If simple anti-Catholicism had animated his work, why would he put so much effort into reproducing the work of Catholic engravers?[10]

6.3   Picart's use of Catholic imagery. This is the original etching from *Histoire des conclaves depuis Clement V*, 3rd ed., 2 vols. (Cologne: 1703), p. 18. Picart owned this book. (Research Library, The Getty Research Institute, Los Angeles, California)

Picart's depictions of the customs of exotic peoples relied in the first instance on the images developed by his predecessors, especially those of Theodor de Bry, a sixteenth-century Flemish Lutheran engraver who worked in England and then in Frankfurt. De Bry and his sons illustrated scores of accounts of voyages to the Americas, Asia, and Africa. Since De Bry had not traveled to these places himself, he too used models, such as the paintings and drawings of Jacques Le Moyne de Morgues, a French artist who traveled with the expedition of Jean Ribaut and René Laudonnière to Florida in the 1560s, and the watercolor drawings of the English artist John White, who accompanied a voyage to the Outer Banks of North Carolina in 1585 and later became governor of Roanoke colony in Virginia. Picart sometimes simply copied De Bry's plates, but he did so not out of slavish imitation but rather out of his concern for undisputed credibility. In his mind, this practice did not constitute plagiarism. Picart did not invent ceremonial tableaux out of whole cloth; he prided himself on using existing images and written accounts.[11]

In his pursuit of accuracy, Picart paid special attention to ritual instruments and to the exact position of participants in the different religious ceremonies. His interest in ritual paraphernalia can be seen in

L'ENTRÉE des CARDINAUX au CONCLAVE. | La MESSE du SAINT ESPRIT.

Premiere CONGREGATION generale des CARDINAUX.| Le SCRUTIN des CARDINAUX pour L'ELECTION d'un PAPE.

MANIERE dont on porte les VIVRES au CONCLAVE. | L'EXAMEN des VIVRES.

6.4 Picart's own depiction of Catholic ritual. Picart took the separate originals from *Histoire des conclaves* (see Figure 6.3) and combined them to create a visual narrative of the meeting to elect a new pope. He clearly insisted on copying the originals quite faithfully. The comparison is to the upper left-hand section. Tracing and reinscribing on a copperplate creates the inversion of the image. B. Picart sculp. dir. 1724; CC, vol. I, second section, facing p. 45. (Research Library, The Getty Research Institute, Los Angeles, California)

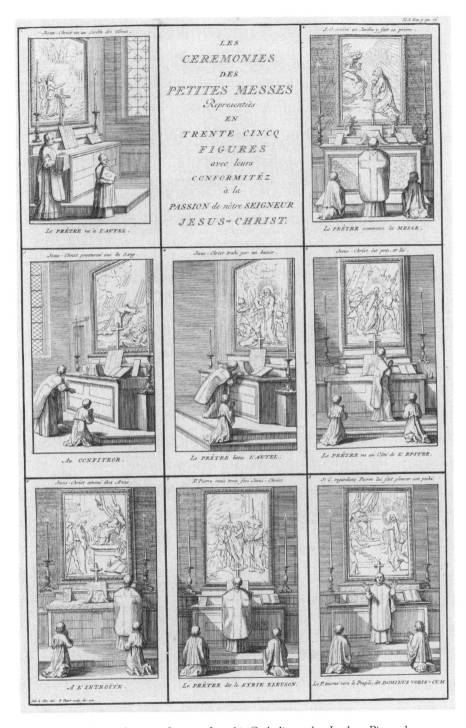

6.5   Picart's reproduction of images from his Catholic teacher Leclerc. Picart also provided a detailed caption, too long to reproduce here, and his signature clearly recognized his debt to his Paris teacher Leclerc: "Seb. Le Clerc del. B. Picart sculp. Dir. 1722" [Sebastien Le Clerc drew it; Bernard Picart supervised the engraving]. CC, vol. I, second section, facing p. 76. (Research Library, The Getty Research Institute, Los Angeles, California)

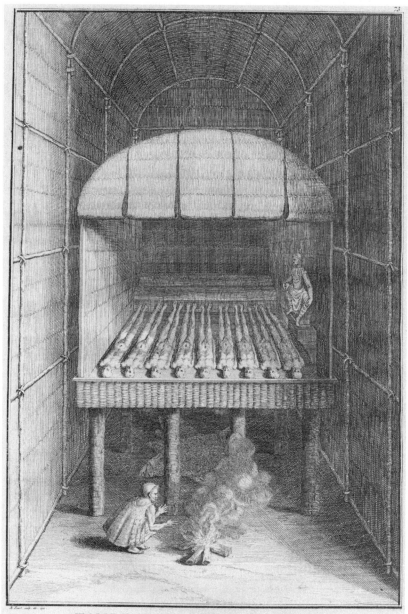

TOMBEAUX des Rois de la VIRGINIE.

6.6 Tombs of the kings of Virginia. Picart's engraving is a mirror image of De Bry's print of 1590, which in turn was an adaptation of a watercolor by John White from 1585–1586. B. Picart sculp. dir. 1721; CC, vol. III, facing p. 122. (Research Library, The Getty Research Institute, Los Angeles, California) every volume, but it is especially evident in the opening section on the Jews. Among the twenty plates of Jewish ceremonies in volume 1 are no fewer than three full-page engravings devoted to ritual instruments and items of dress, ranging from the taled or prayer shawl to the Sefer Torah and its ornaments, known as Rimonim. Although Picart's depiction of pagan religions necessarily lacks the same ethnographic detail, he nonetheless provided a full-page engraving of Indian ritual items that included the hut for the initiation of young men, two kinds of peace pipes, a tomahawk, and a "casse-tête," or instrument for cracking heads.

Even the most cursory glance at the engravings uncovers the artist's determined quest for authenticity. Among the plates, for example, are a picture of the ballot used in electing popes, a huge, double-page engraving that compares the funeral service in Amsterdam with that in The Hague, and a four-part plate depicting the variations in mourning dress of women in Zurich, Augsburg, Frisia, and Zaandam. Picart drew the funeral services himself in the year before his death and supervised the plate on mourning dress the very year he died. He insisted on capturing every detail of dress and ceremonial disposition. This level of accuracy was essential to the credibility of comparisons between religious practices that were developed in the text.

Picart's use of Mughal miniatures in the section on Indian religions in volume 3 exemplifies his search for accurate models. He had first worked with these images a few years earlier when providing the engravings for Henri Chatelain's sumptuously illustrated, seven-volume *Atlas historique*. As models for the *Atlas* engravings he had used Indian miniatures supplied by the Italian diplomat Count Abate Giovanni Antonio Baldini from his personal collection. Baldini had not traveled to South Asia himself, but he developed an extensive collection in a very short time while taking part in the Congress of Utrecht, which ended the War of Spanish Succession with a general peace settlement in 1713. Baldini's ability to collect these miniatures while sojourning in the Dutch Republic serves as another reminder of the remarkable access the Dutch had to goods from all over the world. Given that Baldini returned to Italy in 1716, Picart must have seen the miniatures sometime between 1713 and 1716 (volume 5 of the *Atlas historique* on the Mughal empire appeared in 1719, four years before the publication of volume 3 of *Religious Ceremonies of the World*).[12]

When he supervised the reproduction of his engravings from the

CEREMONIES FUNÈBRES comme on les fait à AMSTERDAM & en plusieurs villes de la HOLLANDE.

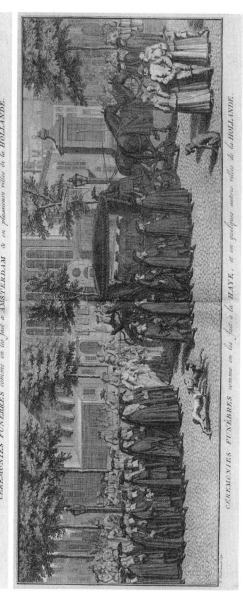

CEREMONIES FUNÈBRES comme on les fait à la HAYE, et en quelques autres villes de la HOLLANDE.

6.7 Funeral ceremonies in Amsterdam and The Hague. Picart drew these scenes as a firsthand observer and prided himself on his accuracy. B. Picart invenit 1732; CC, vol. V, following p. 378. (Research Library, The Getty Research Institute, Los Angeles, California)

6.8   Picart's version of Mughal miniatures. B. Picart sculp. dir. 1723; CC, vol. III, second section, facing p. 134. (Research Library, The Getty Research Institute, Los Angeles, California)

Atlas historique, Picart insisted on perfect copies. He signed these new engravings as supervisor *(B. Picart sculps. dir.* meant that Picart had directed the engraving). He had someone trace and then re-engrave the images, which, as a consequence, are mirror images of the original engravings. It seems likely that the original engravings also closely imitated the Indian miniatures, now lost, for both the engravings in the *Atlas historique* and their copies in *Religious Ceremonies of the World* attempt to capture what is now known as the provincial Mughal style, albeit in the black and white of engraving rather than the watercolors that are characteristic of such miniatures. Picart followed a similar strategy with a few of the Chinese and Japanese subjects, recognizing in these cases that his sources had endeavored to imitate the style of the Chinese or Japanese originals.

Since indigenous images of unfamiliar religions were difficult if not impossible to find in Europe, Picart most often relied on engravings produced by earlier artists such as De Bry or the Dutch artists

Coenrat Decker and Jacob van Meurs, who had illustrated some of the most influential travel accounts of the late seventeenth century. Still, on occasion Picart composed his own images using a mixture of written accounts and elements of preceding images as his sources. Whether choosing which images to copy from his predecessors, altering those choices to suit his purposes, or devising his own new ones, Picart consistently strove to make foreign deities, practices, or processions more palatable to European viewers while still remaining true to the sources. He achieved this effect in various ways: by adding familiar landscapes or architectural elements, by putting unfamiliar deities on classical pedestals, by excluding the scenes of greatest violence depicted by his predecessors, by promoting a sense of identification with those depicted, and ultimately, by setting up subtle comparisons between Western and non-Western, civilized and savage, or Christian and pagan rituals.

A comparison of two plates created by Picart himself (signed *B. Picart invenit),* both with "sacred fire" as their subject, brings some of these techniques into sharper relief. In volume 3 Picart offers a plate with two scenes of Inca sun worship. In volume 5 he depicts Greek Orthodox Christians waiting for and then distributing the holy fire at the Church of the Holy Sepulchre in Jerusalem (the fire was believed to appear at Easter). The Greek Orthodox Christians clearly seem the more chaotic and uncontrolled of the two groups. In the top image of the Incas, the participants are lighting the sacred fire on the eve of their festival of the sun, and in the bottom image, they fall down in worship on the first day of the festival. Picart frames the top scene with classical architecture and landscape and the bottom scene with a pastiche of late medieval European houses (thatched roofs, no less), a gate, a tower, and an Italianate church dome. It is unlikely that he thought such buildings could actually be found in Peru; rather, he seems to have chosen them as frames for the action so that the practices invoked would appear less outlandish. Although the Greek Orthodox are fully clothed, they do not seem more civilized than the Incas in their behavior. In fact, the Inca men in loincloths placed in the foreground of both engravings have the defined musculature that Europeans regularly saw in paintings of mythological scenes by the great masters. Picart's Incas resemble the male figures in his favorite painters Rafael and Annibale Carracci.

As Paola Von Wyss-Giacosa has shown so forcefully for the engravings of India, Picart's own visual language becomes fully comprehen-

Maniere d'alumer le FEU SACRÉ, chez les PERUVIENS, la Veille de la grande FÊTE du SOLEIL, nommée le grand RAMY.

Le premier jour de la grande FÊTE du SOLEIL, L'YNCAS lui presente un Vase plein de Liqueur, et l'invite a boire.

6.9   Inca sun worship. Picart gave special importance to this engraving, as he signed it "B. Picart, invenit 1722," signaling that it was his original creation. CC, vol. III, facing p. 192. (Research Library, The Getty Research Institute, Los Angeles, California)

MANIERE dont les GRECS attendent la descente du FEU SACRÉ dans le St SEPULCRE.

La DISTRIBUTION du FEU SACRÉ aux GRECS par le PATRIARCHE

6.10   Holy fire among the Greek Orthodox. Again, Picart's signature (B. Picart invenit 1730) testifies to his particular interest in these scenes. CC, vol. V, facing p. 143. (Research Library, The Getty Research Institute, Los Angeles, California)

sible only when his engravings are systematically compared with those of his predecessors. Sixteenth-century woodcuts of Indian deities made their subjects look like flesh-and-blood devils, monsters, or witches, even when the texts they were illustrating spoke of metal statues. After the 1660s such figures began to appear more like statues, sitting or standing on pedestals, and, more important, they appeared with their symbolic attributes. Picart relied heavily on his late seventeenth-century predecessors for his Indian images, but even here he did not hesitate to make alterations to serve his aims. For the engraving of Shiva that he based on Coenrat Decker's illustration of a 1672 Dutch travel account, for example, he replaced the flask-shaped object in one of the figure's sixteen hands with a European violin. The aim was clear: give the otherwise strange image of a god with multiple hands a more European resonance. Even while picking and choosing and on occasion altering images, Picart achieved something yet more important: he gathered together in one place and therefore made much more systematic the existing European knowledge about the pantheon of Indian gods.[13]

Since Picart had a large storehouse of images of the Americas from which to choose, he exerted even more control over the visual program of these sections. Although he included an occasional violent image, and even added to the gore on occasion, as in the engraving of a Mexican sacrifice (Figure 6.12), derived from a De Bry book illustration first published in 1602, for the most part Picart left out the most bloody and especially cannibalistic images of natives of the New World that were available to him. Among De Bry's images of the Florida Indians, for example, Picart chose scenes of ceremonies that were celebrated before men went off to war and of the widows performing funeral rites afterward, but he left out the images of warfare and of savage celebration of victory that came in between. So the reader does not see the shaman figure dancing in front of poles decorated with human legs that had appeared in De Bry, even though the reader has seen that same shaman figure divining the future for an Indian king before battle in Picart.

Picart's images almost always avoid references to specific individuals and events. So whereas De Bry's image had referred to a chief named Outina consulting his sorcerer before battle, Picart refers instead to "a king of Florida consulting his magician before going to face the enemy." Similarly, whereas De Bry had shown Spanish soldiers in many scenes, especially those of warfare against the native peoples, Picart leaves them

6.11 Familiarizing the strange. Copies were not always copies. Here Picart puts an unlikely violin in one of Shiva's many hands. B. Picart sculp. dir. 1722; CC, vol. III, second section, facing p. 112. (Research Library, The Getty Research Institute, Los Angeles, California)

Captif ecorché apres avoir été vaincu .   *Captif combattant contre un Prêtre MEXICAIN.*

6.12   Human sacrifice. The role of priests in sacrifice and violence is underlined here. The captions read: "A Captive Skinned after Having Been Vanquished," and "A Captive Fighting against a Mexican Priest." B. Picart, sculp. dir. 1722; CC, vol. III, facing p. 150 (top half of engraving). (Research Library, The Getty Research Institute, Los Angeles, California)

out. Two reasons no doubt influenced this kind of decision. For the Indians of the Americas, Picart was using as prototypes images that dated from the late 1500s and early 1600s, and they often referred to events at that time. He wanted to update them for the 1700s and therefore took out markers associated with a specific time period. But a more profound reason also entered into his calculation. He aimed to capture the general, ritualistic aspects of ceremonies and not specific, historically located instances of them.

In short, Picart's images, especially when read alongside Bernard's text, essentially created the category "religion." Whereas the text sometimes wandered off on tangents about the sources of particular ceremonies, the similarities between rituals across space (Jewish and Catholic) and time (Roman antiquity and American Indian), or the disputes be-

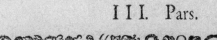

III. Pars.   71

CAPVT XL.

*Mancipium quoddam me apud Barbaros frequenter calumnia-
batur, optans, ut ab illis deuoratus perirem: vice autem versa
id ipsum casum, me præsente, voratur.*

6.13   Depiction of cannibalism by De Bry. European readers were familiar with this
kind of image of the "savages" of the new world, but Picart chose to downplay cannibalism and brutality. *Americae tertia pars* (Frankfurt, 1592), p. 71. (Research Library, The Getty
Research Institute, Los Angeles, California)

tween scholars on the origins of different peoples, the images kept the focus on the most commonly found religious ceremonies—birth, marriage, death rituals, and grand processions—or on the most strikingly different practices, which could range from the arcane procedures for the election of popes in Rome to human sacrifice in Mexico. Implicitly, the images transformed religion from a question of truth revealed to a select few of God's peoples (the Jews, the Catholics, and then the Protestants) to an issue of comparative social practices.

Although the comparability of social practices fully emerges only when all the engravings are considered together as a set, a few large tableaux, often double-page prints, serve as showcases or summaries of the various religions. Examples include the dedication of the Sephardic Synagogue in Amsterdam and a huge papal procession in volume 1; an Inca parade of sun worshippers in volume 3; Indian fakirs performing penitential rites around a holy Banyan tree, and a Japanese Buddhist temple in volume 4; an Anglican service in St. Paul's Cathedral in London in volume 6; and the great mosque at Mecca with the Kaaba shown in volume 7. Picart not only gathered together the latest evidence (his source for the mosque at Mecca was a print in a book published in 1717 that was based on a drawing by a Muslim eyewitness, the first such depiction available in the West), but also put it in a form that was both accessible to Western readers and amenable to comparison. The very fact of showing Inca sun worshippers and Catholics engaged in similar-looking processions or putting a Jewish synagogue, an Anglican cathedral, and a Buddhist temple in similar perspectives inevitably suggested parallels, and the analogies could only be unsettling to those accustomed to thinking of their own religion, or Christianity, or monotheistic religions more generally, as superior in their difference and separateness.[14]

Picart employed his aesthetic talents to draw his viewers into a direct experience of this religious analogy, which as a result transcended the level of intellectual exercise. Although he usually positions the viewer outside the frame, as if he or she is standing at the edge of the ceremonial space watching the ritual unfold, he still compels the viewer to identify with the ordinary people depicted, whether they are Chinese, native Americans, or European Jews. In the image of a "Canadian" couple marrying, for example, the reader does not have to consult the text to see that the bride and groom resemble any other young couple in love. Even if they dress differently from Europeans, they hold themselves in dance or theater postures that are familiar to any European reader. With a simple change of décor, the young man could be dancing a ballet at the court of the French king Louis XIV. The presence of an Oriental carpet highlights the underlying sense of familiarity, even as it distorts the evidence. But the reader also sees, without the aid of any explanation, that no priest, no church, and no liturgy is required to make a marriage of this sort official. The families watch while the couple says its vows holding what appears to be an arrow.

Switch to the image below the marriage rite on the same page for the unhappy ending to the story. The couple is divorcing after having children. The "ceremony" of divorce is not much of a ceremony by European standards. The reader knows, of course, that divorce is not allowed in any Catholic country and is not all that easy in most Protestant ones, either. Again, there is no priest, no church, no lawyer, no court official. The kneeling man in the center may be mediating the divorce settlement, as it appears the children will be divided between the spouses, but no one looks convulsed with grief. Indeed the man and wife who are divorcing seem positively serene. The savages of the New World are not so savage after all. Moreover, the artist implies that the woman is an equal player in the divorce action, something almost unknown in Europe.

The images thus relativize religious rituals with an incredible economy of expression. Because the native Americans seem familiar—in this case they most resemble in their dress ancient Greeks or Romans— the viewer cannot simply dismiss their practices as odd or scandalous. Nothing speaks of scandal in these two images. True, the nearly 3,500 pages of the work offer a multitude of different ways to approach the meaning of religious ceremonies and customs, and not all the images are as anodyne as these. One or even many images cannot answer all the questions asked, either explicitly or implicitly, by the text. Yet the images do suggest some striking answers. Everyone in the world—monotheists and "idolators" alike—has some kind of religion, and their ceremonies share many characteristics. All peoples, in particular, pay special attention to birth, marriage, and death, though with varying levels of participation on the part of priests and officials. Peoples are alike more than they are different in their attitudes toward religion.

Even when the deities depicted seem strange or bizarre, Picart resists

CEREMONIE NUPTIALE du CANADA.

MANIERE dont les PEUPLES du CANADA font le DIVORCE.

6.14 Marriage and divorce among the Canadians. B. Picart delin. 1723; CC, vol. III, after p. 92. (Research Library, The Getty Research Institute, Los Angeles, California)

the all-too-common European urge to ridicule them. The giant Chinese god Ninifo, for example, towers over those who worship him. Described in the accompanying text as an idol or deity who presides over mirth and voluptuousness, he seems an entirely jolly figure, though he does come with two rather devilish companions or guards. In a work published half a century later, in contrast, the Dutch philosopher Cornelius de Pauw described this same god as "hydropic" (suffering from dropsy or what is now called edema), sitting on his claws like an orangutan or a baboon. De Pauw was interested only in contrasting the fat figure, that "horrible package," to the statues of Greek gods with their majestic air. Picart's aims are quite different, and so he does not show Ninifo sitting on his claws.[15]

In other words, Picart resists the negative stereotyping of unfamiliar cultures that had been so common in preceding generations and that would gain renewed momentum with the rise of European imperialism in the nineteenth century. Picart could not always avoid invidious depictions given that he had to rely on his predecessors for many of his images. He continued the tradition, for example, of portraying Asian or American deities as oversized people or monsters. Yet when it came to choosing among many available images, and especially when inventing his own portrayals of unfamiliar peoples and practices, he almost always chose to emphasize the nonviolent ritual or the less horrifying practice. In this respect, *Religious Ceremonies of the World* reflected an unusual moment in European intellectual and religious life, the time after the first discoveries of new places and strange customs and before the crystallization of new European attitudes of racial superiority. In the early eighteenth century, men like Picart and Bernard wanted to understand before they judged, and the more they compared, the less distinctive and superior did European customs appear. The desire to universalize religious impulses led them to unpack the prevalent stereotypes and turn them against Europe itself.

A universal truth of great importance to Picart and Bernard was the inherent untrustworthiness of priests. The suspicion of priests runs through the prints and becomes much more apparent in the accompanying text. In the engravings of Jewish and Protestant ceremonies, rabbis and pastors are either absent or they blend in with their congregations, hardly standing out at all from the others. Picart and Bernard clearly preferred this kind of intermingling, where religious leaders

VITEK ou NINIFO.

MATZOU.

6.15 Picart's representation of Ninifo, an incarnation of the Buddha. B. Picart, sculp. direx. 1726; CC, vol. IV, after p. 222, top half. (Research Library, The Getty Research Institute, Los Angeles, California)

functioned more as teachers of their equals than as a separate caste. Most of the depictions of Catholics, in contrast, either show priests performing official duties without a congregation present or portray them overseeing and overshadowing the proceedings. Priests dominate the images of Catholicism. Yet the evils of priestcraft appear even more pronounced among the heathens, perhaps because it was easier to make the point in reference to practices that were already strange. When human sacrifice takes place among the natives of the Americas, for instance, priests almost invariably preside over the proceedings, usually wielding the knives themselves. Priests pour oil onto the flames while promising Indian widows eternal happiness if they will jump on the funeral pyre of their dead husbands. It is not the heathen idols, then, that prove to be so menacing but rather the priests who serve their own interests and mislead their flocks. The ordinary Chinese in a huge Buddhist temple seem small and unthreatening, whereas the begging monks depicted on nearby pages resemble nothing so much as the magicians, sorcerers, and charlatans who are portrayed alongside them.[16]

The imposture of priests is difficult to represent in a static image, but the text makes it very clear: "As religion loses its simplicity, it needs human means to maintain itself, and these means with time displace religion so completely that it is then nowhere to be found." If it is true that the ancient Chinese were not idolatrous, Bernard continues, the systems and superstitions that have appeared in China since ancient times have corrupted the religion of that country. And why expect otherwise? After all, "Judaism and Christianity have suffered the same fate; their priests regarded them as systems subject to aging that required repairs to protect them against the effects of time." Priests resemble "mercenary workers" who are not content to invent tasks to increase their pay but rather ruin what is good in order to make themselves more valuable to those who employ them. After a while the priests exercise "so openly and with such impunity their charlatanism" that people see in it something holy suggested by a superior mind. Bernard here comes very close to suggesting that all contemporary religions are fraudulent. Religion was originally pure and holy according to his account, but could it ever regain its primitive simplicity?[17]

Picart did not put his own views on this subject into print, perhaps because he feared for his reputation and for his market. *Religious Ceremonies of the World* was after all just one of his many projects. When he wrote his "Discourse . . . Concerning Engraving" he seemed almost exclusively concerned with his reputation as an artist who produced fine art reproductions for collectors. After his death his widow did everything possible to capitalize upon both that reputation and that market. She quickly published under her own name (not Jean Frederic Bernard's) *Impostures innocentes,* which included a catalogue of Picart's work for prospective buyers. Her catalogue organizes his work not by subject matter or medium but by reference to his level of participation. First in the list, in chronological order, come Picart's engravings of master painters because she wanted to highlight his constant affiliation with the higher art of painting. In addition to his hundreds of book illustrations, ranging from the Bible to *Robinson Crusoe,* Picart engraved or etched scores of paintings (and drawings and etchings) by Rembrandt, Rubens, Rafael, the Carraccis, Poussin, Coypel, Le Brun, and other famous artists. Nearly eighty of these works are also reprinted in *Impostures innocentes.*

The catalogue then lists in descending order the works Picart "invented," drew, and engraved himself; those he created or drew and had engraved by others or corrected in the print stage; those he created or drew but had engraved entirely by others; and finally those he neither drew nor engraved but had engraved under his supervision. In this way, his widow's catalogue set a new standard for a print maker's status, implicitly arguing that a print's value derived from the hand of the print maker rather than from the original painter (or ultimate source of the image). Among the hundreds of plates in *Religious Ceremonies of the World,* only the frontispiece merits its own line in the catalogue. A single entry covers the 100 folio plates for the first three volumes of the work, though special mention is given to the fact that "the Jews and some of the Catholics are drawn very exactly after nature by B. Picart in 1721, 1722, 1723, 1724, and 1725." Another entry is devoted to the 43 plates of volume 4 executed between 1724 and 1729, and still another to 18 plates of volume 5 prepared between 1730 and 1732 and published in 1733.[18]

Can aesthetic or intellectual value be measured by market price? In the case of Picart, we are fortunate enough to have three catalogues of his work, two Dutch and one French, that include either printed or handwritten entries of prices for individual works. The highest prices were asked for rare drawings by Picart in India ink. The Getty Dutch

catalogue from 1737 lists an extraordinary price of 415 florins for a drawing in India ink based on a painting of a biblical theme (Abraham dis-
missing Hagar and Ishmael) by Adriaen van der Werff, a contemporary
of Picart. The second most expensive item (200 florins) was another
drawing, of Rinaldo and Armida (characters in a sixteenth-century
poem by Tasso), but this time the work was not based on any previous
source but rather created entirely by Picart himself. In contrast, a copy
of the first five volumes of *Religious Ceremonies of the World* fetched only
52 florins (perhaps because it was an incomplete set).[19]

A comparison of the three catalogues with price listings reveals a hierarchy of values with drawings at the top, followed by the original copperplates (one based on Annibale Carracci's painting "The Triumph of
Galatea" fetched 153 florins), then prints after famous paintings, then
prints published in books or for decorative purposes. Within each category, price also depended on the size of the image and the materials
used (the quality of the paper and the ink). Picart's large print of a political assembly in the French region of Languedoc, for example, fetched
1 florin, 10 stuivers, whereas very small engravings were priced at only
one stuiver (one-twentieth of a florin).[20]

Most of the engravings in the French catalogue are listed at under
one florin; only the very large engravings based on famous paintings are
priced higher, and then usually between one and two florins each. Buyers did not let go unremarked the huge gap between the higher prices
demanded by the Dutch agents for Picart's widow and those deemed
appropriate in Paris. In a sale catalogue of 1744 that included a number
of Picart engravings, the renowned Parisian art dealer Edme-François
Gersaint complained that Picart's widow had astutely controlled the
engraver's production to keep prices high. She did this by keeping in
reserve a certain number of drawings and printer's proofs of engravings, rather than permitting publication, so that collectors would have
to pay high prices to complete their series of Picart holdings. Gersaint
had seen the India ink drawing, "which was only a copy based on Van
der Verf, and which in one inventory was pushed up to 200–300 florins,
which is more than 600 livres in our money, and his widow would not
have sold this drawing during his lifetime for less than 600 florins."[21]

Picart—and his widow—had clearly succeeded in creating an independent value for an engraver's hand. A catalogue of the fine art and
natural history collection of Antoine-Joseph Dézallier d'Argenville

published in 1766 underlines their success. Only three engravers merited mention in the table of contents: Jacques Callot, famed for his prints of the Thirty Years' War of 1618–1648; Sébastien Leclerc, Louis XIV's favorite engraver and Picart's teacher in Paris; and Bernard Picart. Despite moving to Holland, Picart still ranked as the premier French engraver of his epoch.[22]

II

THE BOOK OF
THE WORLD

7

Familiarizing Judaism

AMSTERDAM, with its large and relatively protected population of Sephardic and Ashkenazi Jews, offered an ideal vantage point for anyone interested in Judaism. In no other city in Western Europe could an observer learn more about Jewish customs and ceremonies than amid the canals and gables that encircled the Kalverstraat. If contemporary Judaism troubled and even repulsed Christians, historical Judaism was unavoidable. Without Judaism, there would have been no Christianity. However capacious their vision, Europeans of the early eighteenth century, even unorthodox ones like Bernard and Picart, thought that religion began with the first monotheists and hence the Jews. When analyzing the foibles and commonalities found among all religions in his opening "Dissertation on Religious Worship," Bernard never failed to make analogies to Jewish practices. With an open mind and great perseverance, Picart entered synagogues and homes, pen and pencil in hand, ready to bring to the world the joys and sorrows of Jewish life. Not many of their contemporaries would have brought as much sympathy and curiosity to a faith and way of life so often reviled by Christian commentators.

By the early eighteenth century anti-Semitism had centuries-old roots in Europe, and the Dutch were certainly not immune to its influence. Despite this long history of anti-Jewish prejudices and actions,

Picart and Bernard clearly felt confident that they could make Judaism more comprehensible and therefore less strange and disturbing to their readers. The stakes were high, for the Jews came first in volume 1. Treatment of them had to be convincing, interesting, and even enticing, if readers were to go on to subsequent tomes, or even to part two of volume 1, which concerned the Catholic Church. For reasons partly personal and partly programmatic, Picart and Bernard portrayed the Jews respectfully. Picart, in particular, established friendly personal relations with leading members of the Amsterdam Sephardic community

7.1 The Pentateuch. Picart engraved this title page in 1725 for what became a famous edition of the Pentateuch, well known to collectors to this day. At its top is the crown of Torah sustained by two putti angels; two other angels beneath hold an unfurled Torah scroll. Three cartouches surround the Hebrew title and the names of the three publishers—Samuel Rodriges Mendes, Moses Zarfati De Gerona, and David Gomez Da Silva. Each cartouche has an engraved biblical scene depicting an event in the lives of the biblical namesakes of the publishers: Samuel, Moses, and David. (Courtesy University Library / Print Room, Leiden)

and even produced the title page for what became a famous edition of the Pentateuch (the first five books of the Old Testament). Both men wanted to emphasize the kinship between Judaism and Christianity and the ways Judaism exemplified characteristics found in all the world's religions, so they sought commonalities where others had always found differences. Bernard noted, for example, that like Christians, the Jews devoted one day of the week to worship.[1]

Bernard and Picart could take this more positive view because they lived in a city that not only had many Jews but also had gradually, if grudgingly, allowed them access to positions and influence denied them elsewhere in Europe. When Picart and his friend Prosper Marchand moved from Paris to The Hague in 1710, they would have encountered there a sizeable Jewish population that supported two synagogues. The contrast with Paris must have been stunning. A mere 17 names appeared on the list of Jewish residents compiled by the Paris police in 1715, and even in 1789 there were barely 500 Jews in the French capital. Foreign Jews had to apply for special permission from the French crown to reside in Paris, and most Jews lived in eastern or southwestern France, far from the capital. Yet substantial as it was, the Jewish population of The Hague could not compare to that of Amsterdam; with 13,000–16,000 Jews in the 1720s Amsterdam was the incontestable center of Dutch and West European Jewish life. Larger Jewish populations could be found in the German states and especially Poland, but Amsterdam's Jewish population dwarfed that of Paris or London, with its 2,500 Jews. Even in the mid-eighteenth century only 7,000–8,000 Jews resided in the whole of Great Britain.[2]

Since the Dutch Republic had fewer than 2 million people, compared with 7 or 8 million in Great Britain and 20 million in France, the Jewish presence was all the more visible. No one could have missed it after the 1670s, when both the Great Synagogue of the Ashkenazi Jews and the even more imposing "Portuguese" (Sephardic) Synagogue were built right in the heart of Amsterdam. The renowned Jewish poet Miguel de Barrios (d. 1701) said of Amsterdam, "Its greatest glory is that, having such diverse peoples, of different religions, it maintains them in peace with few officers, but with much justice. It shines like the moon and sheds the light of rectitude and charity . . . the city benignly shelters the people of Moses." By far the most famous of all those immigrant peoples and their descendants was the philosopher Baruch de Spinoza,

7.2   The dedication of the synagogue of the Portuguese Jews in Amsterdam. Picart drew and then supervised the engraving of this print using elements from an earlier engraving by Romeyn de Hooghe of the 1675 dedication. Engraving signed B. Picart delineavit sculp. direx. 1721; CC, vol. I, after p. 100. (Research Library, The Getty Research Institute, Los Angeles, California)

born in Amsterdam in 1632. Like many other Jews in Amsterdam, his father was a merchant who had migrated from Portugal.[3]

The arrival of relatively poor, Yiddish-speaking Ashkenazi Jews from middle and eastern Europe rapidly transformed the city's Jewish community. Although the Ashkenazim numbered only about 500 in the 1640s, by the mid-1700s they made up three-fourths of the Jewish population of Amsterdam, overshadowing in numbers the Sephardim from Spain and Portugal. Amsterdam soon became the publishing capital of Yiddish in Europe, but many disdained the new immigrants, including even the Sephardic Jews. Like most other artists of his time, Picart chose to focus on the Sephardic Jews, who were generally much better off than their Ashkenazi counterparts. Because many of the Sephardic Jews engaged in international commerce, they were wealthy, sophisticated, and generally more assimilated into Dutch culture than the Ashkenazim. Although Picart emphasized the elegant clothing and dignified comportment of the Sephardic Jews, thus making them seem very similar to Dutch Protestants, he did not entirely ignore the Ashkenazim, carefully distinguishing, for example, between the ceremonies of "the German Jews" and "the Portuguese Jews." Picart may have imbibed some of the prejudices against the Ashkenazim, for his German Jews appear less prosperous, more tradition-minded, and perhaps a bit more closed in on themselves. Still, they are hardly caricatured, and Picart obviously intends to show both that the Jews, even the Ashkenazim, resemble other Dutch religious groups, and that Jewish families are much like other Dutch families.[4]

Despite the tension between Sephardic and Ashkenazi Jews—Bernard says in the text that in Holland they are "sworn enemies"—Amsterdam offered unique opportunities to the Jewish community as a whole. No enforced ghetto and no mandatory clothing or hats set the Jews apart. No Catholic Inquisition like those in Spain and Portugal troubled their lives. The Inquisition in many Catholic countries focused its attention on Jews as blasphemers or as false converts who continued to secretly practice Judaism. In 1698 in the southern French town of Avignon, still under the sovereign rule of the papacy, a Christian girl took it upon herself to baptize a ten-month-old Jewish child. The Inquisition then ordered the baby removed from the home of her parents and put into the city's orphanage. We know about this legal abduction because in 1709 papal officials tried to compel the girl's Jewish father, who lived in the local ghetto, to continue providing for her upkeep. By contrast, from the 1650s onward Amsterdam officials prohibited Jewish minors from converting to Christianity against the will of their parents. In 1719 the clerics of the Inquisition in Avignon finally agreed to stop forcibly baptizing Jewish children, but only after the local Jewish population had vociferously protested to Rome.[5]

The relative freedom of Jews in the republic drew the attention of other Europeans. The more charitable ones hypothesized that this policy contributed to the growth of Dutch commerce, wealth, and power. But the Jews did not gain toleration without a struggle. When the

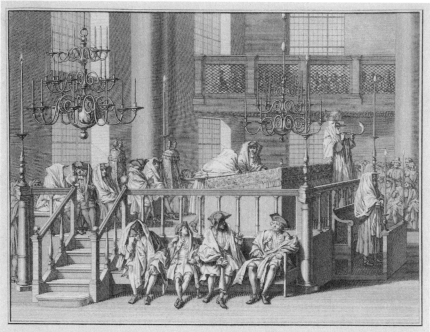

Le SON du COR au PREMIER JOUR de L'AN.

Le CHIPUR, ou le JOUR du PARDON tel qu'il se célèbre chez les JUIFS ALLEMANDS.

Dutch successfully wrenched their independence from the Spanish, formally in 1648, but already in practice two generations earlier, persecuted Jews from Spain and Portugal flocked to the republic. The Dutch municipal authorities applied all sorts of restrictions, but still they kept arriving. At first Jews could not worship in public, sell retail, or gain access to various trades and guilds. Well into the eighteenth century learned academies refused to admit them.

Nevertheless, by the mid-seventeenth century Jewish students had begun attending Dutch universities and soon graduated as doctors and lawyers. Jewish shops appeared in Amsterdam and The Hague offering tea, tobacco, books, textiles, diamonds, and jewelry. Prosperous Jewish families founded literary and philanthropic societies. When inaugurated in 1675 "with all the solemnity imaginable," the Portuguese synagogue counted as the finest in Europe. Numerous descriptions of it appeared in travel literature. In *Religious Ceremonies of the World* Bernard claimed that its opening day "ought to be ranked among the happiest their nation has seen since the destruction of Jerusalem," and Picart devoted a sumptuous double-page plate to the event. In 1691 King William III of England—also the stadholder of the Dutch Republic—paid the synagogue a visit. At his side stood Moses Curiel, one of its founders. A generation or so later Picart would paint and engrave himself proudly seated at the Passover dinner table of the Curiel family, the son of Moses at its head. The oil painting of that evening—one of the very few attributed to Picart—may have been intended as a gift for the family (see Figure I.1). Dutch toleration nonetheless had its limits. The law explicitly forbade sexual contact between Christians and Jews, and Jews could still not become magistrates or leaders in Dutch cities. It took Napoleonic conquest to create Dutch citizenship as a category and offer it to Jews as well.[6]

7.3 *(facing page):* Celebrating the Jewish New Year and the Day of Atonement. Picart's signature tells us that he drew these scenes "from Nature" in 1725. The top half shows Portuguese (Sephardic) Jews celebrating the new year (Rosh Hashanah) in their synagogue, and the bottom half shows German or Ashkenazi Jews observing Yom Kippur in their synagogue. The Ashkenazi Jews appear less well dressed than their Sephardic counterparts, a difference noted by other contemporary sources. CC, vol. I, between pp. 116 and 117. (Research Library, The Getty Research Institute, Los Angeles, California)

7.4 The Passover meal. Picart gave great importance to this work; he signed it "drawn from nature and engraved by B. Picart 1725," which meant that he controlled its execution from start to finish. Scholars still debate which of the figures in the painting is Picart, with candidates being the man without a hat and the figure on the far right with the three-cornered hat. CC, I, following p. 120. (Research Library, The Getty Research Institute, Los Angeles, California)

Bernard and Picart played separate but complementary roles in making Jewish ceremonies and customs more familiar to the public. In laying out the text, Bernard began with two major book-length extracts, the first written by a seventeenth-century Venetian rabbi and the second by a French Catholic priest on the similarities between Jewish and Catholic practices. Because neither of these sources gave sufficient attention to Jewish rites or to the differences between Jews, Bernard appended to them a "third dissertation" that was almost certainly his own compilation drawn from various contemporary sources. It began with the dispersion of the Jews, recounted their persecution at the hands of

Romans and then Christians, and offered a detailed description of Jewish ceremonies, including the differences in practices between "German" and "Spanish and Portuguese" Jews. The engravings by Picart all appeared in this section written by Bernard. For his part, Picart worked hard to gain admission to Sephardic ceremonies in Amsterdam, which he then drew firsthand. In his depictions of Jewish rituals he did everything possible to evoke an affirmative response in the viewer. Picart invested more of his interest, energy, and skill in the Jewish engravings than in those of any other religious group covered in the 3,500 pages of *Religious Ceremonies of the World.* The Portuguese synagogue in Amsterdam, which survived the German occupation of the 1940s and the vicissitudes of time, still includes one of Picart's Jewish engravings in its permanent public exhibition.[7]

Despite the relative toleration afforded Jews in the Dutch Republic, Picart and Bernard still had to overcome a pervasive anti-Semitism when making their case for the exemplary nature of Jewish rituals. Anti-Semitic writings emanating from Germany complained that the freedom enjoyed by Jews in Holland, especially in Amsterdam, made it possible for them to convert Christians. The English freethinker John Toland distinguished himself as one of the few intellectuals who vehemently defended the Jews. He recounted how one acquaintance of his had tried to persuade him that "every *Jew* in the world had one eye remarkably less than the other. . . . Others will gravely tell you, that they may be distinguish'd by a peculiar sort of smell, that they have a mark of blood upon one shoulder." Not surprisingly, Toland's readership extended to Jews living as far from Amsterdam and London as Livorno.[8]

In response to the growing influx of Jews from the east, a new derogatory ethnic label appeared in Dutch at the end of the 1600s: *smous* (pl.: *smousen*). In English slang by the first decade of the eighteenth century, *smouse,* or more commonly *smouch,* matched the Dutch word. The term derives from the verb *schmusen,* which in both Yiddish and German meant to talk engagingly, to bargain, or to haggle. In Yiddish and German, however, the word was used only to describe an activity, whereas in English and Dutch it became a negative term for Jews as persons.[9]

Although Rembrandt, who lived in the Jewish quarter of Amsterdam, showed great interest in Ashkenazi customs and often used Ashkenazi Jews as models for his biblical figures, most artists in Europe

Anno 1475. Am Grünendonnerstag ward das Kindlein Simon 2½ Jahr alt
von den Juden umbgebracht.

Diese Abbildung stehet zu Franckfurt am Oncyn am Brucken Churn.
abgemalet.

7.5 A crude anti-Semitic print of German origin. The image assembles all the stereotypes into a particularly vicious insult. At the top sits the Christian child murdered by Jews who then devoured her blood. In the main frame Jews are forced to consume the milk and feces of a pig. They are depicted with devils' horns and made to kneel before swine. The accompanying text makes much of the distinctive caps, depicted as jester-like in some cases, worn by Jews. From Johann Jacob Schudt (a rector in a local gymnasium), *Jüdische Merckwürdigkeiten* (Frankfurt and Leipzig: Verlag Hoder, 1714). A version of the text appeared in Berlin in 1934. (Courtesy Harry Sondheim, personal collection)

failed to distinguish between Ashkenazi and Sephardic Jews when they demonstrated any interest in the Jews at all. As Toland recounted, various stereotypes had developed over time in the depiction of Jews: artists frequently portrayed them with large, round eyeglasses, swarthy complexions, or large noses, sometimes carrying money boxes or bags or working as lowly peddlers. More vicious representations, which can still be seen in some German cathedral sculpture dating from the Middle Ages, depicted them holding a pig, sucking a sow's teats, or taking the devil as a companion. If color was available, the Jew could be shown with a red beard, because red was the imagined color of Judas's hair. Many of these images first applied to the Ashkenazim and came from Germany and Poland, but they easily migrated and turned into stereotypes for all Jews.[10]

Even though they aimed to counter prejudices against the Jews, Bernard and Picart chose not to lay out an explicit program for their examination of Jewish ceremonies and customs. They wanted their documents and images to speak for themselves. They also wanted readers to draw their own conclusions, with some guidance to be sure, but also with some autonomy. They expressed no interest in contributing to the theological polemics that roiled the relations between different religious communities in most parts of Europe. In his introduction to the whole enterprise, therefore, Bernard focuses on religion and humankind in general. He makes constant reference to the Jews, but always as one example among many of religious practices. He compares Jewish customs with those of the Romans, the Brahmins in India, and especially the Christians.

The ceremonies and customs of the Jews are presented in three distinct parts in volume 1, each of which has its own separate logic. The account by the Venetian rabbi Leon Modena was the first work written in the vernacular to explain Jewish rites and beliefs to Christians. In addition, it provided a wealth of ethnographic detail, describing how houses were to be constructed, the ritual implements found in the Jewish kitchen, and customs of dress for men and women. Composed in 1614–1615, the book was published in Italian in 1637 and then translated into English in 1650 and French in 1674. It may have been suggested to Bernard and Picart by Marchand, who carried the French translation in his Paris bookstore and also kept a copy in his private library.

By 1723, when Bernard and Picart published this volume, Modena's work was in some respects dated, but it still suited their purposes as rare eyewitness testimony. Modena had written his book to refute one of the best-known Christian sources on Jewish rites, *Jewish Synagogue*, published by Johann Buxtorf in German in 1603. A learned professor of Hebrew at Basel University, Buxtorf aimed to show how biblical Judaism had degenerated into the rabbinical Judaism of his day. He believed that Christians needed to understand Jewish rites in order to convert the Jews. Modena's aims were clearly very different from Buxtorf's, yet he himself denigrated practices he considered superstitious and thus unworthy of the Jews. What made him especially attractive to Bernard and Picart, one suspects, was his criticism of excessive rules and regulations ("minutiae") introduced by rabbinical authorities, which was just the kind of criticism that Bernard and Picart would level at all other religions, including Christianity.[11]

The choice of Richard Simon for the second section was as inevitable as that of Modena for the first, though the goal was a bit different. Modena explained Jewish rituals from the inside. Simon then used Modena's account to show the comparability of Jewish to Christian practices. A French Catholic priest, Simon had translated Modena into French in 1674, and then in 1681, using a different pseudonym, he added his comparison of Jewish and Catholic ceremonies. Nothing could have suited Bernard and Picart better: by reproducing Simon's supplement they were simply reporting the comparisons already developed by none other than a Catholic priest.

But Simon was hardly a run-of-the mill priest. In 1678 he had published a critical history of the Old Testament that had gotten him into hot water. He treated the Old Testament like a literary work, tracing inconsistencies and contradictions to show how the text had evolved over time under anonymous hands. The book was denounced by Jesuits and Jansenists alike, and French authorities ordered its confiscation. Simon was thrown out of the Oratorian order. Needless to say, the book continued to circulate in Holland, home of forbidden books, and Simon soon ranked as a martyr for enlightened thinking. Bernard and Picart each had the 1685 Rotterdam edition of the Old Testament book in their personal libraries, as well as a four-volume collection of Simon's writings put out by De Lorme in 1708. It is hardly accidental, then, that Bernard begins with Simon's translation of Leon Modena and then provides Simon's own profoundly ecumenical commentary.

Simon's preface to Leon Modena's text sets the tone for his own subsequent comparisons. He reminds readers of the bonds that tie Christianity to Judaism: Jews wrote the New Testament, some Christian ceremonies are taken directly from the Jews, and Christians and Jews share adherence to the Ten Commandments. Bernard must have been especially struck by one of Simon's asides, which accords with the overall message of *Religious Ceremonies of the World:* both Judaism and Christianity can produce "chimeras," Simon suggests, "but that is not so much the fault of the tradition as of those who are its depositories [priests and rabbis]." Bernard and Picart repeatedly draw attention to the dilution and distortion of original beliefs by those who claim to be religious leaders.[12]

Simon also appended to the Modena text a section on Jewish heresies that reinforced Bernard and Picart's message. That section, "Supplement Concerning the Karaites," gives a very sympathetic account of the Jewish sect that supposedly relied only on the Old Testament and not on rabbinical interpretation and commentary. The Karaites therefore represented a kind of primitive or pure Judaism. As Simon says in the supplement, the Karaites blamed the "Rabbinists," who confused the "fables of the Talmud" and "the daydreams of their ancestors" with "the sacred Books of Scripture." The Karaites did not reject all traditions, insisted Simon, only the false and absurd ones. This was precisely what Bernard and Picart hoped all believers would do: sift through the chaff of superstitious, unthinking traditionalism to find the golden kernels of true faith. To make this point stick, however, they also needed to establish the comparability of religions, their ethnographic and ritual similarities. Simon's text—taken from his *Comparison of the Ceremonies of the Jews with the Discipline of the Church*—fit the bill, even if he did not share Bernard and Picart's more global ambitions. The topic also enjoyed contemporary resonance, for in the second decade of the eighteenth century three men in the Amsterdam synagogue were actually expelled for their beliefs in Karaitism.[13]

The third "dissertation" compiled and adapted by Bernard himself might seem at first glance to be largely descriptive. He devotes eight pages, for example, to a chronology of important dates in Jewish history since the creation of the world, as dated by the Jews, and to the ritual calendar as it would apply, more or less, to the year 1722 (the Jewish calendar does not run January–December). In the long part detailing all the ceremonies, including birth, circumcision, marriage, funerals, and each of the major Jewish festivals, Bernard repeatedly refers back to Leon Modena, adding some details but not disagreeing with his account in any major way. But Modena does not appear at all in the beginning of the section, when Bernard tells the early history of the Jews, details the ways in which they have been persecuted, and analyzes the differences among major sects, including Samaritans, Karaites, Sadducees, Pharisees, and even Chinese Jews, whom he considers a sect because they differ in their practices from other Jews.

The pell-mell quality of this third section derives from the variety of Bernard's aims. He devotes so much space to the ritual calendar because he will provide a parallel calendar in the Catholic section that is much longer, thus subtly making the point that Catholicism is even more "ceremonialist" than Judaism. He gives even more elaborate descriptions of Jewish ceremonies than can be found in Leon Modena because they will form the foundation of his ethnographic analysis; the third volume of *Religious Ceremonies of the World,* for example, will include a long extract from an anonymous work published in 1704 on the parallels between Jewish customs and those of the Indians of the East. Readers could not determine the validity of such comparisons without the detailed knowledge of Jewish ceremonies that Bernard provided. He takes his additional material on Jewish ceremonies from Buxtorf, which he uses as an ethnographic source without endorsing Buxtorf's aim of conversion. Bernard is not just uninterested in converting the Jews. He clearly has little patience for the incessant Christian efforts to convert the Jews by persecuting them, and he praises the Jews themselves for not trying to convert others to their religion.[14]

Beneath this seemingly scattershot approach lies a unifying agenda: Bernard devotes so much attention to the history of the Jews, the proliferation of their sects, and the elaboration of their ceremonies because he wants Judaism to serve as his model of what happens to natural or primitive religion in general. To do this, he must first valorize Judaism rather than denigrate it as so many Christian writers had done. Picart's engravings reinforce this message again and again (see Figure 7.4, for example). Insofar as Jewish rituals went through a process of ossification over time, that process very much resembles the corruption of Catholic practices. Indeed, though Catholicism will provide a prime target for Bernard and Picart, the lesson will be even more universal:

under the influence of priests, virtually every religion has tended to slide into emphasizing externalities rather than holding fast to its original, much simpler truths.

The storyline of corruption—and the original valorization—both come from a book on which Bernard relied heavily for his historical narrative, Jacques Basnage's history of the Jews, first published in 1706–1708. An exiled French Huguenot pastor in Rotterdam, Basnage wrote his history with the same dual purpose as Bernard and Picart. On the one hand, he wrote more positively about the Jews and their long history than had any Christian before him. So affirmative was his account that it was translated into Hebrew and influenced a Yiddish-language history, too. On the other hand, Basnage developed an implicit analogy between the degenerative state of rabbinical Judaism and the corruptions of Catholicism; the history of the Jews thus provided ammunition in the Protestant struggle against Catholicism. Bernard takes his account of the decay of Jewish practices from Basnage. The Jews demonstrated courageous endurance after the destruction of the Temple in Jerusalem and their subsequent flight, Bernard insists, but they progressively gave in to the blind traditionalism of their leaders. Persecution at the hands of the pagan Romans and then the Christians and Muslims hastened the process. Over the centuries repression produced a spate of Jewish impostors and false messiahs, various heretical movements, and increasing ceremonial rigidity. Only the Karaites resisted these superstitious tendencies because they clung closely to the original text of Scripture and left statues and images out of their homes; in short, they resembled Protestants, and perhaps especially Waldensians, in relation to Catholicism![15]

It would apparently follow, then, that the rabbis would come in for some harsh criticism. But here Bernard draws the line. True, he occasionally criticizes the rabbis, whom he portrays as pretentious, "regarding themselves as infallible in their decisions." The thicket of obligations and rules, the multiplication of prayers and benedictions, might seem excessive. Bernard objects, for example, to prayers given in thanks for the birth of a male child since, he argues, God regards women as no less agreeable than men. Yet on the whole, Bernard remains respectful of the rabbis, who are chosen with relatively little ceremony and receive little payment in exchange for their labors. Bernard—and certainly Picart—wanted to stay firmly on the side of valorizing Judaism, including its rabbis and its ceremonies. They therefore underline the similarities between Jewish practices and those of other religions. Like the ancient Greeks, the Jews set aside days for purification. Like Catholics and most heathens, Jews worship at altars and feature music in their ceremonies. Their habit of covering the head likewise has analogues in the customs of other religions, pagan or monotheistic. Bernard owned many books about Judaism and continued to publish about it until the end of his life.[16]

There is no evidence that Bernard and Picart's sympathetic rendering of the Jews and Judaism ever got them into trouble, but one of Picart's best-known predecessors had not been so fortunate, and his experience must have been cautionary. A generation earlier, Romeyn de Hooghe (d. 1708) had produced many sympathetic engravings of Jewish life and customs. Indeed, so much is known about Amsterdam's Jews in the seventeenth century because De Hooghe devoted many etchings and engravings to them. He engraved the facade of the Curiel home as well as a large print of the inauguration of the Portuguese synagogue in 1675 that served as Picart's model. De Hooghe reached the height of his fame in the 1690s, but he also made many enemies. By engraving Orangist propaganda for William of Orange, Dutch stadholder and king of England after 1689, he earned the enmity of the city fathers in Amsterdam, who were anti-Orangist because they feared the stadholder's encroachment on their autonomy. Some of them may also have known that in 1688 William financed his English invasion with help from Don Francisco Lopes Suasso, a Jewish financier. A crash on the Amsterdam exchange in the very autumn that William undertook his invasion also stirred up anti-Jewish feelings that soon spilled over onto De Hooghe, who found himself the target of a relentlessly scurrilous campaign.[17]

De Hooghe's detractors accused him of slandering God by engraving the sixteen erotic postures that accompanied sonnets by the sixteenth-century Italian poet Aretino. If De Hooghe did those engravings they have never been found. The original illustrations of the "postures of Aretino" dated from the 1520s and remained infamous well into the eighteenth century. Even by today's standards they are considered pornographic. At the time, the libertine was closely associated with the heretical. Not surprisingly, then, De Hooghe's disparagers prepared sworn statements, subsequently printed, claiming that De Hooghe had defamed the sacrament, pronounced Jesus the lover of Mary Magdalene, lewdly caressed his own daughter, and said that God does not keep his word. De Hooghe was supposedly overheard in a coffee house pronouncing that "dead is dead and as a result men in this world must do nothing but take Pleasure." His enemies went on to maintain that he allowed his wife to have intercourse in the next room with Jews as well as Christians while he sat eating in his shop. Witnesses came forward to attest to the wife's behavior. De Hooghe's "open atheism and God-lessness" supposedly included drawings of his wife and three of her male friends, members of the Portuguese synagogue, all done in imitation of the postures of Aretino. The artist did not hesitate, they asserted, to sell these lewd creations.[18]

Although the local Jewish population may not have known of these attacks on De Hooghe, since many Jews knew only enough Dutch to conduct business or greet their neighbors, they almost certainly heard loud echoes from the nearly simultaneous stock market crashes of 1720 in Paris, London, and Amsterdam. While some, like Jean Frederic Bernard, made fortunes in the speculative frenzy set off by the creation of the South Sea Company in London and the Mississippi Company in Paris, others, like Picart's in-laws, lost nearly everything when the bubble burst. In Amsterdam, and to a lesser extent in London, Jews got a goodly share of the blame for the collapse. Even though Jews constituted only a small minority of those trading shares in the new companies (probably less than 10 percent in the Dutch market), their presence aroused malicious commentary. The terms "actionist" and "stock-jobber" became associated with Jewish traders. In the English slang of the period, *stock-jobbing* described "a sharp, cunning, cheating trade of buying and selling shares of stock in East-India, Guinea and other companies, also in the Bank, Exchequer, etc."[19]

Picart lived on the Kalverstraat, the eye of the trading hurricane, and he immediately produced a satirical engraving of the events that had that taken place right down the street, "Monument Consecrated to Posterity in Memory of the Incredible Folly of the Twentieth Year of the Eighteenth Century." It also appeared, though perhaps without his permission, in *The Great Picture of Folly,* a large, folio-size volume on the crash that included seventy prints, poems, satirical plays, pamphlets, and even copies of the stock subscription agreements. The engravings in this collection circulated, often crudely copied, throughout

7.6 Picart's satire on the follies of stock speculation. Picart's image of the 1720 bubble makes fun of the naive but avoids the anti-Jewish sentiments found in so many of the plates produced at the time. "Monument consacré a la posterité en mémoire de la folie incroyable de la xx. anneé du xviii siècle," plate 21 in *Het groote Tafereel der dwaasheit*. (Research Library, The Getty Research Institute, Los Angeles, California)

England, France, Holland, and the German states. Unlike many of the other contributors to the book, however, Picart made no connection between the collapse and the trading activities of Jews. The collection included, among other items, previously published anonymous letters violently attacking the role of "Jews and *smousen*" and attributing the entire bubble to their sharp practices. One of the many engravings in the collection that includes Jewish figures shows a *smous* using his staff to pry money from his victim's pockets before the unfortunate fellow can escape to Vianen, one of the so-called free towns where the Dutch authorities could not prosecute debtors. Yet another adaptation of the hunchbacked Jew has him taking pliers to a man's testicles or prying worthless stones out of his anus.[20]

The contrast, then, between Picart and Bernard and many of their contemporaries could not have been more sharply drawn. Just when some began to capitalize on the burst of anti-Semitic feeling in the wake of the 1720 collapse, the two men began to prepare a work that would treat Judaism as a kind of prototypical religion, comparable to all others, including Christianity. Picart started work on his cherished drawings and engravings of Jewish life in the city and beseeched his Jewish contacts to allow him to attend their ceremonies in person. While Picart and Bernard labored to capture the diversity of Jewish demeanor and behavior, many of their contemporaries seemed obsessed with a new, negative stereotypical figure, Bombario or Bambario, a sinister hunchback sometimes depicted in prints carrying a spectacle case. Bambario might seem to be a fool or a harlequin, straight out of the popular Italian and French farces, but he was always shown lurking wherever stocks were being traded, sometimes manipulating the outcome. In one of the prints of *The Great Picture of Folly* "Actie Roth" has his harlequin bring him money, which he stores in his money box, "Bambario's gold chest." The name Bambario or Bombario might have come from the Dutch word *bombarie*, which meant "noise, tumult, or fuss," or it might have been a play on a well-known Jewish name, that of the poet Miguel de Barrios (alias Daniel Levi).[21]

Although Bambario is not labeled as Jewish in the prints in *The Great Picture of Folly*, contemporaries would not have missed the meaning. In one engraving the central figure holds a banner inscribed with the name Bambario and wears a cap frequently seen in anti-Jewish imagery from the period. He is accompanied by the devil. An especially explicit en-

7.7 Sexual caricature of Jews. In this example of anti-Semitic iconography that appeared on the Dutch scene in 1720, elements from an earlier print against women are used to denigrate Jews. Detail from plate no. 12, "By veele zit de kei in 't hoof om dat men in de wind gelooft," in *Het groote Tafereel der dwaasheit*. (Research Library, The Getty Research Institute, Los Angeles, California)

graving, a reworking of an older one satirizing women, converts the shrew of the original into a hunchbacked usurer. Here Bambario twists at the private parts of his victim. Legends on some engravings made the target even clearer by referring explicitly to "Hebrews" or "Smous Levi," for example.[22]

These characterizations fell short of the relentless malignity of the anti-Semitic literature coming out of the German states and Eastern Europe and often reflected a general xenophobia about the ways foreign traders might take advantage of the naive Dutch. There can be no doubt, however, that they often specifically targeted Jews. Originally used to belittle Ashkenazi Jews (when provincial Dutch cities tried to restrict the entry of German Jews they specifically referred to them as "smousen"), by 1720 *smous* could refer as well to Sephardic Jews (Levi being a Sephardic name), even though the two groups rarely intermarried or even had much contact with each other. Sephardic Jews were much more likely than their Ashkenazi counterparts to trade on the emergent stock markets.[23]

7.8   Caricaturing Jews among others. The anti-Semitic image depicted in Figure 7.7 often occurred amid many other satirical scenes created by the bubble of 1720. Here is the print as a whole. (Research Library, The Getty Research Institute, Los Angeles, California)

In the year of the market crash Amsterdam's licensed theater presented to packed audiences Pieter Langendyk's play *Quincampoix,* a satire on the crisis named after the street in Paris where stocks were traditionally traded (also the nickname of the coffee house in the Kalverstraat where much of the speculative frenzy in 1720 took place). The main character, a naive Dutchman, exclaimed that if he wanted to know what was happening to particular *acties,* or stocks, he would ask "a swarm of Smousen." "A following of Jews and others" accompanies "Monsieur Windbuil," the deceptive speculator. When seen on their own, the Jews keep outbidding one another, chanting "the Bubble, the Bubble." They are followed by their Bambario, now harlequin of the Jews. Frequently the Dutch they speak is heavily accented and ungrammatical. In the end money is made and lost, and Windbuil must flee to

7.9   Bombario. This image from the financial bubble of 1720 plays on stereotypes of Jews: note the glasses, the cap, the money box, and so on. This is a detail from plate no. 16, "Uitslag der Wind Negotie," in *Het groote Tafereel der dwaasheid* (1720). (Research Library, The Getty Research Institute, Los Angeles, California)

Vianen. The play, and others like it, depict the Jews as blithely trading on, unconcerned with the mayhem around them.[24]

The denigration of Jews as *smousen* and money-grubbers lived on for years afterward. In the 1720s the label even appeared in a learned journal in the course of a discussion of the supposed ethical difference between a Jewish trader, who is only interested in money, and a Christian one, who has a real conscience. An article published in the 1730s claimed that Jews were natural "actionists," an assertion that continued to appear into the 1760s and 1770s: "'Actie' [stock trading] and 'Windhandel' [wind-trade or speculation] should be shut down; too many people have been ruined. The Jews should also find a new kind of commerce." Some stereotypes die hard.[25]

When Picart and Bernard prepared the first volume of *Religious Ceremonies of the World,* these negative images were well known to them. They did not say why they rejected them, but reject them they clearly did. As refugees who had experienced religious persecution firsthand, they must have felt a certain kinship with the children of Abraham. They read and heard Protestant sermonizing that made constant reference to the persecutions of the Jews, however much the ministers might have ultimately blamed these misfortunes on Jewish "insolence." Moreover, they and their many friends in the book trade knew and admired the work of Spinoza, who had died in 1677 but continued to exercise great influence in intellectual circles in the Dutch Republic. It seems likely, too, that Picart knew of Abraham ben Jacob, a Protestant minister in the Rhineland who converted to Judaism in Amsterdam, where he subsequently worked as an engraver. Ben Jacob produced the first-ever copperplate engravings for a Hebrew book in 1695, a Passover *haggadah.* In 1725, the same year that Picart produced his engraving of the Passover dinner, he also did the drawing, with Hebrew letters, for his title page of a Hebrew Pentateuch. It celebrated the lives of the three Sephardic Jews of Amsterdam who funded the publication. At about the same time he also did a lavish plate on the Torah in a book intended for use at a Seder. Picart's connections to the Sephardic Jewish community were nothing less than extraordinary for the time.[26]

In his engraving of the Passover dinner (Figure 7.4) Picart did not include any young children around the table, though children appear in some of his other Jewish engravings. Since children are so important to the ritual feast, some commentators have suggested that the omission

L' EXAMEN du LEVAIN &c.

A. La Maîtresse de la maison, qui met du PAIN LEVE en divers endroits, afin que son Mari qui en fait la recherche en trouve.

7.10 Searching for the leaven. Here a Jewish mother and her children prepare the household for Passover by removing the leavened bread. This engraving appeared as the top half of Figure I.1, the Passover dinner. In both images Picart aims to make Jewish families seem much like ordinary Dutch households with the same interiors and dress. CC, I, facing p. 120, "L'EXAMEN du LEVAIN &c." Signed "Dessiné d'apres nature et gravé par B. Picart 1725." (Research Library, The Getty Research Institute, Los Angeles, California)

reflects a continuing fear of persecution in the family. The Curiels (or da Costas, as they were also known) had migrated from Portugal, where for decades they had practiced their Judaism in secret. Such families had not allowed children at the Passover Seder because their presence (the ceremony begins at nightfall) might have alerted the authorities to the falseness of their supposed conversion to Christianity. As the next volume of *Religious Ceremonies of the World* would make abundantly clear, the Portuguese and Spanish Inquisitions often targeted secret or crypto-Jews and continued to execute them for the "crime" of Judaism right into the 1700s. Given the recurrent blasts of anti-Semitism even in

Holland, could they afford to let down their guard? Beneath the serene countenances of the Curiel family's celebration lay a long history of trial and tribulation that neither they nor our two authors had forgotten. Yet in the end, because they constituted no competition to the Reformed Church, Jews enjoyed greater freedom for public worship than did Roman Catholics in the Dutch Republic.[27]

8

Cutting Roman Catholicism
Down to Size

As Protestants who had left Catholic France, Bernard and Picart attached great importance to the Catholic section of their encyclopedia. At slightly more than 500 pages of text, it is the longest section of the work, comprising the second half of the first volume and all of the second; and it is the most copiously illustrated, as well, with 55 folio plates of engravings. Yet the Catholic section also posed a serious challenge. If the book simply ridiculed Catholicism, it would have driven away hundreds or even thousands of potential francophone readers. Since the two collaborators clearly aimed to reach an international public, they had to find some kind of intermediate strategy that fostered criticism and a good measure of satire without reducing the entire endeavor to a vendetta against one religion. Moreover, a work on religious ceremonies and customs by two Protestants could hardly afford to ignore the worldwide influence of Catholicism, especially since they began their project with a third collaborator, Antoine-Augustin Bruzen de la Martinière, who remained a Catholic. *Religious Ceremonies of the World* opens with Judaism as the fount of the major monotheistic religions, then Catholicism logically comes next as the first successor to Judaism. Protestantism would make sense only if seen in this lineage.

The work evidently succeeded in creating at least the impression of evenhandedness, for its most prominent Catholic critics complained that it targeted Catholics and Protestants almost equally. When revising the volumes in 1741 for a new Parisian French-language edition that would be acceptable to Church authorities in France, the Catholic clerics Antoine Banier and Jean-Baptiste Le Mascrier insisted that

> this author [Bernard] seems to have decided, one can reasonably conclude, to try to entertain himself at the expense of both parties. Having declared for the most extreme "tolerationism," he can be seen equally ridiculing the fanaticism of the Protestants and seeking continually to give an odious idea of the ceremonies of the Catholics, of their saints, their devotions, their miracles, their relics, etc.

The French clergymen no doubt had complicated motives of their own in revisiting an encyclopedia that had recently been officially condemned by the Church in Rome. Why not simply ignore it altogether? Why bother revising some of the most subversive passages only to leave untouched others that might prove equally troubling?[1]

The French Catholic Church claimed a large measure of independence from the pope, so the 1738 condemnation of the book did not deter the two clergymen. Although they altered the text in many places, they retained not only all the original Picart engravings but also most of Bernard's original text, however much rearranged and recontextualized. They even reproduced the concluding section of volume two on the notorious Catholic Inquisition, which included engravings of torture, humiliations, and executions at the hands of Church authorities. The Inquisition, it should be noted, had no authority in France, and Bernard based his account on exposés published by French Catholics. Might what seemed at first glance to be anti-Catholic actually have been anti-Rome, anti-Spanish, and anti-Portuguese?

Although Banier and Le Mascrier certainly disagreed with Bernard on many points of doctrine, they professed particular offense at the tone of his text: "Over the most serious matters, he has sloshed a certain air of jest and playfulness that is always contrary to good taste when it is out of place. And it is all the more insufferable in this writer because it often degenerates under his pen into bad jokes and gross antics." History, they maintained, should resemble an honest woman, not an actress or a courtesan, much less a fishwife. In short, for them, the doctrinal

Diverses Manieres dont le S.t OFICE fait donner la QUESTION.

8.1   The Inquisition as depicted by Picart. Although Picart made this image famous, he took it directly from an unsigned print in a book by Louis Ellies Dupin published in 1716. Dupin's book is reproduced in the text of *Religious Ceremonies of the World*. B. Picart sculp. dir. 1722; CC, vol. II, second section, facing p. 26 (bottom half). (Research Library, The Getty Research Institute, Los Angeles, California)

defects of the section on Catholicism paled in comparison to Bernard's irritating stance of amused incredulity about religious practices more generally.[2]

The difference between the two versions is best captured by a brief comparison between the very first sentences of the opening "Dissertation on Religious Worship." In the 1723 original (on the left below), Bernard went for the jugular of religious worship in general, basically reducing all religious practices to the same level and even implicitly comparing devout Christians to heathens. In contrast, Banier and Le Mascrier (below right) strove to maintain a clear distinction between Christian and pagan practices:

Most men would not know there is a God, if the worship that one renders him was not accompanied by some exterior signs. The less one knew of the supreme Being, the more these signs were bizarre and extravagant. Ignorance has even pushed devotion to the point of inhumanity, and the wisest among an infinite number of redoubtable pious people [*dévots*] have been ridiculed. Some believed that to serve God it was necessary to kill men in a barbarous and cruel fashion; others, that it was necessary to make oneself dizzy by pirouetting, by striking the ground with one's chest, by torturing oneself and walking on a fire, or by maintaining an ecstatic trance for several hours.	One would often forget there is a God, if the worship that one renders him was not accompanied by some exterior signs. The less one knew of the supreme Being, the more these signs were bizarre and extravagant. Ignorance has even pushed zeal to the point of inhumanity, and an infinite number of peoples such as the Scythians, Mexicans, Peruvians, ancient Gauls, etc., believed that to serve God it was necessary to immolate men in a barbarous and cruel fashion; others, like the Turkish dervishes, the Brahmins, the Quakers, etc., believed that one should make oneself dizzy by pirouetting, by striking the ground with one's chest, by torturing oneself and walking on a fire, or by maintaining an ecstatic trance for several hours.

Similarly, Banier and Le Mascrier refused to emulate Bernard and Picart in devoting a full volume to Islam; the followers of Muhammad do not deserve the distinction of an entire volume, the clerics insisted, though they do have the right to be considered a kind of middle ground between Christianity and idolatry. But that is all.[3]

These first sentences of the book indicate that the reader will have to pay close attention to get all of Bernard's plays on words and satires. *Dévot* in French [devout or pious], for instance, referred both to a religious disposition and to a political party at the French court. The *dévots* advocated an end to tolerance of Protestants in France and so were directly responsible for the fate of refugees such as Bernard and Picart. Here, at the very beginning of the book, Bernard has cleverly slipped in the remark that devotion can lead to "inhumanity," an inhumanity, moreover, that is comparable to human sacrifice or any other barbarous pagan practice. Devotion could turn out to be deadly.

As even this brief passage demonstrates, Bernard and Picart did not choose to confront Catholicism head on. To maintain a modicum of evenhandedness and symmetry in their treatments, they had to follow an approach like that already employed in their account of Judaism. So they relied as much as they could on descriptions and images of Catholic ritual drawn from Catholic sources. Picart based seventeen of his Catholic plates, some with as many as six separate images each, on the engravings found in his 1663 copy of the *Roman Pontifical,* the official liturgical book for Catholic ceremonies. Virtually all the other plates, even those on the Inquisition, came from Catholic sources too. An unsuspecting reader might leaf through the Catholic section and simply be overwhelmed by the complexity of the ceremonies depicted. That reaction would probably have pleased our two Protestants, who wanted readers and viewers to see for themselves how Catholics emphasized ceremony more than inner belief.[4]

Nonetheless, Bernard and Picart refrain from making any explicit pronouncements. They hold no brief for the superiority of Protestant doctrine. Instead, they use the most authentic sources available to develop a historical and ethnographic approach that puts Catholicism on the same level with all other religions. True, the emphasis on history allows them to show that many supposedly central practices of the Catholic Church did not come into usage until many centuries after the death of Jesus, but they seem more interested in setting up potential comparisons to the practices of Jews, Protestants, Turks, and various pagan peoples. Although the historical and ethnographic approach might challenge Catholicism's claims to absolute truth in matters of religion, Bernard and Picart leave it to the reader to draw that or any other conclusion.

To underline the historically variable nature of Catholic doctrine, Bernard calls attention to the conflicts among Catholics. In the general preface to volume one he remarks that the book will offer "considerable detail" about Jansenism and Quietism, even though they have been denounced as heretical or schismatic by Church authorities. Following the writings of the Flemish theologian Cornelius Jansen, adherents of Jansenism took Catholic doctrine and practice part of the way toward Calvinism by emphasizing the inherent sinfulness of all humans, the overwhelming power of God's grace, and the sinner's need for prayer and rigorous self-examination. Less doctrinally consistent

CEREMONIE *de la* CONFIRMATION.

Autre Maniere de CONFIRMER.

8.2 Copies of images from *Roman Pontifical*, 1663. All the images that Picart took from this source were copied as meticulously as possible. Picart sculp. dir. 1723; CC, vol. II, second section, facing p. 68. (Research Library, The Getty Research Institute, Los Angeles, California)

than Jansenism, Quietism emphasized a personal and mystical union with God through meditation and contemplation. A papal bull condemned the sect in 1687, just two years after the revocation of the Edict of Nantes, and Louis XIV had its most prominent French exponent, Jeanne-Marie Bouvier de la Motte-Guyon, imprisoned in the Bastille for seven years. Bernard and Picart clearly sympathized with these dissident Catholics and may have intended to hold them out as examples of how Catholicism might still be reformed from within.[5]

Because the book focuses on religious ceremonies, however, not much space is devoted to explicit discussion of these theological differences. The fundamentals of Catholic doctrine are laid out in respectful but summary fashion, with direct quotes from standard Catholic sources. The reader has to make her or his own judgments about the doctrinal disputes between the orthodox Catholics and the Jansenists and Quietists, for Bernard simply presents them without drawing any conclusions. His disinterest in doctrine becomes most evident when he distinguishes between Roman Catholicism and Christianity more generally. The divinity of Christianity, he maintains, is proved by the excellence of its moral teaching. This teaching has nothing to do with philosophical speculations or doctrinal affectations; it is simply the individual's best effort to imitate the conduct of the "great teacher" Jesus on this earth. It will become clear, as the text proceeds, that the Catholic preoccupation with ritual and external conformity only detracts from this original Christian emphasis on moral behavior. At the same time, an attentive reader must have been struck by this shockingly minimalist definition of Christianity: Jesus is simply a teacher, not unlike Confucius or other religious teachers across the globe and throughout history. Bernard does not call him the Son of God, and he makes no mention of the Trinity or the Bible.[6]

By referring repeatedly to Catholic "mystagogues," as if Catholics had simply taken over the practices of ancient mystery religions, Bernard suggests his dislike for the Church's focus on the externalities of faith. Yet he does not develop this position explicitly; he lets the long catalogue of ceremonies and liturgical prescriptions speak for itself. His disdain for external conformity can be traced, in part, to the influence of Protestant polemicists such as Jean Claude, whose work helped convert Picart and Marchand back in Paris. Just as Claude cited the differences between Roman Catholicism and Greek and Russian

Orthodoxy on the subject of the Eucharist in order to contest the doctrine of transubstantiation, so, too, Bernard underlines the difference in ritual practice and doctrine in the various Catholic countries and between the Roman Catholics and the Jansenists or Quietists. The Greek and Russian Orthodox churches, for example, have saints who do not appear in the Western calendar. It follows, though Bernard leaves it to the reader to draw the implication, that there is no one Catholic faith and that therefore its oneness cannot be held out as a virtue that separates it from the multiplicity of Protestant sects. Yet unlike Claude, Bernard shows virtually no interest in the doctrine of transubstantiation. This indifference may reflect his Waldensian heritage and certainly follows from the position he had been working out in the books, both his own and those of others, that he had been publishing in the years leading up to *Religious Ceremonies of the World.*[7]

Even the criticism of Catholic ceremonialism remains for the most part implicit, becoming evident only to the reader who wants to draw conclusions from the mountain of evidence about the complexity of Catholic rituals. Bernard could not leave everything to chance, however. For the more interested readers, he provides occasional witty asides, hidden like nuggets amid pages recounting various ceremonies. Editorial intervention comes in the form of ethnographic observation—for example, kissing the foot of the pope is compared to honors rendered Roman emperors—or cunning remarks inserted unexpectedly: only a Jansenist or a Calvinist could doubt that the pope should be considered greater than any mortal king. There is no clear rhythm to these asides; they seem to ebb and flow as the mood of the author changes or perhaps different authors are involved at different places in the text. After describing in exquisite detail a mass in the pope's personal chapel, Bernard finally cannot resist an acerbic comment: the strictly prescribed ceremonies, the richness of the cloth, and the sparkle of the jewels that were meant to draw the believer's attention to the mysteries of the faith instead take their place. All that matters is following the formulas. As Bernard notes, "If the custom of twirling like dervishes . . . had been introduced several centuries ago into the Christian religion, it is to be presumed that we would have accustomed ourselves to it."[8]

But after this brief outburst the author returns to his task of chronicling ceremonies of all sorts. For most of the two volumes, Bernard offers reasonably accurate depictions of the rituals mixed in with an oc-

casional short, often satirical, observation about them. Masses, for example, are too often devoted to frivolous matters, which the Church
permits as a way of making money. Purgatory is nothing but an invention of the Catholic clergy designed to satisfy their avarice. "Heretics"
make fun of the huge number of relics of the cross of Jesus: between
them the reliquaries of Christendom have enough wood from the cross
to keep cabinet makers busy for years. There are so many relics of the
Virgin Mary, the author insists, that it seems as if every strand of her
hair was conserved, not to mention every drop of milk in her breast,
each of which somehow found its way to a reliquary the moment Jesus
was born. Any Protestant would have recognized these snide remarks as
staples of anti-Catholic rhetoric, but they are embedded in long sections that are simply adapted from Catholic books of ritual.[9]

More than any specific criticisms, however, the sheer number of different rituals and ceremonies underlines the central argument: Catholicism is the most "ceremonialist" of all religions. To drive home this
point, Bernard and Picart do not limit themselves to the holy rites that
most concern the ordinary believer, such as the parts of the mass or the
celebration of the major sacraments like baptism or marriage. They include every ritual found in the literature written for the Catholic clergy,
from the blessing of a new church bell to the procedures for canonization of saints. The list of major feast days alone takes up nearly sixty
folio pages. Clearly, the reader is not meant to read those sixty pages
line by line; the sheer bulk of evidence makes the point, and demonstrating the bulkiness is crucial to Bernard and Picart's aims.[10]

Almost always the book gives a generic account, in part because the
Catholic sources offer general prescriptions and stereotyped woodcuts
or engravings of how to conduct a confirmation, for example, or celebrate communion. In one instance, however, a recent event is highlighted: the procession and ceremony at St. Peter's for the canonization
of four saints on May 12, 1712. Bernard and Picart may have chosen to
focus on this occasion to make their account more concrete and therefore even more credible, and Picart probably relished the opportunity
to produce something more interesting than yet another insipid print
from the *Roman Pontifical*. Other motives may have entered in as well.
In 1712 Clement XI was preparing his papal bull Unigenitus against
Jansenist teachings in France (highlighted in Picart's frontispiece to
Religious Ceremonies of the World), and it was Clement XI as well who

decreed in favor of the Dominicans in the Chinese rites controversy in 1715. He declared Confucianism incompatible with Christianity and forbade Chinese converts to practice ancestor worship.

Picart's two double-page fold-out engravings of the canonization ceremonies in many ways constitute the centerpiece of *Religious Ceremonies of the World*. Although not obvious to someone viewing them in isolation, these two engravings set the visual template for what follows; all the depictions of processions and religious ceremonies that appear in subsequent volumes will be developed in reference to them. Pagan ceremonies will not appear any more extravagant than these events in Rome, Protestant rites will seem distinctly more sober, and in retrospect, even Jewish rituals (shown in the first half of volume one) look restrained in contrast. The effect is all the more dramatic because Picart based the plates, whose production he directly supervised, on original etchings by Catholic artists who worked for Clement XI himself.[11]

An ethnographic impulse is already visible even to someone who has not yet seen the other prints. Picart chose these large etchings to reproduce in part because they had detailed keys to identify those participating in the ceremonies. Moreover, the viewer is positioned just outside and above the action and thus is meant not only to follow what is happening but also to feel a certain distance. The viewer's location is the same as those implied in the engravings of pagan religions (but also of the Anglican service at St. Paul's and the dedication of the Portuguese Synagogue in Amsterdam). In no other engraving, not even those of Chinese or Japanese temples, does the architectural decor so thoroughly overwhelm the individuals participating. Does Picart intend to hint at Oriental despotism in Rome? In the first engraving, of the procession into St. Peter's, the ordinary people genuflect as the pope is carried by like a satrap, and the architectural decor, especially on the left side of the second engraving (shown in Figure 8.3), strikes a note of strangeness: a lifelike figure in the niche hardly looks like a religious statue, and below her are dancing cherubs who look positively pagan in their riotousness. Picart's choice of these two prints could not have served his purposes any better.

Whereas the images rely on relatively subtle cues or cross-volume comparison to make their ethnographic point, the text instructs readers more directly, though only if they add together comparative remarks made as asides. The Catholic Jubilee, Bernard notes, is half-Jewish and

8.3 The ceremonial staging of St. Peter's, 1712. Picart chose to reproduce with some adaptations an etching drawn by Pietro Ostini and engraved by Federico Mastrozzi, "Theatrum canonizationis SS. Pij V. Andreae Auellini, Felicis à Cantalicio, et Catharinae de Bononia à S. Smo d. n. Clemente Pp. XI. an. 1712. celebratae." He chose the image because Ostini was presumably present at the event, because the depiction is beautiful, and because the message it conveys is ambivalent. Individual faith is overshadowed by ceremonial pomp and circumstance. B. Picart sculp. dir. 1722; CC, vol. I, second section, after p. 150. (Research Library, The Getty Research Institute, Los Angeles, California)

half-pagan in origin. The rosary comes from the Muslims, who got it in turn from the East Indians. Processions are pagan in origin and also appealed to the early Jews. Carnival was invented by fourth-century libertines who wanted to revive pagan bacchanalias. The commemoration of the dead comes from the Romans. The Greeks also paid the priest to say mass at a funeral. The idea of purgatory resonates with ideas expressed by Plato and with the South Asian notion of the migration of souls, which had its origins in turn in beliefs of the Egyptians. Nuns are compared to vestal virgins in Roman times. Many of the important elements in Catholicism thus have their origin in other religions and cannot be considered uniquely true.

Yet in many ways, the section on Catholicism simply brings into higher relief problems and paradoxes that Bernard and Picart find in all religions. What might have begun as an exercise in undermining Catholicism turns into a broader examination of religion itself. Images are a good case in point. "Images are almost as ancient as religion," Bernard notes, "which is hardly surprising, since they have their origin in the weakness of the human mind. Not being able to fix its attention for very long on purely spiritual objects, it turns unconsciously toward the material and tries to render palpable, as it were, the object of its cult." Whereas most Protestants may reject miracles, Muslims, Jews, and pagans believe in them just as much as do the Catholics. In the end Bernard seems to advocate a middle position: "A balance is necessary. Those who want the vulgar masses to be deprived of these exterior aids that attach the common people to God presume too much of those souls who are little accustomed to meditating on spiritual things, while those who speak too magnificently of these exterior aids are hypocrites or bigots." Although Catholic practices may occasionally seem bizarre, they appear less so precisely when viewed ethnographically: "Almost all of the pagan peoples, both ancient and modern, seem to have exhausted their imaginations seeking the most bizarre conceivable practices concerning the dead." The coming volumes, Bernard explains, will show just how strange these practices of other peoples can be.[12]

Every religion has rituals concerning birth, marriage, and death, yet Catholicism appears distinctive not only in the sheer number and complexities of its ceremonies but also in its penchant for hierarchy. Bernard devotes the last of five "dissertations" on Catholicism and then a supplement, more than seventy pages total, to the question of Church hierarchy. Once again he and Picart need only follow Catholic manuals to make their main point. For example, Picart simply reproduces, albeit with considerable improvement in the quality of the engraving, the illustrations for the ordination of subdeacons, deacons, priests, and so on, taken from his copy of the *Roman Pontifical*. Bernard, too, sticks quite closely to the Catholic manuals when describing the ordinary clergy, but his commentary becomes more caustic when he addresses two major *bêtes noires*, monks and papal pretensions. Monks are "this fertile nursery of the idle devout [*dévots*] and *useless servants* of the militant church." They are relatively easily dismissed, however, in part because monks are the subject of so much criticism even from Catholics.[13]

The pope requires much more extended treatment. Contrary to what readers might have expected, however, Bernard does not launch into the usual Protestant polemics on this subject; the pope does not appear as the Anti-Christ pure and simple, and Bernard mentions none of the well-known theological disputes about the pope's authority. Instead he impresses upon the reader the enormous size of the papal bureaucracy by reviewing each part of it, department by department, giving the functions of each set of officials and often noting their revenues as well. Chancellors, regents, auditors, prefects, lieutenants, registrars, scribes, secretaries of state, masters of the palace, chamberlains, major-domos, and librarians pass by in review, and no fulminating asides are needed to make the reader question whether these proliferating authorities are all really necessary to good religion. Papal bulls, Bernard maintains, must pass through the hands of at least 1,000 officials in 15 offices, each of whom has to be paid. It is clear that the pope's household rivals that of any leading monarch, but equality with his temporal peers does not suffice. A rescript of Pope Nicolas III is cited for its claim that "the Roman Pontiff cannot be judged in his person because he is GOD." Bernard simply cites the claim and then moves on.[14]

The reader might have expected the text to end with the discussion of the papal bureaucracy, as the culminating point in Catholic ceremonialism, but from the beginning he or she has been forewarned that the section on Catholicism will end even more controversially with the Inquisition. The Inquisition was the most notorious and most contested of Catholic practices; secret courts run by clerics used torture or threats of torture to gain confessions of heresy from various Catholic dissidents (Galileo being the most famous), Jews, Muslims, and even Indians in the Americas. Since it was not a ceremony or a ritual strictly speaking, what could justify its inclusion in the text? Bernard insisted in his opening preface that it should be included as an integral part of the Catholic religion. It had been authorized by the popes, cardinals regularly participated, and the judges were ecclesiastics motivated by their zeal for the glory of God. What he did not admit was, no doubt, the most important motivation; readers gobbled up the newly published accounts of the secrets of the Inquisition, so why would he pass up an opportunity to make his weighty tomes all that more attractive?[15]

Although treating what might have been considered a tangential subject, this final section offers the reader sensational exposés of secret Catholic practices even while managing to encapsulate many of the methods and aims of the work as a whole. Bernard lets extensive extracts from recently published works make his case for him. His principal source is an anonymous book published in French in 1716, now known to be authored by a French theologian with close ties to the Jansenists, Louis Ellies Dupin. Using an approach similar to Bernard's own, Dupin compiled and extracted material from two recently published books, *History of the Inquisition and its Origin,* published anonymously in 1693 under the fictitious imprint Pierre Marteau, and *Account of the Inquisition of Goa,* published anonymously in Leiden in 1687 with six engravings showing various stages in the punishment of heretics, including burning at the stake. These two books were also written by French Catholics, the first by a Catholic priest, Jacques Marsollier, who aimed to protect the independence of the French Catholic Church from Rome, and the second a dramatic firsthand account by the French Catholic physician Charles Dellon of his misadventures with the Portuguese Inquisition at Goa, a Portuguese colony on the west coast of India.[16]

Dupin condensed and rewrote these narratives but kept their basic form and message. His work could not have failed to attract Bernard and Picart's attention; Dupin's "Historical Memoirs Serving as a History of the Inquisitions" criticized the Inquisition from a Catholic point of view, that is, from the inside. In reproducing the text, Bernard and Picart could hardly be accused of anti-Catholic prejudice, especially since Dupin himself identified Dellon as the author of the Goa section. Without Dellon's eyewitness history, the portrayal of the Inquisition would have remained too oriented toward the formal and external, relating the judicial procedures and ritual punishments of the Inquisition without offering any firsthand descriptions. Dellon's tale reads like a novel, an effect that is undoubtedly intentional, for from the very beginning he draws the reader into the twists and turns of his fate. In the end, he barely escapes with his life.

The Picart engravings that accompany the section on the Inquisition reflect the same intentions found in the text. Picart reproduces the images found in Dupin and Dupin's sources, especially those in Dellon. He does not invent scenes but rather uses those that have some credibility because they derive from firsthand accounts. While sticking remarkably close to the originals, Picart does on occasion embellish his prints with additional details about people or decor. He corrects obvious mistakes in earlier artistic renditions and changes the titles to make them more general; for example, his title "Various Ways in Which the St. Office [Inquisition] Administers Torture" replaces the title given in Dupin, "The Way of Administering Torture in the Basement of the Inquisition of Madrid." Picart and Bernard also provide detailed legends to bring out the significance of the action. In fact, some of Bernard's most pointed remarks can be found in his explanations of the legends to the plates.[17]

Bernard draws his own conclusions in the end, but only after letting his sources have their own say. He does not simply reproduce Dupin's work, though he does reprint large sections of it under Dupin's original title. When it suits his purposes, he condenses parts of the Dellon narrative. The use of a smaller font and double columns allows him to compress Dupin's 690 pages in sextodecimo format (smaller than most modern paperbacks) into 69 folio pages. Bernard's main conclusion echoes an argument found throughout the book: religion itself is to be respected, but the evil influence of certain kinds of priests has to be revealed and rebuffed. Wherever the Inquisition gained a hold, princes and even bishops of the Church had to bow before "the caprices of a rabble of monks." Rulers agreed to establish the Inquisition only under false pretenses. They thought they would gain the favor of Rome but in fact lost control over affairs within their own territories. Ordinary priests are not the problem; the monastic orders, especially the Dominicans and the Franciscans, are the true source of deception and distortion of the Church's purposes.[18]

Despite offering this far-from-neutral judgment, Bernard wants to insist on a careful sifting of the sources. His essay "Clarifications about the Historical Memoirs Serving as a History of the Inquisition," which comes at the very end of the second volume, orients his book toward the future of history writing. He (Bruzen de la Martinière may have lent a hand here) emphasizes the need to compare documents and analyze biases rather than just repeat the usual religious polemics of the era in which authors single-mindedly pressed their own case and ignored any evidence that failed to fit into it. Having jumped into the fray with his section on the Inquisition, Bernard nonetheless tries to assume a posture of impartiality. "The Inquisition in itself," he says, "is a strange matter for those who are indifferent as to whether to praise it or blame it: the state which should characterize every writer who speaks about it."[19]

He then reviews the current writing about the Inquisition, beginning with the Dutch Protestant Philip Limborch's history of the Inquisition in Latin, published in 1692 and then reworked in French by Marsollier. Although Bernard apparently did not know that Marsollier was the author of the 1693 book in French, he had detected the hand of a Catholic author at work. Dellon's authorship of the book on Goa had been known since 1709, but the identity of the writer behind the "Historical Memoirs" evidently still escaped Bernard. Nonetheless, he had traced the anonymous hand's compilation of the previous works and was not entirely satisfied with the result, though he had to admit that the work was written with the kind of freedom that made its passing the French censors very unlikely. Bernard consequently offered specific corrections of the text, which he discusses in some detail. He includes in his analysis several pages on the Inquisition in Venice that had been left out of the "Historical Memoirs." He incorporates them because the Venetian Republic "put a brake on the ambitious tyranny of the priests" by ordering limits on the Inquisition. He never mentions, however, that he has slightly modified the title of "Historical Memoirs" in this last section; what began as memoirs about the Inquisitions in Dupin are now memoirs about the Inquisition, rendered singular. This is not a minor point: referring to the Inquisition in the singular made it seem a more systematic and unified practice of the Catholics.[20]

In case anyone failed to grasp just how cruel the Inquisition could be, Bernard ends the volume with a list of those punished at an auto da fe (burning at the stake) in Lisbon, Portugal, on November 6, 1707. Since the Inquisitors often kept their deliberations secret, such lists were hard to come by. This one includes names, professions, ages, accusations, and the punishments ordered. Most of the 56 men and women named were guilty of the "crime of Judaism"; they were so-called new Christians who practiced Judaism secretly. Four were condemned to burn at the stake. Although Bernard does not cite his source for this list, there was in fact an auto da fe at Lisbon on that date. Modern studies have shown that 115 auto da fes took place in Portugal between 1705 and 1749. Bernard and Picart published their book as criticism of the Inquisition was gathering steam, but the institution was far from moribund.[21]

On the subject of the Inquisition, then, the views of Bernard and Picart were unequivocal: they wanted to combat what they saw as a moral outrage. When explicating the legend for the print on methods of torture used by the Inquisition, Bernard wrote, "Chapter IV [on torture by the Inquisitors] should horrify everyone possessed of humanity." But this was not Protestant indignation; many Catholics, especially French Catholics, also denounced the institution as a perversion of Catholicism. In the end, then, the reader might well decide that Bernard and Picart had refrained from simply joining the Protestant chorus of criticism of Catholic doctrine and practice. They had bigger fish to fry than Catholicism, which was only one religion, however powerful.[22]

9

Idolatry

West and East

IDOLATRY is a slippery concept, despite its emphatic condemnation by all the monotheistic religions. According to the Second Commandment, "You shall not make for yourself an idol, whether in the form of anything that is in heaven above, or that is on the earth beneath, or that is in the water under the earth" (Exodus 20:4). Never short on horrific images, the Book of Revelation by St. John lumped together "the fearful, and unbelieving, and the abominable, and murderers, and whoremongers, and sorcerers, and idolaters" and consigned them to "fire and brimstone" (Revelation 21:8). The Koran advises the followers of Muhammad "to slay the idolaters wherever you find them" (Immunity 9:40). None of the holy books of the major monotheistic religions found anything redeeming about idolatry, yet as the voyages of Europeans increasingly revealed, it seemed to be everywhere.

In the early centuries of the Christian Church idolatry flourished among the Romans, prompting the Church father Tertullian to proclaim it humanity's greatest crime. Christianity has nonetheless faced recurrent conflicts on the question of images. When does an image become an idol? The Spanish Jesuit José de Acosta explained in 1590 that images or objects became idols when the devil tricked the Mexicans, just as he had deceived the ancients, "making them believe that these noble creations—sun, moon, stars, elements—had power and authority of their own to do good or evil to men." His countrymen, Spanish Catholic conquerors, in turn destroyed idols in the Americas. Yet at the same time, followers of the Protestant reformers in Europe were smashing pictures and statues in Catholic churches because they believed that Catholics were actually worshiping these images of the Virgin Mary and the statues of the saints. In addition, Protestants considered the Catholic mass, in which the priest converts ordinary bread and wine into the body and blood of Christ, tantamount to idolatry. In his exposition of the doctrine opposed by the Church of England, published in 1699, Bishop Burnet explained, "This we believe is plain Idolatry, when an Insensible piece of Matter, such as Bread and Wine, has Divine Honors paid it." How different, then, was Catholic idolatry from the practices of the pagans of antiquity or the heathens of the Americas?[1]

That it was not very different seemed to be the implication of Bernard and Picart's treatment of idolatry. Time and again in Bernard's opening essay on religious practices in volume one, he makes reference to idols or idolatry in present-day India or ancient Egypt only to offer a comparison to Catholic practices. The "Banians," Indian merchants who were often devotees of Jainism (an ancient religion that emphasized the equality of all beings, even insects), bow before their idols with their hands on their heads, for example, but almost every religious group bows in one fashion or another, including the Catholics and the Greek Orthodox. Protestants are less obsequious in that they pray without bowing. The peoples of the Americas and India kiss the feet or even the lips of their idols; Muslims kiss the black stone of the Ka'ba in Mecca; and Catholics kiss the cross and relics of saints. Protestants are not mentioned in this passage, presumably because they shy away from this kind of physically charged adoration. The supposed idolatry of the indigenous peoples of the New World or those of Asia and South Asia is thus persistently aligned with Catholic practices, serving both to undermine Catholicism as no better than pagan idolatry and to elevate pagan or heathen customs as comparable to those of the other monotheistic religions. The "connection" between them is nothing short of "quite remarkable."[2]

Yet though Bernard and Picart may have begun with the intention of bashing Catholic practices as idolatrous, their consideration of the religions of the heathen world in two weighty volumes led them inevitably to more far-reaching examinations. Rather than revealing the superiority of Christianity or of Protestantism within Christianity, comparison could effectively reduce all religions to the same plane, especially if pursued in an evenhanded and thoroughgoing fashion. If all religions shared certain qualities, then distillation of those qualities might reveal a universal underlying religion—or it might reveal that all religions suffered from the same defects. It might lead to greater toleration of religious difference—or to general disbelief.

Bernard and Picart placed great emphasis on their aspiration for accuracy and balance, and before the reader could draw conclusions, author and engraver had to establish the credibility of their comparative method. That meant demonstrating the intrinsic interest and merit of pagan and heathen practices. As the Jesuit Joseph-François Lafitau explained in his 1,100-page book on the mores of the American savages, published only one year after Bernard and Picart's volume on the Americas, the first voyagers to the New World had concluded that the Americans had no religion at all, and most of those who followed knew too little of local languages to make much sense of indigenous practices. Lafitau wrote in order to correct the error of the first voyagers. As a Catholic priest, moreover, he had to confront the profound theological issue posed by the discovery of the Americas: the Bible never mentions North or South America. How could its inhabitants be integrated into the story of a single divine creation? At the beginning, some Christian commentators even doubted whether the native Americans were human, and controversy raged about the meaning that should be ascribed to their practices and beliefs.[3]

Like Lafitau, but without the Jesuit priest's firsthand knowledge, Bernard and Picart wanted to get at the logic of native American practices. But they went further still. They juxtaposed the native American practices to those in the Far East and Africa as well as to those found in Judaism. Circumcision could be found in the Yucatan; the "savages" of Canada believe in the devil and a God who created all things. Other parallels could be established among the religions of the East and between those beliefs and the sources of Western religion. The followers of Fo (the Buddha) believe him to be their savior, and the Brahmins (an upper caste of Hindus) gave him the name of Ram. Finally, among the ancient peoples Fo may have been understood as being either Pythagoras or the ancient Egyptian sage Hermes Trismegistus. The Chinese and the Japanese also have a single philosopher who is the font of their

their argument would only be valid if it was global → exceptions couldn't exist

religious wisdom, and he, too, appears to be related to Fo. All seem to have a belief in a Supreme Divinity or a Master of Heaven. Moreover, a secret doctrine held by some Confucians equated the divine being with nature, and "this doctrine would appear to have a character approaching Spinozism." The doctrine is in turn similar to that preached by Fo. Only such a global set of comparisons enabled Bernard and Picart to offer an analysis of religion in general.[4]

Idolatry, then, like religion, was as old as human nature. In its forms Bernard and Picart detected a kernel of truth remarkably akin to the innovations in the Western understanding of God supplied independently by the Hermetic tradition and by Spinoza. Suddenly the core of the idolatrous religions starts to look like what some of Picart and Bernard's contemporaries dismissed as pantheism or materialism. Like their contemporaries, Bernard and Picart are ascribing to the Chinese, in particular, the religiosity they themselves favored. The Catholic Church ultimately condemned Chinese practices as idolatry pure and simple, yet accommodationists like the Jesuits and the German natural philosopher Leibniz said that the Chinese were originally true monotheists and that therefore their practices might not be incompatible with Christianity. In his version of the argument, in contrast, Bernard presents the Chinese as possessing the heresy *du jour* of the eighteenth century, or the one true natural religion, a pantheistic materialism.[5]

Whereas Lafitau wrote his book about the native North Americans to refute atheists, Bernard and Picart displaced atheism from the center of the debate. Detractors would have said that they simply redefined it. In the view of Lafitau atheists were authorizing their own incredulity by "persuading themselves that the barbarian peoples have no religious sentiment" and that therefore these peoples had been duped into their cults by leaders intent on shoring up their power through fear. *The Treatise of the Three Impostors* had offered just this kind of argument about the three forms of monotheism, though without emphasizing the ethnographic basis for it. Lafitau believed that he could bolster Catholic orthodoxy even while digging deeply into what he termed the new "science of mores and customs of different peoples." Bernard and Picart drew radically different conclusions from some of the same evidence. Whereas Lafitau argued that the inner kernel of idolatrous practices resonated with the divinely inspired monotheism of Christianity, Bernard and Picart discerned a universal religiosity born out of the fragility of the human condition that was not the result of a divine spark. Lafitau maintained that the parallels between savage practices and ancient paganism showed a "unanimous consent" planted in the human heart by God, whereas the approach taken by Bernard and Picart pointed toward an embrace of pantheistic naturalism.[6]

Bernard and Picart did not have access to Lafitau's work when they prepared their volume on the Americas, but they cited the Jesuit frequently in the next volume, which covered Eastern idolatry, and clearly shared his concern for giving full due to religions that seemed bizarre and even scandalous to Europeans. Like many intellectuals who came after him in the eighteenth century, Bernard insisted that nothing proved the superiority of the moderns over the ancients more decisively than the discovery of the New World. The Greeks and the Romans knew nothing of the Americas. While many travelers had luridly depicted the savagery, barbarity, and cannibalism practiced in the Americas, Bernard and Picart resolutely took the side of those, like Lafitau, who saw similarities between the idolatrous peoples, West and East, and the pagan Greeks and Romans. Analogies between indigenous American and Greco-Roman customs had long been a staple of travel writing, but Bernard and Picart's aim for a global vision took the discussion in new directions. They did not provide their detailed accounts in order to facilitate the conversion of those still ignorant of the message of Christianity, nor did the devil ever make an appearance. Yet neither did they follow their skeptical mentor Bayle in aiming to uncover the absurdity of all heathen religions. For them, the truth or inner core of idolatry they wanted to find was still hidden in the diversity of religious expression and required serious and sustained study.

The two French Catholic priests who prepared a bowdlerized version of *Religious Ceremonies of the World* clearly understood the nature of the challenge to Christianity posed by Bernard and Picart's approach. Banier and Le Mascrier not only refused to follow Bernard in devoting an entire volume to Islam but also included in the same volume with Islam an essay written by Banier himself on the origin and progress of idolatry in general. They extracted the essay from a work on fables that Banier first published in 1711 but did not give definitive formulation until the late 1730s, after Bernard and Picart had published their volumes on the idolatrous peoples. Banier's book, *The Mythology and Fables of the Ancients, Explained from History* (1738–1740), participated in the ongoing debate about atheism: when it arose, how it was connected to idolatry, whether Buddhism was atheistic, and so on. Banier pointedly insisted that idolatry was preferable to atheism because at least it offered some kind of curb on human evil, which atheism did not. He felt it necessary to take this position because Bayle had mischievously suggested that God would prefer atheism to pagan idolatry. Banier used his brief comparative history of idolatrous religions to support an orthodox conclusion: "the Mind of Man, left merely to its own light, is carried out to nothing but Error and Delusion." Only knowledge of "the true Religion," he maintained, could bring mankind out of that everlasting darkness.[7]

In their rearrangement and reworking of Bernard's original text, Banier and Le Mascrier changed the order in which they considered idolatrous peoples; they began with the most civilized Orient and then took up the Americas and finally Africa. Most authors writing about the world's religions began with the East, and in the seventeenth century many had put Africa before the even more savage Americas. The influential compilation *Purchas, his Pilgrimage; or, Relations of the World and the Religions observed in all Ages,* first published in 1613, put Africa after East Asia and before the Americas. Bernard and Picart chose a more surprising line of attack: first the Americas, then India, China, Japan, and finally Africa. Why did they choose to plant their standard in this fashion? Bernard himself had published travel accounts of the Americas in his series *Voyages au Nord,* and as the title of his highly successful series indicates, he took more interest in explorations of northern countries than southern ones. But was it simply a question of what he knew best, that is, North America?[8]

Africa, meaning sub-Saharan Africa, comes last, it appears, because Bernard and Picart knew it least well. Travel reports of the region were less rich, especially in knowledge of the interior of the continent. The page that opens the rather perfunctory section on Africa in *Religious Ceremonies of the World* simply reports that few comparisons had been developed between African religions and those of the Greeks, Romans, or even Egyptians. In contrast, a rich and ever-expanding literature compared Chinese, Indian, and even American religions with those of pagan antiquity, Egypt and the Phoenicians, and the Jews. Africa did not come last, it is worth emphasizing, because Bernard and Picart judged it more primitive. The only characteristic that sets Africa apart, other than relative lack of European knowledge of it, is the black African penchant for fetishes. But Bernard does not cite these as signs of the primitive nature of African religion, as his successors would do. He suggests, instead, a possible comparison with the Manitous among the native Americans and the forest gods of antiquity. In general, Bernard and Picart exhibit little interest in aligning peoples along a spectrum running from primitive to civilized. They find civility, modesty, and politeness in virtually all cultures. In other words, they are more concerned with the similarities between peoples than with their differences.[9]

The Americas come first because Bernard found there the most telling evidence of universal religious impulses. But that evidence could be telling only if there was some relationship between the Americans and other peoples. Therefore Bernard opens the first volume on idolatry with a general essay on the peoples of the Americas and "the conformity of their customs with those of other ancient and modern peoples." He begins by reviewing the literature on the origin of the Americans and concludes that they must have come by land from "Tartary," the northern Asian lands that now comprise Siberia, Turkestan, Greater Mongolia, and Manchuria. Bernard was hardly original in advancing this view, which had already been articulated by José de Acosta at the end of the sixteenth century. Europe, Asia, and Africa were all populated from the same source, Bernard concludes, which means that all peoples share a common origin. He did not hold this position, it goes almost without saying, because it facilitated the expectation that all peoples could be converted to Christianity. He held to this belief because it made it possible for him to talk about "human nature" and in particular its penchant for idolatry.[10]

With common origins established and the universality of his findings made possible, Bernard then goes on to consider the question of idolatry in general. There are two kinds of idolatry, he writes. The first renders to the stars and the elements what is properly due to God. The second, which takes men as its object, is much more pernicious. The first tries to make God more palpable and in the process ennobles mankind; it errs primarily in multiplying the idea of God many times over. The second, based on pride and fear, builds temples in God's name and stocks them full of "baubles" supposedly agreeable to him. These temples and their objects promote all the "bizarre opinions" that have not ceased to multiply ever since. Should the reader not get the drift, Ber-

L'INITITIATION des JEUNES GENS reçeus au rang des HOMMES.

Les FUNERAÏLLES des CAFRES et HOTTANTOTS.

9.1   Picart's depiction of Africa. Picart drew these scenes himself, and they show some of his characteristic landscape effects. They also set up comparisons to other cultures since they focus on initiation (top) and a funeral ceremony (bottom). B. Picart del. 1729; CC, vol. IV, Africa section, facing p. 47. (Research Library, The Getty Research Institute, Los Angeles, California)

nard asks the Bayle-inspired rhetorical question: "Are all these different cults, all these extraordinary feelings less disagreeable to God than the incredulity of an Atheist? It is doubtful." But Bernard does not stop there; rather than making an argument for atheism, he is using the threat of atheism to hammer home his larger point that natural religion is threatened everywhere by the self-interested institutional elaborations controlled by priests and other authority figures.[11]

Power distorts, in other words, and takes people away from an inner simplicity. It could happen anywhere. In a matter of a few centuries, Bernard insists, a "Christian prince . . . who banished the arts and the sciences from his state" would render his people as "savage as those in Brazil." In every religion the clergyman puts himself forward "primarily to establish his dominion over the consciences" of the people. To accomplish their aims the clergy must appear to possess "particular secrets" that enable them to intercede in heaven. Similar manipulations can be seen among savages, Brahmins, dervishes, and the bonzes and talapoins of the Buddhists. Perched in their temples, they work their charms by words and gestures and aim to convince their people that "God is always miraculous and an enemy of simplicity." The priests claim that God never communicates with humans in a natural way; he communicates only by extraordinary signs. Not surprisingly, the priests are best placed to interpret his message.[12]

These criticisms of idolatry notwithstanding, compared with their predecessors who had often lumped idolators together in a negative way, Bernard and Picart split them into distinctive groups with separate cultures. Nothing makes the contrast clearer than a fascinating engraving published by Pieter van der Aa in 1729 but no doubt based on earlier models. It juxtaposes the most bizarre religious practices that Europeans had discovered in their travels. In this one print Japanese beggars; hermits eating excrement; Indians hanging over burning coals and even killing themselves; and Mexicans committing human sacrifice for their god Vitzliputzli compete for the viewer's attention. The only place where Picart makes similarly global comparisons is in his opening frontispiece (see Figure I.2), in which pagans are shown rather indistinctly and benignly in the background while the allegorized evils of Catholicism take center stage. Picart's engravings sometimes group together different gods or practices within a given culture, but not the gods of separate cultures (see Figure 9.5 below). Readers must infer his

9.2 Taking cultural comparison literally. In this Dutch print, idolatrous religions from around the world are presented side by side. Picart did not mix cultures in this way. From "Prêtres mendians et sacrifians aux Divinitez des Mexiquains," plate 7, vol. 28, Amérique, tome 1–2, *La galerie agreable du monde*, 66 vols. in 27 (Leiden: Pierre vander Aa, [1729?]). (By permission of The New York Public Library)

analogies and comparisons among religions by juxtaposing engravings of different groups. True insight can be achieved only by careful and systematic examinations.

Bernard designed his text to guide the reader through the comparative process. Both the section on the Americas and those on Eastern religions begin with essays that emphasize commonalities. His opening piece on the Americas compares birth, marriage, and funeral ceremonies in both North and South America and in addition considers language, dress, agriculture, commerce, and warfare. Analogies with European practices abound. The polygamy found in the Americas, for example, "is the polygamy of the ancient Jews." Bernard starts the section on India, which comes right after that on the Americas, with an essay by a French traveler first published in 1704; it analyzes the similarity between the customs of the East Indians and those of the Jews and other ancient peoples. John Toland translated that essay into English the following year, and clearly he saw in it grist for his own mill of religious speculation. Like Bernard and Picart, he believed that in the end there is just one universal natural religion.[13]

After laying out commonalities in the introductory essays, Bernard then directs the reader's attention to the practices and customs of particular groups, one by one. Picart's engravings play a major role in these ethnographic sections. The opening essays, by contrast, are not usually illustrated, except for a vignette on the first page of the essay on the Americas. While Bernard and Picart cannot offer a view of the idolatrous religions from the inside, as they do with Judaism, Catholicism, and Protestantism, they can present eyewitness accounts of missionaries and travelers, often very recent ones. In both text and engravings they consistently shine the most favorable light possible on customs and practices. They never announce this strategy, instead define their work as an attempt to offer just "a simple historical report" rather than a philosophical disquisition. Several tactics stand out nonetheless, ranging from the order in which they present religions to their choice of customs to illustrate and the manner in which they depict such rites.[14]

They begin their discussion of the Americas with the indigenous peoples of Canada and only gradually move southward toward the much better known, if not infamous, Aztecs and Incas. In the pages on the "Canadians" (mainly the Iroquois and Hurons of New France) and the peoples of the Mississippi Valley, both text and engravings focus on their courtship, marriage, and funeral rites, which emphasizes their relatively pacific nature. Picart based his engravings of Canadian courtship and marriage (see Figure 6.14) on prints that had appeared in a 1703 book by a renegade French military officer turned explorer, Louis Armand de Lom d'Arce, baron de La Hontan. La Hontan had gone to New France to fight the Iroquois but ultimately found them hardly more savage or brutal than the French themselves. He spent the last years of his life in exile in England, Holland, and northern Germany. His books about New France enjoyed great success in the early eighteenth century, appearing in several French and English editions as well as in Dutch, German, and Italian translation. Picart did not follow La Hontan's lead slavishly, however, for whereas the illustrations in La Hontan reproduced simple and even crude sketches, showing the sticklike figures in static, unadorned poses, Picart's engravings sought to elevate the Canadians, rendering them either classical or contemporary European in appearance and setting them in a vibrant scene with engaged spectators gathered around an unlikely Oriental carpet.[15]

A similar strategy is evident in Bernard's accompanying text. He uses the best sources available, including La Hontan, the Catholic missionary Louis Hennepin, and the French official Claude-Charles Bacqueville de la Potherie, who published a four-volume book on the natives of New France in 1722, just as Bernard and Picart were preparing their volume. Bernard claims to prefer the simple style of Hennepin to the literary embellishments of La Hontan, yet he cannot agree with the Catholic missionary's insistence that the peoples of North America have only the most confused notions of the Divine and no religious practices worth analyzing. All the different names that appear in the many languages of these peoples, Bernard contends, most likely "express the same idea. It is the universal Spirit that gives being and movement to matter." They too are, in short, natural pantheists.[16]

At the same time, Bernard cannot simply rely on La Hontan, who is more interested in showing the despotism and incomprehension of the Jesuits than he is in understanding the range of native religious practices. La Hontan assures his readers that the natives have meaningful and consistent religious beliefs, but he does not endeavor to understand them ethnographically; he simply asserts that they are not as nonsensical as portrayed by the Jesuits. He glosses over the differences between

9.3 Canadian courtship in La Hontan. This is a wonderful example of Picart's adaptation of previous sources. Even the Oriental carpet in Figure 6.14 had its rationale. From Louis Armand de Lom d'Arce, baron de Lahonatan, *Nouveaux voyages de Mr. le baron de Lahontan dans l'Amérique septentrionale*, 2 vols. (The Hague: Frères l'Honoré, marchands libraires, 1703), II: following p. 130. (Reproduced by permission of The Huntington Library, San Marino, California)

groups in favor of one native point of view, represented by his interlocutor Adario, chief of the Hurons, who is clearly a fictionalized character devised to serve La Hontan's aim of deriding the Jesuit missionaries.[17]

Bacqueville de la Potherie shares none of La Hontan's disdain for the missionaries or for the French military, and unlike La Hontan he frequently labels native beliefs absurd and ridiculous, though deserving of compassion. Yet Bacqueville provides a wealth of firsthand information about the differences in religious and secular practices not only between Hurons and Iroquois but among the different tribes within each nation. Bernard exploits the information provided by his sources to develop an ethnographic view that is not only sensitive to differences but also discerns underlying similarities between cultures that will make strange practices less incomprehensible. When he gives a brief rendition of La Hontan's much longer account of the way the Iroquois kill their prisoners, for example, Bernard refers to the ritual as "a kind of sacrifice," thereby establishing a link between religious and martial practices and between the native Americans and the ancient pagans. Even scalping has an ethnographic past. None of Bernard's contemporaries took such a large step toward cultural relativism.[18]

After Canada and the Mississippi Valley come "Virginia" and "Florida," where the engravings show the indigenous peoples before and after—but not during—war, once again reflecting Picart's desire to downplay the battle itself in favor of scenes of mourning. Although Bernard mentions the practice among some Floridians of sacrificing their firstborn children to the sun and remarks that scalping of defeated enemies is common, his text also focuses on priests, festivals, and gods rather than on acts of brutality. Picart contributes an engraving, which he drew himself, about the sacrifice of a firstborn to the sun, but he chooses to show the ritual dance beforehand rather than to render the moment of sacrifice itself.[19]

Only upon arrival in Mexico and then Peru are any scenes of violence graphically depicted. Yet even here, given the lurid representations of human sacrifice that were available to them from earlier works, Bernard and Picart choose to downplay cruelty in favor of descriptions of festivals, processions, marriages, and especially funerals. Bernard and Picart do not try to efface human sacrifice from the account; engravings based on well-known prototypes show the sacrifice of captives in Mexico and Peru (see Figure 6.12). Bernard asks, "Can one find some

FLORIDIENNES, qui ayant perdu leurs maris, a la guerre, viennent implorer l'assistance du ROY.
HERMAFRODITES, destinez a servir les malades, et a enterrer les morts.

Veuves de la FLORIDE, qui sement leurs cheveux sur les Tombeaux de leurs Maris.

9.4   Florida Indian women in mourning. The captions read: (top) "Floridian women who, having lost their husbands in war, now implore the the king for assistance. Hermaphrodites, destined to serve the sick and to bury the dead." (bottom) "The widows of Florida, who spread their hair in the tombs of their husbands." The original De Bry image of the top half showed armed Spanish soldiers and Floridian men with bows, arrows, and clubs, rather than hermaphrodites, who appear elsewhere in Theodor De Bry's *Grands Voyages,* part IV. B. Picart, sculp. dir. 1721; CC, vol. III, facing p. 132. (Research Library, The Getty Research Institute, Los Angeles, California)

idea of humanity in the barbarism of these Sacrifices?" He answers that
these practices must have arisen out of the need to appease angry gods.
In any case, he insists, the brutalities of Aztecs and Incas have to be
viewed in the harsh light cast by their conquerors: "It would be difficult
to reconcile the civility of these peoples with the barbarism of their religion, whose worship consisted principally of sacrificing men and offering their blood to idols: but one would have the same trouble reconcil-
ing the gentleness and humanity of Christianity with the barbarism of
the Spanish toward the peoples that they subjugated in this powerful
empire of the New World."[20]

The text and engravings usually refer to Mexicans and Peruvians,
rather than to Aztecs and Incas, in part because Bernard and Picart believed that life had changed dramatically for these peoples in the after-
math of Spanish conquest and conversion. Still, Bernard follows standard practice in ascribing to the Aztecs and Incas a higher degree of
civilization than characterized the more savage Indians of North America: the Aztecs and Incas replaced a profusion of idols with organized
cults and savage tribes with peoples governed by laws and political hier-
archies. In this, their trajectories resemble that of the Jews. For once,
Bernard does not seem intent on tracing the corruption of Aztec and
Inca religion over time, perhaps because the intervention of the Spanish
changes the storyline. He nonetheless draws attention to the overween-
ing role of "priests," especially in human sacrifice.[21]

In general, then, the account valorizes the peoples of the New World,
especially those of North America: they are more egalitarian and contented than Europeans, they live simple lives, and they are less dissi-
pated and more devoted to their families, especially their children, than
are Christian Europeans. Even in matters of dress, Bernard compares
seemingly bizarre native ornamentation to the powder used by "little
modern masters" to whiten their hair or their wigs. Although it was difficult to give good press to human sacrifice among the Aztecs and Incas,
Bernard and Picart came very close to articulating the "noble savage"
that Rousseau would idealize thirty years later.[22]

The section on the Americas is immediately followed by a long consideration of India, which opens the treatment of Eastern religions because Indian religious practices had been most often compared with
those of the ancient pagans and Jews. From India, readers proceed
to places less often compared with Europe and less familiar to them.

Within India, the discussion opens with the Banians and then takes up the Brahmins because their practices had long intrigued Europeans. First come four "dissertations" from recent or well-known published works, beginning with that of the French traveler from 1704 drawing comparisons to the practices of the ancient Greeks and Romans. This piece is followed by a French translation of a work by Henry Lord first published in English in 1630, a French translation of a Dutch work by Abraham Roger (or Rogerius) first published in 1651 (and considerably reworked), and one by an unnamed author, who was Portuguese according to the preface, on the gods of the Indians. This last dissertation, which first appeared in print in 1709, is followed by a long letter written by a Jesuit missionary in India to one of his colleagues, which was first published in Paris in 1711 in a collection of Jesuit missionary letters.[23]

In this letter the Jesuit priest Bouchet assures his correspondent that most Indians have nothing at all to do with "the absurdities of atheism"; they drew their religion in the first place from the books of the Old Testament and the prophets, and their fables and worship of idols have only corrupted, not completely effaced, these original notions about the Divinity. The general framework thus established in an apparently evenhanded fashion, Bernard then appends his own supplement that parallels his long essay on the Americas. Here the Indian gods, religious practices, and social customs are described in great detail. The supplement carries over into the next volume, which then goes on to discuss Burma, Thailand, Tonkin (Vietnam), the Moluccas, Java, and Ceylon (Sri Lanka) before proceeding to a more detailed examination of China, Japan, and Africa. Picart's engravings of India appear for the most part in this original "supplement," which was written by Bernard himself and set in a larger font than the preceding dissertations taken from other sources.[24]

Although Bernard and Picart depict many of the same exotic practices in India that had attracted the attention of their predecessors, such as *sati* (widow burning) and various forms of asceticism, they do so in a generally more respectful fashion. At the end of the seventeenth and beginning of the eighteenth centuries, European representations of Indian gods started to move away from the earlier denigration of them as monsters, and Europeans began to develop a genuine interest in the customs and religious practices of other peoples. Knowledge of other peoples no longer served only the purpose of religious conversion; increasingly it served as a platform for questioning the previously unquestionable nature of European customs. Bernard and Picart were developing their approach at an important turning point in European understanding of non-Western religions. The almost obsessional focus on linguistic etymologies, allegories, and attempts to trace the diffusion of Egyptian beliefs, Judaism, and even early Christianity that had characterized sixteenth- and seventeenth-century scholarship now increasingly gave way to more sustained efforts to get at the internal logic of exotic beliefs. Bernard had elements of both these types of analysis in his text, but he gave much greater weight to the latter than to the former. This emphasis is most apparent in the lengthy discussions and frequent depictions of birth, marriage, and funeral ceremonies found in each culture. Moreover, neither Bernard nor Picart showed any interest in repeating the much-published stories of the persecution of Christian missionaries by stubborn idolatrous natives. They remained entirely focused on the natives and their religions.[25]

Picart's opening engraving for the second volume on idolatry is a particularly telling example of his effort to capture the essence of an exotic set of practices. In this stunning double-page plate, Picart renders many of the most commonly depicted ascetic penances, such as hook swinging, but he does so in an invariably more aesthetic fashion than his predecessors. He also includes a mischievously pornographic moment on the far right (a scene sanitized in the Catholic bowdlerization and in the English translation) in which the ascetic's sexual temptation is taken to extremes. Picart based his print on a simpler plate in Jean-Baptiste Tavernier's *Six Voyages*, first published in French in 1676 (a book in his personal library). For some of the figures Picart used Indian miniatures that he had seen and reproduced for other books (the two women in the group on the lower left, for example, see Figure 6.8). Even amid temptations, none of the "fakirs" depicted seem absurd or clownish despite their long hair and nakedness. In the text, the ascetic practices are compared to those of the early Christians. Seemingly in passing and somewhat incongruously, Bernard raises a question about the belief that informs asceticism: Is the famous late seventeenth-century Huguenot voyager Jean Chardin right in attributing them to metempsychosis (the transmigration of souls) and other such more or less irrational doctrines?[26]   → *re.incarnation*

Repeatedly in the discussion of pagan idolatry Bernard returns to

9.5   Indian practices of penance. Personally drawn by Picart from various sources, the image is one of his most remarkable. B. Picart del. 1729; CC, vol. IV, after p. 8. (Research Library, The Getty Research Institute, Los Angeles, California)

this curious doctrine. He reprints a long letter on metempsychosis from the missionary Bouchet and puts it between the second half of his supplement on India and the section of the volume that covers China and Japan. The letter identifies idolatry with a specific belief, and it claims widespread adherence to the doctrine across Asia even, as Bernard points out, among the Siamese and the Javanese. Indeed, so well does the Bouchet letter on metempsychosis fit the purposes of Bernard and Picart that one can only wonder about the Jesuit's orthodoxy. Bouchet finds the "monstrous," "ridiculous," "extravagant," and "chimerical" doctrine in India, Siam (Thailand), Cambodia, Indochina, China, Japan, Africa, and even the Americas. La Hontan, too, had found metempsychosis alive and well among the natives of New France. Belief in the transmigration of souls could be found closer to home, too, says

229

9.6 Detail from Figure 9.5. It is not surprising that the kneeling woman was effaced in both the English translation and the bowdlerized Catholic version of 1741. (Research Library, The Getty Research Institute, Los Angeles, California)

Bouchet, among the Druids, the original Christian heretics like the Manicheans and Gnostics, and the Jews as well. Some scholars, Bouchet reports, believed that metempsychosis had its origins among the ancient Egyptians, others among the ancient Indians. The doctrine constituted, in other words, something like an original, foundational belief existing outside the established doctrines and churches, just the kind of belief that Bernard and Picart were seeking. They did not have to argue for its appeal across cultures; Bouchet did that for them. The comment

9.7   The prototype from Tavernier's *Six Voyages*. Jean-Baptiste Tavernier, *Les six voyages de Jean-Baptiste Tavernier*, 2 vols. (Utrecht: Guillaume, 1712). (Courtesy Young Research Library, UCLA)

on metempsychosis with which Bernard opens his introduction to the section on India is revealed to be a tease: "No one among us believes in it, at least not in the manner of the Brahmins."[27]

Although it was widely known at the time of Bernard and Picart's labors that the ancient Greeks, not least among them Plato, believed in the transmigration of souls, what may not be self-evident from our distance is the heretical potential the doctrine offered intellectual radicals and seekers after religious truth in the eighteenth century. Metempsychosis perfectly captures the complexity of religious perspectives—born out of the "crisis of the European mind"—found in the first generation that forged the principal ideas of the European Enlightenment. Benjamin Furly, of Quaker background and from whose library the Knights of Jubilation got the manuscript that became *The Treatise on the Three Impostors,* privately held to the originally Pythagorean notion that after death the soul lives on by migrating into the body of another. Furly may have gotten the idea from his close friend Francis Mercury van Helmont, who took it from Kabbalistic sources. In his pantheistic and materialist work *Letters to Serena* (1704) Toland argues that when we die we only "cease to be what we formerly were, so to be born is to begin to be something which we were not before." There is only birth and death followed by rebirth. Some Quakers given to heterodoxy might imagine metempsychosis as preceding an ultimate salvation, while deists with materialist leanings could incorporate it into their search for a universal religion entirely human in origin.[28]

Bernard knew the writings of Toland well and may even have known him personally during the brief period when both were living in the Dutch Republic. It is possible, then, that Toland was the source of this interest. In any case, Bernard signaled his personal investment in the matter by republishing in 1714 a work that had appeared only two years before, Michel Mourgues's *Plan théologique du pythagorisme.* Mourgues, a Jesuit like Bouchet, had examined metempsychosis as one of the three cardinal moral principles of ancient philosophers (along with the immortality of the soul and the judgment of souls after death). He presumably wrote his work for entirely pious reasons, using metempsychosis to show the superiority of the analytical powers of the early church fathers who combated it. Yet even he thought of Pythagoreanism as a kind of primitive philosophy and theology, and he used the occasion to recount the many ancient Western forms of the doctrine and also told of its presence in India and Siam. He related the doctrine to the belief among the Indians that all of nature is animated and interchangeable; all souls participate in this constant movement to other bodies. Bernard may well have republished this work because he, like Picart, had encountered the idea in the vast network of internationally connected and enlightened seekers after alternatives to absolutist forms of Christian orthodoxy. Like Furly, Toland, and Collins, Picart and Bernard belonged to that network.[29]

Freethinkers also encountered metempsychosis through the works of Giordano Bruno. When living in Holland Toland carried with him one of his favorite books, a rare copy of Bruno's *Lo Spaccio della bestia trion-fante* [The expulsion of the triumphant beast], first published in London in 1584, a work that advocated, among various heresies, metempsychosis. It appeared in an anonymous English translation in 1713, probably inspired if not translated personally by Toland. The translation found its way into the library of Furly. Bruno, a renegade Dominican, was burned at the stake in Rome in 1600 for his heretical views. A pantheist before anyone had invented the term, Bruno argued for the interchangeability of all matter and spirit. A century after Bruno's death at the hands of the Roman Inquisition, Toland revived interest in his philosophy and provided a new vocabulary (pantheism) for what others previously had described with disdain as materialism, pagan naturalism, or hylozoism (the doctrine that life is inseparable from matter). Although Bernard might have come to his interest in metempsychosis by way of Toland or the Jesuit's account that he reprinted, Picart turned out to be the one most interested in Bruno, for he owned six of his works, never easy to find, including the Italian original of *Triumphant Beast*. With Toland's help Bruno brought back into European thought an ancient strand of speculation and provided yet another weapon in the arsenal aimed at Christian orthodoxy. Metempsychosis also appeared in 1669 in Naudé's *Apology for All the Great Men who have been Accused of Magic,* a key text for freethinkers and a book owned by both Picart and Bernard and republished by Bernard. In the 1720s when the young Benjamin Franklin turned toward deism he also gave credence to the doctrine. Later, Romantic poets and philosophers would celebrate the soul's migrations. At least one of them, the English Romantic poet Robert Southey, got his information directly from *Religious Ceremonies of the World,* for he cites it in his notebooks.[30]

Metempsychosis rendered hell—and for some people, eternal life in general—irrelevant. It also offered a tidy way of getting around the Calvinist doctrine, so central to much of orthodox Protestantism, of predestination. The soul of someone predestined to go to hell, despite that person's having lived an exemplary life, was given a second chance at death. In Bernard's account the doctrine was to be found everywhere among the religious beliefs of the East. It had treacherous associations because the belief in the transmigration of souls usually went hand in hand with a metaphysics that reduced nature to matter in motion and allowed nature to be coterminous with God. Although not a believer in metempsychosis, Spinoza believed in such matter, as did Toland, though Toland added his own particular twist on materialism that enlisted Newton's science to the cause. Motion can be inherent in matter, so in a sense everything can turn into something else eternally, because the Newtonian laws of motion are imbedded in nature. From Toland's science-based materialism through to that of Diderot and d'Holbach later in the eighteenth century there is a straight metaphysical line to Marx.[31]

To materialism Bernard added an ethnographic dimension by reminding Europeans, by means of Bouchet's account, that the ancient books of the Indians of the East held to the same pantheistic metaphysics that made transmigration possible: "One finds in the books of the ancient Indians that the souls are a fragment of the substance of God himself." This sovereign being "has scattered himself in all the parts of the Universe in order to animate it," and he vivifies and renews all beings. Indeed Father Bouchet claims to have spoken to a Brahmin who thought that "a portion of the Divinity . . . animates men." Yet others among the Indians believe "that God is an extremely subtle air . . . that souls reunite themselves with God . . . and are purified by multiple Metempsychoses." The Jesuit's letter on metempsychosis ostensibly decries the belief while detailing the many versions of it found in the world. Always insisting on letting readers decide for themselves, Bernard has managed to give one of the most detailed accounts of metempsychosis to be found in print. He simultaneously lends credibility to a notion that had circulated among heterodox Protestant visionaries and draws attention to the multicultural origins of the emerging European Enlightenment. Bernard used his Jesuit sources well.[32]

The sections that follow Bouchet's letter, first on China and Japan, and then on Persia, do not give the same prominence to metempsychosis as a doctrine, but they concern, in essence, some of the same issues, both religious and metaphysical. Is there a natural religion that precedes the known official religions? If so, what are its core beliefs? The section on Persia, for example, focuses on Zoroastrianism as a kind of primitive religion that precedes Islam in the region and that shares many elements with primitive Judaism and primitive Christianity. The section on China and Japan is even more hard-hitting because in it Bernard begins immediately with the question of atheism. The section opens, "Father Martini maintains that in the Chinese language there is no

[margin handwritten note: Jesuit, credible source + widespread belief]

particular name that can suitably refer to God. That establishes a kind of prejudice favorable to those who believe that the Chinese are atheists."[33]

Martini's conclusion echoed those of missionaries to the peoples of the New World, who mistakenly considered the natives atheists. Bernard would have none of it, but when he turned to China and Japan, the issue of Eastern religiosity was at that moment a hot topic. For many years a controversy had raged within the Catholic Church about the so-called Chinese rites. The Jesuits had been allowing Chinese converts to continue ancestor worship on the grounds that it was a civil and not a religious practice and therefore not incompatible with Christianity. In 1700 the theology faculty of the Sorbonne condemned the books on Chinese religion by the Jesuit Louis Le Comte as "false, brazen, scandalous, impious, contrary to the word of God, and heretical." Le Comte had argued, most controversially, that the Chinese had known the true God for centuries before the birth of Christ. He insisted that they had honored God in ways that could serve as an example to Christians, that they worshiped God in the oldest temple known in the world, and that their morals were pure at a time when Europe and most of the rest of the world lived in error and corruption. The Chinese had only become idolators, Le Comte maintained, five or six hundred years after the death of Christ. Who was to be Bernard's most-cited source on China? Louis Le Comte.[34]

An analogy would have leapt to the minds of contemporaries: the Chinese lapsed into idolatry at roughly the same time—after the emperor Constantine (d. 337)—that altars and Christian icons came to replace the pagan domestic gods so beloved by the Romans. In vain had iconoclastic Christian reformers tried to remove or deface the images of God and the saints that then proliferated, only to lose the struggle to a form of Christianity that reveled in images of saints, the Virgin, Christ, and even God himself. The Chinese followed the same pattern of descent into idolatry as had the Christian Church itself. Bernard once again cites Le Comte in arguing that the first Chinese emperors knew a true religion, but that superstitions gradually crept in and corrupted this original religion over the long run. In general, moreover, Bernard's own editorializing and comparisons find every occasion to accent the similarities between "idolators" and monotheists. Even some of the medical magic practiced by the Chinese, like prescribing rice and fish as cura-

[handwritten margin note: → and at the same time]

tive, resembles the Dutch tradition of selling herring as a cure for ill-ness. Although many religions see the body as "the prison" of the soul, both the peoples of the East and the peoples of the West seek to nur-ture and conserve it: "One senses the conformity that is found between these ideas."[35]

Like Le Comte, Bernard paid special attention to Confucius, whom he depicted in the most laudatory terms: "Who would not believe on reading the story of such a beautiful moral system and of such an excel-lent practice of its injunctions that *Confucius* was Christian and that he had learned the teachings of J.[esus] C.[hrist]. Notice in particular *this integrity, which was a gift from Heaven and of which man has been de-prived.*" Confucius, then, served as a kind of universal moral exemplar, parallel to Jesus. Since he preceded Jesus by some 500 years, his very existence might be taken as proof of the universality of natural religion. Still, Confucius could not hold back the inevitable decay of that natu-ral religion in China any more than Jesus could prevent the subsequent deterioration of the Christian Church.[36]

Bernard and Picart did the best they could to present an accurate view of Chinese, Japanese, and other Asian religions, which was no easy matter given their complexity and variety. Bernard offered capsule his-tories of Laotun (Laozi, founder of Daoism) and Fo or Foe and his followers (Buddhists) in China and Sintos (Shintos) and Budsdoists (Buddhists) in Japan, for example, almost always in a relatively positive light. For Japan he relied quite heavily on a book by Engelbert Kaempfer that had appeared for the first time, in English, in 1727, the year before he published the volume that included Japan. Its French translation only appeared in 1729. In short, Bernard spared no effort to get the best up-to-date information.

Similarly, Picart's engravings stayed close to the depictions available to him in the travel literature. Although Picart did not neglect the op-portunity to portray exotic gods and goddesses in striking, even life-like poses, he did so when the models he had to hand permitted those interpretations. Many of his Asian prints are based on those in Olfert Dapper's collection of voyages by merchants from the Dutch East In-dia Company; Dapper published his collection in Dutch in 1670, and it appeared in English and German soon afterward. Picart's double plate engraving of the Temple of 1,000 Idols (the temple of Sanjūsangen-dō in Kyoto still stands today) is based on a print in Arnoldus Montanus's collection of voyages to Japan that was first published in Dutch in 1669 and immediately translated into English. In this case, however, Picart did not simply copy the preceding work. He changed the placement of the human figures to create a greater sense of vivacity, and he turned some shadowy sculptural reliefs on the top tier in Montanus into much scarier half-human, half-animal figures. In the text, Bernard compares the descriptions of the temple available to him and concludes that the central figure must be Amida and the thousand idols representations of Canon, his son. But he notes that Kaempfer insists that the temple is dedicated to Quanwon (the next engraving in the volume is of Quanwon copied from Kaempfer's book). These approximations turn out to be reasonably accurate, as the temple is now thought to be dedicated to the god or goddess of mercy Kannon (represented as either male or female), whose Chinese name is Guanyin, and Kannon is considered to be an assistant or companion to Amida, who is a reincarnation of the Buddha. Bernard even speculates that Canon, Quanon, and Quanwon probably all refer to the same god.[37]

Bernard and Picart had to work with the names handed down in the sources, and they can hardly be blamed if early eighteenth-century travelers did not understand that many of the different gods, such as Xekia, Ninifo, and Daybot, were different incarnations of the Buddha, though Bernard in a footnote explicitly says that Budso is the same as Fo, Xaca, Sommonacodom, Budhu, Witznou (Vishnu), Chacabout, and so on. Europeans did not understand all the connections between forms of Buddhism in different countries, and indeed they did not yet use the label "Buddhism" as an all-encompassing category, but Bernard read his sources carefully enough to see the religious similarities across Asian cultures. He knew that Fo and Budso both had sources in India and that they were somehow related to each other. Buddhism would not become the object of sustained study in the West until the 1820s and even later.[38]

Whereas Confucius interested Bernard from a moral point of view, the sect of Fo fascinated him for philosophical reasons. Most Chinese and Japanese were not atheists, according to Bernard. He knew that the "philosophers" or "new philosophers" (neo-Confucians), Shintos, and Buddhists (followers of Fo or Foe, as he was known in the early 1700s) were often accused of atheism, even by Le Comte, who claimed that the followers of Fo promoted metempsychosis and atheism as well as idola-

TEMPLE du JAPON en il y a mille IDOLES.

9.8   Temple of 1,000 Idols in Japan. B. Picart sculp. dir. 1726; CC, vol. IV, following p. 310. (Research Library, The Getty Research Institute, Los Angeles, California)

try. But here Bernard wanted to separate himself from Le Comte by distinguishing between doctrines held privately by an intellectual elite (the literati) and those taken up by the masses. There may well be "systematic atheists" in China and Japan, he confesses, just as there are "among us." But Bernard ascribes to the Chinese a natural religion far more interesting and nuanced than mere atheism.[39]

In Bernard's words, the esoteric literati doctrine, unfit for the masses, resembles "Spinozism." To lay out the principles of this doctrine, Bernard relied on the synthetic account of Chinese religion provided by Charles Le Gobien, one of the most prominent defenders of the Jesuit position in the Chinese rites controversy. Le Gobien had not himself been to China, but he was procurator (agent) of the French Jesuit mission in China and organized the publication of Jesuit accounts in *Lettres édifiantes*, a series that began in 1702 and continued, with different editors, until 1776. Le Gobien had distinguished between the neo-Confucian philosophers and the Buddhists, condemning in particular the latter, but Bernard emphasizes the similarities between the literati, whether followers of Fo or of Confucius.[40]

The literati adhered to a secret doctrine according to which they saw in nature "only Nature itself" (and no transcendent divine presence). "One would not dare to hazard a guess," Bernard comments wryly, "as to whether this Nature is a Being different from Matter." This coyness is typical of Bernard; he would not take a stand in print on that most controversial and heretical of issues in Europe, pantheistic materialism. Beginning in the late seventeenth century, freethinkers, deists, and heretics of various stripes had challenged what they considered the simplistic notion of a transcendent Deity. Some jumped ship altogether and became systematic atheists, as Bernard calls them. Others, like Toland, with help from Bruno and Spinoza, articulated a metaphysics of matter in motion within Nature that could also be divine (the divine being immanent in nature rather than nature's creator).[41]

Bernard's subsequent exposition makes the literati also seem like believers in metempsychosis, though he does not use the term explicitly. Man was created by the accidental conjunction of gross and subtle forms of matter (therefore not directly by God), and the soul, which is the purest portion of matter (and not something else in substance), "finishes with the body when its parts are disturbed and is reborn with it when chance returns those parts to their first state." The literati believe that the world has a beginning and an end, Bernard explains, but once the world ends another commences and so on infinitely into the past and infinitely into the future (therefore defying the biblical chronology). Most Europeans would have read the Chinese and Japanese as atheists if that was what their most learned wise men believed. Bernard sets out to complicate the picture while at the same time allying the Eastern religions with the most virulent Western heresies. But he does not want to use the label atheism; "there is as much injustice in calling them atheists (the term atheist taken in its most precise meaning) as there would be in regarding the idolators of antiquity as such." That categorization would violate the tenets of the universal natural religion that his text and Picart's images seek to recapture.[42]

Consequently, Bernard denies that even the literati are atheists in the strict sense of the word (holding that there is no God at all), though it is clear that they adhere to materialist and pantheist views that would be considered atheistic by orthodox Christians. Bernard does not deny, however, that the Chinese and Japanese are for the most part idolators. Even the literati can be considered idolators with their ceremonies of ancestor worship, but like Bernard and Picart and their cosmopolitan friends in Holland, the literati resist the "gross" forms of idolatry so common in both the ancient and the modern world, that is, they do not mistake statues or other objects for real beings. The literati have seen through the idolatry peddled by the clergy of the various sects. They are not taken in, as are the common people, by the trickery and manipulation of the bonzes, talapoins, and monks. The priests got their fabulous temples and monasteries by convincing their followers that disobedience would lead after death to a cruel and constant metempsychosis in which their souls would return as rats, mice, mules, or asses.[43]

In case the parallel to Western religions is not evident, Bernard compares the appearance of some Chinese clerics dressed in black and wearing prayer beads with their Catholic counterparts. Once again the fundamental tension in the work becomes apparent: on the one hand, Bernard and Picart want to align idolatry with a universal story of the decline of natural religion, exemplified in particular by the corruption of Roman Catholicism; but on the other hand, they want to show the intrinsic interest of all the varieties of religious practice around the world. They do not simply echo the line taken in *The Treatise of the Three Impostors,* which summarily dismisses all the monotheistic religions as products of fear and the superstitions inculcated in the masses by manipulative priests. That was a short treatise; in contrast, Bernard and Picart supply more than 3,000 pages, most of which concern the inner workings of the different religions. So after recounting the intellectual complexity of Chinese doctrines in 19 folio pages that include only 1 page of engravings by Picart of Xekia (the Buddha), Bernard then goes on to offer 30 sumptuously illustrated pages on different Chinese gods and idols; 30 pages on Chinese priests, festivals, and medicine (with some of the more stereotypical images of Chinese mendicants); 2 smaller sections on Chinese science and the emperors; and finally, 22 pages on marriage and funeral ceremonies and the education of children.[44]

This last section is graced by only a single engraving, but it is one of Picart's most striking efforts, a double-page plate titled "Funeral Train for an Important Person in China." Picart's engravings of the Chinese gods and idols in earlier sections often emphasized their monumental size and the way they dwarfed their human worshipers, yet the funeral idol featured in this procession is smaller than the humans who carry it. The artist has clearly labored to make the Chinese funeral procession seem familiar rather than strange. With its mixture of children, priests, musicians, acrobats, and even fireworks, the procession includes elements of Roman Catholic processions and European municipal parades; if anything, this procession is less alien than the Roman Catholic processions in volumes one and two. Picart goes out of his way to aestheticize the event in ways intelligible to Europeans; the landscape on the left is Italianate, for example, while the architecture on the right is Chinese. Other than the curious idol, nothing in this depiction seems particularly strange or bizarre. Picart's print gives visual form to Bernard's formulation in the Chinese section of the essential similarity among all religions: "All religions resemble each other in something. It is this resemblance that encourages minds of a certain boldness to risk the establishment of a project of universal syncretism. How beautiful it would be to arrive at that point and to be able to make people with an overly opinionated character understand that with the help of charity one finds everywhere *brothers*." On that masonic-style note (freemasons called each other brothers, as did the Knights of Jubilation), Bernard makes crystal clear the syncretism at the heart of his message.[45]

Somehow this syncretism could be extracted out of a travel litera-

CONVOI FUNEBRE D'un GRAND de la CHINE.

9.9 Chinese funeral procession. Picart adapted an image that appeared in Olfert Dapper's 1670 compilation of Dutch East India Company missions to China. Dapper was in his personal library. B. Picart sculp. dir. 1729; CC, vol. IV, following p. 264. (Research Library, The Getty Research Institute, Los Angeles, California)

ture that was often more biased than curious. Consider, for example, the people of Java, where the Dutch had major commercial interests. Very early in the travel literature the Javanese appear in a work by Jan Huygen van Linschoten, *Itinerario,* first published in 1595 and then reworked by the De Bry family of engravers in Frankfurt. In Linschoten and De Bry the Javanese appear barely clothed and are said to "have a stubborn and harsh character." A mere ten years later another set of De Bry images began to soften their character and clothe their bodies. Later in the seventeenth century the Dutch artist Romeyn de Hooghe took up the Javanese but engraved them in such a way as to once again render them exotic. Picart had a clear choice in depicting this island people, and he chose to humanize them and evoke in his viewers a feeling of shared civility.[46]

Picart's engravings of the Javanese focus on a joyous wedding scene and feature a winding parade where first the groom goes to the house of the bride and then leads her along to the anticipated ceremony. All the participants are dressed sumptuously. The houses are made to appear sturdy and spacious (perhaps even European in style), and the fantastic images found in many other travel accounts are missing entirely. These hardly seem like cannibalistic savages, though Bernard does say in the text that some Javanese sold their old folks to cannibals. Bernard distinguishes between the idolators of the interior, who subscribe to metempsychosis but still worship one God, Creator of the Universe, and the coastal Muslims and Christians converted by the Dutch. The reader leaves the island with the set of images provided by Picart, that of a decorous marriage ceremony, much like marriage ceremonies in other places, whether exotic or closer to home.

Countless other examples of Bernard's analysis or Picart's visualization might be cited, but the piling up of examples would not change the bottom line. The peoples of the East, like the peoples of the Americas, are most often depicted with a cosmopolitan sympathy. Strange or even repellent ceremonies and customs are not overlooked, but they do not take center stage. The emphasis is on likeness and similarity, comparability above all, not incommensurability. Idolatry appears unthreatening and, moreover, highly significant for the history of humankind. When idolatries are put side by side and sifted for their essential elements, they tell the story of a universal natural religion, an impulse to believe

Premiere CEREMONIE NUPTIALE, des PEUPLES de JAVA. Le MARIÉ va chercher la MARIÉE.

Seconde CEREMONIE NUPTIALE des PEUPLES de JAVA, le MARIÉ conduit la MARIÉE chez lui.

9.10   Javanese marriage ceremonies. The captions read: (top) "First marriage ceremony of the peoples of Java. The husband goes to get his bride." (bottom) "Second marriage ceremony of the peoples of Java. The husband takes home his bride." B. Picart sculp. dir. 1726; CC, vol. IV, facing p. 134. (Research Library, The Getty Research Institute, Los Angeles, California)

that takes various forms and yet reveals, underneath its dazzling diversity, a set of universal fears and hopes.

A generation later, the great dreamer of democracy Jean Jacques Rousseau would search for a similarly universal natural religion. In his attempt to integrate religion into his new civil society shaped by the social contract, he rejected the atheism and pantheistic materialism that flourished among the Paris intelligentsia of the mid-eighteenth century. The common people, Rousseau believed, craved something simpler and more emotionally satisfying. To this end, in *Emile* he created his Savoyard vicar whose profession of faith explicitly rejected materialism:

> Imagine all your philosophers, ancient and modern, having exhausted their strange Systems of force, chance, fate, necessity, atoms, a living world, animated matter, and every variety of materialism. Then comes the illustrious [Samuel] Clarke who gives light to the world and proclaims the Being of beings and the Giver of things. . . . I believe, therefore, that the world is governed by a wise and powerful will; I see it or rather I feel it, and it is a great thing to know this.

Rousseau embraced theism as the beginning and the end of his religion. His God was probably further from Nature than Bernard or Picart would have placed him, but Rousseau nonetheless ran into trouble with some of the same religious authorities who had condemned *Religious Ceremonies of the World*. Protestant magistrates in Geneva and Catholic officials in France ordered the burning of *Emile* after its publication in Holland in 1762. The search for a universal natural religion, even a straightforwardly theistic one, remained dangerous even twenty years after Bernard and Picart finished publishing their volumes. Despite their very real differences, Rousseau, like Bernard and Picart, sought to articulate the core of a pure natural religion that no longer existed in the world.[47]

In the story told by Bernard and Picart, the demise and corruption of that natural religion occurred everywhere in the world. From Java and the Mississippi Valley to Rome, human hopes were deceived by priests and institutions that built their fortunes on fear. Yet Bernard and Picart did not rest content with simply reiterating that argument; they wanted their readers and viewers to grasp the wonder of religious diversity for themselves and draw their own conclusions. Unlike Rousseau, they never invented a wise vicar who preached the doctrine of a renewed natural religion. Instead, they urged readers to seek understanding of all the world's religions, with the hope of learning from the differences they could see in the world around them. Even the life of Muhammad and his teachings, as we shall see, could be approached with a similar open mind and found revealing for what they could tell about the people who followed Islam.

10

Rehabilitating Islam

For the most part Europeans regarded the other monotheists in the world, Muslims and Jews, as infidels. The vast majority of Europeans had laid their eyes on very few Jews and even fewer Muslims. Only in the port city of Venice in the 1570s were the number of Muslims sufficient to warrant the city's installing a special residence for these foreign visitors, the Fondaco dei Turchi, in a palazzo facing the Grand Canal. Its windows and doors were screened off so that residents could commit no "scandalous and indecent acts." For extra protection a Christian sentry stood ready at the only remaining access, prepared to stop Christian women or boys from entering. At night he locked the building up and the Muslims in. Resident Muslim ambassadors were unknown in Europe into the 1790s. When Bernard, Picart, and Picart's students set out to describe the religious beliefs and customs of Islam, they had their work cut out for them. They were utterly dependent upon what travelers and observers returning from the Middle East could tell them. In general, theirs was not a pretty story.[1]

Bernard and Picart showed their colors when they decided to devote an entire volume to Islam, or what they called, like many Europeans of the time, Mahometism. Bernard explained this choice somewhat disingenuously in the preface to the preceding volume, which covered Anglicans, Presbyterians, Quakers, Anabaptists, and various sects, including the Jansenist "convulsionaries," who believed in the healing miracles that took place at the tomb of a Jansenist priest in Paris in the 1720s. In that introductory piece Bernard claimed that the volume did not have enough space for Mahometans, and that it "might perhaps be odious" to put them with the Christians, even though they could hardly be included with the idolatrous peoples, since they were monotheists. Bernard had other reasons to give so much space to Islam, as we shall see. By offering the most comprehensive account of the time, Bernard effectively made Islam into a test case for monotheism more generally. He used it to raise a series of troubling and even subversive questions. Since Muslim rulers offered toleration to Christians and Jews, might not Christian rulers learn at least to tolerate differences within Christianity, if not to extend the same toleration to Jews and Muslims? Did the enduring success of Islam suggest the validity of deism or even atheism? Deists believed in the existence of one God but not in the Trinity or the literal truth of the Bible. Like Muslims, it could be argued, they put more emphasis on good moral conduct than on theological niceties. If Muhammad was an impostor, as Christians believed, then was Jesus one as well, as *The Treatise of the Three Impostors* had argued? Many European critics of Islam at the time worried about the connection to deism, in particular. Islam, for Bernard and Picart, therefore, was much more than the alarmingly successful story of imposture that even many educated Europeans still read into the religion of Muhammad.[2]

Bernard's treatment of Islam follows his established pattern: he compiles and adapts information from the most recent and reliable sources to develop an evidently balanced and even sympathetic account that nonetheless serves his own intellectual and moral purposes. Picart died four years before the publication of the volume on Islam, so only some of the engravings are his, though we can safely assume that he had a part in the planning for the volume. By Bernard's own report, for the first parts of the volume he relied on Henri de Boulainvilliers's life of Muhammad published in French in 1730, Jean Gagnier's life of Muhammad published in French in 1732, and George Sale's introduction to his English translation of the Koran published in 1734 (Sale, in turn, had used the new Latin translation of the Koran by the Italian Catholic priest Ludovico Marracci that was published in 1698). Since Bernard's volume appeared in 1737, it is clear that he was keeping up with new publications even as he pursued his other interests in the book trade.

Following a practice he had developed for the earlier volumes, Bernard put extracts from other works in quotation marks and footnoted them, and when he reproduced whole sections, making quotation marks too cumbersome, he clearly signaled the original source in the footnote. Thus, for example, his account of the genealogy of Muhammad came straight out of Gagnier, though the unsigned illustration of that genealogy and the similarly unsigned engraving of the Temple of Mecca both came from the 1721 French translation of a book by the Dutch Orientalist Adrian Reland.[3]

Bernard and Picart's volume brought together the best of recent work on Islam in order to show readers that Islam, like Christianity, had a long and complex history worthy of their attention and respect. Europeans had almost never taken this position before the end of the 1600s. From 711, when the Moors (Muslims) of North Africa invaded Spain, until 1683, when the Turks lifted their siege of Vienna, Europeans viewed the Arab and Turkish followers of Islam as their mortal enemies. Muhammad was the anti-Christ, an Arab devil, a polygamist and impostor. Viewed already by the Romans as robbers and wolves, the Arab followers of Muhammad were demonized twice over during the Crusades. Undertaken between 1095 and the 1270s by European Christians who aimed to push out the infidels occupying the Holy Land, the Crusades cemented the negative image of Arabs. Pope Urban II, who launched the First Crusade, pointed to the savagery of this reputedly cruel and treacherous people, who murdered Christians and pillaged churches. After the Turks of the Ottoman Empire conquered Constantinople (Istanbul) in 1453, the Turks replaced the Arabs as enemy number one. When Martin Luther wanted to attack the Catholic Church in the early sixteenth century he aligned the pope with the Turks: "The Pope is the Spirit of the Antichrist and the Turk the body of the Antichrist."[4]

Yet cracks did appear in this monolith of hostility, if only because Christian rulers sought allies wherever they could find them in their conflicts with one another. A few Europeans began to pursue a serious interest in Islam in the sixteenth and especially the seventeenth century, as increasing diplomatic and commercial relationships with the Ottoman and Safavid (Persian) empires stimulated more sustained intellectual engagement with Islam. When King Francis I of France sent an ambassador to the Ottoman ruler in 1535, one of the men sent with the ambassador, Guillaume Postel, learned Arabic, collected Arabic manuscripts, and wrote the first Arabic grammar. Similarly, Edward Pococke learned Arabic while serving as chaplain to the Levant Company in Aleppo and in 1636 became the first professor of Oriental languages at Oxford University. Persian was also the subject of increasing study, in part because Persian was the lingua franca in the eastern Islamic world, used in spoken or written form in Afghanistan and much of South Asia, and not just Persia (Iran). In 1684 Joseph Labrosse, a French Carmelite missionary to Persia, published in Amsterdam (of course!) a dictionary of Persian with translations into Latin, French, and Italian.[5]

Even as knowledge of Islam and Middle Eastern languages progressed, however, negative stereotypes still predominated. The most enduring of these concerned the founder, Muhammad, who was considered by almost all Europeans to be an impostor. On this missionaries, travelers, and even Enlightenment giants like Voltaire concurred in their judgments. Voltaire wrote a play, first performed in 1741, with the telling title *Mahomet or Fanaticism*. In it Mahomet (Muhammad) appears to be ambitious, scheming, and megalomaniacal. He promotes his new religion, not out of conviction, but rather for political reasons:

> Let us raise Arabia on the ruins of mankind:
> The blind and tottering universe demands
> Another worship, and another God. (Act II, Scene V)

"Another God" appears not through true revelation but by political calculation. Voltaire's Mahomet, not surprisingly, stops short of nothing, including murder, to achieve his ends.

Yet Voltaire's depiction of the impostor had a barely hidden motivation. The playwright uses Muhammad and Islam more generally as a way of criticizing all the monotheistic religions. Although Voltaire would never go as far as *The Treatise of the Three Impostors*, his viewers and readers got the subversive point. One police official in Paris reported to another in 1742 that the people who had seen the performance of Voltaire's play complained that it was filled with "infamies, villainies, irreligion, and impiousness." Mahomet could be seen, and was seen by many spectators, as standing in for all the founders of monotheistic religions. Similarly, in his article on the Koran in his *Philosophical Dictionary* of 1764, Voltaire repeated all the caricatures of Muhammad ("a

10.1   Romeyn de Hooghe's depiction of Muhammad. Most European artists emphasized Muhammad's martial character. From Gottfried Arnold, *Historie der Kerken en
ketteren van den beginne des Nieuwen Testaments tot aan het jaar onses Heeren 1688*, 2 vols.
(Amsterdam: Sebastiaan Petzold, 1701), vol. 1, facing p. 468. (Research Library, The Getty
Research Institute, Los Angeles, California)

[handwritten annotation: Not peaceful, like all the depictions Bernard an Picart made]

sublime and bold charlatan") and of the Koran ("a collection of ridiculous revelations") only as a way to mock the Catholic monks who had so persistently misunderstood both. "If his book is bad for our time and for us," Voltaire concluded, "it was very good for his contemporaries, and his religion even better. It must be granted that he drew almost all of Asia out of idolatry. He taught the unity of God." Voltaire himself was a deist.[6]

Gradually between 1683, when the Turks fell back from Vienna, and the high Enlightenment of the mid-1700s, Islam came to be viewed less as a cesspool of sexual licentiousness, error, and imposture (though this portrayal still had its adherents, as it does today) and more as a kind of intellectual and cultural foil for European customs and religions. It could never occupy the same place as idolatry pure and simple because Muhammad explicitly built upon the Jewish and Christian traditions and abhorred idolatry as much as they did. Muslims were not ignorant of the Christian message; they agreed with it on many points but considered Jesus only one of many prophets who had preceded Muhammad, the last of the prophets, who received the word of God himself in the Koran. The New Testament, in contrast, tells the story of Jesus and his early followers, but its contents were not revealed to Jesus and took form only after his death. Moreover, Islam was, like Christianity (and unlike Judaism), a proselytizing religion; they actively competed with each other for souls.

Islam took on new significance after the Protestant Reformation because it, too, was a breakaway religion. Protestants did not consider themselves friends of Islam, but they saw elements in that religion that they could use in their conflicts with Catholics. Protestants attributed the rise and persistence of Islam to the corruption of Roman Catholicism, and they cited Muslim toleration of other religions against Catholic rejection of any accommodation. Catholics, including Marracci in the introduction to his Latin translation of the Koran, accused Protestants of being followers of Muhammad, while Protestants retorted that Catholicism resembled Islam in its emphasis on pilgrimage, fasting, and good works. In short, Islam provided a shifting point of triangulation for European Christians; Muslims went from being the absolute other at the beginning—the despised enemy—to a potential political ally and religious touchstone.[7]

still a bad thing to be, though

Islam, rather than Judaism, also served as a point of departure for the discussion of deism. Christians had a settled narrative about their relationship to Judaism; the first Christians were Jews, after all, and the New Testament of Christianity promised the fulfillment of the prophecies of the Old Testament of the Jews. Christianity had superseded Judaism, not negated it. Islam, however, claimed to have superseded Christianity, which posed an altogether different kind of problem for Christians and explains their insistence that Muhammad was an impostor. For Christianity to be true, he had to be a false prophet. → because the 2ⁿᵈ coming of christ = Appocalipse

Deists, by contrast, could view Muhammad as no more (or less) false than Jesus; both might be seen as prophets or wise men without special access, however, to revealed truth. Moreover, deists were not particularly troubled by the existence of three different forms of monotheism. They believed that God had created the universe but that he no longer intruded in affairs on earth. They agreed, therefore, with the most fundamental tenet of all monotheisms—that there is one God, creator of the universe—but they saw little value in the trappings of organized religion. Deists could cite the very existence of three monotheistic religions as evidence for their position; if three major religious groups recognized the same one God, then belief in that one God was surely true, but, conversely, no one monotheism had a special purchase on that truth since there were after all three of them. John Toland, one of the inspirations for Bernard and Picart, claimed to have recovered a lost "Gospel of Barnabas"—in fact an early modern forgery—in which Jesus appears solely as a man and as such fits the later account offered by Islam at its founding.[8]

Contemporaries had come to expect such insults to Christianity from Toland. Although considered less subversive than outright atheism, deism was nonetheless viewed as deeply heretical by Catholics and orthodox Protestants alike, as Rousseau discovered when his *Emile* was censured in Catholic Paris and burned in Calvinist Geneva in 1762. The offending passages in the profession of faith of the Savoyard vicar might seem like a very bland form of deism to present-day readers, but they shocked authorities at the time. Moreover, Rousseau did not hesitate to vaunt Islam's positive qualities. In *The Social Contract* (1762), he even praised Muhammad for bringing his religion and the leadership of his state together. Such opinions remained problematic even a generation after the 1730s when the big shift in understanding of Islam took place.[9]

Bernard published his volume on Islam right in the thick of the transformation in European attitudes toward Islam. He took the side of interpreters such as Reland, Gagnier, and Sale, who were less hostile to Islam than previous writers like the Anglican minister Humphrey Prideaux. The title of Prideaux's immensely popular book of 1697 announced his position: *The True Nature of Imposture Fully Display'd in the Life of Mahomet*. His subtitle was no less significant: *With a Discourse annex'd for the Vindicating of Christianity from this Charge, offered to the Consideration of the Deists of the Present Age*. Prideaux had first published the discourse in 1696 as *A Letter to the Deists* and then appended it to his life of Muhammad, explicitly written to combat deism, which he saw as responsible for "the great prevailing of Infidelity in the present age." If he could show that the doctrines of Muhammad were impostures and that Christian doctrine had nothing in common with them, then Christianity, and especially belief in the Trinity, would be confirmed. Prideaux's book appeared in many different English, French, and Dutch editions over the next two decades and was reprinted repeatedly for more than a century. Although Prideaux granted the success of Muhammad's message and avoided some of the most fantastic stories about the prophet, he nonetheless concluded in the tried and true Christian manner that Muhammad's two chief passions were ambition and lust and that the Alcoran (Koran) promoted war, bloodshed, and an obsession with women both on earth and in the afterlife.[10]

Like most people of his time, Prideaux did not clearly separate religion and politics. Religious toleration was necessarily a political issue because it required a state decision, whether on the local or the national level. While a tutor of Hebrew at Christ Church, Oxford, Prideaux spied on John Locke for the Tory government. When Parliament passed the Act of Toleration of 1689 granting toleration to dissenting (non-Anglican) Protestants, Prideaux was convinced that moral breakdown would soon ensue, even though Catholics and anti-Trinitarians were expressly excluded. It is not surprising, then, that he, like many of his contemporaries, conflated deism with Quakerism, Socinianism (Unitarianism), and even atheism.[11]

Bernard prepared his volume on Islam while debates over religious toleration, deism, and atheism were just heating up to the boiling point. He intended to contribute to all of them. He did this by reproducing the least prejudiced previous accounts about Islam and adding to them his own emendations and commentary, which seized every opportunity to link considerations of Islam to debates about toleration, deism, and atheism within Europe. In the middle of his discussion of the sects of Mahometism, for example, he inserts the sentence, "Tolerance being founded on a natural principle, nothing, it would seem, is more worthy of a reasonable man." The exact location of this sentence is significant and exemplifies Bernard's subtle technique. He is considering one last sect among the Mahometans, that of "the indifferent," a term he associates with English Latitudinarianism (the belief held by many in the Anglican Church that doctrine, liturgy, and church organization mattered much less than the state of individual souls), deism, and even atheism in Europe. "Indifferentism" can refer to the belief that all religions are equally valid or that no one of them is uniquely true. It can also refer to a caricature of the position of the Latitudinarians, attributing to them the belief that agreement on doctrine, liturgy, and church organization is irrelevant (indifferent) to salvation. The indifferent among the Mahometans, recounts Bernard, believe that it is not necessary to prefer the orthodox to the heretical; all can be good Mahometans. These "Latitudinarian Mahometans," as Bernard calls them, are rejected by Sunnis and Shiites alike. The Orient is like the Occident in this respect, he remarks: people are always being forced to take sides. In the footnote to his sentence on toleration as a natural principle, Bernard gives the Latin *(Quod tibi non fieri vis etc.)* for the golden rule: "Do unto others as you would have done unto you." In just a few sentences, then, Bernard raises some of the most controversial questions facing Christians in his time, but he does so almost in passing and without drawing attention to his maneuver.[12]

Deism would be the focus of much of the discussion of Islam, though atheism and materialism also appeared on occasion. In his discussion of the Koran, for example, Bernard compares Islamic teachings to Latitudinarianism, Pyrrhonism (extreme skepticism), deism, Spinozism, and hylozoism:

> All these beautiful terms [of Islam for the Supreme Being] incorporate either the Platonic idea, which makes of God the general principle behind all Beings, or that of the Stoics, which makes God the soul of the world; or that of the Hylozoites, who vivify matter; or finally that of some Jewish savants and followers of Ar-

istotle, who, by establishing the co-eternity of God and matter in such a way that there is in God only the priority of Nature, unite them nonetheless necessarily one to the other.

Still, Bernard refuses to explicitly hold up Islam as an example of deism or pantheistic materialism. He lets the reader decide, or at least he implies as much. He denies any desire to examine whether the religion of the Mahometans "is effectively that of the Spinozists and Deists of Europe," though he has obviously provided evidence for just such a consideration.[13]

Rather than pronouncing on the subject, Bernard circles back to the broader syncretism that runs like a red thread through all the volumes: "the Mahometans whom one taxes with libertinage and with *Deism,* teach that God is a circle that incorporates every thing, and that it is in this that the immensity of God consists. *All these lines, all these different paths of religions end up in this circle.*" Bernard italicizes key elements in the passage to draw the reader's attention, but he does not spell out his own interpretation. He took the italicized passage about "all these lines" from one of his most cited sources, Barthélemy d'Herbelot's *Bibliothèque orientale,* a dictionary about peoples of the East published in 1697. D'Herbelot had the sentence, without italics, under the article "Din," Arabic for "way" or "path" (or for Europeans, "religion"). D'Herbelot was citing an Arabic source and concluded from it that there were deists among the Muslims. Bernard sees in it grist for his own syncretic mill.[14]

It would be hard to overstate the distance between Bernard and Picart and most of their predecessors. When Marracci produced his new Latin translation of the Koran in 1698, for example, he did so explicitly in order to refute it. Even the English translator of Reland's more sympathetic account of Islam claimed that his only interest was to "expose this Deceiver, and his Reveries, to the Laughter and Contempt of all the sensible part of Mankind." In 1734 George Sale still took an apologetic stance; while Muhammad cannot be considered equal to Moses or Jesus because their "laws came really from heaven," he nonetheless gave his people "the best religion he could, as well as the best laws, preferable, at least, to those of the ancient pagan lawgivers." Bernard, in contrast, uses the word "imposture" or "impostor" mainly when it occurs in his sources, and he makes every effort to universalize it.

Thus, the founder of the Catholic Inquisition was an "impostor monk," the Jews had any number of impostors and false Messiahs, and a Catholic priest used imposture to convince native Americans to worship the cross.[15]

Picart's visual interpretations are harder to pin down than Bernard's textual ones because the authenticity of his depictions depended on their fidelity to their sources. A picture might be worth a thousand words, but the reader would not necessarily know just what those thousand words might be. Picart's visual program is most easily traced in the choices he makes among the images available to him. In general, his and his assistants' engravings make Muslims seem comparable to Europeans and certainly less exotic than "the idolatrous peoples." Picart drew many of his plates about Islam from a collection of one hundred engravings of paintings by the Flemish painter Jean-Baptiste Vanmour that had been originally commissioned by the French ambassador to the Ottoman Turks from 1699 to 1710, Marquis Charles de Ferriol. The plates were first published in Paris in 1714. The Ferriol collection began with depictions of the sultan and his court and then moved down the social scale. Picart and Bernard naturally emphasized religious practices and after that social customs such as marriage and burial ceremonies, so the sultan appears only much later in their volume and then dressed in special robes for the festival of Beiram (or Bairam) that celebrates the end of fasting in the month of Ramadan. Picart ignores the plates that concern the officials and women of the sultan's harem. His first plate drawn from the Ferriol collection reduced and combined four different folio-size engravings on one folio plate showing three different kinds of dervishes and one Turk at his prayers. All four look dignified, even the one dervish who is dancing. Like most of the engravings drawn from the Ferriol collection, this one is signed *B. Picart sculp. direxit,* meaning that Picart supervised the process of engraving. Most of the engravings of Islam that are signed by Picart are dated 1731—when they are dated at all—two years before his death.[16]

Picart clearly found dervishes fascinating. The only engraving on Islam directly drawn by his hand is the double plate engraving of dancing dervishes, also dated 1731 and engraved by his student Jacob Folkema. It is an exact copy of a plate added to the 1715 edition of the Ferriol collection, but Picart has changed the title, which in the original read, "The Dervishes in their Temple at Pera [a district of Istanbul], Having Just

DERVICH ou Moine Turc qui tourne par dévotion. | *SAKA Charitable Derviche qui porte de l'eau par la ville et la donne par charité.*

TURC qui fait sa prière. | *DERVICH des Indes.*

10.2 Picart's depiction of three dervishes and one Turk at prayer. B. Picart sculp. dir. 1731; CC, vol. VII, facing p. 142. (Research Library, The Getty Research Institute, Los Angeles, California)

Finished Whirling," to the more generic, "Dance of the Dervishes." The caption supplied in the 1715 edition of the Ferriol collection is relatively nonjudgmental: it says that music is essential to the dance, which is preceded by a reading of the Koran. The dervishes "twirl with their arms open and appear ecstatic," but they are not ridiculed, as they would be in many other accounts. In 1793, for instance, the British compiler Reverend John Trusler would tell his readers of dervishes fainting with ecstatic visions after intense dancing, their hair flying, with much shouting and "the dome re-echoing the wild and loud music and noise, as it were, of frantic bacchanals."[17]

Bernard seems not to have shared Picart's interest in the dervishes. Picart, not Bernard, owned a copy of Postel's *De cosmographica disciplina et signorum coelestium* [Cosmography and celestial signs], which tried to incorporate Arabic astrology and Greek hermetic philosophy into a truly cosmic religion under the authority of the pope. Postel was eventually arrested by the Roman Inquisition and spent his last eleven years under house arrest in a French monastery. Postel's search had its equivalent in Islam in Sufi circles, which sought a more mystical and inner-directed form of worship. The whirling dervishes were Sufis. Yet despite his interest in syncretism Bernard failed to see the connection that Picart seems to have discerned. Perhaps the difference arose from the fact that Picart had lived much longer in France. He was a teenager in Paris when the French physician and traveler François Bernier published a letter that included an explanation of Indian Sufi practices linking them explicitly to Quietism, which similarly emphasized the annihilation of the self and mystical union with God. Quietism was condemned by a papal bull in 1687. Although Bernier had to publish his letter in 1688 in a periodical coming out of Rotterdam, the Quietist controversy, like that over Jansenism, was the kind of issue that set Picart to thinking about his allegiance to Catholicism. Moreover, Picart, unlike Bernard, owned Bernier's multivolume "abridgement" of the works of his teacher Pierre Gassendi that highlighted the atomistic and materialistic implications of the philosopher's writings. Gassendi had been linked to the libertine freethinkers including Gabriel Naudé. Gassendi and Bernier both fit well with Picart's capacious interests in natural philosophy, travel literature, and unorthodox religious views.[18]

From his sources Bernard knew about the thirteenth-century Turkish Sufi master Mevlana Celaleddin-i-Rumi (Mewlana or Mevelava in

10.3   Picart's dancing dervishes. Since this is the only engraving in the Islam volume
that was drawn by Picart himself, we can assume that he gave considerable importance
to it. Although he died four years before the volume was published, he had directly supervised the production of eleven of the plates (thirteen if the double plates are counted
as two) in this volume. From Picart's personal library, it is clear that he had developed a
serious interest in Islam, for he owned Marracci's 1698 Latin translation of the Koran, a
1717 edition of Reland in Latin, as well as a 1649 edition of the first translation of the
Koran into French by André du Ryer. B. Picart delin. 1731; J. Folkema sculp.; CC, vol.
VII, after p. 226. (Research Library, The Getty Research Institute, Los Angeles, California)

his sources), who he says invented the dance. Nonetheless, after a brief
discussion, Bernard switches to considering the dervishes monks, one
of his prime *bêtes noires*. He describes another dervish depicted in the
clothes of a traveler (by Folkema with no participation by Picart) as
claiming to preach the Muslim faith but in reality serving as a spy and

special agent: "Monks are always monks wherever they may be found," he concludes derisively. His obsession with the evils of priestcraft and especially monks kept him from seeing the potential interest in dervishes. After all, one of his favorite authors, Pierre Bayle, had cited information he got from Bernier about Sufis in one of the many long notes to his key article on Spinoza in his *Historical and Critical Dictionary.* Bayle clearly saw the connection to Western forms of heresy, including atheism. Dervishes aside, Bernard recognized the heretical potential in Islam because he reports that some have seen atheism, stoicism, Pythagoreanism, and metempsychosis among various Shiite sects, and he even draws a brief but explicit parallel there between Quietism and Persian sufis.[19]

Although Bernard may not have appreciated dervishes as much as Picart did, he gave his "dissertations" on Mahometism straightforward and unbiased titles. They show the gap between his and other contemporary depictions, such as Marracci's 1698 "Refutation of the Koran": (1) "Introduction to the History of Mahometism"; (2) "Dissertation on Mahomet"; (3) "Dissertation on the Beginnings of Mahometism"; (4) "Dissertation on the Prejudices and False Ideas That Have Been Formed against Mahometism"; (5) "Dissertation on the Koran"; (6) "Confession of Faith of the Mahometans"; (7) "Catechism of the Mahometans"; (8) "Clarifications about the Mahometan Religion"; (9) "Dissertation on the Various Precepts and Customs of the Mahometans"; (10) "Dissertation containing the Description of the Ceremonies of the Mahometans"; and (11) "Dissertation on the Sects of Mahometism." From the outset, then, Bernard signals his allegiance to the new-style interpreters of Islam. If the prophet whipped up enthusiasm and claimed the ability to perform miracles, for example, he was only making the most of "the common ideas" of men. "Did he fail to prevail against the state of Christianity of his time?" Bernard asks rhetorically.[20]

While blending together Boulainvilliers, Gagnier, Sale, and d'Herbelot in dissertations 1–3 and 5, Bernard relied on the French translation of Reland for sections 4 and 6–8. The Confession of Faith in section 6 reproduces a section with the same title added by the French translator to Reland's original work in Latin. The translator (not named in the work, identified as M. D** by Bernard, and known to be David Durand, a French Huguenot living in London) claims to have taken it from a Latin manuscript translation of a manuscript originally written in Spanish with Arabic characters (now called *aljamía*). For the discussion of false ideas in section 4, the catechism in section 7, and the clarifications in section 8, Bernard reproduces most of the French translation of Reland's sections with the same titles, but here he announces that he has suppressed some of the footnotes of the translator, added his own, and corrected the translation where he thought it suitable to do so.

Even when reproducing the work of another, Bernard can use typography to underline his position. On the first page of the clarifications section, for instance, he copies the French translation of Reland word for word but italicizes a phrase that Reland's translator did not: "From the moment that the *Mahometan* Doctrine infected the known world, several Authors have worked to stop the contagion, by refuting with all their powers a Religion that is very pernicious, *& fatal to Christianity, but nevertheless rather attractive for the mind and for the heart, which are naturally enemies of mortifications.*" Below he notes that the translator added this phrase. Did Bernard italicize it to draw attention to the fact that it was not there in the original? That seems unlikely since he did not hesitate to correct the translation wherever he saw fit. It seems more probable that he wanted to draw the reader's attention to the point added by the Protestant translator: Islam may be fatal to Christianity but it is intellectually and emotionally attractive in ways that conflict in particular with Catholicism (hence the reference to "mortifications").[21]

Although Bernard is critical of Durand's translation of Reland, it proves essential to his purposes. Reland made a clear argument for toleration:

> If the good pleasure of God had been that all the men of the world agreed unanimously on all the points of religion like they agree on all the truths of arithmetic, nothing would have been easier than to guide them to this universal consent. But experience teaches us that God did not find this appropriate; that is why full and complete liberty for each to follow his own lights and to believe true that which appears to him to be such [is required]. For there is nothing more absurd than to want to oblige people to receive as truth that which they do not regard as true: and it is a shame for Christians to refuse to other Christians, as they do, the usage of

this precious liberty and thus to oblige them by their bad ways to take refuge in the empire of the Turks, where they find more repose and charity than with their brothers.

Durand also made crucial additions to Reland's original Latin text in order to highlight Reland's argument for toleration and make it more Protestant. He inserts a sentence, for example, claiming that Muhammad explicitly recommended tolerance to his followers, and he adds references to the pope to draw attention to Catholic intolerance in particular: "The *Great Lord* [Sultan] is gentler than the *Pope,* and the *Mufti* more charitable than a *Bishop.*" Durand's motives may have gone beyond the defense of Protestantism against Catholicism, for he also had connections to freethinking circles. He wrote a sympathetic life of Vanini (d. 1619), who had been burned at the stake for atheism, a work that he could get published only in the Dutch Republic by one of the Knights of Jubilation, Gaspar Fritsch.[22]

After extensively reproducing sections from Reland, Bernard then turns in dissertations 9 and 10 to social customs and religious ceremonies, and not surprisingly, these are the sections that are the most heavily illustrated, in part by Picart himself and in part by Picart's students and followers. Twenty-two of the 26 folio-page engravings of Islam (85 percent) appear in these two sections, which include only 47 of the 291 (16 percent) pages of text. For the text, Bernard begins with Sale again but then picks and chooses among a long list of prominent travel writers who visited the Middle East: the French Protestant jeweler Jean Baptiste Tavernier, who traveled relentlessly across Europe, the Middle East, and Asia between 1629 and 1668, returning to France only to be forced to flee as a Protestant after the revocation of the Edict of Nantes; the English consul in Turkey in 1667–1668, Paul Rycaut; the French Huguenot refugee Jean Chardin, who traveled extensively in the Middle East and India in the 1660s and 1670s; the French scientist Jean de Thévenot, who traveled in the Middle East and India between the mid-1650s and the mid-1660s and learned Turkish, Persian, and Arabic; and the French botanist Joseph Pitton de Tournefort, who traveled in Turkey and surrounding lands between 1700 and 1702. As he had in earlier sections, Bernard repeatedly cites and often quotes extensively from d'Herbelot's *Bibliothèque orientale.* Yet though Bernard's method seems the same in these sections as in previous ones, his text here reproduces more of the enduring European stereotypes than had the previous sections.[23]

[*handwritten margin note: for commerce? for religious reasons?*]

In these sections Bernard cannot resist titillating the reader, so he begins with a discussion of the Islamic prohibition of alcohol and goes on to coffee and the use of drugs such as opium and "heng" (hemp). He makes a point similar to those he makes about other religions, however: people often do what their religious leaders forbid them to do. An obvious tension runs through these pages on ceremonies and customs. On the one hand, Bernard gives prominence to all the practices that Europeans found most strange, not to say repugnant: whirling dervishes, the exclusively civil celebration of marriage, polygamy, the ease with which divorce is granted to men, the role of eunuchs, the punishment meted out to women who commit adultery, and so on. On the other hand, even here Bernard is always ready to make an undercutting comparison. True, Muslims are allowed to have sex with their slaves. This observation is immediately qualified by two other remarks: Muslims can marry women of any religion, and among the Turks, all children, even those born to slaves, inherit equally from their fathers. Are Christians so superior, then? he seems to ask. Moreover, though Bernard mentions eunuchs very briefly, neither he nor Picart pay any attention to the harem, as it has no connection to religion. Still, there is no denying that in these sections Bernard's penchant for the erotic (present in many of his other works, too) carries him rather far from his more serious designs. Nonetheless, both text and image manage to distinguish clearly between the practices of the Sunni Turks and the Shiite Persians, which is much more than can be said for many of their European contemporaries.[24]

[*handwritten margin note: their customs might be taboo, but they're still honorable*]

The magnitude of Bernard and Picart's accomplishment in their treatment of Islam can be brought into greater relief by comparing it with the version offered by their bowdlerizers Antoine Banier and Jean Baptiste Le Mascrier. Banier and Le Mascrier reproduced Picart's engravings for the Islam section, as for the other volumes, but they subtly downgrade the engravings on their title pages throughout, which put in red letters *Histoire, Cérémonies, Peuples du Monde, Banier, Mascrier, Paris,* and *1741* (their publication date) but not Picart. Their title page vignette by Charles Nicolas Cochin, a favorite engraver of the French king Louis XV, elevates the figure of Catholicism and seriously downgrades the two followers of Muhammad, who are falling away from

10.4 Sunnis and Shiites. "The Carnival of the Turks" (above) and "The Festival of Hussein" (below) are clearly designed to contrast Sunni and Shiite practices. (Hussein was the grandson of Muhammad killed at the battle of Karbala; Shiites commemorate his death on the Day of Ashura.) L. F. D. B. inv. [Louis Fabrice Dubourg was a student of Picart's] B. Bernaerts Sculp.; CC, vol. VII, following p. 258. (Research Library, The Getty Research Institute, Los Angeles, California)

heaven and covered in darkness. The vignette appeared on the title page of each volume, indicating that Banier and Le Mascrier gave priority to challenging Picart's more positive representation of Islam in his frontispiece (see Figure I.2). In addition, they diluted the overall message of Bernard's text by not giving Islam its own volume. Right after Islam they offer Banier's essay on the origins of idolatry and then proceed to Bernard and Picart's section on Chinese religion. Islam thus leads into idolatry.[25]

Banier and Le Mascrier nonetheless kept Bernard's basic divisions of the text and even added to it an essay published under a pseudonym in 1684 by Richard Simon. Simon aimed at combating prejudices against Muslims. Simon, like them, was a Catholic priest, and Le Mascrier may well have identified with the trouble Simon found himself in with the authorities because Le Mascrier, too, was sometimes found wanting in orthodoxy. Le Mascrier is best known as the editor of Benoît de Maillet's posthumous *Telliamed,* a book of conversations between a French missionary and an Indian philosopher published in 1748. De Maillet offered heretical and proto-Darwinian ideas about the origins of the earth, the plurality of worlds, and the source of humankind in aquatic forms of life (all contrary to biblical accounts). Le Mascrier supposedly toned down the heterodox ideas, but his involvement attracted the attention of the inspector of the book trade. We can conclude, therefore, that Le Mascrier's interest in the Bernard and Picart work was not perhaps as completely orthodox as one might assume. Not surprisingly, the Parisian police had opened a dossier on him.[26]

It is less surprising, then, that Banier and Le Mascrier did not alter much of the text on Islam because they obviously considered it valuable. Still, they did add notes to at least keep the censors at bay (remembering that the original work was put on the Index of Forbidden Books in 1738, only three years before). Thus at the end of the paragraph on the sect of "the indifferent," which they reproduce exactly, they say in the footnote: "One should not be surprised to hear the Dutch publisher [Bernard] speak in this way in favor of *Tolerantism.* We have drawn attention elsewhere rather precisely to his sentiments on this subject." Similarly, at the beginning of the clarifications section (no. 8 in Bernard), they take out the italics introduced by Bernard and put the phrase in parentheses, because this part of the sentence had been introduced by Reland's French translator. Later in the same section they keep the sen-

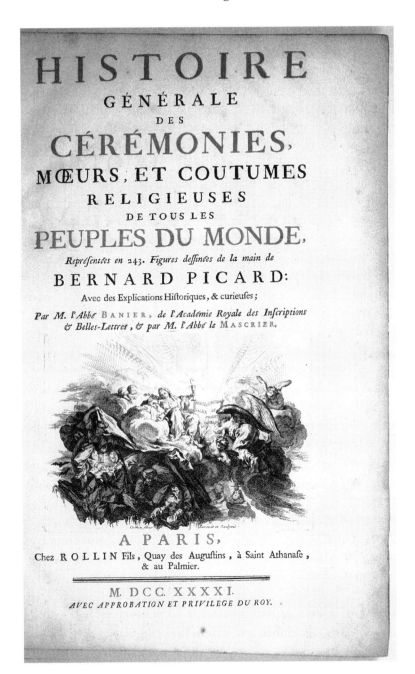

10.5 Title page of *Histoire générale des cérémonies* by Banier and Le Mascrier. Note how the female figure of the Catholic Church is bathed in light while all others are threatened with darkness. Cochin filius invenit et sculpsit. (Courtesy Young Research Library, UCLA)

tence on the pope but add a note at the bottom that reads: "All this is again an addition by the translator [of Reland], who speaks as a Protestant, and as a Refugee."[27]

At the end of the volume on Islam, standing alone, is a final disquisition on the religion of the Sabians. Bernard presumably included the Sabians in this volume because they were tolerated, like Christians and Jews, by the Muslims and because, according to Jean Chardin, they could still be found on the banks of the Tigris and Euphrates rivers. Bernard includes them to suggest that the sources of a universal natural religion might still exist in the lands long since conquered by Islam. Who were its progenitors? Sophocles, Empedocles, Socrates, Cicero, and the constantly recurring Pythagoras are to be considered forerunners, according to Bernard, because they believed in the unity, indivisibility, infinity, and immutability of a supreme being.

The first Sabians believed that the sun, moon, and other celestial bodies were the home of this single, infinite Intelligence that was superior to all nature. With vows, prayers, and supplications, but especially with good moral conduct, the Sabians praised this supreme being and recognized its presence in all living beings. The inevitable decline was one that befell all systems of belief: "when tradition began to become obscure, fear began to engender superstition." The superstitious then related to God as subjects do to kings, explains Bernard; they believed that they needed mediators rather than being able to approach God directly. This corruption of an originally pure practice constituted nothing less than the origin of pagan idolatry itself. In the later 1700s both Freemasons and Rosicrucians would on occasion trace their origins to these same Sabians, who were linked with Brahmins in an imagined hermetic chain that went back to the Egyptians, Zoroaster, Hermes Trismegistus, Moses, Solomon, Pythagoras, Plato, and the Essenes (a Jewish mystical sect contemporaneous with Jesus and made famous in our time by the discovery of the Dead Sea Scrolls). Once again, Bernard has fastened readers' attention on an obscure group whose beliefs and practices have clear affiliations with radical religious beliefs in his own time. Once again, he in effect shows that the Enlightenment with its search for a universal natural religion has roots in a distant past in faraway places and not just in Europe.[28]

We are now able to read Bernard and Picart's volume on Islam with the help of computerized search functions that reveal interconnections we might not glean from reading straight through a text and its images. Do we see things that contemporaries would have missed? The answer is probably not, for Bernard provides no fewer than 159 pages of indexes to the book at the end of volume seven that would have allowed readers to cross-reference the subjects that interested them. True, Hermes and metempsychosis do not appear in the index to the Islam volume, perhaps because Bernard had run out of gas in preparing this last volume after nearly twenty years devoted to the project. Pythagoras does appear under the article "Fo" [Buddha] and is cross-referenced to Hermes Trismegistus. Still, by the time they reached the volume on Islam, readers had become familiar with Bernard's technique. They knew to look for the description of heretical sects and to read selectively for Bernard's interpolations from his sources, if they wanted to follow that thread. But they were not compelled to read for this or any other hidden agenda. They could read the volume as an up-to-date compendium of the best sources available on Islam, as did even those severe Catholic critics Banier and Le Mascrier. They could learn the history of Muhammad and the Koran and get a firsthand feeling for Islamic practices, see the differences from and similarities to Judaism and Christianity, and draw their own conclusions. At the very least they would have to recognize that Islam was as riven by division as were Catholicism and Protestantism alike. Dissent was everywhere. Toleration of differences over doctrine and practice was unavoidable, as the Dutch had been the first to discover.

II

Dissent, Deism, and Atheism

PROTESTANTS who identified with the Enlightenment—indeed were among its progenitors—knew the range of available religious beliefs, and how significantly options had widened in one generation. They understood the boundaries of orthodoxy and heresy and the difference between what might be said in public and what had to remain private. They were among the first generation of Europeans for whom deism, even atheism, could be not only discussed in print but also lived. These new boundaries are on display in what became the sixth volume of Bernard and Picart's massive book. Their by-now-familiar habit of addressing beliefs with a modicum of skeptical but respectful restraint continues in this volume. Bernard refuses to affirm the orthodoxy or veracity of any one religion. Most important, new possibilities finally get their due: deism, Spinozism, and atheism all receive serious and sustained attention.

Bernard's treatment of these heresies at times throws up as much smoke and fog as it casts light. As author and engraver well knew, deism and atheism were the burning philosophical and religious issues of the first half of the eighteenth century. As the contents of his library makes clear, Bernard read in all those controversies. When he addressed them, we may assume that he chose his words carefully but also cautiously. He was keenly aware that Protestant sects as diverse as Anabaptists, Socinians, and Dutch Collegiants had been labeled as deists just for having "described the faults of the ecclesiastics." When discussing deism as derived from Spinoza, for example, he acknowledged that Spinoza was, indeed, "a dangerous Philosopher."[1]

At first glance something of a grab bag, the sixth volume (bearing "volume four" on its title page and meant to be a continuation of the monotheistic religions) possesses a certain enlightened logic. It begins with a look at what the age called with disdain "enthusiasm." Even before his preface to the volume (thus indicating perhaps that he came across this piece only at the last minute) and separately paginated from the rest, Bernard prints a letter about the latter-day Jansenists known as convulsionaries who experienced miraculous cures and convulsive trances at the tomb of a cleric in the cemetery of St. Medard in Paris in 1731. The anonymous author of the letter cannot make up his mind what to think about them; are they impostures foisted upon a credulous people or are they real? Since no amount of research and reason seems to resolve the issue, the author concludes, tongue in cheek, that only the Church can decide on the truth or falsity of the miracles.[2]

Enthusiasm, which Bernard equates in this volume with "violent fanaticism," had long worried him. Already in *Moral Reflections* (1711) he discussed the Anabaptists and cast a fairly cold eye on their practices. He also had nothing but contempt for the French Prophets, who roamed the streets proclaiming the demise of the anti-Christ, Louis XIV. Fanaticism had come to be associated with political disorder, even upheaval and mob rule. By the 1730s negativity about enthusiasm and what one English commentator called "a strange medley of Phanatiques" could be found on either side of the Channel, in a Dutch, or French, or English intellectual context. Bernard knew all of them remarkably well.[3]   *fanaticism as the opposite of Rationality?*

Enthusiasts and fanatics occupy a central place in volume six, but Bernard does not open with them. The stage has to be set. Having discussed the Lutherans and continental Calvinists in volume five, he turns first in this volume to the Anglicans, to whom he devotes more than one hundred pages. The Presbyterians and Quakers each merit about twenty pages, the Puritans only four. Only then does he turn to his "Dissertation containing a Historical Description of several Fanatical Sects and Assemblies, few in number, or little known, having ceased to exist." Then he offers separate essays on Anabaptists, so-called Adamites, mystical sects, Labadists, Quietists, Socinians, and Collegiants. At the very end comes the true *pièce de résistance,* the deists. Bernard does not reveal the rationale for this ordering, except to say in the preface that he will end with "some opinions that have not resulted in the formation of religious sects, but which should not be forgotten, if only to protect oneself from their poison."[4]

The turn away from belief in the miraculous and the extremes of behavior found in some religious sects introduced the very notion of religious psychology. Sensibility, taste, and decorum required mental discipline, even a degree of privacy about matters religious. In the case of Bernard, as shown in chapter five, this new emphasis on psychology, on the emotional impulses permitted a person of religious temperament, led to the insight that human sexuality and the guilt associated with it sparked the religious impulse. In his emphasis on the more cerebral forms of religiosity Bernard is implying that such groups have achieved an inner discipline, a psychological state of reasonableness that renders them immune to the hysteria he associates with enthusiasm. In the last paragraph of this volume, as a kind of summing up, Bernard defines the religious man as one who "renders to God what he is due and in the course of his life submits to him to the full extent of his reason; who in adoring him does not take fright like the vulgar; who strips himself of all servile fear in rendering to him his homage; who, religious by his recognition and duty toward God, despises the terror that death inspires in the superstitious and the falsely devout; and finally who renounces the false ideas of an inexorable destiny [predestination] that many Christians dare to conceive." These were not the words of an orthodox Calvinist![5]

Bernard is now, incidentally, the key player in this volume. Despite the fact that Picart's name appears again in bold red letters on the title

---

11.1 *(facing page):* The Collegiants. The similarity in styles between Picart and his pupil Louis Fabricius Dubourg can be seen in these two images. Both engravings designed by Dubourg could have been drawn "from nature," from a Collegiant meeting in Amsterdam in the 1730s, when Dubourg worked there. The top engraving illustrates the male egalitarianism that made any man a preacher; the bottom depicts a communion service. Designed by Louis Fabricius Dubourg (L. F. D. B. del.) (Dutch, 1693–1775), engraved by Pieter Tanjé (Dutch, 1706–1761); CC, vol. VI, between pp. 328 and 329. (Research Library, The Getty Research Institute, Los Angeles, California)

ASSEMBLÉE de ceux qu'on appelle COLLEGIANS a Amsterdam.

L. F. D. B. del.   P. Tanjé sculp.

Leur CENE a Rynsburg.

page, by the time of its appearance in 1736—well after the volumes on Judaism, Catholicism, and idolatry—Picart had been dead three years. Most of the engravings in volume six were produced by his students or assistants, and their artistic style clearly resembled that of their master. Picart had trained them well. But, alas, we know little about their religious convictions or reading habits. We may safely assume that most were Protestant in background, if no longer in conviction.[6]

When it came to the vice of enthusiasm, whether Catholic or Protestant in origin, Bernard did not mince words. The undated letter from Paris that opens the volume describes the so-called *convulsionnaires* as "fools." Assembled in and around a Parisian church, they believed that the remains of its dead abbé had the power to effect miracles and to cure ailments. In the face of that power believers went into involuntary trances and convulsions. Their devotees left spiritual diaries that recorded dreams, trances, and prayer sessions as being equally true events, all indicative of one's spiritual state. Thousands flocked to see the spectacle and young, yet-to-be-famous *philosophes*, like Voltaire, recorded their horror at the folly of humankind. Although published five years after the main events it describes, the account Bernard printed would have registered favorably with anyone proud to be self-described as enlightened. Although most of the fuss about the group had died down by the late 1730s, in that decade devout followers were still recording their visions and dreams.[7]

The letter that opens the volume is accompanied by an unsigned engraving of Parisian men and women hurling themselves to the ground in one scene and in various states of hysterical collapse in the other. Bernard must have been troubled by the fact that the *convulsionnaires* were widely said to be Jansenists, the brand of French Catholicism thought by some to be closest to Protantism. Yet as the volume made clear, he knew that Protestants could also be "fanatiques" guilty of "enthousiasme." Famous in the first two decades of the century, the so-called French Prophets were Protestant visionaries from the Cevennes mountains in southern France who rebelled against Louis XIV in anticipation of his demise and traveled throughout Protestant Europe in search of converts. They were given to trances and talking in tongues. Bernard did not miss the chance in volume six to describe them, too, as "fanatics," saying that they suffered from "a malady." We know from his *Moral Reflections* that he had seen representatives of the Protestant

Le CIMETIERE *de* S^T MEDARD.

Differentes AGITATIONS *des* CONVULSIONAIRES.

11.2　The *Convulsionnaires* of Paris. An offshoot of the Jansenists, the sect or cult met in and around a Parisian church, the parish church of St. Medard. Unsigned; CC, vol. VI, opposite p. 4. (Research Library, The Getty Research Institute, Los Angeles, California)

group who had made their way to Holland in the second decade of the century. In 1711 Bernard described the leader of the prophets, or Camisards, as they were also known, as "the chief of a troupe of bandits." Bernard, like many of his contemporaries, had been horrified by the behavior he witnessed.[8]   → strong reactions

For devout Protestants of an earlier era, like Isaac Newton (b. 1642), the French Prophets foretold the retribution that Christ would visit on the Anti-Christ (often identified as the pope in Rome) upon his millennial return. The Prophets were no more "fanatical" than many good seventeenth-century Protestants, like Newton himself, who was also (more cautiously to be sure) a millenarian. Bernard notes that the recording secretary for the Prophets was none other than the famous Swiss mathematician Fatio de Quillier, but he appears not to have known that Fatio's friend and confidant Newton also approvingly watched the Prophets on the streets of London. Nor could Bernard possibly have known that a generation later the Shakers in the New World may have traced their ancestry back to the French Prophets. Newton died in 1727, and within his lifetime a sea change occurred within European Protestantism. "Enthusiasm" and "fanaticism" became labels that denoted the irrational, the beyond-the-pale ranting of deluded people who imagined they had a divine voice at work within themselves. The labeling and dismissal of enthusiasm opened a space into which enlightened notions of reason and common sense rushed.[9]

thinking god was talking through then was a bad thing

Bernard's skepticism about "the extravagant practices of various fanatics of our century" pervades the account of enthusiasts, whether they are Catholic, Protestant, or less easily identified with any religion, such as the Rosicrucians or various small millenarian groups such as the Massalians from ancient times who are lumped under the general category of "Bohemians" (gypsies). Yet his censoriousness did not foreclose the possibility of titillating his readers. In the case of the enthusiastic Adamites—of whose existence there is little to no evidence—their ranting naked in the streets of Amsterdam offered the engraver, here François Morellon La Cave, a golden opportunity to depict naked men entertainment and women for the delectation of his audience.

An underlying grid of rationality structures Bernard's account in this volume. First he moves from Anglicanism, acerbically noting that it is closest to Catholicism, to Presbyterianism and Quakerism, where ceremonies become more minimalist. Although he is not very favorable to

ASSEMBLÉES nocturnes des ADAMITES.

ADAMITES d'AMSTERDAM.

11.3 The Adamites by night and by day. Adamites are depicted here ranting in the streets of Amsterdam and disrobing at night, but there is little historical evidence for the existence of the group. The reality or imagination of them allowed the artist to depict nudity and libertinism. Engraved by François Morellon La Cave (Dutch, 1696–1768); CC, vol. VI, between pp. 212 and 213. (Research Library, The Getty Research Institute, Los Angeles, California)

Anglicanism in general, Bernard may have given prominence to it in part because he admired the writings of its contemporary liberal or Latitudinarian wing, exemplified by Newton's friend Samuel Clarke. Bernard repeatedly republished Clarke's most notable works. After dispensing with the fanatics in the central section of the volume, he turns first to the Anabaptists, presumably because they had once—during the sixteenth-century turmoil of the Reformation—been fanatics but were no longer. Following a brief interlude on the Adamites, he considers various mystical sects, both Protestant and Catholic, and then gets to the true heart of the argument with the most rationalistic religious forms: these are first the various anti-Trinitarians such as Socinians and Unitarians, then the Dutch Collegiants, who emphasize reasonable ecumenical discussion, and finally deism.

Although *Religious Ceremonies of the World* tries to give every religion its due, clearly Bernard is most at home when describing the varieties of the more cerebral forms of Protestantism. And he knew whereof he spoke. The grasp of both English and Dutch religious history that the volume displays, with its attention to millenarianism, the Puritan movement, and the distinctions between Anglicans and Presbyterians, the Dutch Remonstrants, Arminians, and Mennonites versus strict Calvinists, is testimony to the amount of research and lived experience that went into the writing of the volume. We know that Bernard worked hard to find contemporary sources. In 1731 he wrote to London to Pierre Desmaizeaux, John Toland's biographer and a key player in the Republic of Letters, to ask if Desmaizeaux could provide him with engravings or drawings of Anglican ceremonies. He wanted to depict what was actually to be seen within the category of "religion." Correspondence—often hidden or carried by friends—contributed mightily to the exchange of images and views; so, too, did books and loosely organized clubs like the Knights of Jubilation or the circle of Huguenot refugees and their English friends who met in London at the Rainbow Coffee House. Desmaizeaux acted as a major go-between for the circles to which Bernard and Picart belonged in the Dutch Republic.[10]

The attention Bernard lavishes on the wide spectrum of Protestant sects and disputes found uniquely in the Dutch Republic suggests that he was fascinated by its religious diversity. He discusses in detail the quarrels between the followers of the theologians Voetius and those of Cocceius, a seventeenth-century rehearsal for what became on both sides of the Channel by the next century the bitter contest between science-inspired freethinking and Christian orthodoxy. In the 1640s Voetius thought that he spied in Descartes's philosophy the foundation of atheism, and the antidote as he saw it was a rigid adherence to orthodox scholasticism in philosophy and strict Calvinism in matters religious. Cocceius sought a liberal interpretation of Christianity and flexibility toward science and the new philosophy. The dispute roiled the Dutch Reformed Church into the early eighteenth century.

Bernard was always on the look-out for heresies conceived within the bosom of orthodoxy. He dwells at some length on Quietism, a mystical form of Catholicism that vexed the French church during the 1690s. He is especially interested in any hint of syncretism, arguing at one point that Siamese and Chinese mystics embrace a form of Quietism, finding God utterly mysterious and remote, reached only, if ever, by tranquility and passivity. With typical incomprehension their enemies have called them atheists just as they have decried the Spinozists. Many are the forms of heresy associated with atheism.[11] → everything that's not church is Atheism

When surveying the gamut of religious expression, no group proved too small to interest Bernard, and if they were important to his purposes, he would grant them more space than their actual numbers in the 1730s would have warranted. Unitarians, Collegiants, and one mystical sect that may never have existed, the Brethren of the Rosy Cross, or Rosicrucians, all receive coverage and even, in many cases, engravings. Curiously Bernard displays no particular sympathy for the Rosicrucians. Widely regarded in the seventeenth century as dangerous Protestant reformers, they take their inspiration in Bernard's account from Arab magicians and the Kabbalism encountered in Spain. They came to see themselves as "illuminated" and "as the sole possessors of all the graces that Nature bestows." They publicly identified the pope as the Anti-Christ, but they also condemned Muhammad. Not least, they thought they had the power to exorcize demons, but in the end they came to most resemble "charlatans and alchemists."[12] → anyone that has power = bad

In a rather curious spot, in the middle of a discussion of the mystical sects, Bernard suddenly inserts a reference to contemporary events in the republic. He complains that the republic has apparently become less tolerant of late because it has forbidden meetings of the freemasons, who had no animosity toward religion, good morals, or social order. They had been in existence for "a long time" in Great Britain, he insists. In December 1735 the States of Holland had indeed forbidden such meetings, most likely because the leaders of the first Dutch lodge had come out of the entourage of the British ambassador and presumably sympathized with the pro-Orangist policies of the British government. The British hoped to restore the stadholderate at a time when the Dutch political elite wished to keep the claimant to that title from ever assuming it. Dutch suspicions were only heightened by the fact that the stadholder-in-waiting had recently married Anna of Hanover, the daughter of the English king, George I. The States spied Orangism masquerading as a fraternal (and secret) order and moved against the freemasons. Other than a brief mention in the text, Bernard limits his consideration, no doubt out of caution, to an extended footnote.

There Bernard takes up the masonic cause, noting that while the

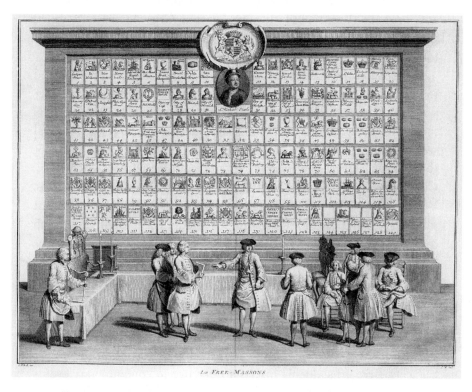

Les FREE-MASSONS

11.4   Freemasonry. Other sources contemporary to this engraving of the 1730s confirm the authenticity of the symbols and ceremonies. Sir Richard Steele (of *Spectator* fame), whose portrait sits atop the display, may indeed have been a freemason. L. F. D. B. inv. (Dubourg); I. F. Scul.; CC, vol. VI, between pp. 252 and 253. (Research Library, The Getty Research Institute, Los Angeles, California)

masons' secret is said to be "impenetrable," the freemasons are "distinguished by the illustrious persons who are members." He tells the reader that some people have assumed that the freemasons are "libertines and deists, others that they are debauched people of every sort of rank, estate and profession." Some claim that "they seek to make cabals against the state." A few go further and associate them with the scandal of 1730, with "the S . . ."— the sodomites. Even Bernard will not put that in print. In 1730 hundreds of men in the republic were accused of sodomy and some were executed. The panic about secret networks of sodomites led to a more general reaction against libertinism and nonconformity. People in the Marchand-Picart-Rousset circle were questioned by the authorities, but in the end they were left in peace. Off and on in the course of the eighteenth century freemasons would be accused of the vice that Bernard cannot name.[13]

In this long footnote that extends across the better part of two folio pages, Bernard shows that he had done his homework on freemasonry. He gives a reasonably accurate account of early British masonic history complete with the information that the lodges began to surface in London during the 1690s. He notes that many English princes and aristocrats as well as clergy belong to the order. Moreover, the note is accompanied by a double plate engraving. The lodges depicted come from an engraving by the English freemason John Pine. Dubourg, the draftsman of Bernard's plate, had spent time in London and might have known Pine through the coffee house on St. Martin's Lane that artists and engravers made their haunt. Dubourg adds a masonic ceremony with the gentlemen attired in the fashionable long jackets favored at the time in polite circles on either side of the Channel. This particularly ornate costume is closest to the French model and would easily have been seen on elite men in the Dutch Republic. The squares and trowel, sun and moon, were authentically masonic. From the engraving's placement in the section on the Labadists, we might conclude that Bernard was uncertain about just what to do with the freemasons. But he may just have wanted to cover his tracks given the contention surrounding the issue in Holland. The English edition pulled out almost the entire account and pointedly noted that freemasonry is not a religion. The later French edition of 1741 pirated by two Parisian abbés expanded the section on freemasonry and became a major source of information on it in that decade.

Bernard may have had help with his discussion of freemasonry. Picart's lifelong friend Marchand was very close to Rousset de Missy. In 1735 Rousset was already participating in the new lodges and eventually became the leader of Amsterdam freemasonry. If Rousset supplied information about the new lodges, perhaps he also told Bernard that a Jew had been among its founders. Rousset welcomed Sephardic Jews into his own Amsterdam lodge, and one—a member of the elite Cappadoce family—was so emboldened by his masonic experience as to demand entry into a lodge in Bordeaux. It refused him twice and banned all Jews from membership, thus making palpable for us the degree of religious toleration that could be found in some places in the Dutch Republic.[14]

Did Bernard consider freemasonry a new form of religion? We do not know. But we do know that the more cerebral the form of religiosity, the more sympathetic the attention he gives it. A good measure of this preference is provided by the thoughtful engravings of groups like the Collegiants, the Quakers, and even contemporary Anabaptists. The enemies of the last two saw them as ranters potentially dangerous to the state. By contrast, Bernard focuses on the Quakers' famous willingness to allow women to preach. The Anabaptist scene, clearly set in the republic, is orderly and pious, though Bernard holds members of that sect at arms length and gives their suspect behavior, including the practice of polygamy in the previous century, extended treatment. That they have reformed is, however, duly noted. The same tranquility may be seen in the meeting of the Collegiants, seated in orderly rows, discussing matters religious under the watchful eye of the clock. As friends of Spinoza, they, too, were suspect in many quarters and were seen to be as heretical as the Socinians or the anti-Trinitarians. By the time Bernard presented the Collegiants so prominently, they numbered in the mere hundreds. We may legitimately ask, is he trying to use the images to influence the reader, only now to tip his hand as to type of religiosity to be preferred? The Collegiants privileged the moral life over doctrinal conformity and eschewed deference to pastors. In their own way they were freethinkers who by the 1730s had come to identify reason as the spirit that moves men (see Figure 11.1).[15]

Although Bernard carefully described the broad spectrum of Protestant sects, he was clearly fascinated by more heretical positions, such as those linked to anti-Trinitarianism. This section of Bernard's text in

Le BAPTEME *des* MENNONITES.

La BENEDICTION *qui suit le* BAPTEME.

11.5   Mennonites of the 1730s. By this time the Anabaptists had merged with the Mennonites, resulting in a newfound respectability and prosperity. L. F. Du Bourg del.; B. Bernaerts sculp.; CC, vol. VI, facing p. 207. (Research Library, The Getty Research Institute, Los Angeles, California)

volume six repays careful reading. Always labeled as deeply heretical, the refusal to acknowledge the person of Christ as divine—variously known as Socinianism or Unitarianism—receives such lengthy treatment, and is made to seem so disciplined and reasonable in terms of its practices, that we can only question the author's motives. If these are books—if not people—whom the orthodox would burn, why discuss their beliefs at such length? Certainly Bernard would have known the vast literature in every European language that attacked anti-Trinitarianism mercilessly. Even John Locke, the great apostle of religious toleration, said nothing in print about his own anti-Trinitarianism (both he and Newton believed in the unity of the Godhead and not in the Trinity). The question of why Bernard devotes so much attention to heresy becomes more pressing when the volume turns its attention to "the dangerous system of another Englishman who has pretended *that Christianity is not mysterious.*"[16]

Like the proverbial bad penny, John Toland has returned. He is, in many ways, the key to understanding Bernard's views, which are developed in dialogue with him in these pages. The keeper of the record by which we can identify at least some of the Knights of Jubilation receives extended consideration in volume six. In his famous—most would have said infamous—book *Christianity not Mysterious* (London, 1696), Toland proposed the principle, in his own words as quoted by Bernard: "that Reason is the unique foundation of certitude and revelation . . . should be no less subject to the examination of Reason" than "the phenomena of nature." Even while claiming at one point that Toland slides imperceptibly from incredulity to atheism, Bernard devotes page after page to his ideas and leaves a final judgment hanging: Bernard will neither render him "odious" nor support his opinions. After all, Bernard says, only "a few superior minds" can use reason to examine their beliefs.[17]

Does Bernard think that Toland is too heady for the common people but appropriate for men like himself? Or does he worry about the implications of the views of this "famous and bold libertine?" Toland appears again at the very end of Bernard's discussion of the deists, who are then defined as those "who believe that all religions are equally agreeable to God." They accept this diversity and offer as an analogy the many ways that men honor the great princes. Even at this late moment in the text, Bernard takes the time to summarize the thesis of Toland's 1709 Latin text *Adeisidaemon* (published in the republic), noting that under the guise of explicating Livy's criticism of Roman superstitions, Toland was indicting all religions that rely on superstition. Toland claimed, asserts Bernard, that he was not an enemy of the church *"but of those who govern it, for whom superstition will be eternally necessary."*[18]

Bernard takes Toland's opinion on the psychology of blind faith a step further: "And I would happily add please God that false zeal, which is the result for some of a decadence of the passions and for others the result of fear—in the great the result of ambition and in the small that of politics and ignorance—would never have authorized the establishment of fables." Toland's view of priestcraft is also similar to what we find throughout *Religious Ceremonies of the World;* as Toland puts it, "the people therefore were obliged to admit everything as sacred & authentic that fell from the lips of the high priest." Bernard departs from Toland when it comes to the English freethinker's belief, put forward in *Letters to Serena* and repeated in *Adeisidaemon,* that "the gods and goddesses of the heathen nations were in reality human beings." Bernard thought that the gods stood as representations of the universal substance (as Spinoza called it) or God. Yet he would have agreed with Toland, who, like Spinoza, thought that natural philosophy provided an account of the laws of Nature, which is the universal substance. Bernard endorses their skepticism about how, as Toland puts it, "the illiterate multitude unacquainted with natural philosophy, converts . . . appearances . . . into portents and prodigies."[19]

Bernard himself had a lifelong interest in superstition, and in two volumes contemporaneous with volume six he reprinted French texts about Catholic superstitions and lumped them with magic and sorcery. With some self-satisfaction Bernard produced what he believed to be a veritable catalogue of the varieties of superstition found in the world. It is hardly surprising, then, that when Bernard addresses superstition in volume six of *Religious Ceremonies of the World,* the voice in the text suddenly shifts from the third person to the "moi" and "je" of the author. In old age—and at the time of writing Bernard would have been in his early fifties, old in that time—"the soul" seeks ever stronger superstitions, just as those debauched by too much wine can get high only by resorting to liquors specially invented for them by doctors. As if cautioned by Hobbes about the sources of religious belief, boldly Bernard asserts the necessity of never adopting a servile fear. He proclaims the need not only to avoid the fear of death that is the hallmark of the superstitious but also to eschew the false ideas about death beloved by some Christians. The allusion could only be to the falsity of any notion of predestination or possibly even of the existence of heaven or hell. Bernard closes the volume with these lines from Virgil (in Latin): "Happy is he who understands the causes of things / and tramples underfoot all terrors and inexorable fate / and the clamour of greedy Acheron [the river of pain]."[20]

The English edition steered clear of any element in these final pages that smacked of heresy. Indeed, the English editing and expurgating of Bernard's views, particularly on deism and atheism, can be taken as a guide to the more audacious elements in his thinking. In the English edition the account of Toland's views simply disappears. *Christianity not Mysterious* is mentioned, but the reader is instructed to also read Toland's opponents. Bernard's views too are significantly diluted. Where Bernard had defined the religious man as one who "renders to God what he is due and in the course of his life submits to him to the full extent of his reason," the English translation added a crucial phrase about God's revelation: "we must then conclude, that a truly religious man renders to God what is due to him, submits himself, and the whole extent of reason, *to his infallible Word.*" Talk about fear is tempered: "ancient and modern wits . . . have been forced at last to own the necessity of some religion, not only to keep men in awe, not out of fear, but because they were convinced of the being of God by Dint of Demonstration." The English translator has given readers an altogether sunnier, even pious rendition of the one true faith, and crucially it includes a reference to providence, something missing entirely in *Religious Ceremonies of the World.* But other English contemporaries of the altered translation evinced no such inhibitions. The famous engraver Hogarth never missed an opportunity to ridicule superstition and to castigate the Anglican Church and its preachers for mendacity and sloth. His style, if not his thinking, had been influenced by Picart.[21]

Toland was an essential foil for Bernard, but in some ways Bernard's stakes were even higher. He was giving new meaning to the category of religion itself. He was contributing to an intellectual shift of major importance in the European conceptualization of religion. In the ancient world at the time of Cicero or Virgil, *religio*—simply scruples—meant ritualistic aspects of public or private behavior that followed rules. Not until the time of St. Augustine did the Church fathers distinguish a specifically Christian religion that opposed the pagan. Medieval monks in turn fashioned terms like "faith," "law," and "sect" to describe Christianity, but scholars now believe that the abstraction "religion" emerged only with the Protestant Reformation. The plurality of competing and hostile religious cults and customs required people to reflect on the larger phenomenon of religion. Religion started to mean a set of doctrines specific to one Christian religion or another. From there it was a short step, taken incidentally by a thinker often accused of deism, Lord Herbert of Cherbury (d. 1648), that enabled people to speak in the abstract about the characteristics of all "religion." Almost simultaneously religion began to be seen, not as rituals and ceremonies *tout court,* but as an intellectual system.[22]

Bernard pushes the envelope of abstraction even further when in volume six he includes under the rubric of religion groups as disparate as the Brothers of the Rosy-Cross, or Rosicrucians, the Freemasons, the Adamites, the Polish Brethren (Socinians), and finally Spinozists and deists. Perhaps Bernard is able to make that intellectual move precisely because he was intimately familiar not only with deism and atheism as ways of thinking but also with accusations hurled by theologians who did not like a sect's doctrines. Late in the seventeenth century an unprecedented set of quarrels had erupted around the thought, first of Thomas Hobbes, then of Spinoza. Indeed the polemics consistently joined them, saying that Spinoza preached more openly a naturalism that Hobbes kept more covert. In different ways both transgressed a fundamental tenet of the Judeo-Christian tradition and called into question the absolute separation of matter and spirit, body and soul, Creator from creation. In so doing they were said to collapse the supernatural into nature.

Both Hobbes and Spinoza occupied places in the libraries of Bernard and Picart. Both presented to the pious the possibility of there being atheists, the most extreme variety of heresy, it was said, ever to find a place on the intellectual agenda of Western Europe. German theologians attacked Spinoza as a fatalist and labeled the derivative "ism" as resting on precarious, confused, and ambiguous principles. Those were some of the kinder things said about Spinozism. Hobbes's denial of the existence of spirits and his conviction that Christianity should become a kind of civil religion firmly under the control of the state meant that neither he nor Spinoza could have imagined their followers being labeled religious. But that is just how Bernard describes the orthodox vision of them at one point, "Spinozists, Papists, Jews, and Mohammedans." Bernard also knew these labels to be extremely slippery, citing one Dutch sect that tried to combine the philosophy of Spinoza with a "new system of mysticism" similar to that found among the Pietists of the period. Often condemned, the sect met in secret because the States of Holland had outlawed it for "libertinism and irreligion." Central to the heresies associated with Hobbes and Spinoza was a new biblical criticism pioneered by Richard Simon that treated the sacred texts as historical documents. Simon himself intended no threat to religion, but his work opened the door to considering the Bible as simply a historical document. To the orthodox all these heresies, with materialism at their root, were a many-headed hydra.[23]

Suddenly, by the last quarter of the seventeenth century, what the pious labeled nonbelief threatened to become a *religious* alternative, and there were actual persons, with philosophical treatises, who could be read as being atheists, regardless of what may have been their heartfelt convictions. Increasingly abstracted as a category, religion became in effect more like science or philosophy with a distinct set of styles, practices, philosophical convictions, and truth claims. Churches, sects, fraternities, small clusters of people with rituals, or groups without them possessed of a set of beliefs—like deists—became objects of Bernard's rigorous gaze. He refuses to fling insults because to do so would only "take away from the reader the liberty to judge and examine." Perhaps his restraint rested on his conviction that none of these heretics were actually atheists.[24]

In this sixth volume, as in all the others, Bernard argues for the impossibility of Atheism. It, like Deism, is always capitalized. Everyone, he claims—including Spinoza—has come to see that there is a universal self-sufficient substance, a supreme being with authority and dominion over humankind: "No matter how all these Libertine, Deist, Freethinking philosophers etc may have reasoned, they were all compelled to recognize a supreme authority." It may coexist, or not, with matter. The supreme authority may or may not "exist before Matter; [be] Matter itself or [be] only soul of this Matter; coexisting and co-eternal, space that contains bodies; substance infinite and universal." Let the reader decide.[25]

kind of a summary of everything he has seen so far

In so describing God's relationship to the world, Bernard admits the possibility that Spinoza, when he conflated God with substance, had just possibly come close to the way the world may be. But labels need to be accurate. Calling Spinozists and others "atheists" results from an overactive imagination finding false resemblances between different positions. The aim of those who slur them is to authorize the prejudices found among elements of the public. Bernard considers Spinoza to be a "Deist Philosopher." Had Bernard known Hobbes's response to the accusation that he was an atheist, Bernard could only have smiled in agreement: "Do you think I can be an atheist and not know it? Or, knowing it, durst have offered my atheism to the press."[26]

The point that Bernard makes about atheism, hence about Spinoza, is an important one and a corrective to the recent interpretation of the Enlightenment that makes Spinoza the main progenitor of its radical phase and, quite simplistically, an atheist. To be sure, Spinoza did not make it easy for his contemporaries—nor for future readers and scholars—to know what he meant in his posthumously published *Ethics* (1677). In the opening section "Of God" he proclaimed: "we have demonstrated . . . that Nature does not act with an end in view; that the eternal and infinite being, whom we call God, or Nature, acts by the same necessity whereby it exists. That the necessity of his nature whereby he acts is the same as that whereby he exists has been demonstrated." The overwhelming majority of devout Christians and Jews who read passages like that in 1677 said to themselves, "this is rank and horrendous atheism." To make God out to be like Nature destroyed the distinction between creator and created. Some Spinoza scholars have agreed, and argue that Spinoza's intention when he elided God with Nature, and both with Substance, was to collapse God into Nature so as to eliminate him once and for all.[27]

Others recognize the nuances present in the immensely difficult terminology employed by Spinoza in his philosophical masterpiece and see him as wishing to affirm God as the lawgiver of nature. They argue that "saying God is in all things is not the same thing as saying that he *is* all things." They take seriously Spinoza's statement: "By God, I understand a being absolutely infinite—that is—a substance consisting of an infinity of attributes, of which each expresses eternal and infinite essence." Sometimes words mean what they say; at least that is what Bernard thought when he argued that Spinoza was not an atheist but

[handwritten margin note: Atheism x deism ↓ collapse of God and Nature*]*

a deist. Toland had coined the term "pantheist" to describe someone thinking along the lines laid down by Spinoza. Prosper Marchand's close friend Jean Rousset de Missy used it with approval in his private letters to Marchand, but Bernard never uses the term. Pantheism only began to be associated with Spinoza much later in the eighteenth century, when the English and German Romantics rediscovered Spinoza. The Romantics rehabilitated Spinoza and thought that he had inserted God into Nature because—far from being an atheist—he was obsessed with God. By late in the century the English Romantics had found another way of describing Spinozism's radical tenets, best summed up by the phrase Samuel Taylor Coleridge used to describe his close friend the poet William Wordsworth: he is "a republican and at least a semi-atheist."[28]

In an earlier volume Bernard uses the term "Spinozism" and consigns it to a very special group of non-European thinkers, the Confucians. Europeans of Bernard's day held China as a true and old civilization and regarded the Confucians as among its most serious philosophers. In describing the views of the Indochinese, gleaned from the accounts of travelers, Bernard claims that the followers of Confucius postulate that there are five "elements . . . wood, fire, earth, water, and metal," and that these create all men and animals, who are composed "of a subtle matter." In effect Bernard paints Confucianism as a form of materialism, a conflation of everything into matter. Like most Europeans of his day Bernard would have taken Asians to be more learned than—for example—the peoples of the New World. In other volumes he tells his readers that the idolatrous peoples of America are less philosophical in general and most likely have little understanding of matters as deep as materialism, pantheism, or deism. Yet even the Americans, Bernard informs, "recognize spirits in inanimate things" in ways not unlike the Ancients, who believed in "a universal Spirit that penetrates all beings." Although such metaphysical speculations "are too philosophical for the Savages," they are present, diffused among their wisest men.[29]

The philosophical insights—most would have said errors—that in the West were associated with Spinoza (and in the case of materialism also with Hobbes) turn out to have been sprinkled throughout the thoughts of humankind. Bernard wants all people to have religion and to have an idea of a supreme being, regardless of how many idols or gods they also invoke. But however infusing of matter, this Being is remote, indebted to science in that it is, to use Spinoza's words, "the efficient cause of all," the originator of the laws of nature. Derived from the most outrageous thinkers of the previous generation and of their day, deism made the Bernard and Picart exploration of all the religions of the world compelling. The conclusion seems inescapable: disbelief in the central doctrines of Christianity, what Bernard calls "the false ideas [of so] many Christians," anchored Picart and Bernard's toleration of human religious diversity. Their effort of imagination gave the name of deism to the thing that brought God and nature, spirit and matter, together. Deism sufficed for "giving the idea of the moral" as much in speculation as in practice. It also dispensed with the notion of a watchful, providential God, described by Rousset writing to Marchand as "the god of the lazy."[30] →someone looking over your shoulder

Bernard also finds Spinozism closer to home. He tells the story of an obscure Dutch sect founded late in the seventeenth century by Pontiaan van Hattem and based partly on the ideas of Spinoza. Van Hattem was a Dutch Reformed preacher who was banned from the ministry in 1683 for his heterodox opinions. Bernard devotes pages to enumerating van Hattem's various doctrines, which appear to be a strange jumble of Quietism and other heresies. At one point Bernard uses the term "complicated deism," even though the Hattemites claimed to believe in the Trinity and therefore considered Jews, Muslims, and Socinians to be atheists. It seems entirely possible that Bernard devoted so much attention to them because van Hattem preached religious tolerance and the abolition of all the requirements of confessionalism. Bernard insisted that van Hattem (d. 1706) still had followers in the Dutch Republic, which is true since they were being persecuted into the 1730s. Bernard refers explicitly in his footnotes to writings about the persecutions. He ridicules those who claimed that the Hattemites were raising an army of atheists who were asked to drink a glass of wine containing a piece of paper on which was inscribed the name of the Devil. Like the mystical Hattemites, Bernard was another freethinking heretic of the spirit.[31]

Toland may have offered tools for criticizing the superstitions that had crept into Christianity, but Spinoza and Spinozism remained central preoccupations for Bernard, as can be seen from his extended treatment of the Hattemites. Bernard insisted that Spinoza and his followers believed in an abstraction known as "God." Finding the religious dimension in Spinozism required a rare insight that did not become commonplace until the late eighteenth and early nineteenth century, when European intellectuals rediscovered Spinoza. Bernard's account of him and his Dutch followers stands as one of the most extensive treatments available outside of Dutch-language polemics and Toland's own somewhat garbled presentation in *Letters to Serena* (1704). Bernard's version is worth taking seriously—especially by those who think that Spinozism could only mean atheism. Indeed it is on the subject of atheism that Bernard is at his most subtle, if not coy, and difficult to decipher. It was hardly accidental that he titled his concluding essay in the volume "Dissertation that contains the particularities concerning Deism and the Dogmas of a sect accused of libertinism and of Deism, Etc." Just what was included in that Etc.?[32]

No one has a window into anyone's inner beliefs. Through a glass darkly we pry, conjecture, and look for clues, left hundreds of years ago, purposefully or not. But one central tenet runs through *Religious Ceremonies of the World:* everyone, all of human kind, entertains a belief in some kind of supreme deity. The opening dissertation, written when Picart was very much alive, makes this claim and also states clearly that the religious and ceremonial forms that belief takes are entirely inventions of the human psyche. At the end of volume six, the conclusion to Bernard's treatment of all the monotheistic religions, the same assertion appears again: "It is, it seems to me, very unlikely, not to say impossible, for there to be true Atheists. The existence of a Supreme Being is too visible, and the characters of good and evil, with their consequences, are depicted too vividly in the conscience of all men for it to be possible to absolutely take away from them the idea of a Being sovereign over nature." This belief in a supreme being can be found among the Chinese and the Japanese as well as in the monotheistic religions. Yet Bernard is maddeningly elusive about what or who God might be.[33]

After introducing the Hattemites near the beginning of his essay on deism, Bernard breaks off to take on Spinoza himself, on the grounds that only then can the doctrines of the Hattemites be reasonably compared to those of the philosopher. Bernard gives a lengthy account of the life of Spinoza (it is removed in the English translation), parts of which come directly from a short, sympathetic biographical piece by Jean Maximilien Lucas. That biography had also appeared as the first part of *The Treatise on the Three Impostors.* Having had a hand many years earlier in calling attention to the Lucas biography (see chapter one), Bernard is quite precise in identifying it *(La Vie)* and the *Three Impostors* treatise itself (*L'Esprit de Spinosa*—the original 1719 title was *La Vie et l'esprit de Spinosa*). The reader correctly learns of the efforts "of the Inquisitors of books" to suppress the work in the Dutch Republic. In this same section Bernard sympathetically discusses Spinoza's earlier expulsion from the synagogue in 1656, noting that after that event Christians put Spinoza under their protection, and he in turn "thought only of advancing the human sciences."[34]

In his detailed exposition of Spinoza, Bernard renders him a deist. He carefully considers Spinoza's understanding of God as Nature and never identifies his set of beliefs as atheism. Bernard does admit to Spinoza's having been "a dangerous philosopher" and recommends that readers also consult Bayle's interpretation of Spinoza, as found in his *Dictionary*. Bayle's account is decidedly negative compared with Lucas's biography. Nonetheless, Bernard tells the reader that he will avoid labeling Spinoza "impious." In effect Bernard offers the definition of God found in Spinoza's *Ethics:* there is such a being, a single universal Substance that has authority over humankind. The Spinozist definition of God was completely removed from the English translation.[35]

Bernard was keenly aware that the accusation of atheism had been leveled by just about every form of Christianity against its rivals, Protestants versus Catholics, Anglicans versus Puritans, and always Trinitarians against Socinians. It is precisely this sort of rigidity that Bernard never fails to highlight: "It is not difficult to make the *Rigid* understand that all of that necessarily comes back to the same thing; for whoever is not Orthodox is indubitably either a *Jew,* a *Papist,* a *Mahometan,* or a *Spinozist,* from which he falls finally into the most profound abyss, which is decided Atheism." When approaching the accusation that one or another form of belief is dangerous to the state, Bernard even notes that if Socinians—for example—were to become dominant then they would take the same turn as did the Anabaptists and abandon their most extreme beliefs.[36]

Being a member of the first generation of Europeans able to embrace the new religions, the deism, materialism, and pantheism bequeathed by thinkers as diverse as Bruno, Vanini, Naudé, Hobbes, Spinoza, and Toland, among others, Bernard thought deeply about theology, metaphysics, and natural philosophy. As the son of a Protestant minister, could he have done otherwise? His *tour de force* account of the heresies of the age turns finally for resolution not to Dutch or French sources, although he knew them well, but to English thinkers as diverse as the liberal Anglican Samuel Clarke and Toland. Bernard ignores Clarke's attack on Toland, Hobbes, and Spinoza, and instead uses Clarke to affirm that Christianity has its foundation in natural religion. In company with Toland, Bernard laments the mysteries and superstitions that have accrued over many centuries within a priest-driven Christianity. Bernard's obvious sympathy for the writings of Clarke and Toland, as well as those of the Socinians, permits him to speak in a contemporary voice, often quoting them speaking about "today," and to affirm that the very diversity of heresies now found in the world confirms that "the grace of God is spread among all men." Bernard repeats Toland's claim that "*divine faith* is today founded on nothing more than reason (and on reasoning)."[37]

Bernard has arrived at a place where enlightened religiosity may be said to be divinely inspired yet humanly invented. Born into the most monotheistic form of Christianity, Calvinism with Waldensian associations, Bernard has retained its psychology of certainty that human knowledge can reach for veracity because there is a Supreme Being. God may be largely unknowable—even if part of nature—but the world and its many religions can be understood through a posture of scientific detachment because reason, like grace, is spread among all of humankind. This first generation of enlightened thinkers who could embrace deism or Spinozism came out of Christian backgrounds. They brought the custom of sincere belief and the search for moral guidance to their quest for an alterative and coherent system of truth. In effect they could take the deism of Toland, the insights of Hobbes, the metaphysics of Spinoza, the liberal religiosity of Clarke and forge yet another religion. In so doing they were moving into uncharted intellectual terrain. They knew that religion could not be shelved, yet the religion Bernard favors has no resemblance to the existing and churched varieties. He knew what Christians thought about such a religiosity, about the disrespect accorded heresy and unorthodoxy. It was a disdain normally reserved for idolatry or Islam.

The heart of Christianity had become, for thinkers like Bernard and Picart, as well as many others, not a way of life guided by clergy but a series of abstractions. Deism and Spinozism, no less abstract, also became in an unprecedented way confessional and reinforced their quest.

Now as mature thinkers settled in Amsterdam, Bernard and Picart set upon examining the religious ceremonies and customs of the world. They searched for the common core found in the East and the West, in the old and the new worlds. They covered their own version of natural religion with the claim of universal validity. Everyone believed in their own version of God, only Deists knew that all the rest of religion relied upon human contrivances, reinforced by clergy and temple, rich and variegated by virtue of our imagination. What better than to dispense with customs and inventions, to pursue the life of the mind in reading and writing, in drawing and etching? Such arts afforded the possibility of a new kind of immortality, a chance to articulate a visionary new confession based solely upon reason that could inform, guide, and perhaps also enlighten. Their natural religion could transcend the interfaith contestations that in every Western country or colony still bedeviled social harmony, or worse, that permitted active persecution. At its conclusion the last volume on the monotheistic religions laid out the deistic creed and offered it, like all the other religions that preceded it, as one choice available to the informed reader.

Conclusion

Literary Fortunes

*R*ELIGIOUS *Ceremonies of the World* was a blockbuster. Its devastating critique of established religion and its almost prohibitive cost never impeded its commercial success. The book was an author's dream, not only because of the striking number of copies and editions that were sold all over Europe and the Americas, but even more because it remained in print for almost a full century. All editions were bestsellers in their own right. The original Amsterdam edition was printed in 1,200 copies, about the maximum amount that could be made in one run.

Between 1733 and 1739 Bernard published two reprints of all seven volumes, some vastly improved. He did not reprint the series in a logical order. The second reprint of the volumes that dealt with the Jews and the Catholics came last, in 1739. The total number of reprint copies is unknown, but it is unlikely that the number of each run would have been lower than 400. They must have sold quickly. According to the letter that Jean Frederic Bernard sent to the editors of The Hague journal *Nouvelle Bibliothèque* in 1741, all copies sold rapidly. Besides, the sales catalogue of Jean Frederic's stock after his death in 1744 reveals that he had only a few incomplete copies left. In 1743 Bernard added two supplements, sometimes considered volumes 7.2 and 8, and he even advertised a volume 9. Despite the title pages, no Picart engravings appear in any of these volumes.[1]

Bernard was certainly not the only one to profit. In 1741 the Parisian publishing firm Rollin issued a new edition, employing the same piracy practices that financed Jean Frederic's own company. Rollin at some moment must have acquired the original copperplates sold on auction by Picart's widow in 1733. He commissioned the Parisian clerics Antoine Banier and Jean Baptiste Le Mascrier to produce a new version under a slightly different title: *General History of the Ceremonies, Traditions, and Customs of All the Peoples of the World.* It was printed in 350 copies and sold quickly.[2]

Within Bernard's lifetime the Paris version was the only one produced without his consent. In 1728 the first volume of a Dutch edition was put up for sale. Picart's magnificent "Vignette of the Principal Religions of the World" was specially engraved for this Dutch translation. Its quality was high and true to the original. Unlike the English version, it never omitted radical passages. The Amsterdam author Adriaan Moubach, responsible for the translation, had a reputation to keep up. Bernard knew him well. Moubach was an expert on the Northern seas and the Greenland fisheries, topics Bernard was interested in for his *Voyages au Nord* series. The publishers were trusted colleagues of Bernard's, too. With two of them, Hermanus Uytwerf of Amsterdam and the Rotterdam firm of Jan Daniel Beman, he had just completed a very successful joint venture: the publication of the popular Ostervald Bible. The Dutch edition sold its 550 copies extremely well, almost all to subscribers, a remarkable success if we take the small size of the Dutch market into account and the fact that many educated Dutch already would have subscribed to the original French-language edition.

In 1733 the first volume of an English edition was issued, to be completed six years later. Its translation was less faithful than the Dutch one. The *General Preface,* for instance, which would constitute a major stumbling block for the papal censors some five years later, was omitted, and throughout the text small changes were made, rendering it less offensive to orthodox readers. The six-volume English edition was probably printed in more than 800 copies. It must have sold rapidly, as only three years after its completion, in 1741, the market was able to absorb a one-volume abridged version. It contained most of the engravings, but the volume of the text had been seriously reduced. In 1738 a German abridgment began to appear, made by a pupil of Bernard Picart, David Herrliberger. After having completed his apprenticeship with

Picart, Herrliberger returned to Switzerland, where he became a well-established engraver of topographic scenes. The Herrliberger edition took thirteen years to complete. It was published in a series of small fascicules that in the end made up three folio volumes. Herrliberger cut dramatically the number of text pages but retained most of Picart's engravings, adding a few ceremonies of his own, in use in the churches of the Swiss canton of Zürich. The German-language version consisted of 350 copies.[3]

Thus within a few years after the completion of the original Amsterdam edition, almost 4,000 copies had reached the public. All editions were printed in the expensive folio format, and their cost was seldom

C.1   Funeral procession of a Zurich gentleman. From David Herrliberger, *Gottesdienstliche Ceremonien, oder H. Kirchen-Gebräuche und Religions-Pflichten der Christen* (Zurich: David Herrliberger; Basel: Daniel Eckenstein, 1750–1751), 25. (Author's collection)

lower than 150 florins. Very few works of a similar size and price in eighteenth-century Europe enjoyed a comparable success. Bayle's *Historical and Critical Dictionary,* for instance, which went through many three- and four-folio-volume editions, was much cheaper and sold generally for less than 50 florins. Even in the eighteenth century books had a short life expectancy. After a few years interest dropped off and new titles absorbed the attention of the reading public. *Religious Ceremonies of the World* had a different experience. Its popularity did not end by 1750 and it even got a second life.[4]

In 1783 the Paris publisher Antoine Laporte (1746–1817) published an adaptation in four slim folio volumes on the basis of the pirated edition of 1741. The Laporte version of *Religious Ceremonies of the World* kept all

C.2   Communion service in the Reformed Church of Zurich. From Herrliberger, *Gottesdienstliche Ceremonien, oder H. Kirchen-Gebräuche und Religions-Pflichten der Christen,* 47. (Author's collection)

the Picart engravings but rehashed Bernard's text completely. Its author was Jean Charles Poncelin de La Roche Tilhac (1746–1828), a French cleric who had come to Paris hoping to make a career in the sophisticated world of salons and academies. Like so many other provincials, he ended up as a hack writer and a political intriguer. To enhance the edition's authenticity, Laporte gave it the same title as the Amsterdam original and even an Amsterdam imprint. It was a completely Parisian production, though, as Laporte had never set up shop in Amsterdam. Its 400 copies sold fast. In 1789 the Laporte firm printed another 400 copies that also were soon gone.

Religious Ceremonies of the World was even granted a third life. In 1807 the Paris publisher Prudhomme and Fils decided to put a new edition of the work on the market, as all previous editions were sold out. Louis-Marie Prudhomme (1752–1830), the firm's founder, came from a bookseller's family in Lyon. He was the owner of Paris's most radical newspaper in the first years of the Revolution, *Révolutions de Paris*. He experimented with newspaper illustrations such as the engraving and the woodblock and wrote a famous history of the Terror. The Prudhomme firm operated at the high end of the market and issued the chief biographical dictionary of the French Empire. The new editors' approach was almost scholarly. They made a careful comparison of all previous editions and decided that the only one worth reprinting was the original Amsterdam version. All others, they wrote in their preface, were hopelessly corrupted and misinterpreted Bernard's and Picart's intentions completely.[5]

The Prudhomme team published a comprehensive twelve-volume folio edition that almost surpassed the quality of the Amsterdam original. A new letter type was specially designed, print errors were corrected, the order of the chapters was adjusted to make their sequence more logical, and an extensive index was added. In places the editorial team even corrected Bernard's prose, which they called an unpolished "refugee style." They took much care not to change Bernard's ideas themselves. Jean Frederic might not have been a master prose stylist, but they admired his sense. To complete the set the Prudhomme editors added the two folio volumes of *Ancient and Modern Superstitions,* which Bernard had published separately in the 1730s and which many owners already had bound together with their copy of *Religious Ceremonies of the World.* Finally, to make the series up-to-date, Prudhomme added a

Tom. X.   *Planche. I.*

COSTUME DES ORATEURS DES THÉOPHILANTROPES.

C.3   Orator of the Theophilanthropists. From *Cérémonies et coutumes religieuses de tous les peuples du monde, representées par des figures dessinées de la main de Bernard Picart, avec des explications historiques et des dissertations curieuses. Nouvelle édition entièrement conforme à celle de Hollande,* 12 vols. (Paris: L. Prudhomme, 1807–1810), X, 234. (Author's collection)

volume in which all new religions and sects were discussed. As they did not exist or had not yet been discovered in Bernard's time, they had been left out of the original edition. At first sight this survey of the religions of the South Seas, Methodists, Theophilanthropists, and Freemasons, as well as of a large group of smaller sects, actually enhanced the encyclopedic character of *Religious Ceremonies of the World*, something that Bernard had tried to avoid. However, the editors followed Bernard's reasoning throughout and looked at these new religions for a universal natural religion. Finally, the Prudhomme team had recovered all the original plates from which the engravings had to be printed. They could not locate the title vignette of 1727 and feared that it had been destroyed in the Revolution. They copied it from the original and included it in their reprint. The Prudhomme edition was an erudite tribute to both Picart and Bernard, and it is difficult to imagine that they would not have applauded it themselves.

Apparently the demand was still great. In about six years the market absorbed the 400 copies printed by Prudhomme, and in 1816 a new edition went to press. Though it kept a substantial part of the text and the engravings intact, it imposed a new order and added much new material once again, especially on the developments in the French Catholic Church and on recently emerged sects, stressing even more its encyclopedic character. Owing to reduction of the text and a smaller letter type, the new publisher, the Paris firm A. Belin, succeeded in condensing the material into six quarto volumes (mostly bound as four) that could be much more attractively priced. To fit the engravings into the quarto format an engraver had developed the technique (and won a prize at a Paris industrial exposition for its use on the Picart volumes) that allowed each image to be reduced in size with exact faithfulness to the original dimensions. A new chemical process, they told their prospective clientele, would ensure that the engravings would look just as fresh as a century before. In 1819 the last volume of the complete *Religious Ceremonies of the World* was ready for sale, again in 400 copies. Nearly a century after Bernard and Picart had decided to offer tolerance and natural religion as a remedy against Europe's devastating religious divisions, and after almost 6,000 copies had sold, their message was still in demand and still available.

Readers often buy their books for reasons completely different from the author's intentions. That happened with *Religious Ceremonies of the World* as well. The few available documents about reader reactions reveal the wide range of expectations and experiences of buyers, readers, and donors. The wealthy Swedish aristocrat Jan Jacobus de Geer, for instance, bought a subscription for his son Charles, chiefly because the son "loved travel books which contain such extraordinary stories." The

C.4   Lodge of the Mopses. There is some question about whether the Mopses ever actually met; their depiction may have been satirical. *Cérémonies et coutumes religieuses de
tous les peuples du monde . . . Nouvelle édition entièrement conforme à celle de Hollande*, X,
435. (Author's collection)

British-Dutch nobleman Willem Bentinck was of the opinion that the work taught an educated man exactly what he needed to know about religion. A tutor to the future Dutch stadholder William V, he presented him with a copy at the age of fourteen. Pieter Teyler van der Hulst, a very wealthy Haarlem clothier of Mennonite stock, originally had bought *Religious Ceremonies of the World* for encyclopedic reasons. Its tolerant message, however, inspired him to set up a well-endowed learned society, explicitly devoted to the study and promotion of natural religion, even though his conception of natural religion was a bit more orthodox than the one entertained by the two Bernards.[6]

Analyzing the book's reception is seriously hampered by the instability of the text. It is often very difficult to establish precisely which version of *Religious Ceremonies of the World* readers have consulted, and they differed widely. The issue of authenticity, inherent to the mass reproduction of books, was a problem even before the invention of printing. In the era of the large medieval copy shops, universities and church authorities tried to impose strict rules, but the number of corrupted copies continued to grow, giving rise to the demand for authenticated texts that would not perplex readers and scholars alike. The printing press was an enormous step forward in the standardizing process, but the printed book did not definitively resolve the issue of corrupted texts. It just gave them a larger scope. Printing, after all, was a commercial enterprise, and there were always enough unscrupulous publishers on the look-out for quick profits. At the lower end of the market small-time booksellers sold large numbers of unauthorized books patched together from many sources. At the high end plagiarism and the reprint of unauthenticated texts were just as common, and the publishing history of *Religious Ceremonies of the World* is a perfect illustration.[7]

The 1741 Banier and Le Mascrier edition of the work constituted flagrant plagiarism, and it made Jean Frederic livid. It is very likely that the Parisian piracy frustrated his next reprint project, but what really angered him was Banier and Le Mascrier's interference with the text, their compromising of its integrity. Not only did they change the title; they also made numerous alterations and added a series of supplementary essays. In a long, fulminating essay Bernard vented his anger. He denounced their theft of his work, the pettiness of their scholarly critique, their condescending treatment of a Dutch bookseller/author without any formal standing in the learned world, and the poor quality of their copies of Picart's engravings. Particularly infuriating to Bernard was their attempt to Catholicize his work. He cited other cases of plagiarism committed by French clergymen who brazenly pilfered the work of fellow scholars. The most famous instance was the appropriation of Jacques Basnage's *History of the Jews,* adapted to French Catholic taste by Abbé Dupin. Bernard certainly had a case there. The French publisher Rollin, on learning that the Papal Office of the Inquisition had put *Religious Ceremonies of the World* on the Index, probably decided to act quickly and ordered the two mercenary clergymen (one with a police file on his activities) to produce a version of the work suitable for the Catholic market.[8]

There can be no doubt about the Catholic flavor of the Parisian *General History of the Ceremonies, Mores, and Customs of All the Peoples of the World.* The two abbés complained about the libertine ethos of the original edition, about Bernard's refusal to take sides in the Protestant-Catholic debate, and most of all about his advocacy of universal religious tolerance without exceptions. For the Prudhomme team in 1807 the "Catholic remedy" was exactly the reason to discard the work of the two "servants of the altar," as they were now dubbed. But there was more to it. In the long term the Catholic reception of the *General History* was not altogether favorable; far into the nineteenth century it was still frowned upon. Moreover, though Banier may have been an orthodox believer, Le Mascrier's credentials as a devout Catholic are much more doubtful. He had a hand in the Parisian publication of the subversive tract of Jean Baptiste Mirabaud on the materialist character of ancient philosophy, a treatise that some eleven years before had been published by Bernard in a shorter version. Even the *General History* reveals a dissident subtext. For example, the section on freemasonry in volume six was vastly expanded upon and became an important source of information about a fraternity the papacy had condemned in 1738.[9]

The editions of the 1780s constitute the next stage in the ongoing corruption of the original text and intentions of Bernard and Picart. The Poncelin version also employed the idea of a natural religion, but its message was stripped of Bernard's radical implications. Poncelin tailored his reworked copy to a rather primitive enlightened idea of the progress of civilization. Toward that end he added a new volume of his own: *Superstitions of All the Peoples of the World,* which he sold separately as well. *Superstitions* explained how religious follies had destroyed an-

cient civilization and even threatened modern ones, presenting Newton as proof. The Englishman might be a modern genius of science but
Poncelin blamed him for his outdated views on the coming apocalypse;
such beliefs stood in the way of progress. The Laporte edition displayed
precisely the derogatory view of other civilizations that Bernard and
Picart had tried to avoid. To Poncelin, Muslim culture and society, for
instance, offer the antithesis of the qualities revered in the West. The
East is a hotbed of despotism, backwardness, and eccentricity that in-
hibits progress. The harem where women are subordinate and sensual,
and men feminine and cruel at the same time, is the epitome of Arab
culture. Whereas Bernard and Picart had tried to rehabilitate Islam,
Poncelin's version of *Religious Ceremonies of the World* constituted an
early contribution to the discourse we now identify as orientalism. Poncelin, who was quick to realize that exotic religions and superstitions
were marketable topics, hurriedly authored another single-volume folio
sequel that he entitled *Oriental Superstitions* and published in 1785. All
these later editions done without Bernard's controlling vision reflected
new ideologies about "the other" that under the guise of "progress" created negative stereotypes.[10]

In the world dominated by the French language, *Religious Ceremonies
and Customs* in its various editions and adaptations transmitted fundamentally conflicting messages, ranging from full tolerance on the basis
of a radical concept of natural religion, to Catholic orthodoxy with radical and subversive undertones, and eventually to varieties of orientalism. In the English-speaking world a comparable process was under
way, even though after 1741 no new editions were issued. The fundamental transformation of the ideas and images of the two Bernards took
place here much more covertly.

The English hack William Hurd took the first step and published in
1780 *A New Universal History of the Religious Rites, Ceremonies, and Customs of the Whole World.* Hurd's *History* went through many reprints and
became the standard reference work on religion for generations of En-
glishmen and women. Nowhere did Hurd make any reference to *Ceremonies and Religious Customs of the Various Nations of the Known World*,
as the English translation of Bernard and Picart's work was called. His
title, however, amounted to a clever plagiarism, the more so because
almost all his plates were crude copies of original Picart engravings.
The text told a completely different story. The idea of the fundamental

equality of beliefs was discarded, and Hurd's book should be character-ized as a modernized version of the bias found in seventeenth-century works by Purchas and Ross. For Hurd religion was a battlefield and his-tory showed the final triumph of Protestantism over Catholicism. The Jewish and Greco-Roman traditions were manifestations of a crum-bling past, and the heathen and savage peoples proved that without di-vine guidance the number of absurd and inhumane superstitions would only continue to grow.

A central figure in the next stage of the transformation of Bernard's original message was the British savant and administrator of Scottish descent Sir Colin Mackenzie (1754–1821), the first surveyor-general of British India and one of the founders of British colonial science and scholarship. In 1826 he published *The Religious Rites and Ceremonies of Every Nation in the World.* Mackenzie did not hide the fact that the "splendid Bernard Picart" was his source of inspiration, but he made it perfectly clear that he intended to modernize the book. Mackenzie used Picart's engravings only sparingly and subjected Bernard's text to a much newer interpretation of the idea of history. Mackenzie was con-vinced that in the past men and women were different, more primi-tive and unfamiliar with modern rational and scientific reasoning. In his native Scotland enlightened philosophers such as Lord Kames, Adam Ferguson, William Robertson, and Adam Smith had developed these embryonic eighteenth-century notions into their theory of the progress of society in four stages, a model that became central to Mackenzie's view of the history of religion. The imperial version of Picart was now ready to be clearly formulated.[11]

The final step was taken by an American author, Charles Goodrich, who lived by the pen, contributing to magazines, writing schoolbooks, and producing adaptations of famous works. Goodrich almost com-pletely copied Mackenzie's historical narrative relegating the tribes of the Sandwich Islands to the most primitive stage of civilization while locating Anglo-Saxon Christianity at its apex. Goodrich added the ele-ment of a Western civilizing mission that was still incompletely ex-pressed in Mackenzie's survey. As Goodrich observed in his introduc-tion: "the anti-Christian systems and the idolatrous superstitions of the world are rapidly approaching their fall . . . Idolatry has been over-thrown in the islands of the Pacific; and in India, that massive, gorgeous, venerable superstition . . . has been undermined and a breach made in its outworks." In the nineteenth century many English-language reprints and adaptations would hammer this message home, the most important addition being William Burder's *Religious Ceremonies and Customs* (1841), which claimed to be an abridgment and adaptation of the original English translation of the 1730s. A work invented in the 1720s to address the global had morphed into an imperialist credo.[12]

In the end, Picart's brilliant reputation as an engraver turned out to be a liability as well as an asset for the mission of the two Bernards. His name on the title pages and his engravings were the only permanent elements in all versions and editions. They transformed *Religious Ceremonies of the World* from a book title into a brand name. Under the cover of his continuing presence, diluted, weakened, and eventually corrupt versions of the original text appeared, even to the extent of contradicting the original propositions of Picart and Bernard. The impressive sales of the Prudhomme edition of the early 1800s contributed greatly to keeping their original ideas alive. But it alone could not halt the growing chorus of orientalizing and Christian-supremacy voices. Commerce and a rough and vibrant capitalism—what had made a radical venture such as *Religious Ceremonies of the World* possible in the first place—ultimately worked to undermine its message.

One would have expected the emerging disciplines of anthropology and especially of comparative religion to recognize the pioneering qualities of *Religious Ceremonies of the World* and to make it part of their canon. If we consult the standard textbooks, however, we look for the names of Picart and Bernard in vain. Louis Henry Jordan's 1905 groundbreaking overview of the newly emerging field of comparative religion relegated Picart and Bernard to the appendix. Today's most firmly established textbook history of the discipline, Eric Sharpe's *Comparative Religion*, fails to mention the two Bernards at all. Even a specialized monograph such as David Pailin's survey of comparative religion in the seventeenth and eighteenth centuries hardly appreciated the revolutionary qualities of their work, characterizing their views as "morally eccentric." Most studies attribute great value to *Religious Ceremonies of the World* as an early reference work, but its approach is judged too diffuse and lacking in scientific rigor. The two Bernards were a stepping stone toward the modern disciplines at best.[13]

The work of Bernard and Picart has fallen victim to the same development that has eliminated the artisan from the history of the emergence of the natural sciences. Only authors who behaved in accordance with the later nineteenth-century images and ideals of scholarship were selected as crucial to the formation of these disciplines. As booksellers and engravers the two Bernards failed to reach the scholarly standards the emerging discipline was expecting of its pioneers. The fact that by the later nineteenth century the intellectual accomplishment of Bernard and Picart was very difficult to decipher, contaminated as it was by more than a century of rehashing and diluting of their words in the many bowdlerized editions, must have played a central part. We are now on the brink of restoring them to their rightful place.

Bernard and Picart themselves were uninterested in founding new disciplines. They were confronted with a crisis of dramatic proportions. All over Europe religion had become a divisive factor that threatened to destroy the fabric of politics and society. They made use of all modern scholarly disciplines and techniques then available to them to find a solution to this tragedy. Their *Religious Ceremonies of the World* was an impressive intellectual achievement. Thanks to efforts like theirs religion would cease to be the most central issue on the European agenda. After 1750 the problems of political participation and social equality would dominate Enlightenment debates. But today, now that religious divisions are animating world politics again and even wars of religion between states seem a serious possibility anew, their work has lost none of its relevance.

How pleased Bernard and Picart would have been to know that their many volumes are still being read today. How could it be otherwise? Their enquiries encompassed much of what was then known about the peoples of the world and their religious customs. With clarity and rigor Bernard and Picart offered an unprecedented synthesis, novel primarily in two ways. They sought, wherever possible in word and image, to slip out from under the biases found in most accounts of religion and then to search for the universals seen in the religions of Europe, Asia, the Americas, and Africa. They blended encyclopedic erudition with the style of late Baroque realism, using engravings to give aesthetic pleasure and enlightened perspectives. They brought art into the service of curiosity and tolerance while setting new standards for documentation and the citation of evidence. They never forgot that they were refugees (with a bias against Catholicism) who had found a new intellectual life based upon their experiences in the Dutch Republic and vast reading in the most avant-garde texts to be found in French, Dutch, Latin, German, and English. These artisans of Enlightenment tell us more about the foundations of that movement than does the simple explication of classic texts (however famous the author) or a monochrome history of a single cluster of ideas. They bring us closer to what the experience of early modernity might have been.

The Seven Volumes of
Religious Ceremonies of the World

Table A.1 The seven volumes of *Religious Ceremonies of the World*

Vol. no.[a]	Date	Subject	Length[b]	Text	Plates[c]	<1	1	2	3–6	>6	Two-page spread	Fold out
1	1723	Jews/Catholics[d]	506	404	44	3	6	10	11	4	2	3
2	1723	Catholics	360	301	29			12	13		2	
3	1723	Americas, India	510	410	47	2	9	23	12	1		
4	1728	India, Asia, Africa	638	504	65		5	22	24		7	
5	1733	Greek Orthodox, Protestants	444	396	24		2	6	6		5	
6	1736	Anglicans, Quakers, Deists, etc.	404	363	19		1	7	1		5	
7[e]	1737	Islam, Additions	553	323	35	2	11	8	8		6	1
Total			3,415	2,701	263	7	34	80	75	5	27	4

a. The order of the original seven volumes varies from library to library. We have used the numbers given to the volumes by the Getty Research Institute library. Their volumes are numbered by the date of publication. The title pages of the original French edition divided the volumes into two groups: 1–5 on the monotheistic religions and an additional two on idolatrous religions. The Getty numbering of the volumes is the same as that of the English translation, published between 1733 and 1739.

b. The total page count includes blank pages on the back of engravings as well as plates of engravings, tables of contents, and the like. Text pages are listed in the next column. Pagination within the volumes is irregular: prefaces often have no numbers at all, and sometimes sections within volumes begin again at page 1. Fonts vary, so not every page of text is alike.

c. The first column of Plates gives the total number of folio plates with engravings (in which double plates and fold-out plates are counted as two). This number is somewhat misleading, however, as some folio plates include an image on only part of the page (< 1); some are full-page engravings (1); some plates have two (2), three, four, five, six (3–6), eight, or nine (> 6) separate images on one folio-size page; still others are double page (2x) or fold-out ("fld out" or larger than double page) plates. Thus volume 1 might be thought to have some 130 engravings. Purely decorative *culs de lampe* or "printer's flowers" are excluded from the count.

d. Volume 1 starts with a 6-page general preface and a 36-page essay comparing forms of religious worship around the world.

e. Volume 7 includes 352 pages on Islam; 41 pages of supplements, including a double-page engraving of the Jewish festival of Purim; and 160 pages of indexes to the previous volumes.

Editions of
Religious Ceremonies of the World

Editions in French

1. *Cérémonies et coutumes religieuses de tous les peuples du monde représentées par des figures dessinées de la main de Bernard Picard: avec une explication historique, & quelques dissertations curieuses.* 7 vols. Amsterdam: J. F. Bernard, 1723–1737. Folio.[1]

2. *Cérémonies et coutumes religieuses de tous les peuples du monde representées par des figures dessinées de la main de Bernard Picart: avec une explication historique, & quelques dissertations curieuses.* 7 vols. Amsterdam: J. F. Bernard, 1733–1739. Reprint. Folio.

3. *Histoire générale des cérémonies, moeurs et coutumes de tous les peuples du monde; représentées en 243 figures dessinées de la main de Bernard Picard, avec des explications historiques & curieuses, par M. l'Abbé Banier & par M. l'Abbé Mascrier.* 7 vols. Paris: Rollin fils, 1741. Folio.

4. *Supplements.* 2 vols. Amsterdam: J. F. Bernard, 1743. Folio.

5. [Jean Charles Poncelin de la Roche Tilhac], *Cérémonies et coutumes religieuses de tous les peuples du monde représentées par des figures dessinées & gravées par Bernard Picard, & autres habiles artistes: Ouvrage qui comprend l'histoire philosophique de la religion des nations des deux hémisphères; telles que celle des Brames, des Peguans, des*

Chinois, des Japonois, des Thibetins, & celle des différens peuples qui habitent l'Asie & les isles de l'Archipélague Indien; celle des Mexicains, des Péruviens, des Brésiliens, des Groënlandois, des Lapons, des Caffres, de tous les peuples de la Nigritie, de l'Ethiopie & du Monomotapa; celle des juifs, tant anciens que modernes, celles des musulmans & des différentes sectes qui la composent; enfin celle des chrétiens & de cette multitude de branches dans lesquelles elle est subdivisée. Nouvelle edition, enrichie de toutes les figures comprises dans l'ancienne edition en sept volumes, & dans les quatre publiés par forme de supplement. 4 vols. Amsterdam [Paris]: Laporte, 1783. Folio.[2]

6. *Cérémonies et coutumes religieuses de tous les peuples du monde représentées par des figures dessinées & gravées par Bernard Picard, & autres habiles artistes: Ouvrage qui comprend l'histoire philosophique de la religion des nations des deux hémispheres; telles que celle des Brames, des Peguans, des Chinois, des Japonois, des Thibetins, & celle des différens peuples qui habitent l'Asie & les isles de l'Archipélague Indien; celle des Mexicains, des Péruviens, des Brésiliens, des Groënlandois, des Lapons, des Caffres, de tous les peuples de la Nigritie, de l'Ethiopie & du Monomotapa; celle des juifs, tant anciens que modernes, celles des musulmans & des différentes sectes qui la composent; enfin celle des chrétiens & de cette multitude de branches dans lesquelles elle est subdivisée. Nouvelle edition, enrichie de toutes les figures comprises dans l'ancienne edition en sept volumes, & dans les quatre publiés par forme de supplement.* Par une société des gens de lettres. 4 vols. Amsterdam [Paris]: Laporte, 1789. Folio.

7. *Cérémonies et coutumes religieuses de tous les peuples du monde, représentées par des figures dessinées de la main de Bernard Picart, avec des explications historiques et des dissertations curieuses. Nouvelle édition entièrement conforme à celle de Hollande.* 12 vols. Paris: L. Prudhomme, 1807–1810. Folio.

8. *Histoire des religions et des moeurs de tous les peuples du monde / avec 600 gravures, représentant toutes les cérémonies et coutumes religieuses, dessinées par B. Picart. Publiées en Hollande, par J.-Fr. Bernard.* 6 vols. Paris: A. Belin, 1816–1819. Quarto.

9. [Jean Charles Poncelin de la Roche Tilhac], *Cérémonies religieuses de tous les peuples du monde, avec 50 fig. en taille douce par Bernard Picard.* Paris: E. Babeuf, 1821. 1 volume in octavo.

Editions in Dutch and German

10. [Abraham Moubach], *Naaukeurige beschryving der uitwendige godtsdienstplichten, kerk-zeden en gewoontens van alle volkeren der waereldt; in een historisch verhaal met eenige naaukeurige verhandelingen ontvouwen, door verscheiden aanmerkin-*

gen opgeheldert; en in kunstige tafereelen afgemaalt: geteekent door Bernard Picard. 6 vols. Rotterdam, Amsterdam, and Den Haag: Uytwerf, Beman en Van der Kloot, 1727–1738. Folio.

11. [David Herrliberger], *Heilige Ceremonien, Gottes- und Goetzen-Dienste aller Völcker der Welt: oder eigentliche Vorstellung und summarischer Begriff der vornehmsten Gottes-dienstlichen Pflichten. Nach des berühmten Picarts Erfindung in Kupfer gestochen.* 3 vols. Zürich: David Herrliberger, 1738–1751. Folio.

Editions in English

12. *The Ceremonies and Religious Customs of the Various Nations of the Known World; together with historical annotations and several curious discourses. Written originally in French, and illustrated with a large number of folio copper plates designed by Mr. Bernard Picart, and curiously engraved by most of the best hands in Europe.* 7 vols. London: William Jackson and Claude Dubosc, 1733–1739. Folio.

13. *The Ceremonies and Religious Customs of the Various Nations of the Known World; with additions and remarks omitted by the French author Written originally in French, and illustrated with copper plates all beautifully design'd by Mr. Bernard Picart; whereby the reader will be informed (in a concise, clear and intelligible style) of the customs and ceremonies; in what manner, and under what forms, representations and signs &c the several nations under both hemispheres worship a supreme being. Faithfully abridg'd from the French original.* London, 1741. 1 volume in quarto.

14. William Hurd, *A New Universal History of the Religious Rites, Ceremonies, and Customs of the Whole World: or, a complete and impartial view of all the religions in the various nations of the universe.* London: Alexander Hogg, 1780.[3]

15. Colin Mackenzie, *The Religious Rites and Ceremonies of Every Nation in the World: Impartially described and beautifully Illustrated with Engravings on Steel & Wood. Modernized from the Celebrated & Splendid Work of Bernard Picart.* London: John Williams, 1826.

16. Robert Huish, *The Religious Ceremonies and Customs of Every Nation of the World, Abridged from the Celebrated and Splendid Work of Barnard Picart. Illustrated by Beautiful Engravings on Steel and Wood.* London: John Williams, 1828.

17. Charles A. Goodrich, *Religious Ceremonies and Customs, or the Forms of Worship practised by the several nations of the known world, from the earliest records to the pres-*

ent time; on the basis of the celebrated and splendid work of Bernard Picart; to which is added, a brief view of minor sects, which exist at the present day. Hartford: Hutchison and Dwier, 1834.

18. William Burder, B.A., *Religious Ceremonies and Customs; or the Forms of Worship practised by the several nations of the known World, from the earliest records to the present time; on the basis of the celebrated and splendid work of Bernard Picart.* London: Thomas Tegg, 1841.

Abbreviations

Bernard cat.   *Catalogue du fonds de librairie de feu Jean Frederic Bernard consistant en un bel assortiment de livres. . . .* (Amsterdam: Pierre Humbert and Son, S. and P. Schouten, Marc Michael Rey, 1747).

CC   *Cérémonies et coutumes religieuses de tous les peuples du monde / representées par des figures dessinées de la main de Bernard Picard* [i.e. Picart]; *avec une explication historique, & quelques dissertations curieuses,* 9 vols. (Amsterdam, Chez J. F. Bernard, 1723–1743).

Imp Inn   *Impostures innocentes, ou Recueil d'estampes d'après divers peintres illustres, tels que Rafael, Le Guide, Carlo Maratti, Le Poussin, Rembrandt, &c. Gravées à leurs imitation, & selon le gout particulier de chacun d'eux, & accompagné d'un Discours sur les Préjugés de certains Curieux touchant la Gravûre. Par Bernard Picart, dessinateur et graveur: avec son Eloge historique, et le catalogue de ses ouvrages.* (Amsterdam: Chez la Veuve de Bernard Picart, sur le Cingel, à l'Etoile, 1734).

Picart cat.   *Catalogue de livres curieux tant en françois qu'en Latin & . . . , rassemblez par feu M. Bernard Picart . . . ces Livres se vendront chez S. Schouten dans le Kalverstraat le 13 Octobre 1733* (Amsterdam: J. F. Bernard & Salom. Schouten, 1733).

VWG   Paola Von Wyss-Giacosa, *Religionsbilder der Frühen Aufklärung: Bernard Picarts Tafeln für die Cérémonies et Coutumes religieuses de tous les Peuples du Monde* (Wabern/Bern: Benteli Verlags, 2006).

Notes

Introduction

1. All translations are our own unless otherwise noted. We have chosen to quote from the French original with our own translation rather than use the English translation, which is not always true to the original. We give titles as they appeared in the first edition even when they lack modern diacritical markings and render Bernard's name Jean Frederic without accents because it appears in the sources with inconsistent markings. Bernard published two supplementary volumes to the work in 1743 that are not included in our consideration. The first is subtitled *TOME SEPTIEME SECONDE PARTIE. Qui contient plusieurs Dissertations de Mess. les Abbés Banier & Le Mascrier, sur des matiéres qui ont quelque raport aux Cérémonies Religieuses &c.* After a preface severely criticizing the two Catholic clerics Banier and Le Mascrier, who published a pirated and expurgated edition of *Religious Ceremonies of the World* in 1741, Bernard then printed some of the additional material they had included in their edition, presumably to counter their efforts to better him. The second supplement, subtitled *TOME HUITIEME. Qui contient un paralléle historique des Cérémonies Religieuses de tous les Peuples anciens & modernes, & la description de divers Usages singuliers, prétendus Religieux, ou qui ont quelque raport à la Religion,* contains various additional "dissertations" on civil ceremonies that Bernard claims to have intended to consider in *Religious Ceremonies of the World,* but in fact the volume seems an ill-considered attempt to capitalize on the success of the original work. It includes titillating essays on the feast of fools, the use of satire, the masquerades of Carnival, and the similarity between the practices of the Jews and ancient bacchanalias. These two volumes contain no engravings by Picart,

the title pages notwithstanding. In some libraries the book can be found with volumes numbered in a different order. (In his personal library Bernard lumped all the monotheistic religions together, for example.) For Picart's influence on Hogarth see William Bates, *Notes and Queries,* 6th series (1880), 332; and William Hogarth, John Nichols, et al., *The Genuine Works of Hogarth* (London: Longman, 1817), 3: 193.

2. Our thinking about the sacred has been nudged by Dan Diner, *Lost in the Sacred: Why the Muslim World Stood Still* (Princeton: Princeton University Press, 2009), introduction.

3. The essential starting point for any discussion of *Religious Ceremonies of the World* is VWG. She provides important background to the publication and an indepth analysis of the prints about India. An excellent overview, especially of Picart's career, can be found in the introduction to a contemporary reproduction of the images in the work by Odile Faliu, *Cérémonies et coutumes religieuses de tous les peuples du monde/dessinées par Bernard Picart* (Paris: Herscher, 1988).

4. Jonathan Sheehan, "Sacred and Profane: Idolatry, Antiquarianism and the Polemics of Distinction in the Seventeenth Century," *Past and Present,* 192 (2006): 35–66.

5. On discovery see Harold Cook, *Matters of Exchange: Commerce, Medicine, and Science in the Dutch Golden Age* (New Haven: Yale University Press, 2007); and Deborah E. Harkness, *The Jewel House: Elizabethan London and the Scientific Revolution* (New Haven: Yale University Press, 2007). For works on the Enlightenment that largely ignore *Religious Ceremonies of the World* see Jonathan I. Israel, *Radical Enlightenment: Philosophy and the Making of Modernity, 1650–1750* (New York: Oxford University Press, 2001), 134–135, where it receives two sentences out of 810 pages, and 696n, where the circle around Marchand is dismissed as "a joke" and Marchand described incorrectly as "a providential deist" (576). Bernard, Picart, and their masterpiece receive better treatment in Israel, *Enlightenment Contested: Philosophy, Modernity, and the Emancipation of Man, 1670–1752* (New York: Oxford University Press, 2006), 377–380 (where Bernard is incorrectly identified as an atheist *tout court*). The book is overlooked in Henry Vyverberg, *Human Nature, Cultural Diversity and the French Enlightenment* (New York: Oxford University Press, 1989). To spare the reader a list of everything after 1989, we suggest Larry Wolff and Marco Cipolloni, eds., *The Anthropology of the Enlightenment* (Stanford: Stanford University Press, 2007), where neither Bernard nor Picart receives a footnote and ethnography is seen to begin with Montesquieu's *Persian Letters.* In a book that wants to denigrate the irreligious impulse in the Enlightenment and in which Bernard and Picart might have served as allies, they are also absent: S. J. Barnett, *The Enlightenment and Religion* (Manchester, UK: Manchester University Press, 2003).

6. Peter Dear, "The Church and the New Philosophy," in S. Pumfrey, Paolo Rossi, and M. Slawinski, eds., *Science, Culture and Popular Belief in Renaissance Eu-*

rope (Manchester: Manchester University Press, 1991), 119–139; and Rienk Vermey, *The Calvinist Copernicans: The Reception of the New Astronomy in the Dutch Republic, 1575–1750* (Amsterdam: Koninklijke Akademie van Wetenschappen, 2002), 335–348.

7. For the first published edition of the *Treatise* we must go to its original title, [Anon.], *La vie et l'esprit de Mr. Benoit de Spinosa* [Amsterdam: Charles le Vier, 1719]. Almost every copy of this edition was confiscated or destroyed. Levier belonged to the Marchand circle. A copy exists at UCLA as #307 in the library of the late Professor A. Wolf; see *Spinoza, Benedictus de (1632–1677): The Library of the Late Prof. Dr. A. Wolf, Catalogue No. 150* (Amsterdam: International Antiquariaat, 1950). The quote from Bernard comes from CC, I: v.

8. Bernard cat. and Picart cat. Roger Chartier and Henri-Jean Martin, ed., *Histoire de l'Édition française,* 4 vols. (Paris: Fayard, 1982–1986), II, *Le livre triomphant 1660–1830* (1984): 266.

9. Picart signed six of the Jewish plates *B. Picart dessiné d'après nature* ("drawn from life"). No other plates in the volumes carried this mention, but three Protestant plates were signed *B. Picart invenit* (Latin for "he devised it"). *Invenit* appears only nine times and the abbreviation *inv.* twice with Picart's signature. Five images of the Inquisition come from the French Catholic traveler Gabriel Dellon, *Relation de l'Inquisition de Goa* (Paris: D. Horthemels, 1688). Guillaume Calafat, "The Gallicano-Jansenist Roots of the Bernard-Picart Vision," in Lynn Hunt, Margaret Jacob, and Wijnand Mijnhardt, eds., *Bernard Picart and the First Global Vision of Religion* (Los Angeles: Getty Publications, 2010).

10. Bernard's passage is emphasized in VWG, p. 210. She provides an in-depth analysis of the India engravings more generally. The Bernard passage appears in a footnote to CC, III, 2nd part: 111.

11. José de Acosta, ed. Jane E. Mangan, introduced by Walter D. Mignolo, trans. Frances M. López-Morillas, *Natural and Moral History of the Indies* (1590; Durham, NC: Duke University Press, 2002), 251, 289–291, 303. For an English translation of Bartholomé de Las Casas that put his text to good propagandic use see [Anon.], *An Account of the First Voyages and Discoveries Made by the Spaniards in America. . . . By Don Bartholomew de Las Casas, Bishop of Chiapa* (London: J. Darby, 1699). Las Casas spoke about the simplicity and weakness of the Indians. See also Anthony Pagden, *The Fall of Natural Man: The American Indian and the Origins of Comparative Ethnology* (with corrections and additions, Cambridge, UK: Cambridge University Press, 1986).

12. *Atlas Geographus: Or, a compleat system of geography, ancient and modern. Containing what is of most use in Bleau, Verenius, Cellarius, Cluverius, . . . ,* 5 vols. ([London], 1711–1717), III: 752.

13. On Chinese philosophy and Spinozism see CC, IV: 205. See also Thijs Weststeijn, "Spinoza sinicus: An Asian Paragraph in the History of the Radical Enlightenment," *Journal of the History of Ideas,* 68 (2007): 537–561.

14. Joseph-François Lafitau, *Moeurs des sauvages ameriquains comparées aux moeurs des premiers temps* (Paris: Saugrain and Hochereau, 1724), I: 99–102. He also made extensive use of ancient thinkers like Cicero and Seneca. On the Marchand circle see Margaret C. Jacob, *The Radical Enlightenment: Pantheists, Freemasons and Republicans* (London: George Allen and Unwin, 1981; 2nd ed., Cornerstone Books, 2006). Also available at http://www.cornerstonepublishers.com/radical.pdf.

15. Professor Kishwar Rizvi of Yale University provided crucial insight on the representation of Islam in the frontispiece and in the text and images in volume 7. See Kishwar Rizvi, "Persian Pictures: Art, Documentation, and Self-Reflection in Bernard and Picart's Representations of Islam," in Hunt, Jacob, and Mijnhardt, eds., *Bernard Picart*.

16. John Marshall, *John Locke, Toleration and Early Enlightenment Culture* (Cambridge, UK: Cambridge University Press, 2006), 154. See also Joris van Eijnatten, *Liberty and Concord in the United Provinces: Religious Toleration and the Public in the Eighteenth-Century Netherlands* (Leiden: Brill, 2003), 17–27; and by the same author, *Mutua Christianorum Tolerantia: Irenicism and Toleration in the Netherlands. The Stinstra Affair 1740–45* (Florence: Leo S. Olschki Editore, 1998).

17. For a brilliant account of the process see Marshall, *John Locke*. See also on toleration Nabil Matar, "Islam in Britain, 1689–1750," *Journal of British Studies,* 47 (April 2008): 284–300.

18. Quote from CC, I: iii. For the sense of guilt, see p. iv.

19. CC, I: x. Picart's students produced engravings for the later volumes.

20. Gustave Leopold van Roosbroeck, *Persian Letters before Montesquieu* (New York: Publications of the Institute of French Studies, 1932). Bernard's work, also published anonymously, was *Reflexions morales satiriques & comiques, sur les moeurs de nôtre siécle* (Cologne: Chez Pierre Marteau le Jeune, 1711). Van Roosbroeck concludes in terms that we can only salute: "As a precursor of Montesquieu, as one of the libertines of the early eighteenth century, who formulated on the traces of Bayle, the tenets and opinions of the later 'philosophes,' who gathered the materials they used and evolved their very methods, J. F. Bernard deserves richly the attention of the history of ideas and the history of literature" (p. 81).

21. According to the prospectus published in the *Journal des Sçavans* 69 (January 1721): 53–58, a complete edition in folio cost fifty florins and the grand folio format seventy-five florins. This version of the *Journal* may be a pirated Dutch edition because a prospectus for eight quarto volumes at the same price appeared in December 1720 in *Journal des Sçavans* 39: 622–624 (copy owned by the Bibliothèque Nationale de France). The rising price per volume can be found at the beginning of CC, VII. Information on Dutch average wages comes from Jan de Vries and Ad van der Woude, *The First Modern Economy: Success, Failure, and Perseverance of the Dutch Economy, 1500–1815* (Cambridge: Cambridge University Press, 1997), 580.

22. *Grub Street Journal,* London, March 1, 1733, Issue 166. Weekly installments

for volume 4 are advertised in *St. James Evening Post,* London, issues of May 22 and May 29, 1733. The tables for placement of engravings were not always included in the bound volumes (the UCLA copy of the English translation, for example, does not have them, but the British Library copy does). Average annual wages can be found in William J. Christmas, *The Lab'ring Muses: Work, Writing, and the Social Order in English Plebeian Poetry, 1730–1830* (Newark: University of Delaware Press, 2001), 160.

23. Dr. William Michael Short of Loyola College in Maryland provided the translation from the Latin. Dr. Gene Ogle obtained copies of the records. Archivio della Congregazione per la Dottrina della Fede, Vatican City, Rome, MS ACDF, Index, Diari 16 (1734–46) ff. 36v–39r; Index, Protocolli Ridolfius, NNNNN (1737–1740), ff. 69r, 70r, 100r–103v, 533r. The quote is from 100 verso. Quote from CC, I: unnumbered second page of "Préface générale." This "general preface" is to be distinguished from the preface that precedes the section on the Jews that is retained in the English translation. Bernard Picart, *The Ceremonies and Religious Customs of the Various Nations of the Known World: Together with Historical Annotations, and Several Curious Discourses Equally Instructive and Entertaining. . . . Written originally in French, and illustrated . . . by Mr. Bernard Picart, . . . translated into English, by a gentleman, . . . ,* 7 vols. (London: printed by William Jackson, for Claude du Bosc, 1733–1739).

24. Michel Marion, "Quelques aspects sur les bibliothèques privées à Paris entre 1750 et 1759," in *Buch und Sammler. Private und öffentliche Bibliotheken im 18. Jahrhundert. Colloquium der Arbeitsstelle 18. Jahrhundert. Gesamthochschule Wuppertal, Universität Münster, Düsseldorf vom 26–28 September 1977* (Heidelberg: Carl Winter, 1979), 97. *Histoire générale des cérémonies, moeurs, et coutumes religieuses de tous les peuple du monde / représentées en 243 figures dessinées de la main de Bernard Picard* [*i.e. B. Picart*]; *avec des explications historiques, & curieuses par M. l'Abbé Banier, & M. l'Abbé le Mascrier* (Paris: Rollin Fils, 1741). This altered version changes the order of the volumes and modifies the text to make it less anti-Catholic. Guillaume Calafat brought us crucial insight into the section on the Inquisition and its connection to Jansenism.

25. *The Life and Correspondence of Robert Southey. Edited by his son, the Rev. Charles Cuthbert Southey* (New York: Harper and Brothers, 1855), 287. Southey claimed to read "Picart" in an entirely Christian frame, but he was writing to a clergyman.

1. A Marketplace for Religious Ideas

1. British Library, London, MSS ADD 4292, ff. 18–19.

2. For the career of Marchand and the uncertainty about the exact date of his arrival in The Hague, see Christiane Berkvens-Stevelinck, *Prosper Marchand et*

l'histoire du livre: Quelques aspects de l'érudition bibliographique dans la première moitié du XVIIIe siècle, particulièrement en Hollande (Bruges: Drukkerij Sinte Catharina N.V., 1978), xxiii–xxiv.

3. Isabella Henriette van Eeghen, *De Amsterdamse boekhandel, 1680–1725,* 6 vols. (Amsterdam: Scheltema en Holkema, 1960–1978), see esp. vol. IV: 41–43. On the Fritsch and Gleditsch connections see Robert L. Beare, "The So-Called 'Neukirch Sammlung': Some Speculations," *Modern Language Notes,* 77 (1962): 411–434.

4. The letter of Vincent was addressed to B. Moretus, 26 January 1713, Museum Plantin Moretus MS 642–010. Inger Leemans, "Picart's Dutch Connections: Family Trouble, the Amsterdam Theater and the Business of Engraving," in Lynn Hunt, Margaret Jacob, and Wijnand Mijnhardt, eds., *Bernard Picart and the First Global Vision of Religion* (Los Angeles: Getty Publications, 2010). Bruno Liesen and Claude Sorgeloos, eds., *Le Rayonnement des Moretus. Catalogue* (Brussels: Bibliotheca Wittockiana, 2006).

5. *Journal littéraire* [sic], I (May–June 1713), published in The Hague by T. Johnson: iv.

6. Sarah Hutton, ed., *Benjamin Furly, 1646–1714: A Quaker Merchant and His Milieu* (Florence: Leo S. Olschki Editore, 2007).

7. *Journal littéraire,* I (May–June 1713): iii–v, xviii. Bernard cat. and Picart cat. On the club, the journal, and its context, see Margaret C. Jacob, *The Radical Enlightenment: Pantheists, Freemasons and Republicans* (London: George Allen and Unwin, 1981), 182–214.

8. *Journal littéraire,* I (May–June 1713): xviii, 207; Léonie Maass, *Het Journal littéraire de la Haye (1713–1723): De uitwendige geschiedenis van een geleerdentijdschrift,* Proefschrift (Deventer: Drukkerij de Bruijn, 2001); "Journal littéraire, 1713–1737," *Documentatieblad Werkgroep Achttiende Eeuw,* 18, no. 2 (1986): 117–329.

9. Myriam Yardeni, *Le Réfuge huguenot: Assimilation et culture* (Paris: Champion, 2002), 15–16; H. Bots and G.H.M. Posthumus Meyjes, eds., *La Révocation de l'Edit de Nantes et les Provinces-Unies* (Amsterdam-Maarssen: APA Holland University Press, 1986). See also http://gemeentearchief.amsterdam.nl/schatkamer/300_schatten/vreemdelingen/hugenoten/.

10. J. A. I. Champion, "'The Fodder of Our Understanding': Benjamin Furly's Library and Intellectual Conversation c. 1680–c. 1725," in Hutton, ed., *Benjamin Furly,* 111–148.

11. "La colonie française" was coined by Jean des Champs; see Uta Janssens-Knorsch, *The Life and "Mémoires secrets" of Jean des Champs (1707–1767): Journalist, Minister and Man of Feeling* (London: Huguenot Society of Great Britain and Ireland, 1990), 235. On the perils posed by censorship, see Anne Sauvy, *Livre saisis à Paris* (The Hague: Martinus Nijhoff, 1972).

12. For a history of the editions and the Picart vignette, see http://www.lib.uchicago.edu/efts/ARTFL/projects/dicos/BAYLE/bayle.1720.jpeg.

13. University Library, Leiden, Marchand MSS 2, Anthony Collins to Levier, October 1, 1713, London.

14. See Peter Harrison, *"Religion" and the Religions in the English Enlightenment* (Cambridge: Cambridge University Press, 2002), 87–95; and for a recent treatment of the text that sees it as indebted to Toland's reading of Anaxagoras, Jeffrey Wigelsworth, "A Pre-Socratic Source for Toland's *Pantheisticon*," *History of European Ideas*, 34 (2008): 61–65. For a copy of a French translation see http://libsysdigi. library.uiuc.edu/oca/Books2007-10/henryclintonhutcoo/henryclintonhutcoo_djvu. txt. On Toland's relationship with the French Huguenots see Anne Dunan-Page, ed., *The Religious Culture of the Huguenots, 1660–1750* (London: Ashgate, 2006).

15. For Bernard's treatment of Spinoza, see CC, VI: 335–339.

16. Daniel Defoe, *Reformation of Manners* (London: n.p., 1702), 21. See also Justin Champion, *Republican Learning: John Toland and the Crisis of Christian Culture, 1696–1722* (Manchester: Manchester University Press, 2003).

17. Public Record Office, Kew, UK, Shaftesbury MSS 30/24/22/2 6 March 1705/6 to Jean Le Clerc.

18. *Reflexions morales satiriques & comiques, sur les Moeurs de nôtre siécle* (Cologne: Chez Pierre Marteau le Jeune, 1711), 8.

19. *Reflexions morales*, 170.

20. *Reflexions morales satiriques & comiques, sur les Moeurs de nôtre siècle. Nouvelle Edition corrigée & augmentée d'un tiers* (Amsterdam: Chez J. F. Bernard, 1713), 55–56, for the cafés.

21. *Reflexions morales satiriques & comiques, sur les Moeurs de nôtre siècle. Troisiéme ed. corrigée & augmentée. On y a joint une clef.* (Amsterdam: Chez J. Frederic Bernard, 1716). The 1716 edition differs little from the 1713 edition except for the key with its identification of Basnage and Saurin, pastors in The Hague, Prince Eugene, Louis XIV, the duke of Marlborough, and so on. See pp. 199–200 for the description of Amsterdam in both the 1713 and the 1716 printings.

22. Museum Plantin, Antwerp, Moretus MS 641.360, 27 June 1712. On the circle into which Picart married, see Dr. Maurits Sabbe, *De Moretussen en hun Kring* (Antwerp: Resseler, 1928), esp. p. 210. Inger Leemans provided us with the marriage act: Gemeentearchief, Amsterdam, Trouwacte, 9 September 1712, Bernard Picard van Parijs, Wed. Cloucina Pros, in de Nes & Anna Vincent Van Angouleine oud 28 Jaar, op de Cingel, geassisteerd met haar Vader Eijsbrant. Vincent. 25 september Acte.

23. Bernard cat. and Picart cat. Our study of the catalogues was immensely aided by Jessica Buskirk and Susan Cribbs, who prepared *Endnote* versions of the catalogues.

24. For an example of the pornographic element, see the unsigned and undated engraving that appears after p. 139 in "Dissertation sur l'usage de la satire," in *Religious Ceremonies of the World*, IX (the second supplementary volume published after

Picart's death). Silvia Berti questions the radicalism of the libertines in "At the Roots of Unbelief," *Journal of the History of Ideas,* 56 (1995): 555–575. As an antidote to her approach see Jean-Pierre Cavaillé, "Libertinage ou Lumières radicales," in Catherine Secrétan, Tristan Dagron, and Laurent Bove, eds., *Qu'est-ce que les Lumières "Radicales,"* 61–74 (Amsterdam: Éditions Amsterdam, 2007). Even in 1868, when the Bernard translation was republished in a limited edition for bibliophiles (often known for collecting erotica and pornography), the writer of the biographical preface signed himself only "un bibliophile." *État de l'homme dans le péché originel.* "Tirage à 237 exemplaires numérotés: 2 papier de Chine, 235 papier de Hollande" (Brussels: C. Muquardt, 1868).

25. *Bibliotheca Furliana; sive catalogus librorum . . . Doctiss. Viri. Benjamin Furly, inter quos excellunt Bibliorum editiones, mystici, libri proprii cujuscumque sectae Christianae . . . Auctio fiet die 22 Octobris, 1714, etc.* (Rotterdam: Fritsch and Böhm, 1714). The copy at the British Library, BL 11901.A.11, lists the price paid for each book. Luisa Simonutti, "English Guests at 'De Lanterne': Sidney, Penn, Locke, Toland and Shaftesbury," in Sarah Hutton, ed., *Benjamin Furly,* 31–66, quote p. 64.

26. Prosper Marchand, *Dictionnaire historique: ou Mémoires critiques et littéraires, concernant la vie et les ouvrages de divers personnages distingués, particulièrement dans la république des letters,* 2 vols. (The Hague: P. De Hondt, 1758–1759), I: 325. See Silvia Berti, "The First Edition of the *Traité des trois imposteurs* and Its Debt to Spinoza's *Ethics,*" in Michael Hunter and David Wootton, eds., *Atheism from the Reformation to the Enlightenment,* 182–220 (Oxford: Clarendon Press, 2003). The article on Spinoza in Bayle's *Dictionary* can be found at http://colet.uchicago.edu/cgi-bin/BAYLE.sh?MILESTONE=Spinoza&PAGEIDENT=. The only American copy of the 1719 edition is located at Young Research Library, UCLA.

27. Edwin Marcel van Meerkerk, *Achter de schermen van het boekbedrijf: Henri Du Sauzet (1687–1754) . . .* (Amsterdam: APA-Holland University Press, 2001), 81–83. For a discussion of Lucas as the author, which argues without much proof that Jan Vroesen is the actual author of the biography, see Silvia Berti, "L'Esprit de Spinosa: ses origines et sa première édition dans le contexte spinozien," in Silvia Berti et al., *Heterodoxy, Spinozism and Free Thought in Early Eighteenth Century Europe: Studies on the Traité des Trois Imposteurs* (Dordrecht: Kluwer, 1996), 3–52, esp. 24 ff. Most scholars seem to agree with Berti that Vroesen had a hand in writing or compiling the second, more radical (as opposed to the first biographical) part of the treatise. Sauzet later became a freemason, as did others involved in the publication of the *Three Impostors.* Vroesen can also be spelled Vroese in this period.

28. Justin Champion, http://eprints.rhul.ac.uk/archive/00000153/01/Champion_IMPOSTOR.DOC; see also A. W. Fairbairn, "Sur les rapports entre les éditions du *'Traité des trois imposteurs'* et la tradition manuscrite de cet ouvrage," *Nouvelles de la république des lettres,* 2 (1988); Silvia Berti, "'La Vie et l'esprit de Spinosa' (1719) e

la prima traduzione francese dell' Ethica," *Rivista Storica Italiana,* 98 (1986): 5–46. Richard H. Popkin, "The Crisis of Polytheism and the Answers of Vossius, Cudworth, and Newton" and "Polytheism, Deism, and Newton," in James E. Force and R. H. Popkin, eds., *Essays on the Context, Nature, and the Influence of Isaac Newton's Theology,* 9–42 (Boston: Kluwer Academic Publishers, 1990). On Rousset de Missy, see Jacob, *The Radical Enlightenment,* 218–220.

29. Margaret C. Jacob, *The Enlightenment: A Brief History with Documents* (Boston and New York: Bedford/St. Martin's, 2001), 101.

30. Jacob, *The Enlightenment,* quote p. 112 from *Three Impostors.*

31. David Durand, *The Life of Lucilio (alias Julius Cæsar) Vanini, Burnt for Atheism at Thoulouse. With an abstract of his writings. . . . Translated from the French into English* [the French original appeared in 1717] (London: W. Meadows, 1730), 101. Jean-Antoine-Nicolas de Caritat, Marquis de Condorcet, *Esquisse d'un tableau historique des progrès de l'esprit humain; texte revu et présenté par O. H. Prior* (Paris: Boivin et Cie, 1933), 106. The tract was originally written in 1794.

32. Th. Bussemaker, ed., *Archives ou correspondance inédite de la maison d'Orange-Nassau,* 4th series (Leiden: A. W. Sijthoff, 1914), IV (1759–1766): 471–472.

33. Museum Plantin Moretus MS 641–381, Anne Vincent from Amsterdam to Balthazar Moretus, Antwerp, 10 October 1712, writing in French. MS 641–382, letter of 21 October 1712 that Douxfils has intervened on their behalf and rescued the goods. University Library, Leiden, Marchand MSS, Marchand 55b, song in the hand of Douxfils: "Le grand Masson, & ses deux Camarades,/ En cette Cour tinrent les plus hauts grades."

2. Bernard Picart

1. Gemeente Archief, Amsterdam, Trouwacte, 9 September 1712; Doopregisters, 134, p. 51; Henry de Wilde was notary for their first will of 1713, inv. nr. 5075, and nr. 129. His widow's will is no. 5075, notary Adrian Baarsz. The notice of his first wife's funeral, dated 5 November 1708, and of her burial in the parish church of Saint Severin, Paris, appears in University Library, Leiden, Marchand MSS, MS 21:2, f. 46. See Marchand MS 29, ff. 5–6 for Picart's second wife's control of their business after his death.

2. Ecole nationale supérieure des beaux arts, Paris, MS 40 Registre, beginning October 1681. The king has been informed that various members are Protestant and they are to be "deposedez de leurs fonctions. . . ." Catholics are to be put in their place; MS 36 and 39 are inventories of works presented to the academy and include sculptures on the theme "against heresy." See also Bibliothèque de la Société de l'Histoire du Protestantisme Français, Paris, MS 1570. V/a, Fonds Romane Musculus, taken from notes made about Etienne by Musculus in the postwar period.

3. University Library, Leiden, Marchand MSS, MS 12, ff. 28–29; he does also have translations by Catholics. Marchand wrote a treatise on how to read all these versions comparatively (f. 34).

4. The engraving, located at the Getty Research Institute, has been variously attributed to Etienne and Bernard. In the lower lefthand corner, it is signed "Jouuenet pinx./B. Picart romanus ex. Cum Pri. Regis/1685," but there is some question about the "B". Could the "B" [Bernard] have been an "E" [Etienne] cleverly filled in by either an ambitious boy or a father eager to push his son's career —or even a later collector? A modern monograph on Jouvenet unequivocally attributes the engraving to Etienne Picart; see Antoine Schnapper, *Jean Jouvenet (1644–1717) et la peinture d'histoire à Paris* (Paris: Laget Libraire, 1974), 183–184. On the Swedish invitation see Roger Armand Weigert and Carl Hernmarck, *Les Relations artistiques entre la France et la Suède, 1693–1718: N. Tessen le Jeune et Daniel Cronström, correspondance* (Stockholm: R. A. Weigert and C. Hernmarck, 1964), 146. For a drawing by Picart after a work of Le Brun see Fondation Custodia, Institut Neerlandais, Paris, #1971-T.66.

5. The dispute between the academy engravers and the guild of master printer-engravers can be found in Archives Nationales, Paris, O¹ 1925, Reg. B Fol. 108, 17 April 1703. The dispute was very complex. The master printer-engravers claimed the right to print any engraving for which the academy engravers had not incised at least the face(s) and outline of the figure(s). The academy engravers wanted to retain the right to print engravings that they purchased out of "simple curiosity" in order to study the techniques of old masters or foreign engravers more closely. They won the case.

6. Stadsarchief, Antwerp, MS 4578 bis, gives the Spanish official response to the request that the guild be made into an academy. The response calls for it "to cultivate and maintain the sciences of painting, statuary, perspective and printing of books," an academy *"semblable à celles de Rome en Paris. . . ."* See Maarten Prak et al., *Craft Guilds in the Early Modern Low Countries: Work, Power, and Representation* (Burlington, VT: Ashgate, 2006). Koninklijke Academie, MS 292 (141*), ordinance of the city of Antwerp for good order in and around the Academie and ordering how pupils should be listed, how to punish pupils, what are the duties of the deans etc., 6 November 1690. For members see Philippe Felix Rombouts and Theodore Van Lerius, eds., *De Liggeren en andere historische archieven der Antwerpsche Sint Lucasgilde*, 2 vols. (The Hague: Nijhoff, 1864–1876 [reprinted Amsterdam, 1961]), II: 529–593, for members in the period Picart would have been there.

7. Ernst Vegelin van Claerbergen, ed., *David Teniers and the Theatre of Painting* (London: Courtauld Institute of Art Gallery in association with Holberton Publishing, 2006).

8. Picart's production is best followed through the catalogue given in *Imp Inn*, but this list should be checked against the one in the hand of Marchand that can be

found in Rijksmuseum, Amsterdam, Prentenkabinet, MS C/R MOIII.ASC/174*. David Martin, *Histoire du vieux et du nouveau Testament, Enrichie de plus de quatre cens figures . . . avec privilege de nos seigneurs les Etats de Hollande et de West-Frise* (Amsterdam: Pierre Mortier, 1700), vol. 1. The fifty Picart engravings are listed in *Imp Inn* under the category of being invented but not engraved by Picart. For payment to Picart see University Library, Leiden, Marchand MSS, MS 29, f. 4, a printed *Reekening . . . door den Schilder David van der Plaas . . . Amsterdam,* 1701, p. 10, for a direct payment in name of Picart; p. 22 for payment to "the Frenchman"; and pp. 23–25 for name of Picart. For Pool see M. Pool, *Beeld-Synders Kunst-Kabinet . . . naar de Tekeningen van Barent Graat* (Amsterdam: M. Pool, 1727). The de Larrey folio volumes had a curious publication history. The first volume to appear, which is bound as volume 2, appeared in 1697 with engravings executed by various hands, among them Vermeulen. None are signed by Picart; Monsieur De Larrey, *Histoire d'Angleterre, d'Ecosse, et d'Irlande* (Rotterdam: Reinier Leers, 1697). The second volume containing chronologically earlier parts of the history appeared only in 1707 and was bound as volume 1; its frontispiece was done by Picart but dated 1713, and there are no other engravings in this volume. The volume that appeared in 1698 is bound as volume 3 and contains no signed work by Picart. According to the printed list of Picart's life work in *Imp Inn,* Picart assisted Vermeulen with some of the portraits that were done in Antwerp in 1696; possible candidates might have been the frontispiece; the portrait of Catherine Howard, opposite p. 463; Catherine Parr, opposite p. 486; or Jane Gray, opposite p. 749. Volume 4 (Rotterdam, 1713) was published by Fritsch and Böhm, and the engraving of William III in which Picart had a hand is by E. Desroches, opposite p. 660. Marchand also had business dealings with Mortier in 1708; see University Library, Amsterdam, Gl 27, Marchand to Mortier, 1708(?), that same year listed in body of the letter.

9. On Picart's relationship with De Lorme, see Isabella Henriette van Eeghen, *De Amsterdamse boekhandel, 1680–1725,* 6 vols. (Amsterdam: Scheltema en Holkema, 1960–1978), esp. vol. I: 168–171, and vol. II: 71–192.

10. Bibliothèque de l'Arsenal, MS Bastille 10561. For Namur see the list in *Imp Inn,* where it is said that he conceived and executed it.

11. *Catalogue des livres qui se vendent à Paris chez Prosper Marchand et Gabriel Martin, libraires, rue Saint Jacques, vis-à-vis la fontaine Saint Severin, [rüe du Platre] au Phénix. [à l'Etoile]* (Paris: Prosper Marchand et Gabriel Martin, 1703). University Library, Leiden, Marchand MSS, MS 11 contains a much fuller list of the shop's contents; this catalogue includes the shop's logo of the Phoenix designed by Picart; MS 12 is a hand-written list of Marchand's personal library; MS 72:1 has a copy of the work on geography dated 1707; MS 72:4 has a set of accompanying maps.

12. Prosper Marchand, *Cymbalum mundi, ou dialogues satyriques sur differens sujets, par Bonaventure Des Perriers* [sic] (Amsterdam: Prosper Marchand, 1711), 4. The engraved frontispiece is signed by Picart, as is the logo on its title page. The

English version appeared the next year as Prosper Marchand, *Cymbalum mundi. Or, Satyrical dialogues upon several subjects, by Bonaventure Des Perriers, valet-de chambre to Margaret de Valois, queen of Navarre. To which is prefix'd a letter containing the history, apology, &c. of that work.* Done into English from the French (London, 1712). In his own catalogue of his library Marchand described the letter in these terms: "dans la quelle on justifie cet ouvrage d'Atheisme et d'impieté, par Felix de Commerci (i.e., Prosper Marchand) manuscrit, in 8." University Library, Leiden, Marchand MSS, MS 12, f. 16; Marchand continued to work on the text for many years; see MS 30.

13. Bibliothèque Nationale de France, MSS Fonds Français 21736 (95), thesis defended by Dionysius Rouille du Coudray, a Parisian cleric, on 7 August 1707. This is the only thesis of the time that appears to fit philosophically with the engraving. In University Library, Leiden, Marchand MSS, MS 28, fol. 251, there is a version of the legend for this engraving written in the hand of Marchand and affixed over the printed copy. On the work of Etienne Picart, see Véronique Meyer, *L'Illustration des thèses à Paris dans la seconde moitié du XVIIe siècle: Peintres, graveurs, éditeurs* (Paris: Commission des travaux historiques de la Ville de Paris, 2002). The catalogue of Picart's works in *Imp Inn* lists the 1690s Descartes prints. See Jacques Bernard, *Nouvelles de la republique des lettres,* August 1707, 231–234, for a letter (not identified as by Marchand) describing the son of a merchant named Brillon who studied at the collège of la Marche and decided to order a vignette for the frontispiece of his thesis. I will send it to you, the writer says, and you can judge for yourself if it is a crime. It is on the subject of truth. The letter then describes the Picart engraving. See also the letter in the same journal, August 1708, 224–230.

14. Phillips Son & Neale [auction catalog], *Ancient and Modern Prints; Painters' Etchings; Foreign Portraits* (London, 1834).

15. For the baptism of Roger-Bernard in 1703 see Henri Herluison, *Actes d'état-civil d'artistes français: peintres, graveurs, architectes, etc.; extraits des registres de l'Hôtel-de-ville de Paris, détruits dans l'incendie du 24 Mai 1871* (Paris, 1873; Geneva: Slatkine Reprint, 1972), 345. On De Piles and the status of honorary members see Charlotte Guichard, *Les Amateurs d'art à Paris au XVIIIe siècle* (Paris: Champ Vallon, 2008), 31–42.

16. For an in-depth discussion of Poussin's ideological commitments see Judith Bernstock, *Poussin and French Dynastic Ideology* (New York: Peter Lang, 2000). See also Todd P. Olson, *Poussin and France: Painting, Humanism, and the Politics of Style* (New Haven, CT: Yale University Press, 2002), 181–185 and 199–200; and Thomas Puttfarken, *Titian and Tragic Painting: Aristotle's Poetics and the Rise of the Modern Artists* (New Haven, CT: Yale University Press, 2005). *Conference de Monsieur Le Brun premier peintre du Roy de France, chancelier et directeur de l'Académie de peinture et sculpture sur l'expression generale & particuliere. Enrichie de Figures gravées par B. Picart* (Amsterdam: J. L. De Lorme, and Paris: E. Picart le Rom., 1698), 8. In 1711

Marchand published, with an Amsterdam imprint, a new edition of the Le Brun text with engravings by Picart. For De Piles and Cartesianism see Baldine Saint Girons, "Un nouveau discours de la méthode? La première conférence de Roger de Piles à l'Académie royale de peinture et de sculpture (1699)," in *La Naissance de la théorie de l'art en France, 1640–1720* [*Revue d'esthéthique*], 83–98 (Paris: Editions Jean-Michel Place, 1997).

17. Roger de Piles, *The Art of Painting, and the Lives of Painters: Containing, a Compleat Treatise of Painting, Designing, and The Use of Prints. Done from the French of Monsieur de Piles* (London: J. Nutt, 1706 [first French ed. 1699]), 56–57; many of these views are already present in his *Conversations sur la connoissance de la Peinture . . . la vie de Rubens* (Paris, 1677). For the etchings in Descartes, see René Descartes, *Discours de la méthode pour bien conduire sa raison et chercher la vérité dans les sciences, plus la Dioptrique, les Météores et la Géométrie qui sont des essais de cette méthode* (Leiden: J. Maire, 1637).

18. Roger de Piles, *The Principles of Painting, under the Heads of Anatomy Attitude Accident . . .* (London: J. Osborn, 1743), 273.

19. *Réponse au livre de Monsieur l'Evesque de Meaux, intitulé Conférence avec M. Claude* (n.p.: Veuve d'Olivier de Varennes, 1683), iii. See also University Library, Leiden, Marchand MSS, MS 12, ff. 45–46, 48, showing that Marchand had Claude in his personal library. Ten works by Claude appear in the thirty-five-page catalogue of Protestant books that the archbishop of Paris determined should be confiscated after the revocation of the Edict of Nantes. The catalogue appears in printed form in BNF MS Fonds français 21740.

20. *Réponse au livre de Mr. Arnaud intitulé La Perpétuité de la Foy de l'Eglise Catholique touchant l'Eucharistie défendue* (Rouen: Jean Lucas, 1670).

21. For Protestants arrested, interrogated, and imprisoned, see Frantz Funck-Brentano, *Les Lettres de cachet à Paris, étude suivie d'une liste des prisonniers de la Bastille (1659–1789)* (Paris: Imprimerie Nationale, 1903), 116–160. For those who abjured see Bibliothèque de la Société d'Histoire du Protestantisme Français, MSS E. 39, photocopies of the original from the Archives de l'Assistance publique, Paris, fonds de l'Hôtel Dieu, Liasse 1422, from 1698 to 1713.

22. The account of Picart's tribulations comes from Marchand's "Eloge historique de Bernard Picart, dessinateur et graveur," esp. pp. 3–5, in *Imp Inn*. Marchand's name does not appear as author of the "Eloge," but VWG follows Christiane Berkvens-Stevelinck (*Prosper Marchand: La Vie et l'oeuvre (1678–1756)* [Leiden: E. J. Brill, 1987]) in arguing that Marchand is the author. Funck-Brentano, *Les Lettres de cachet à Paris*, 159.

23. "Eloge historique."

24. University of Leiden, Marchand MSS, Ms 28, letter signed Rotterdam, October 27, 1713. The printed preface to *Recueil de divers traités touchant l'eucharistie* is not signed by Marchand but is found among his papers at the same location

(Marchand 28). On Furly see Stefano Villiani, "Conscience and Convention: The Young Furly and the Hat Controversy," in Sarah Hutton, ed., *Benjamin Furly, 1646–1714: A Quaker Merchant and His Milieu,* 87–110 (Florence: Leo S. Olschki Editore, 2007).

25. For the monies paid to engravers and painters, see Jules Guiffrey, ed., *Comptes des bâtiments du roi sous le règne de Louis XIV,* V (1706–1715) (Paris: Imprimerie Nationale, 1901).

26. Thomassin's decision to go to Holland with Picart and his subsequent career are described in a letter written by François Bernard Lépicié, secretary and historiographer of the Royal Academy, in February 1741, Fondation Custodia, Institut Néerlandais, Paris. Pierre Wachenheim alerted us to the existence of this letter. On Surugue, see Maxine Péraud et al., *Dictionnaire des éditeurs d'estampes à Paris sous l'Ancien Régime* (Paris: Promodis, 1987), 284–286.

27. *Poésies sur la constitution Unigenitus* (Villefranche: Chez Philalète Belhumeur, 1724). The frontispiece is not signed, but it is dated 1723 and appears in the catalogue of Picart's work in *Imp Inn.* See Pierre Wachenheim, "Bernard Picart graveur des jansénistes: Propositions pour un corpus séditieux," in Philippe Kaenel and Rolf Reichardt, eds., *Interkulturelle Kommunikation in der europäischen Druckgraphik im 18. und 19. Jahrhundert,* 333–356 (Hildesheim and Zürich: Georg Olms Verlag, 2007). We are very grateful to Dale Van Kley for alerting us to Wachenheim's work and to Dr. Wachenheim for providing us with a copy of this indispensable article. For the frontispiece to Marchand and friends' journal see *Journal Littéraire* (The Hague: Thomas Johnson, 1714), vol. 4, May–June 1714.

28. Stadsarchief, Antwerp, MS GA 4574, placard of June 19, 1670, against the publishing or dissemination of two books against the Jesuits; March 20, 1690, another ordinance against the sermons of a local preacher, possibly a Protestant or a Jansenist. Cf. Maurits Sabbe, *La Vie des livres à Anvers aux XVIe, XVIIe, et XVIIIe siècles* (Brussels: Editions du Musée du livre, 1926), 135–136.

3. Why Holland?

1. For Dutch propaganda against the French see *Alle de gedichten van J. Antonides van der Goes: hier by komt het leven des dichters,* 4th ed. (Rotterdam: Arnold Willis, 1730), with engravings by Picart; Wijnand W. Mijnhardt, "A Dutch Culture in the Age of William and Mary: Cosmopolitan or Provincial," in Mordechai Feingold and Dale Hoak, eds., *The World of William and Mary: Anglo-Dutch Perspectives on the Revolution of 1688–1689* (Stanford: Stanford University Press, 1996), 223–224.

2. On the French background see Jacob Soll, *The Information Master: Jean-Baptiste Colbert's Secret State Intelligence System* (Ann Arbor: University of Michigan Press, 2009). Bernard and Picart's original collaborator, Antoine Augustin

Bruzen de la Martinière, published a history of the life and reign of Louis XIV that included a very critical section on the revocation of the Edict of Nantes. Bruzen was himself a Catholic, but he worked and published in the Dutch Republic. *Histoire de la vie et du règne de Louis XIV, Roi de France & de Navarre, redigée sur les memoires de feu Monsieur le Comte de ****, 5 vols. (The Hague: Van Duren, 1740–1742), IV: 309–338.

3. Bayle is so described in a letter from La Reynie to Louvois of 1685, quoted in Soll, *The Information Master,* 179–180.

4. For Marteau see http://www.pierre-marteau.com/c/jacob/clandestine.html.

5. Harold J. Cook, *Matters of Exchange: Commerce, Medicine, and Science in the Dutch Golden Age* (New Haven: Yale University Press, 2007), 226–266.

6. Wijnand W. Mijnhardt, "The Construction of Silence: Religious and Political Radicalism in Dutch History," in Wiep van Bunge, ed., *The Early Enlightenment in the Dutch Republic, 1650–1750: Selected Papers of a Conference Held at the Herzog August Bibliothek, Wolfenbüttel, 22–23 March 2001* (Leiden: Brill, 2003), 244–246.

7. Michiel Wielema, *The March of the Libertines: Spinozists and the Dutch Reformed Church (1660–1750)* (Hilversum: Verloren, 2004).

8. Wijnand W. Mijnhardt, "Tolerantie als politiek probleem," *Rekenschap* 43 (1996): 126. Dutch consumption is a much debated question. See, for example, Jan de Vries, "Luxury in the Dutch Golden Age in Theory and Practice," in Maxine Berg and Elizabeth Eger, eds., *Luxury in the Eighteenth Century: Debates, Desires and Delectable Goods,* 41–56 (Houndmills, Basingstoke, U.K.: Palgrave Macmillan, 2003).

9. Linda Frey, Marsha Frey, John C. Rule, eds., *Observations from The Hague and Utrecht: William Harrison's Letters to Henry Watkins, 1711–12* (Columbus: Ohio State University Libraries, 1979), 126, written from The Hague, 5 October 1711.

10. Rietje van Vliet, "De poliep en de luis. Geleerden en boekverkopers in het midden van de achttiende eeuw," *Jaarboek voor Nederlandse Boekgeschiedenis* 11 (2004): 152–155.

11. [Lieven de Beaufort], *Verhandeling van de vryheit in den burgerstaet* (Leiden: Samuel Luchtmans, 1737), see esp. pp. 61 and 135.

12. José de Kruif, "Classes of Readers: Owners of Books in Eighteenth Century The Hague," *Poetics* 28 (2001): 423–453.

13. Roger Chartier, "Magasin de l'univers ou magasin de la République," in Christiane Berckvens-Stevelinck, ed., *Le Magasin de l'univers: The Dutch Republic as the Centre of the European Book Trade.* Papers presented at the international colloquium, held at Wassenaar, 5–7 July 1990 (Leiden: E. J. Brill, 1992). See also P. G. Hoftijzer and Otto Lankhorst, *Drukkers, Boekverkopers en Lezers in de Republiek: Een historiografische en bibliografische handleiding,* 2nd ed. (The Hague: Sdu Uitgevers, 2000), 120. For the depth and breadth of the Dutch book trade see www.

bibliopolis.nl and Hannie van Goinga, "*Boeken in beweging.* Publieke boekenveilingen in de Republiek 1711–1805," *Jaarboek voor Nederlandse Boekgeschiedenis* 11 (2004): 99–126.

14. John Michael Montias, *Artists and Artisans in Delft: A Socio-Economic Study of the Seventeenth Century* (Princeton: Princeton University Press, 1982), 220. We thank Amy Powell for this reference.

15. Gabriel Naudé, *Instructions Concerning Erecting of a Library Presented to My Lord, the President De Mesme,* trans. John Evelyn (London: Printed for G. Bedle, and T. Collins . . . and J. Crook . . . , 1661). For Collins's library see *Bibliotheca Antonii Collins,* sold at St. Pauls Coffee House, 1731, by Thomas Ballard. BL 270 1 23 (1–2) has prices marked; King's College, Cambridge, Keynes MS 431, for *La vie et l'esprit;* information on Collins and Shaftesbury supplied by Justin Champion. See also de Kruif, "Classes of Readers," 435.

16. On such freedom, see, for example, [Anon.] *Zamenspraak tusschen de Haagsche Louw en Krelis, over het request van de vlag-officieren, ter beteugeling der drukpers* (no date or place).

17. Hannie van Goinga, *Alom te bekomen: Veranderingen in de boekdistributie in de Republiek 1720–1800* (Amsterdam: De Buitenkant, 1999), 341.

4. Jean Frederic Bernard

1. A monograph on Jean Frederic Bernard does not exist. For general information: Isabella Henriette van Eeghen, *De Amsterdamse boekhandel 1680–1725,* 6 vols. (Amsterdam: N. Israel, 1961–1978), III: 18–22; and Jean Sgard, *Dictionnaire des journalistes 1600–1789,* 2 vols. (Oxford: Voltaire Foundation, 1999), II: 80–81. In 1934 Elizabeth M. Sheets completed a very perceptive master's thesis on Bernard at Columbia University in New York entitled "Jean Frédéric Bernard. Précurseur du mouvement philosophique du XVIIIe siècle," but it remained unpublished.

2. See http://sitepasteurs.free.fr (accessed March 28, 2008) and Bernard Appy, *De père en fils. Une famille protestante du Luberon (1598–1685)* (Aix-en-Provence: Editions Ampelos, 2008). We wish to thank Mr. Bernard Appy for his help with research into the Bernard family and the Huguenot congregation of Velaux. For Jean Frederic's birth certificate: Archives AD 13 (Aix-en-Provence), 202 E 296: Velaux BMS Protestants 1669–1685, baptêmes; for Jean Bernard, see Eugène Arnaud, *Histoire des Protestants de Provence, du Comtat Venaissin et de la Principauté d'Orange,* 2 vols. (Paris: Grassart, 1884), I: 452–457.

3. Antoine Yrondelle, *Histoire du collège d'Orange depuis sa foundation à nos jours (1573–1909)* (Paris: Honoré Champion, 1912), 47–63; *Relation de ce qui s'est passé au restablissement d'Orange, par Monsieur de Chambrun, Ministre de la Parole de Dieu à Orange* (Orange: Raban, 1666), 82–90.

4. See for the various birth and marriage certificates of the merchant colony in

Marseilles in Velaux: Archives AD 13 (Aix-en-Provence), 202 E 296: Velaux BMS Protestants 1669–1685, *baptêmes et mariages*. Nicolaas Ruts married into the important Swiss merchant family of Zollikofer, originating in St. Gall and active in Marseilles for almost a century. Ruts's business partners, the Martens family, also had their children baptized in Velaux. For Ruts's position as a consul, see O. Schutte, *Repertorium der Nederlandse vertegenwoordigers residerende in het buitenland 1584–1810* (Den Haag: Martinus Nijhoff, 1975), 71.

5. Arnaud, *Protestants de Provence*, II: 295–367; [Jean Claude], *An account of the Persecutions and Oppressions of the Protestants in France* (London, 1686), 19–21, as quoted in John Marshall, *John Locke, Toleration and Early Enlightenment Culture* (Cambridge: Cambridge University Press, 2006), 63–64; Anna Bernard, *Die Revokation des Edikts von Nantes und die Protestanten in Süd-Ost-Frankreich 1685–1730* (Munich: Oldenbourg Verlag, 2003), esp. pp. 123 and 144.

6. Archives AD 13 (Aix en Provence), Fonds Geraudie (310 E 455) Melchior Miljard (1681–1687) Notaire de Velaux, ff 63–653; Gabriel Audisio, "Au Temps de la Révocation: le Luberon, le royaume et l'Europe," *Sixième Journée de l'Association d'Etudes Vaudoises et Historiques du Luberon* (1985): 5–20, quotation p. 14; and Dario Mougel, "Une communauté protestante face à la Révocation," ibid., 33–41. Arnaud, *Protestants de Provence*, I: 412–417. For the church of Velaux see Jean-Jacques Dias, "Le temple caché de Velaux," *La Valmasque, Bulletin de l'Association d'Etudes Vaudoises et Historiques du Luberon*, 71 (2006). At least seventy-five Huguenots would flee from Velaux. See database on the Refuge Huguenot of the Centre d'Analyse et de Mathématique Sociales in Paris.

7. See Hans Bots, G. H. M. Posthumus Meyjes, and Frouke Wieringa, ed., *Vlucht naar de vrijheid: De Hugenoten en de Nederlanden* (Amsterdam: De Bataafsche Leeuw, 1985). Bernard's signing of the orthodox Confession de Foi is documented in the *Bulletin de la Société de l'Histoire du Protestantisme Français: documents historiques inédits et originaux, XVIe, XVIIe et XVIIIe siècles* (1858), 426. For his pension and education, see Suzanne Stelling Michaud, *Le Livre du Recteur de l'Académie de Genève (1559–1878), II, Notices biographiques des étudiants A-C* (Genève: Librairie Droz, 1966), 184. Last will of Barthélemy Bernard, notary public Hendrik Outgers. Municipal Archives Amsterdam, no. 5075–3373–126.

8. Pierre Bayle, *Nouvelles Lettres*, 2 vols. (The Hague: Van Duren, 1739), II: 421, letter of January 1, 1705. Typically Bernard stocked his shops with books he had acquired on credit. For more details about his dealings see Amsterdam Municipal Archives, notary public J. Hoekebak. no. 5922, December 22, 1711; idem, March 18, 1712, no. 5923.

9. [J. F. Bernard], *Reflexions morales satiriques & comiques, sur les moeurs de nôtre siécle* (Cologne: Chez Pierre Marteau le Jeune, 1711), 259–263.

10. The business dealings involving Jeanne Chartier can be documented from the Amsterdam archives of the notaries public: notary public Cornelis van Achthoven, April 3, 1714, no. 6422, 117; notary public Philippe de Marolles, May 12, 1714,

nos. 7964–67 and 7964–68 (two separate transactions); idem, May 16, 1714, nos. 7964–94. Unfortunately no record of the death inventory survives. For the Lacoste family see *De Navorscher,* 4 (1854), pp. 187 ff.

11. *Correspondance de Voltaire,* Theodore Besterman, ed. (Geneva: Institut et Musée de Voltaire, 1953+), Lettre à abbé Moussinot, 27-12-1738. The limited possibilities of a smalltime publisher such as Du Sauzet can be easily demonstrated by his dealings with Voltaire. Voltaire promised Du Sauzet the right to publish his *Siècle de Louis XIV,* but nothing came of it; a Parisian publisher got the work instead. Only in 1733 did the Amsterdam moguls permit Du Sauzet to take part in a profitable group engaged in large-scale privateering of books. See Edwin van Meerkerk, *Achter de schermen van het boekbedrijf. Henri du Sauzet (1687–1754) in de wereld van de uitgeverij en de boekhandel in de Republiek* (Amsterdam/Utrecht: APA-Holland Universiteitspers, 2001), 17–51.

12. Hannie van Goinga, *Alom te bekomen: Veranderingen in de boekdistributie in de Republiek 1720–1800* (Amsterdam: De Buitenkant, 1999), 123–157; Julia Adams, *The Familial State: Ruling Families and Merchant Families in Early Modern Europe* (Ithaca: Cornell University Press, 2005), ch. 5.

13. Van Eeghen, *De Amsterdamse Boekhandel,* III: 179–182.

14. Only a few extant copies bear a Bernard imprint. Most of them carry Humbert's name. For Naudé's libertinism, see Jack A. Clarke, *Gabriel Naudé* (Hamden, CT: Archon Books, 1970).

15. Short-Title Catalogue, Netherlands, Royal Library, The Hague, Records Lombrail. Bernard and Humbert took over some of Lombrail's successful titles, such as Beverley's *Virginia* (published by Bernard in 1718) and Tillotson's *Sermons,* of which they made various editions.

16. See for these reprinting practices *Bibliopolis: History of the Printed Book in the Netherlands* (Zwolle: Waanders, 1999), 35; and Chris Schriks, *Het Kopijrecht: 16e tot 19e eeuw* (Zutphen: Walburg Pers/Kluwer, 2004), 31–47.

17. Van Eeghen, *Amsterdamse Boekhandel,* IV: 34, and VI: 326–331. In the stock lists found in books published by Bernard, the titles he sold on behalf of the Company of Fourteen were distinguished from those he published himself by the phrase "dont il a nombre" ("from which he has many copies").

18. For Bernard's activities as publisher of clandestine manuscripts see Geneviève Artigas-Menant, *Du Secret des clandestins à la propagande voltairienne* (Paris: Honoré Champion, 2001), 35–43, esp. p. 42; Ira O. Wade, *The Clandestine Organization and Diffusion of Philosophical Ideas in France from 1700–1750* (Princeton: Princeton University Press, 1938), ch. 6.

19. For his views on the university-educated, see *Reflexions morales,* 225–226.

20. Gustave Leopold van Roosbroeck, *Persian Letters before Montesquieu* (New York: Publications of the Institute of French Studies, Inc., 1932), ch. 4; *Reflexions morales,* préface and p. 145; *Dissertations mêlées sur divers sujets importants et curieux,* 2 vols. (Amsterdam: Jean Frederic Bernard, 1740), preface. See also J. M. Quérard,

Les Supercheries littéraires dévoilées: Galerie des auteurs apocryphes, supposés, déguisés, plagiaires et des éditeurs infidèles de la littérature française pendant les quatre derniers siècles, 5 vols. (Paris, n.p., 1847–1853), IV: 93 ff.

21. "Quisquis eris cupidus scriptorrem noscere libri, Nominis indicium littera Beta dabit. Gallia me genuit; tenet uvida terra; coactus Exulo, dum reditum tristia fata negant," in *Etat de l'Homme dans le peché originel* (Printed in the World [Amsterdam], 1741). It seems entirely possible that Broncard never published the 1733 edition and that it was printed in Amsterdam.

22. On *Eloge de l'Enfer* [Praise of hell], see Quérard, *Les Supercheries,* IV: 95; and A. A. Barbier, *Dictionnaire des ouvrages anonyms,* 4 vols. (Paris, 1872–1879). At the time of publication *Eloge de l'Enfer* was usually ascribed to a certain Abbé Bénard. The renowned nineteenth-century bibliophile Paul Lacroix assumed Bénard to be Jean Frederic Bernard, an attribution carried forward ever since its appearance in Barbier's *Dictionnaire,* even though the book was published for the first time only fifteen years after Jean Frederic Bernard's death. According to the more recent *Dictionnaire des journalistes,* however, Abbé Bénard was the pseudonym of a French priest of Jansenist leanings, Pierre Quesnel (1699–1774), who was a minor journalist living in The Hague. Quesnel worked as a corrector in the workshop of the publisher Pierre Gosse, according to Jean Sgard, ed., *Dictionnaire des journalistes,* 2 vols. (Oxford: Voltaire Foundation, 1999), II: 815–816. Quesnel contributed to the journal *La Bigarure,* marketed by Gosse. Gosse also published *Eloge de l'Enfer,* a satirical work aimed at the Catholic Church written in the same vein as Erasmus's *Praise of Folly.* In style and composition it has almost nothing in common with the prose of Jean Frederic Bernard. In contrast, it has clear affiliations with an earlier work published by Quesnel in The Hague in 1736, *Histoire de l'admirable dom Inigo de Guispuscoa, fondateur de la monarchie des Inighistes,* 2 vols. (The Hague: Vve de C. le Vier, 1736). A utopian novel, *Histoire de l'admirable dom Inigo de Guispuscoa* ridicules Ignatius of Loyola and the order of the Jesuits. See Christiane Berckvens-Stevelinck and Jeroom Vercruysse, eds., *Le Métier du journaliste au dix-huitième siècle* (Oxford: Voltaire Foundation, 1993). Other than Sgard's two pages, little has been written on this question. In volume two of his trilogy on the Radical Enlightenment, Jonathan Israel incorporates Bernard wrongly into his band of followers of Spinoza. See Jonathan I. Israel, *Enlightenment Contested: Philosophy, Modernity and the Emancipation of Man, 1670–1752* (Oxford: Oxford University Press, 2006), esp. pp. 377–380. Examples of Bernard's interest in sexual politics include his reprints of Jean de la Chapelle's erotic novels based on Tibullus and Catullus and the erotic poetry of Salvator Rosa, a seventeenth-century Italian painter who rebelled against the academic style in painting.

23. Erich Haase, *Einführung in die Literatur des Refuge* (Berlin: Duncker and Humblot, 1959), 416–417; Anne Goldgar, *Impolite Learning: Conduct and Community in the Republic of Letters, 1680–1750* (New Haven: Yale University Press, 1995), ch. 3; Pieter Johannes Wilhelmus van Malssen, *Louis XIV d'après les pamphlets ré-*

pandus en Hollande (Amsterdam: H. J. Paris, 1936); Eric le Nabour, *Le Régent, libéral et libertin* (Paris: J'ai Lu, 1984). For an example of Bernard's dedications, see François Hédelin, abbé d'Aubignac, *Pratique du théatre* (Amsterdam: J. F. Bernard, 1715).

24. Otto Lankhorst, "'Die snode uitwerkzels van een listige eigenbaat'. Inventarisatie van uitgaven bij intekening in de republiek tot 1750," *De Zeventiende Eeuw*, 6 (1990): 129–136. See also Robert Carfray Alston, F. G. Robinson, and C. Wallis, *A Checklist of Eighteenth-Century Books containing a List of Subscribers* (Newcastle: Avaro, 1983).

25. Van Eeghen, *Amsterdamse Boekhandel*, V: 234 ff. Paul Hoftijzer, *Pieter Van der Aa (1659–1733): Leids drukker en boekverkoper* (Hilversum: Verloren, 1999), 60 ff.

26. The indispensable source is Jean Sgard, ed., *Dictionnaire des journaux, 1600–1789*, 2 vols. (Paris: Universitas, 1991), I: 819–820, 167–168, 179–180, and 185–188. J. F. G. Boex, "De *Bibliothèque Françoise* van Henri Du Sauzet, 1730–1746" (Ph.D diss., University of Nijmegen, 2002), 21–52.

27. Hans Bots and Bruno Lagarrigue, "L'Unique exemplaire d'un préambule à *l'Histoire critique des journaux* par François-Denis Camusat (1700–1732) et les remarques manuscrites de Pierre des Maizeaux pour améliorer ce texte," *LIAS* 21 (1994): 95–134. Camusat's exact age when dressing up this proposal, sixteen or nineteen, is in doubt. See "l'Unique exemplaire," 95. For examples of his editing for Bernard, see François-Eudes de Mézeray, *Mémoires historiques et critiques sur divers points de l'histoire de France*, 2 vols. (Amsterdam: J. F. Bernard, 1732) and *Poësies de Monsieur le Marquis de La Farre* (Amsterdam: J. F. Bernard, 1755).

28. Jean Sgard, "F.-D. Camusat et *l'Histoire critique des journaux*," in Marianne Couperus, ed., *L'Étude des périodiques anciens: Colloque d'Útrecht*, 32–54 (Paris: A. G. Nizet, 1972).

29. For the Northwest passage debate in the seventeenth century, see J. F. Gebhard, *Het leven van Mr. Nicolaas Cornelisz. Witsen.* 2 vols. (Utrecht: J. W.Leeflang, 1881), II: 442–448. For Bernard's views, see the preface to volume 1 of the *Voyages au Nord* (Amsterdam: J. F. Bernard, 1715), "Essai d'instructions pour voyager utilement. Où l'on voit ce qu'on doit examiner dans les Voyages, par rapport à la Geographie, l'Histoire naturelle, le Commerce etc," 1–116. See also Anthony Pagden, *The Fall of Natural Man: The American Indian and the Origins of Comparative Ethnology* (Cambridge: Cambridge University Press, 1982), esp. pp. 198–209. The reprint was of René Augustin Constantin de Renneville, *Recueil des voyages qui ont servi à l'établissement et aux progrès de la Compagnie des Indes orientales formées dans les Provinces unies des Païs-Bas*, 7 vols. (Amsterdam: J. F. Bernard, 1725).

30. *Dialogues critiques et philosophiques*, II: 235; *Bibliothèque Françoise*, 12 (1728), pp. 275–297.

31. Charles Etienne Jordan, *Histoire d'un voyage littéraire fait en 1733* (The Hague: Moetjens, 1735), 187; Van Meerkerk, *Achter de schermen*, 312–314.

32. P. G. M. Dickson, *The Financial Revolution in England: A Study in the Devel-*

opment of Public Credit, 1688–1756 (London, 1967), 84–87; Frans de Bruyn, "Het groote tafereel der dwaasheid and the Speculative Bubble of 1720: A Bibliographical Enigma and an Economic Force," *Eighteenth-Century Life* 24 (2000): 62–87; and Frans de Bruyn, "Reading Het groote tafereel der dwaasheid: An Emblem Book of the Folly of Speculation in the Bubble Year 1720," *Eighteenth-Century Life* 24 (2000): 1–42. Colin Nicholson, *Writing and the Rise of Finance: Capital Satires of the Early Eighteenth Century* (Cambridge: Cambridge University Press, 1994), 51 ff. Though the consequences of the bubbles were less dramatic in the Dutch Republic, its publishers produced the most extensive contemporary documentation of the crisis.

33. The full details of all his transactions are missing, but for some of the evidence see Municipal Archives Amsterdam, notary public George Wetstein, September 3, 1720, no. 8296–96 for an investment of 25,000 guilders in the Provincial Commercial Company of Arnhem; idem, George Wetstein, no. 8296–107, August 12 and September 9, 1720, investment in the Commercial Company of Hoorn for 50,000 guilders and in the Provincial Utrecht Company for 15,000 guilders. For Bernard's collection of profits: notary public George Wetstein, May 19, 1721, no. 8298–13.

34. *Relations de la Louisiane, et du fleuve Mississipi: où l'on voit l'état de ce grand païs & les avantages qu'il peut produire &c.* (Amsterdam: J. F. Bernard, 1720); and *Recueil d'arrests et autres pièces pour l'établissement de la Compagnie d'Occident* (Amsterdam: J. F. Bernard, 1720).

35. Van Eeghen, *Amsterdamse Boekhandel,* II: 23. Inger Leemans, "Picart's Dutch Connections: Family Trouble, the Amsterdam Theater and the Business of Engraving," in Lynn Hunt, Margaret Jacob, and Wijnand Mijnhardt, eds., *Bernard Picart and the First Global Vision of Religion* (Los Angeles: Getty Publications, 2010).

36. W. F. H. Oldewelt, *Kohier van de personeele quotisatie te Amsterdam over het jaar 1742,* 2 vols. (Amsterdam: Gemeente Archief, 1945), II: 150. Van Eeghen, *Amsterdamse Boekhandel,* II: 19; Max Fajn, "Marc-Michel Rey: Boekhandelaar op de Bloemmark (Amsterdam)," *Proceedings of the American Philosophical Society* 118 (June 1974): 260–268; Jeroom Vercruysse, "Marc-Michel Rey, Libraire des Lumières," in H. J. Martin and R. Chartier, eds., *Histoire de l'édition française,* 4 vols. (Paris: Fayard, 1989), II: 322–323. Elisabeth Bernard continued to reprint some of her father's titles under his imprint.

5. A Writer's Mental Universe

1. CC, VIII: 8, preface to the reader. On the title page the volume is identified as part two of volume 7, and the author is listed as "Bernard Picart and others."

2. See, for example, Marchand's thoughts on religion recorded at University Library, Leiden, Marchand MSS, MS 28, f. 130–138, renumbered as ff. 166–167, "La

Religion est le Fruit des Réfléxions & Méditations des premiers Hommes qui, uniquement occupés pour la plûpart de cultiver leurs Champs . . . leurs Réfléxions sur le bel ordre de La Nature . . . Telle est l'Origine de la Religion: Origine fondée sur la Raison & le Bon-Sens, que toutes celles qu'on débite ordinairement dans les Sociétes des Pais Orientaux & Occidentaux."

3. Gabriel Audisio, *Les Vaudois du Luberon. Une minorité en Provence (1460–1560)* (Merindol: Association d'Etudes Vaudoises et Historiques du Luberon, 1984).

4. Gabriel Audisio, *Preachers by Night: The Waldensian Barbes (15th–16th Centuries)* (Leiden: Brill, 2007). For Waldensian theology, Euan Cameron, *The Reformation of the Heretics: The Waldenses of the Alps (1480–1580)* (Oxford: Clarendon Press, 1984), 65–124, and Cameron, *Waldenses: Rejections of the Holy Church in Mediaeval Europe* (Oxford: Blackwell, 2000), 209–280. See also CC, V: 282, and esp. 312–324.

5. On Waldensian clandestine behavior, see Cameron, *Reformation of the Heretics*, 21, 81.

6. CC, I: préface générale.

7. James Ussher, *Gravissimae questionis, de christianaruum ecclesiarum, in occidentis praesertim partibus, ab apostolicis temporibus ad nostrum, usque aetatem, continua succesione et statu, historica explication* (London: Bonham Norton, 1613); Jean Léger, *Histoire générale des églises évangéliques des vallées de Piémont ou Vaudoises* (Leyden: Jean le Carpentier, 1669); Cameron, *Waldenses*, 224 ff and 290 ff.

8. CC, I: v.

9. For Bernard's relationship with the French moralizing tradition, Roger Mercier, *La Réhabilitation de la nature humaine, 1700–1750* (Villemonble: Editions La Balance, 1960), 75, 128. In the 1730s Jean Frederic would publish a three-volume reprint of Pascal's *Lettres provinciales*. For the discussion of the behavior of the first Christians, [J. F. Bernard], *Reflexions morales satiriques & comiques, sur les moeurs de nôtre siécle* (Cologne: Chez Pierre Marteau le Jeune, 1711), 217–218. Porrée's original edition was entitled *Traité des anciennes cérémonies, ou Histoire contenant leur naissance et accroissement, leur entrée en l'Église, et par quels degrez elles ont passé jusques à la superstition.*

10. Quotation from *Histoire des ceremonies et des superstitions, qui se sont introduites dans l'Église* (Amsterdam: J. F. Bernard, 1717), 4.

11. J. N. Bakhuizen van den Brink, *Ratramnus, De Corpore et Sanguine Dominis, Verhandelingen der Koninklijke Nederlandse Akademie van Wetenschappen, afd. Letterkunde,* Nieuwe Reeks, vol. 87 (Amsterdam/London: North-Holland Publishing Company, 1974), 128–129; *Superstitions anciennes et modernes: prejugés vulgaires qui ont induits les peuples à des usages & à des pratiques contraires à la religion,* 2 vols. (Amsterdam: Jean Frederic Bernard, 1733–1736), containing contributions of Jean-Baptiste Thiers (1636–1703), Pierre Lebrun (1661–1729), and Bernard himself. In the Laporte reprint of 1807–1810 the *Superstitions* were reproduced as vols. 10 and 11.

12. For Meslier and Giannone, see also Jonathan Israel, *Contested Enlighten-*

ment: Philosophy, Modernity, and the Emancipation of Man, 1670–1752 (Oxford: Oxford University Press, 2005), 716–728, 519–520. For Bekker, Andrew Fix, *Fallen Angels: Balthasar Bekker, Spirit, Belief, and Confessionalism in the Seventeenth Century Dutch Republic* (Dordrecht: Kluwer, 1999); for Bayle's views, cf. *Dictionaire critique et historique,* 4 vols. (Rotterdam: Leers, 1720), article Des Périers. Cf. Antony McKenna, "l'Éclaircissment sur les pyrrhoniens, 1702," in H. Bots, ed., *Critical Spirit, Wisdom and Erudition on the Eve of the Enlightenment: The Dictionaire critique et historique de Pierre Bayle (1647–1706)* (Amsterdam: APA-Holland University Press, 1996), 297–320, esp. 318. For Thiers and Le Brun on superstition, William Monter, *Ritual, Myth and Magic in Early Modern Europe* (Brighton: Harvester Press, 1983), ch. 7.

13. *Reflexions morales,* 323.

14. *Critical and Philosophical Dialogues* (London, 1735), 92–102; *Reflexions morales,* 267, 369.

15. Jack A. Clarke, *Gabriel Naudé, 1600–1653* (Hamden, CT: Archon Books, 1970), 11; René Pintard, *Le Libertinage érudit dans la prmière moitié du XVIIe siècle* (Geneva: Slatkine, 2000); Gabriel Naudé, *Considérations politiques sur les coups d'état* (Rome, 1639), edited by Françoise Charles-Daubert (Hildesheim: Olms Verlag, 1993), 171–172. A personal element might have been involved as well. Waldensians often had been falsely accused of witchcraft and magic: Martine Osterero, Agostino Paravinci Bagliani, and Kathrin Utz Tremp, eds., *L'Imaginaire du Sabbat. Edition critique des textes les plus anciens* (1430c.–1440c.) (Lausanne: Cahiers Lausannois d'Histoire Médiévale, 1999), 301–303; and Cameron, *Reformation of the Heretics,* 97.

16. Marchand and Bernard were the first publishers in more than a century to reissue the work of Des Périers; the text is preceded by a letter from P. M. to B. P., Marchand to Picart. For the Rabelais edition: *Oeuvres de Maitre François Rabelais avec des remarques historiques et critiques de Mr. le Duchat,* 3 vols. (Amsterdam: Jean Frederic Bernard, 1741). Rabelais was one of Bernard's heroes, whom he quoted incessantly. Bernard also published a new edition of the *Roman de la Rose* (Amsterdam: Jean Frederic Bernard, 1735), a medieval tale that had received new attention from the French humanists. Cf. for the Navarre circle, Barbara Stephenson, *Power and Patronage and Marguerite de Navarre* (Aldershot: Ashgate, 2004). The cruelty of Francis I toward the Waldensians was often on Bernard's mind. Cf. *Etat de l'Homme dans le peché originel* (Printed in the World [Amsterdam], 1741), p. 25.

17. Guillaume Postel, *De orbis terrae concordia* (Basel: J. Oporinus, ca. 1544). For a brilliant treatment of Bernard and Picart and the Hermetic tradition: David Brafman, "Picart, Bernard, Hermes, and Muhammad (not necessarily in that order)," in Lynn Hunt, Margaret Jacob, and Wijnand Mijnhardt, eds., *Bernard Picart and the First Global Vision of Religion* (Los Angeles: Getty Publications, 2010). For Bernard's *Plan theologique du Pythagorisme* (Amsterdam: Jean Frederic Bernard, 1714)

and its author, Michel Mourgues, cf. Yves Marquet, *Les frères de la pureté, pythago-riciens de l'Islam. La marque du pythagorisme dans la rédaction des Epîtres des Ihwân as-Safâ* (Paris: S.E.H.A., 2006). For the Pythagoreans see CC, I: xxi.

18. Beverland, *De Peccato Originale* (Leiden: Danielis a Gaesbeeck, 1679). Cf. R. De Smet, *Hadrianus Beverlandus (1650–1716). Non unus e multis peccator. Studie over het leven en werk van Hadriaan Beverland* (Brussels: Paleis der Academiën, 1988). See also Rudolf de Smet, "The Realm of Venus. *Hadriani Barlande* [*He. Beverland*] *De Prostibulis Veterum*, MS Leiden BPL 1994," *Quaerendo* 17, no. 1 (1987): 45–59. Bernard's *History of the State of Man in Original Sin* is the only work he was never prepared to publish under his own imprint. All six editions have fictitious imprints. In 1741 he published the last reprint as Imprimé dans le Monde ("Printed in the World"). In 1774 Marc Michel Rey presumably took care of the 7th edition, also "Printed in the World." The last edition was printed in Brussels in 1868 (based on the 1741 version), an edition that was forbidden in France. According to the biblio-graphical dictionaries, a certain Fontenai was rumored to have published a free adaptation in 1714 too. This edition has not been found, and we presume that it never existed. In Bernard's version the parts of the text that refer to Spinoza and Hobbes have been left out. Rabelais is the most frequently quoted source.

19. CC, I: iii–xxxviii. For libertines in the republic see Michiel Wielema, *The March of the Libertines: Spinozists and the Dutch Reformed Church (1660–1750)* (Hil-versum: Verloren, 2004).

20. Original edition: Joannes Boemus, *Omnium gentes mores, leges et ritus* (1520). Cf. Jöan Pau Rubies, "Theology, Ethnography and the Historicization of Idolatry," *Journal of the History of Ideas* (2006): 139–158, esp. 147.

21. Samuel Purchas, *Purchas, his Pilgrimage; or, Relations of the World and the Religions observed in all Ages and places discovered, from the Creation until this pres-ent* (London: Henry Featherstone, 1617); Alexander Ross, *Pansebeia, or View of all the Religions in the World. With the several church-governments, from the creation, till these times. Also, a discovery of all known heresies in all ages and places . . . To which are annexed, The lives, actions and ends of certain notorious heretics* (London: J. Sal-well, 1655). Quotation is from fifth edition, 1673 preface. Increasingly the fourth category of people came to be called polytheists. Cf. Francis Schmidt, "Polytheists: Degeneration or Progress?" *History and Anthropology* 3 (1987): 3–60. *Pansebeia*, 5th ed. (London: Saywell, 1673), preface.

22. Frank A. Kafker, *Notable Encyclopedias of the 17th and 18th Century* (Oxford: Voltaire Foundation, 1981); Marie Leca-Tsiomis, *Ecrire l'Encyclopédie: Diderot, de l'usage des dictionnaires à la grammaire philosophique* (Oxford: Voltaire Foundation, 1999), 52–67.

23. Peter Burke, "Images as Evidence in Seventeenth-Century Europe," *Journal of the History of Ideas* 64 (2003): 272–296. Francis Haskell, *History and Its Images: Art*

and the Interpretation of the Past (New Haven: Yale University Press, 1995), 131–135. D. O. Hurel and R. Roge, eds., *Dom Bernard de Montfaucon: Actes du colloque de Carcassonne, Octobre 1996*, 2 vols. (Caudebec-en-Caux: Editions de Fontenelle, 1998). Picart never used Montfaucon's plates. Only the plagiarized Parisian edition of 1741 would incorporate a few of Montfaucon's engravings. Cf. Geneviève Artigas-Menant, *Du secret des clandestins à la propagande voltairienne* (Paris: Honoré Champion, 2001), 41, who fails to distinguish between the original and the bowdlerized version. Artigas-Menant, who characterizes *Religious Ceremonies* as an unoriginal hodgepodge that stands out only because of its superb illustrations, unfortunately misses the essence of the enterprise.

24. Peter Dear, "The Church and the New Philosophy," in S. Pumfrey, Paolo Rossi, and M. Slawinski, eds., *Science, Culture and Popular Belief in Renaissance Europe*, 119–139 (Manchester: Manchester University Press, 1991); and Rienk Vermey, *The Calvinist Copernicans: The Reception of the New Astronomy in the Dutch Republic, 1575–1750* (Amsterdam: Koninklijke Akademie van Wetenschappen, 2002), 335–348.

25. For the influence on Montesquieu, see van Roosbroeck, *Persian Letters before Montesquieu*, 59–86.

26. Jean Steinmann, *Richard Simon et les origines de l'exégèse biblique* (Paris: Desclee de Brouwer, 1960), 50–53; Paul Auvray, *Richard Simon (1638–1712)* (Paris: Presses Universitaires de France, 1974); *Les Juifs présentés aux Chrétiens. Textes de Léon de Modena et de Richard Simon* (Paris: Les Belles Lettres, 2004), xlix; Guy Stroemsa, "Richard Simon: From Philology to Comparatism," *Archiv für Religionsgeschichte* 3 (Leipzig: K. G.Saur, 2001): 90–107.

27. For Spencer, see Jan Assmann, *Moses the Egyptian: The Memory of Egypt in Western Monotheism* (Cambridge, MA: Harvard University Press, 1997), 55–90; and Guy Stroumsa, "John Spencer and the Roots of Idolatry," *History of Religions* 41 (2001): 1–23. For Fleury: Bruno Neveu, *Érudition et religion au XVIe et XVIIIe siècles* (Paris: Albin Michel, 1994), 346–349.

28. M. Quak, "De Collegianten te Amsterdam in de periode 1722–1775" (master's thesis, Utrecht University, 1983). Cf. Jesse Sadler, "The Collegiants, a Small Presence in the Republic, a Large Metaphor for the Book," in Hunt, Jacob, and Mijnhardt, eds., *Bernard Picart and the First Global Vision of Religion.*

29. Jacalyn Duffin, "Jodocus Lommius's Little Golden Book and the History of Diagnostic Semeiology," *Journal of the History of Medicine and Allied Sciences* 61 (2006): 249–287. Bernard published editions of Lommius in 1715, 1720, and 1725. His Boerhaave edition was printed in 1726.

30. Pierre Jurieu, *Des droits de deux souverains* (Rotterdam: Henri de Graef, 1687), 14, 145–154. Vgl. F. R. J. Knetsch, *Pierre Jurieu. Theoloog en Politikus der Refuge* (Kampen: Kok, 1967), 270–277.

31. For the Locke and Van Limborch debate: John Marshall, *John Locke, Tolera-*

tion and Early Enlightenment Culture (Cambridge: Cambridge University Press, 2006). For Bayle see Hubert Bost, *Pierre Bayle* (Paris: Fayard, 2006), 181–212.

32. Cf. the membership lists compiled in Quak, "De Collegianten te Amsterdam in de periode 1722–1775," which reveal quite a few of Bernard's and Picart's acquaintances. See also Inger Leemans, "Picart's Dutch Connections: Family Trouble, the Amsterdam Theater and the Business of Engraving," in Hunt, Jacob, and Mijnhardt, eds., *Bernard Picart and the First Global Vision of Religion.*

33. Wijnand W. Mijnhardt, "The Construction of Silence: Religious and Political Radicalism in Dutch History," in Wiep van Bunge, ed., *The Early Enlightenment in the Dutch Republic, 1650–1750,* 231–261 (Leiden: Brill, 2003); Richard Stauffer, *L'Affaire d'Huisseau. Une controverse au sujet de la réunion des chrétiens (1670–1671)* (Paris: Presses Universitaires de France, 1969); and idem, *The Quest for Church Unity: From John Calvin to Isaac d'Huisseau* (Allison Park: Pickwick Publications, 1986). Dutch translation: *De Vereeniging van't Christendom, Aanwyzing van het middel om alle Christenen onder een geloofsbelijdenis weer te zamen te voegen* (Amsterdam: Pieter Arentsz, 1671). In his analysis of the history of Protestantism Bernard supported unification along the lines of Pierre Poiret, one of the famous Christians without a church and a good friend of the high priestess of the seekers, Antoinette Bourignon. See also CC, V: 311 and 386.

34. Anthony Pagden, *European Encounters with the New World* (New Haven: Yale University Press, 1993), 11. For an extensive discussion of the problems of the genealogical relationship of the religions: François Laplanche, *L'Évidence du Dieu chrétien. Religion, culture et société dans l'apologétique protestante de la France classique (1576–1680)* (Strasbourg: Palais Universitaire, 1983); and Alphonse Dupront, *Pierre-Daniel Huet et l'exégèse comparatiste au XVIIe siècle* (Paris: 1930).

35. See also *Emile ou de l'éducation:* "parmi tant de cultes inhumaines et bizarres (. . .) vous trouvez partout les mêmes idées de justice et d'honnêteté, partout les mêmes notions du bien et du mal," in *Oeuvres complètes de J. J. Rousseau,* 5 vols. (Paris: Bibliothèque de la Pleiade, 1959–1995), IV: 597 ff. For a detailed analysis of the relationship of Bernard's daughter Elisabeth with Jean Jacques Rousseau, see J. Bosscha, ed., *Lettres inédites de Jean Jacques Rousseau à Marc Michel Rey* (Paris: Muller, 1858).

6. Picart's Visual Politics

1. Christoph Lüthy, "Where Logical Necessity Becomes Visual Persuasion: Descartes's Clear and Distinct Illustrations," in Sachiko Kusukawa and Ian Maclean, eds., *Transmitting Knowledge: Words, Images, and Instruments in Early Modern Europe* (Oxford, UK: Oxford University Press, 2006), 97–133, and in the same volume see the essay on Vesalius by Sachiko Kusukawa.

2. The original drawings for the prints are dispersed among various collec-

tions. The largest number are preserved in the Teylers Museum in Haarlem. A notarial contract of 1710 between Picart and one of his publishers for an illustrated Bible shows that Picart demanded that his name appear on the title page and that he was able, unlike other engravers, to require royalty payments for each print sold (in that case four livres ten sous per copy). The contract can be found in A. Bredius, "Het Contract van Picart's Bijbelprenten," *Oud Holland* 29 (1911): 185–188. See the indispensable discussion in Sarah Monks, "Bernard Picart's *Impostures innocentes* (1734): Constructing the Early Eighteenth-Century French Reproductive Printmaker" (master's thesis, Courtauld Institute of Art, University of London, 1996).

3. Picart's production can be followed year by year in the catalogue printed after his death by his widow in *Imp Inn.*

4. Roger de Piles, *Abregé de la vie des peintres, avec des reflexions sur leurs ouvrages, et un Traité du Peintre parfait, de la connoisssance des Desseins, & de l'utilité des Estampes* (Paris: Chez François Muguet, 1699), 77–78, 84–85.

5. Picart's "Discourse" can be found separately paginated in *Imp Inn.* See also Ann Jensen Adams, "Reproduction and Authenticity in Bernard Picart's *Impostures innocents,*" and Louis Marchesano, "The *Impostures innocentes:* Bernard Picart's Defense of the Professional Engraver," both in Lynn Hunt, Margaret Jacob, and Wijnand Mijnhardt, eds., *Bernard Picart and the First Global Vision of Religion* (Los Angeles: Getty Publications, 2010).

6. Pierre Wachenheim, "Art et politique, langage pictural et sédition dans l'estampe sous le règne de Louis XV," 2 vols. (Ph.D diss., Université de Paris I Panthéon-Sorbonne, 2004), esp. 39, 317.

7. On Picart's influence on Hogarth, see F. Antal, "Hogarth and His Borrowings," *The Art Bulletin* 29 (March 1947): 36–48. In a brief note in *Notes and Queries,* 6th series, 1880, 332, a William Bates claims to own a drawing by Hogarth signed in his handwriting "Com'union as at St. Paul's for Picart." Van der Schley produced an engraving for volume 6 with the title "La Communion des Anglicans à Saint Paul."

8. On his way of working see pp. 9–11 of "Eloge historique de Bernard Picart, dessinateur et graveur" (each piece is numbered separately in *Imp Inn).* For the list of Picart's books, see Picart cat. The engraving with Chinese characters is "QUANTECONG DIVINITÉ CHINOISE que les CHINOIS disent avoir eté leur premier EMPEREUR," in CC, IV: following p. 222. It is based on a 1670 print by Jacob van Meurs but redrawn by Picart himself.

9. On his efforts to gain admission to the ceremony, see *Imp Inn,* "Eloge," 9. On Nuñes da Costa, see Isabella H. van Eeghen, "Bernard Picart en de Joodse godsdienstplichten," *Amstelodamum* 65 (1978): 58–63. Ann Jensen Adams was kind enough to provide us with this reference. VWG argues that Picart is the man with the three-corner hat on the grounds that the other man is too young to be Picart (then fifty-two years old) and is in fact wearing a kippah or yarmulke. By contrast,

the Sotheby's catalogue for the sale of the oil painting and various others claims that Picart is the hatless man on the left. Sotheby's catalogue for a sale April 12, 1996, in Tel Aviv. Picart's self-portrait probably dates from 1709 or before, when Picart was only thirty-six.

10. Picart cat. gives the date of 1663 for the *Pontificale Romanum* but no date of publication for most works. Picart owned *Histoire des conclaves* (the French translation of the original 1667 Italian work), but no edition is given. We consulted the etchings in *Histoire des conclaves depuis Clement V jusqu'à présent: enrichie de plusieurs memoires, qui contiennent l'histoire du pape & des cardinaux d'aujourd'hui, & celle des principales familles de Rome, où l'on apprend quantité de particularitez de cette cour: avec un discours qui explique toutes les cérémonies qui s'observent depuis la mort du pape, jusqu'après l'élection de son successeur: accompagné de plusieurs tailles douces dans les endroits necessaires,* 2 vols., 3rd ed. (Cologne: [s.n.], 1703).

11. For an in-depth analysis of his approach see Catherine Clark, "Chinese Idols and Religious Art: Questioning Difference in *Cérémonies et coutumes,*" and Verónica A. Gutiérrez, "Quetzalcoatl's Enlightened City: A Close Reading of Picart's Engraving of Chollollan/Cholula," both in Hunt, Jacob, and Mijnhardt, eds., *Bernard Picart and the First Global Vision of Religion.*

12. Baldini's role is discussed in R. W. Lightbown, "Oriental Art and the Orient in Late Renaissance and Baroque Italy," *Journal of the Warburg and Courtauld Institutes* 32 (1969): 228–279.

13. VWG, see the Decker on p. 220. She claims (p. 217) that Ixora is Ishvara—the "highest god" or Shiva. On the originality of Picart's effort to give a complete picture of the Indian deities, see p. 255.

14. VWG, p. 104 on the Mecca print, and pp. 187–197 on the large print of fakirs performing penitential rites.

15. Cornelius de Pauw, *Recherches philosophiques sur les Egyptiens et les Chinois,* 2 vols. (Londres, i.e., Lausanne ?, 1774), I: 305.

16. Picart's use of these earlier stereotypical representations is discussed by Marcia Reed, "Picart on China: 'Curious' Discourses and Images Taken Principally from the Jesuits," in Hunt, Jacob, and Mijnhardt, eds., *Bernard Picart and the First Global Vision of Religion.*

17. Quotes from CC, IV: 225.

18. The catalogue is eight folio pages, follows the "Eloge," is separately numbered, and is not included in the English translation of 1756. The function of the catalogue is examined by Monks, "Bernard Picart's *Impostures innocentes.*"

19. The Getty catalogue is the most extensive and has handwritten prices in an eighteenth-century hand. *Catalogus van een fraaye party Konstige en uytvoerige Tekeningen, onder de welke uytmunt de schoone collectie van eygenhandige Teekeningen van Bernard Picart . . .* [announcing a sale in Amsterdam on November 25, 1737, of the widow's holdings] (Amsterdam, 1737). The theme of Abraham and Hagar was es-

pecially beloved by Dutch audiences, according to Christine Petra Sellin, *Fractured Families and Rebel Maidservants: The Biblical Hagar in Seventeenth-Century Dutch Art and Literature* (New York: T. and T. Clark, 2006).

20. There are no records of eighteenth-century sales of any paintings by Picart, which suggests some doubt as to the authenticity of the oil painting of the Seder attributed to him. For the copperplates see *Catalogus van Schilderyen, van de Wed. Bernard Picart, verkogt den 15 Mey 1737. In Amsterdam* in *Catalogus of Naamlyst van Schilderyen, met derzelver pryzen . . . uytgegeven door Gerard Hoet* (The Hague: Pieter Gerard van Ballen, 1752), 474–477. [The prices are printed.] The French catalogue was located in the Fitzwilliam Museum, Cambridge, UK. *Catalogue des Estampes qui composent la plus grande partie de l'Oeuvre de B. Picart, dessinateur et graveur qui se vendent chez . . .* (n.p., n.d.). The handwritten prices in the French catalogue are also given in Dutch florins. Since the Fitzwilliam catalogue has no date, the prices listed in it are necessarily subject to debate.

21. *Catalogue raisonnée des diverses curiosités du cabinet de feu M. Quentin de Lorangere, composé de tableaux originaux des meilleurs maîtres de Flandres, d'une tres-nombreuse collection de desseins & d'estampes de toutes les ecoles, de plusieurs atlas & suites de cartes, de quantité de morceaux de topographie, & d'un coquillier fait avec choix . . . par E. F. Gersaint* (Paris: Chez Jacques Barois, 1744), 163.

22. Pierre Remy, *Catalogue raisonné des tableaux, estampes, coquilles, & autres curiosités; après le décès de Feu Monsieur Dezalier d'Argenville, Maître des Comptes, & Membre des Sociétés Royales des Sciences de Londres & de Montpellier* (Paris: Chez Didot, l'aîné, 1766).

7. Familiarizing Judaism

1. CC, vol. I, "Dissertation sur le culte religieux," xiii. David Myers provided invaluable assistance in reading the Pentateuch engraving.

2. See Bibliothèque Arsenal, Paris, MS 10229, for requests to reside in Paris made in the 1750s. For The Hague in this period, see Gysbert de Cretser, *Beschryvinge van s'Gravenhage . . .* (Amsterdam: Jan ten Hoorn, 1711), 31. For London's Jews see http://www.ucd.ie/economics/research/papers/2008/WP08.06.pdf. For the Paris and London figures see Arthur Hertzberg, *The French Enlightenment and the Jews* (New York: Columbia University Press, 1968), 133; Lionel Kochan, *The Making of Western Jewry, 1600–1819* (New York: Palgrave Macmillan, 2004), 150–151. For Germany see Johann Jacob Schudt, *Jüdische Merckwürdigheiten* (Frankfurt and Leipzig: Verlegs Samuel Tobias Hoder, 1714), 272. We thank Harry Sondheim for permission to use and cite Schudt.

3. See the etchings of the synagogues by Adolf van der Laan in *Image and Impression: Rare Prints from the Collection of the Library of the Jewish Theological Seminary of America* (New York: Library of the Jewish Theological Seminary of Amer-

ica, 2002), 31, where the date of 1710 may be incorrect. Laan worked from 1717 to 1740. For a description of the interior of both synagogues see [Adolf Van der Laan], *Gebouwen, Gezigten, en Oudheden der stad Amsterdam Met Figuren* (Amsterdam: Marshoorn, 1734), 227–230. By 1796 the Amsterdam Jewish population had risen to around 25,000; cf. Judith C. E. Belinfante, "Utopie of wekelijkheid. Een plan tot positieverbetering voor de arme joden van Amsterdam uit de achttiende eeuw," *Nieuwe Nederlanders: Vestiging van migranten door de eeuwen heen* (Amsterdam: SISWO, 1996), 70–71. Miguel de Barrios, *Triumpho del govierno popular* (n.d., n.p.), as cited in Kenneth R. Scholberg, "Miguel de Barrios and the Amsterdam Sephardic Community," *The Jewish Quarterly Review,* n.s. 53 (1962): 120–159; quote p. 159.

4. Samantha Baskind, "Distinguishing the Distinction: Picturing Ashkenazi and Sephardic Jews in Seventeenth- and Eighteenth-Century Amsterdam," *The Journal for the Study of Sephardic and Mizrahi Jewry* (February 2007), available at http://sephardic.fiu.edu/journal/SamanthaBaskind.pdf. See also Shlomo Berger, "An Invitation to Buy and Read: Paratexts of Yiddish Books in Amsterdam, 1650–1800," *Book History* 7 (2004): 31–61.

5. CC, I, 1st part, third section, p. 90. Margaret C. Jacob, *Strangers Nowhere in the World: The Rise of Cosmopolitanism in Early Modern Europe* (Philadelphia: University of Pennsylvania Press, 2006), 34–35, citing Archives départementales de Vaucluse, MS IG 827, f. 345.

6. [Anon.], *Le Guide, ou Nouvelle Description d'Amsterdam* (Amsterdam: Covens and Mortier, 1753), 69–70. CC, I, first part, third section, p. 101. Hendrik Brugmans and A. Frank claim that William III visited the synagogue in 1690, *Geschiedenis der joden in Nederland* (Amsterdam: Van Holkema and Warendorf, 1940), book 2, chs. 2 and 3. On Moses Curiel see J. S. da Silva Rosa, *Geschiedenis der portugeesche Joden te Amsterdam, 1593–1925* (Amsterdam: Menno Hertzberger, 1925), 97–100.

7. The Jewish Historical Museum of Amsterdam has many Picart engravings in its collection.

8. Toland (in a work published in 1714) is quoted in Frank Felsenstein, *Anti-Semitic Stereotypes: A Paradigm of Otherness in English Popular Culture, 1660–1830* (Baltimore: Johns Hopkins University Press, 1995), 49. See Francesca Bregoli, "Jewish Scholarship, Science, and the Republic of Letters: Joseph Attias in Eighteenth-Century Livorno," *Aleph* 7 (2007): 12.

9. Very little has been written about Dutch anti-Semitism in this period; see F. Van Cleeff-Hiegentlich, "Eerlyke smousen, hoe zien die 'er uit myn heer?' Of hoe er in de achttiende eeuw in de Republiek der Zeven Verenigde Nederlanden over joden werd gedacht—een verkenning," in Anne Frank Stichting, *Vreemd Gespuis* (Amsterdam: AMBO, 1987), 56–65. *Notes and Queries: A Medium of Intercommunication for Literary Men, General Readers, Etc.,* 11th series, 2 (July–December 1910): 225.

10. Felsenstein, *Anti-Semitic Stereotypes,* 83.

11. Stephen G. Burnett, "Distorted Mirrors: Antonius Margaritha, Johann Buxtorf and Christian Ethnographies of the Jews," *Sixteenth Century Journal* 25 (Summer 1994): 275–288. For Leon Modena's negative view of rabbinical introductions, see footnotes c, page 4, CC I, first part.

12. CC I, preface to the Leon of Modena excerpt.

13. CC, I, first part, p. 29. See also Marina Rustow, "Karaites Real and Imagined: Three Cases of Jewish Heresy," *Past and Present* 197 (2007): 58–68.

14. CC, I, first part, third section, p. 138.

15. See, for example, CC, I, first part, third section, p. 80. Jonathan M. Elukin, "Jacques Basnage and the History of the Jews: Anti-Catholic Polemic and Historical Allegory in the Republic of Letters," *Journal of the History of Ideas* 53 (October–December 1992): 603–630. Bernard owned the 1716 edition of Basnage, *Histoire des juifs, depuis Jesus-Christ, jusqu'a présent. Pour servir de continuation à l'Histoire de Joseph* (The Hague: H. Scheurleer, 1716).

16. CC, I, first part, third section, pp. 103 and 108. "Lettre A Monsieur**** sur les juifs," in *Dissertations mêlées, sur divers sujets importans et curieux,* 163–201 (Amsterdam: Jean F. Bernard, 1740).

17. Wayne Franits, "Seks en schandaal: Romeyn de Hooghe en de pamflettenoorlog," *De Boekenwereld* 15 (1999): 232–238. For his depiction of Jews see Romeyn de Hooghe, *Hieroglyphica Merkbeelden der Oude Volkeren: namelyk Egyptenaren, Chaldeeuwen, Feniciers, Joden . . .* (Amsterdam: Joris van der Woude, 1735), 251. Jozeph Michman, Hartog Beem, and Dan Michman, *Pinkas. Geschiedenis van de joodse gemeenschap in Nederland,* trans. from the Hebrew by Ruben Verhasselt (Amsterdam: Contact, 1999), 34–36. On De Hooghe's Jewish prints see Steven Nadler, *Rembrandt's Jews* (Chicago: University of Chicago Press, 2003), 58–61. See also Jonathan I. Israel, "The Republic of the United Netherlands until about 1750: Demography and Economic Activity," in J. C. H. Blom et al., *The History of the Jews in the Netherlands* (Portland, OR: Littman Library of Jewish Civilization, 2002).

18. Adriaen Bakker, *Memorie van Rechten . . . in de crimineele saak tegens Romein de Hooge, etser aldaar. Met de Bylagen Daar toe specterende* (Amsterdam: Jan Rieuwertsz, 1690), 1–17; *Romein de Hooge. Voor den Rechterstoel van Apollo, Verdedigende zich wegens de snoode Misdaaden en vuile Lasteringen, welke hem in een zeker Geschrift, Geintituleerd Vindiciae Amsteladamenses of Contra-Spiegel der Waarheid . . .* (Haarlem: Romulus ab Alto, in de Venusbuurt [clearly a false imprint], 1690), 12.

19. Oxford English Dictionary at http://dictionary.oed.com/cgi/entry/50238096 ?query_type=word&queryword=stock-jobber&first=1&max_to_show=10; for background see Anne Goldgar, *Tulipmania: Money, Honor, and Knowledge in the Dutch Golden Age* (Chicago: University of Chicago Press, 2007), epilogue. On reaction in England, see Dianne Dugaw, "High Change in 'Change Alley': Popular Ballads and Emergent Capitalism in the Eighteenth Century," *Eighteenth-Century*

Life 22 (1998): 43–58, esp. pp. 50–51. The Amsterdam crash occurred in September 1720 but was less severe than those in Paris or London.

20. *Het groote tafereel der dwaasheid [The great picture of folly]: vertoonende de opkomst, voortgang en ondergang der actie, bubbel en windnegotie, in Vrankryk, Engeland, en de Nederlanden, gepleegt in den jaare MDCCXX: zynde een verzameling van alle de conditien en projecten van de opgeregte compagnien van assurantie, navigatie, commercie, &c. in Nederland, zo wel die in gebruik zyn gebragt, als die door de h. staten van eenige provintien zyn verworpen: als meede konst-plaaten, comedien en gedigten . . . : gedrukt tot waarshouwinge voor de nakomelingen, in 't noodlottige jaar, voor veel zotte en wyze* (n.p., 1720). Frans De Bruyn, "Reading *Het groote tafereel der dwaasheid:* An Emblem Book of the Folly of Speculation in the Bubble Year 1720," *Eighteenth-Century Life* 24 (2000): 1–42; Frans De Bruyn, *"Het groote tafereel der dwaasheid* and the Speculative Bubble of 1720: A Bibliographical Enigma and an Economic Force," *Eighteenth-Century Life* 24 (2000): 62–88. The anonymous engraving referring to Vianen is "De Stervende Bubbel-Heer in den Schoot van Madame Compagnie." We found two different versions of this print in the Getty Research Institute holdings, one without the legend referring to *smous* and one with the legend that appears as well in *The Great Picture of Folly:* volume ID P850001* Box 2, VI–35, has the legend; P85001* Box 1, VI–36, does not (they are both boxed with engravings by Romeyn de Hooghe). Inger Leemans brought many of these sources to our attention.

21. On Bombario, see De Bruyn, "Reading *Het groote tafereel der dwaasheid:* An Emblem Book," 23–24. De Bruyn does not make the connection to the Jews or to De Barrios. See also H. den Boer and J. Israel, "William III and the Glorious Revolution in the Eyes of Amsterdam Sephardi Writers: The Reactions of Miguel de Barrios, Joseph Penso de la Vega, and Manuel de Leao," in Jonathan I. Israel, ed., *The Anglo-Dutch Moment: Essays on the Glorious Revolution and Its World Impact* (Cambridge: Cambridge University Press, 1991), 439–461. The fourth edition of *Het groote tafereel* (1780) does not provide any more information about the figure Bombario. Plate 19 in the first edition has become its title page. In April 2008 a colloquium on the book was held at Yale University School of Management; its participants provided helpful background information. See also [Anon.], *De Windhandel, of Bubbles Compagnien. Blyspel* [Gedrukt in Quinquenpoix by Bombario], n.p., n.d., but almost certainly from 1720–1721, Amsterdam.

22. For the cap see Heinz Schreckenberg, *The Jews in Christian Art: An Illustrated History* (New York: Continuum, 1996). See also Thomas Wright, *A History of Caricature and Grotesque in Literature and Art* (London: Chatto and Windus, 1875), p. 418. A similar cap can be seen in *Image and Impression . . . Jewish Theological Seminary of America,* p. 43, the engraving of Jonathan Eybeschuetz (circa 1690–1764), and the engraving on p. 107 dating from 1680. For the original source engraving of the shrew by Hugo Allardt see Cornelis Veth, *Geschiedenis van de Nederlandsche caricatuur en van de scherts in de Nederlandsche beeldende kunst* (Leiden: A. W.

Sijthoff, 1921), p. 95. In reference to another engraving, Veth (pp. 154–155) claims that Bambario is the Scottish financier John Law; in fact Bambario is his accomplice. See also Yosef Kaplan, "De joden in de Republiek tot omstreeks 1750," in J. C. Blom, R. G. Fuks-Mansfeld, and I. Schöffer, et.al., eds., *Geschiedenis van de Joden in Nederland* (Amsterdam: Uitgeverij Balans, 1995), pp. 172–173; and Schreckenberg, *The Jews in Christian Art*. A "Hamburger Judas" appears as well in *The Great Picture of Folly* in an engraving entitled "De Malle Actionisten naar Vianen of t'Peperland." Another example of anti-Jewish caricature can be found in Roeland van Leuve, *'s Waerelds koopslot of de Amsteldamse beurs, bestaande in drie boeken met zeer veele verbeeldingen . . .* (Amsterdam: Jacobus Verheyden, 1723), pp. 56–58. For the usurer as a hunchback see Sara Lipton, *Images of Intolerance: The Representation of Jews and Judaism in the Bible moralisée* (Berkeley: University of California Press, 1999), p. 35. The reference to Hebrews is found at the bottom of the engraving (unnumbered) "De Wind Koopers met Wind Betaald, of de laatste zal blyven hangen." "Smous Levi" comes from the bottom caption for the engraving, "De Windverkopers of Windvangers, die door wind, verliezen Geld en Goed: bederven Vrouw en Kind."

23. For the viciousness of German anti-Semitic prints see Johann Jacob Schudt, *Jüdischer Merckwürdigkeiten vorstellende was sich curieuses und denckwürdiges in den neuern Zeiten bey einigen Jahrhunderten mit denen in alle IV. Theile der Welt, sonderlich durch Teutschland, zerstreuten Juden zugetragen: sammt einer vollständigen Franckfurter Juden-Chronick, darinnen der zu Franckfurt am Mayn wohnenden Juden, von einigen Jahr-hunderten, biss auff unsere Zeiten, merckwürdigste Begebenheiten enthalten: benebst einigen, zur Erläuterung beygefügten Kupffern und Figuren* (Frankfurt and Leipzig: n.p., 1714), part II, print opposite p. 256. For a useful comparison, see Richard H. Popkin, "The Jews of the Netherlands in the Early Modern Period," in R. Po-Chia Hsia and Hartmut Lehmann, eds., *In and Out of the Ghetto: Jewish-Gentile Relations in Late Medieval and Early Modern Germany* (Cambridge: Cambridge University Press, 1995), pp. 311–316; on Schudt as a Jew-baiter, see p. 141. On the relations of the two Jewish communities see Kenneth R. Scholberg, "Miguel de Barrios and the Amsterdam Sephardic Community," *The Jewish Quarterly Review,* New Series, 53 (October 1962): 120–159, and Yosef Kaplan, "The Jews in the Republic until about 1750: Religious, Cultural, and Social Life," in J. C. H. Blom et al., *The History of the Jews in the Netherlands,* pp. 116–131. See also Dorothee Sturkenboom, "Staging the Merchant: Commercial Vices and the Politics of Stereotyping in Early Modern Dutch Theatre," *Dutch Crossing: A Journal of Low Countries Studies* 30 (2006): 216–228. For the decree by officials in Utrecht see *Publicatie tegens het inkomen en vernachten van Hoogduytsche Joden of smousen, derselver wyven or kinderen, binnen de stadt Utrecht: By provisie in de vroedschap gearresteert den 8 october, 1736* (Utrecht: Jac. Van Poolsum, 1736).

24. A copy of the play can be read at www.let.leidenuniv.nl/Dutch/Ceneton/ Quincampoix1720.html. For a useful discussion of Dutch toleration see John Mar-

shall, *John Locke, Toleration and Early Enlightenment Culture* (Cambridge: Cambridge University Press, 2006), ch. 4.

25. William Swaanenburg, *De vervrolykende Momus*, Amsterdam, Monday, July 7, 1727, no. 30, pp. 234–238; *De Hollandsche Spectator*, January 18, 1734, no. 233, pp. 322–323; *De koopman, of bijdragen ten opbouw van Neêrlands koophandel en zeevaard*, Amsterdam, vol. 2, 1769, p. 438.

26. For Protestant preaching see a work that Picart owned in his library, Jean Claude, *La Parabole des Noces* (Geneva: Samuel De Tournes, 1678), pp. 86–95, 117–128. L. and R. Fuks, "Hebrew Book Production in the Northern Netherlands and Their German Connections in the 17th Century," *De Arte et Libris: Festschrift Erasmus, 1934–1984* (Amsterdam: Erasmus Antiquariaat en Boekhandel, 1984), pp. 173–178. VWG, p. 75. For the Picart illustration of the Torah see: http/www.jhm.nl/objecten.aspx?SEARCH=trefwoord%20=%20"Picart,%20Bernard"%20%20or%20vervaardiging.naam%20=%20"Picart,%20Bernard".

27. The discussion of the Seder and the omission of children can be found in the sale catalogue that includes the Picart painting (no. 229, bought by I. I. Perry), Sotheby's, *Important Judaica*, April 12, 1996, Tel Aviv. For the position of Catholics in the republic see Charles H. Parker, "Paying for the Privilege: The Management of Public Order and Religious Pluralism in Two Early Modern Societies," *Journal of World History* 17 (2007): 267–297. See also Yosef Kaplan, "Jews in the Republic until 1750," in Chaya Brasz and Yosef Kaplan, eds., *Dutch Jews as Perceived by Themselves and by Others: Proceedings of the Eighth International Symposium on the History of the Jews in the Netherlands* (Leiden: Brill, 2001), esp. pp. 160–163. See also Silvia Berti, "Bernard Picart e Jean-Frederic Bernard dalla religione riformata al deismo: Un incontro con il mondo ebraico nell'Amsterdam del primo settecento," *Rivista Storica Italiana* 67 (2005): 974–1000.

8. Cutting Roman Catholicism Down to Size

1. *Histoire générale des cérémonies, moeurs, et coutumes religieuses de tous les peuples du monde, représentées en 243 Figures dessinées de la main de Bernard Picard: Avec des Explications Historiques, & curieuses; par M. l'Abbé Banier, de l'Académie Royale des Inscriptions & Belles-Lettres, & par M. l'Abbé le Mascrier*, 7 vols. (Paris: Chez Rollin Fils, 1741), I: iii.

2. Ibid., pp. iv and 307.

3. CC, I: iii and *Histoire générale des cérémonies*, I: 3.

4. We are grateful for the research of Rob Haulton comparing the Picart images with those in the *Pontificale Romanum: Clementis VIII. primum, nunc denuo Vrbani VIII. auctoritate recognitum. In tres partes sive tres tomos divisum, pro faciliori pontificum usu.* (Paris: Societas Typographica Librorum Officii Ecclesiastici, 1663), the copy of Saint Louis University. Picart owned a 1663 copy, but the publisher is not given in Picart cat.

5. CC, I: third unnumbered page of Préface générale.

6. CC, I: second section, "Dissertation on the Christian Religion according to the Principles of the Roman Catholics," esp. p. 6.

7. On the saints, see CC, I: second section, 143.

8. CC, I: second section, 6, 51, 65, 67, 76.

9. CC, I: second section, 167; for purgatory, see CC, II: 95.

10. One of the main sources cited by Bernard was the "Rituel d'Alet," published in 1667 by Nicolas Pavillon, bishop of Alet. It was condemned in 1668 by the pope for its Jansenist tendencies, making it an immediate *cause célèbre*. It was reprinted and revised many times.

11. Picart based his engravings on etchings by Federico Mastrozzi that had been drawn by Pietro Ostini. We were only able to discover this thanks to research undertaken for us by Antonella de Michelis of John Cabot University in Rome. Picart alters some elements: he adds a couple of captions, places them differently, and offers a more vivid rendition. On Clement's art policies see Christopher M. S. Johns, *Papal Art and Cultural Politics: Rome in the Age of Clement XI* (Cambridge: Cambridge University Press, 1993).

12. CC, I: second section, III; CC, II: 91, 106.

13. CC, II: 142.

14. CC, II: 166.

15. CC, I: unpaginated Préface générale.

16. Louis Ellies Dupin, *Mémoires historiques pour servir à l'histoire des Inquisitions, enrichis de plusieurs figures,* 2 vols. (Cologne: Chez Denys Slebus, Libraire, proche l'Eglise Cathédrale [obviously a false imprint], 1716). We were alerted to the importance of this work and to this section of volume 2 by Guillaume Calafat, "The Gallicano-Jansenist Roots of the Bernard-Picart Vision," in Lynn Hunt, Margaret Jacob, and Wijnand Mijnhardt, eds., *Bernard Picart and the First Global Vision of Religion* (Los Angeles: Getty Publications, 2010).

17. Calafat offers a detailed analysis of the changes in the engravings in "The Gallicano-Jansenist Roots of the Bernard-Picart Vision."

18. CC, II: third section, 74.

19. CC, II: third section, 73.

20. CC, II: third section, 78.

21. The number of auto da fes comes from Elkan N. Adlev, "Auto de fé and Jew," *The Jewish Quarterly Review* 15, no. 3 (April 1903): 413–439, chart p. 436.

22. CC, II: third section, 92.

9. Idolatry

1. José de Acosta, *Natural and Moral History of the Indies,* trans. F. M. López-Morillas (Durham, NC: Duke University Press, 2002), 260. See Oxford English

Dictionary, entry for "idolatry." For a discussion of the theological background and its intersection with historical and ethnographic approaches, see Joan-Pau Rubiés, "Theology, Ethnography, and the Historicization of Idolatry," *Journal of the History of Ideas* 67 (October 2006): 571–596.

2. CC, I: xxvi and xxx; III: 4.

3. On Lafitau and the questions he faced, see Andreas Motsch, *Lafitau et l'émergence du discours ethnographique* (Sillery [Québec]: Septentrion, 2001). On Lafitau's comparative method, see Jacques Revel, "The Uses of Comparison: Religions in the Early Eighteenth Century," in Lynn Hunt, Margaret Jacob, and Wijnand Mijnhardt, eds., *Bernard Picart and the First Global Vision of Religion* (Los Angeles: Getty Publications, 2010).

4. CC, IV: 203–205 and esp. 205 for the similarity to Spinozism. See Acosta, *Natural and Moral History of the Indies,* note 1, Book V, chapter 1, where Acosta also claims that the Amerindians "confess a supreme Lord and Maker of all," though they have no single word "with which to name God."

5. Jonathan I. Israel, "Admiration of China and Classical Chinese Thought in the Radical Enlightenment (1685–1740)," *Taiwan Journal of East Asian Studies* 4, no. 1 (June 2007): 1–25.

6. Joseph-François Lafitau, *Mœurs des sauvages ameriquains, comparées aux mœurs des premiers temps,* 2 vols. (Paris: Chez Saugrain l'aîné, 1724), I: 110 and 4. See the chapter on Lafitau in Anthony Pagden, *The Fall of Natural Man: The American Indian and the Origins of Comparative Ethnology* (Cambridge: Cambridge University Press, 1986), 198–209. CC, III: 12–13.

7. M. L'Abbé (Antoine) Banier, *The Mythology and Fables of the Ancients, explain'd from History. By the Abbé Banier, . . . Translated from the original French,* 4 vols. (London: A. Millar, 1739–1740): I, 166, 145.

8. *Purchas his pilgrimage. Or Relations of the world and the religions observed in all ages and places discovered, from the Creation unto this present In foure partes. This first containeth a theologicall and geographicall historie of Asia, Africa, and America, with the ilands adiacent. Declaring the ancient religions before the Floud . . . With briefe descriptions of the countries, nations, states, discoveries, private and publike customes, and the most remarkable rarities of nature, or humane industrie, in the same. By Samuel Purchas, minister at Estwood in Essex* (London: Printed by William Stansby for Henrie Fetherstone, and are to be sold at his shoppe in Paul's Church-yard at the signe of the Rose, 1613). For Banier and Le Mascrier's ordering of idolatry, see *Histoire générale des cérémonies, moeurs, et coutumes religieuses de tous les peuples du monde, représentées en 243. Figures dessinées de la main de Bernard Picard . . . par M. l'Abbé Banier, de l'Académie Royale des Inscriptions & Belles Lettres, & par M. l'Abbé Mascrier,* 7 vols. (Paris: Chez Rollin, 1741), I: xxiv.

9. For Bernard's view of Africa, see CC, IV, "Dissertation sur les cérémonies religieuses des peuples de l'Afrique," 1–7.

10. CC, III: first section, 1–12. On the views of de Acosta on the origins of the Americans, see Pagden, *The Fall of Natural Man*, 194–195.

11. CC, III: first section, 12.

12. CC, III: first section, 12–14.

13. On polygamy see CC, III: first section, 21. The essay on India appeared originally under the name Mr. De la C***, *Conformité des coutumes des Indiens orientaux, avec celles des Juifs & des autres peuples de l'antiquité* (Brussels: G. de Backer, 1704). The author was De la Créquinière, about whom little is known. See Sanjay Subrahmanyam, "Monsieur Picart and the Gentiles of India," in Hunt, Jacob, and Mijnhardt, eds., *Bernard Picart*.

14. CC, III: first section, 12.

15. For the various editions of La Hontan's work see Mary Elizabeth Storer, "Bibliographical Observations on Foigny, La Hontan and Tyssot de Patot," *Modern Language Notes* 60, no. 3 (March 1945): 143–156. Louis Armand de Lom d'Arce, baron de La Hontan, and Nicolas Gueudeville (who may have written part of vol. 2), *Nouveaux voyages de M. le baron de La Hontan dans l'Amérique septentrionale*, 2 vols. (The Hague: Les frères L'Honoré, 1703).

16. For Bernard's remarks on La Hontan's and Hennepin's stylistic differences, see CC, III: first section, 88, note c. For Bernard's critique of Hennepin, see 82–83.

17. Why Jonathan Israel considers La Hontan (and Bernard too) *spinosiste* is not clear from Israel's own account and certainly not evident at all in La Hontan. Jonathan I. Israel, *Enlightenment Contested: Philosophy, Modernity, and the Emancipation of Man, 1670–1752* (Oxford: Oxford University Press, 2006), 600–601.

18. Claude-Charles Bacqueville de la Potherie, *Histoire de l'Amérique septentrionale*, 4 vols. (Paris: Jean-Luc Nion and François Didot, 1722), esp. II, 1–81. The engravings in these volumes apparently had no influence on Picart, which is not surprising since they seem to have been produced by someone (they are not signed) who had never seen native Americans and had no idea at all of their dress. On the treatment of prisoners see La Hontan, *Nouveaux voyages*, II: 175–181. On sacrifice, see CC, III: first section, 104. On the sources available to Bernard and Picart on the Americas, see Peter C. Mancall, "Illness and Death among Americans in Bernard Picart's *Cérémonies et coutumes*," in Hunt, Jacob, and Mijnhardt, eds., *Bernard Picart*.

19. CC, III: first section, 129; the engraving is after p. 128.

20. CC, III: first section, 12, 144.

21. CC, III: first section, 145.

22. CC, III: first section, 24–29.

23. VWG, 122–124. She offers by far the richest account of Picart's images and of the sources of the work in general.

24. CC, III: second section, 100. Bouchet's letter appeared in *Lettres edifiantes et curieuses, ecrites des missions etrangeres par quelques Missionnaires de la Compagnie de Jesus*, 34 vols. (Paris: Nicolas Le Clerc, 1707–1776), IX (1711): 1–60.

25. See, for example, Partha Mitter, who gives considerable credit to "Picart" (by which he means Bernard and Picart) in *Much Maligned Monsters: A History of European Reactions to Indian Art* (Chicago: University of Chicago Press, 1992). The *Lettres edifiantes,* which served as a source for Bernard and Picart, included many tales of the persecution of missionaries, including some by Bouchet, whom they cite frequently as an informant about native practices. See, for example, *Lettre du P. Bouchet à M. Cochet de Saint-Vallier, President des Requetes du Palais,* on the persecution of Christians in India, in *Lettres edifiantes,* XI (1715): 1–74. VWG argues that Picart's engravings constitute a canon of the European views of the time of India, VWG, 131.

26. CC, IV: first section, 6. See the extensive treatment of this image in VWG, 187–197. She includes an engraving from the 1681 German translation of Tavernier that is even closer in some respects to Picart's image than the one in the 1676 French original. Bernard owned the 1718 French edition of Tavernier.

27. The letter first appeared as *Lettre du Pere Bouchet missionnaire de la compagnie de Jesus a Monseigneur Huet, ancien eveque d'Avranches* in *Lettres edifiantes,* XIII (1718): 95–225. It appears unaltered in CC, IV: 157–186 (in folio pages), though Bernard adds a new heading to make the point clear: "Lettre du Pere Bouchet sur la Metempsychose" is printed across the top of every two-page spread. See esp. vol. IV: 157–159 for its diffusion and vol. III: second section, second unpaginated page of the "avertissement" for Bernard's introduction of the subject. For La Hontan on metempsychosis, see *Nouveau voyages,* I: 158.

28. Furly to Desmaizeaux, 20 December 1700, British Library, MSS ADD 4283, ff. 265–266; see also F. M. Van Helmont, *The Paradoxal Discourses . . . Concerning the Macrocosm and Microcosm, of the Greater and Lesser World, and their Union* (London: Robert Kettlewell, 1685), part II, 112–113, 141. See also Stuart Brown, "'Hereticks of the Lanterne': Furly and van Helmont from the Standpoint of Locke," in Sarah Hutton, ed., *Benjamin Furly, 1646–1714: A Quaker Merchant and His Milieu* (Florence: Leo S. Olschki Editore, 2007), 67–86. Margaret C. Jacob, "John Toland and the Newtonian Ideology," *Journal of the Warburg and Courtauld Institutes* 32 (1969): 307–331. The phrase about the crisis comes from Paul Hazard, *La crise de la conscience européenne (1680–1715),* 3 vols. (Paris: Boivin, [1935]).

29. Michel Mourgues, *Plan théologique du pythagorisme, et des autres sects sçavantes de la Grece . . .* (Amsterdam: Jean Frederic Bernard, 1714), 531–540. The work was originally published in Toulouse and respectfully reviewed in *Journal des Sçavans,* vol. XVI (April 17, 1713): 241–250, so its orthodoxy was apparently not in question.

30. The Bruno book appeared in English translation in London in 1713 with no mention of a publisher or translator. For its place in Furly's library see J. A. I. Champion, "'The Fodder of Our Understanding': Benjamin Furly's Library and Intellectual Conversation c. 1680–c. 1725," in Hutton, *Benjamin Furly,* 125–126. For Picart and Bernard's own libraries, see Picart cat. and Bernard cat. Interpreting

Bruno is never easy, and one scholar at least denies that he endorsed metempsycho-
sis, R. G. Mendoza, "Metempsychosis and Monism in Bruno's Nova filosofia," in
Hilary Gatti, ed., *Giordano Bruno: Philosopher of the Renaissance* (Burlington, VT:
Aldershot, 2002), 273–297. See the helpful discussion of the general intellectual atmosphere (though he does not confront the issue of metempsychosis directly) in
Israel, *Enlightenment Contested,* 491–492. We find more convincing the view of Bruno's embrace of metempsychosis found in Karen Silvia De León-Jones, *Giordano
Bruno and the Kabbalah: Prophets, Magicians, and Rabbis* (New Haven: Yale University Press, 1997), esp. pp. 84–87. Gabriel Naudé, *Apologie pour tous les grands hommes
qui ont este accusez de magie* (Paris: Jacques Cotin, 1661), 159–160. Bernard brought
out his edition in 1712. Robert Southey cites the Bouchet letter in "Picart," in Robert Southey and John Wood Warter, *Southey's Common-Place Book,* Fourth Series,
Original Memoranda, Etc. (London: Longman, Brown, Green, and Longmans,
1851), p. 42, under "Ideas and Studies for Literary Composition."

    31. Brown, "'Hereticks of the Lanterne,'" 70–71.

    32. See Donald Durnbaugh, "Work and Hope: The Spirituality of the Radi-
cal Pietist Communitarians," *Church History* 39 (1970): 72–90. See also Brown,
"'Hereticks of the Lanterne.'"

    33. CC, IV: 189 (and not 389, as the printer mistakenly had it).

    34. In one of those delicious twists of history in this period, Louis Ellies Dupin,
the pro-Jansenist critic of the Inquisition, turns up here, as critic of the Jesuits
(not surprising since the Jansenists hated the Jesuits and vice versa). *Defense de la
censure de la faculté de theologie de Paris, du 18 octobre 1700. Contre les propositions des
livres intitulez: Nouveaux Mémoires sur l'état present de la Chine; Histoire de l'Edit
de l'empereur de la Chine; Lettre des Ceremonies de la Chine par Messire Louis Ellies
Du Pin, Docteur en Theologie de la Faculté de Paris, & Professeur Roïal en Philosophie*
(Paris: Chez André Pralard, 1701), p. xxx. Louis Le Comte, *Nouveaux Memoires sur
l'Etat present de la Chine,* 3rd ed., 3 vols. [3rd ed. of vols. 1 and 2, 2nd ed. of vol. 3]
(Paris: Jean Anisson, 1697). On Le Comte, see also David E. Mungello, *Curious
Land: Jesuit Accommodation and the Origins of Sinology* (Honolulu: University of
Hawaii Press, 1989).

    35. CC, IV: 190–191, 102–104, 108–109, 111.

    36. CC, IV: 198.

    37. Engelbert Kaempfer, *The History of Japan, Giving an Account of the Ancient
and Present State and Government; Of Its Temples, Palaces, Castles and Other Buildings; Of Its Metals, Minerals, Trees, Plants, Animals, Birds and Fishes; Of the Chronology and Succession of the Emperors, Ecclesiastical and Secular; Of the Original Descent, Religions, Customs, and Manufactures of the Natives, and of Their Trade and
Commerce with the Dutch and Chinese. Together with a Description of the Kingdom,* 2
vols. (London: The Translator, 1727). Olfert Dapper, *Gedenkwaerdig bedryf der Nederlandsche Oost-Indische maetschappye, op de kuste en in het keizerrijk van Taising of*

Sina: behelzende het tweede gezandschap aen den onder-koning Singlamong en veldheer Taising Lipoui; door Jan van Kampen en Konstantyn Nobel. Vervolgt met een verhael van het voorgevallen des jaers zestien hondert drie en vier en zestig, op de kust van Sina, en ontrent d'eilanden Tayowan, Formosa, Ay en Quemuy, onder 't gezag van Balthasar Bort: en het derde gezandschap aen Konchy, Tartarsche keizer van Sina en Oost-Tartarye: onder beleit van Zijne Ed. Pieter van Hoorn. Beneffens een beschryving van geheel Sina. Verciert doorgaens met verscheide kopere platen (Amsterdam: J. van Meurs, 1670); and Arnoldus Montanus, *Gedenkwaerdige gesantschappen der Oost-Indische maatschappy in 't Vereenigde Nederland, aan de kaisaren van Japan: vervaetende wonderlyke voorvallen op de togt der Nederlandtsche gesanten: beschryving van de dorpen, sterkten, steden, landtschappen, tempels, godsdiensten, dragten, gebouwen, dieren, gewasschen, bergen, fonteinen, vereeuwde en nieuwe oorlogs-daaden der Japanders: verçiert met een groot getal afbeeldsels in Japan geteikent: getrokken uit de geschriften en reis-aentekeningen derzelve gesanten* (Amsterdam: J. Meurs, 1669). For the publication history, see Isabella H. Van Eeghen, "Arnoldus Montanus's Book on Japan," *Quaerendo* 2, no. 4 (1972): 250–272. CC, IV: 299.

38. CC, IV: 277, footnote f. On the study of Buddhism, see Donald S. Lopez, ed., *Curators of the Buddha: The Study of Buddhism under Colonialism* (Chicago: University of Chicago Press, 1995).

39. CC, IV: 194, footnote c.

40. On Le Gobien's views, see Mungello, *Curious Land,* 343–353.

41. CC, IV: 205.

42. CC, IV: 205–206, 285. The parenthetical expression is Bernard's.

43. CC, IV: 226.

44. On the erasure of the comparative impulse in *The Treatise of the Three Impostors,* see Revel, "The Uses of Comparison," in Hunt, Jacob, and Mijnhardt, eds., *Bernard Picart.*

45. Our view of this engraving is shaped by the analysis in Catherine E. Clark, "Chinese Idols and Religious Art: Questioning Difference in *Cérémonies et coutumes,*" and Marcia Reed, "Picart on China: 'Curious' Discourses and Images Taken Principally from the Jesuits," in Hunt, Jacob, and Mijnhardt, eds., *Bernard Picart.* CC, IV: 230–235. "Syncretism" as a precise term comes into French sometime between 1698 and 1762. Bernard uses *réunion* here (which means syncretism). It is possible that Bernard was influenced by the controversial 1670 work of Isaac d'Huisseau, *Réunion du Christianisme,* which proposed the reunification of Christian churches along Latitudinarian lines. Bernard and Picart each owned one of d'Huisseau's books, but not *Réunion.*

46. We are very indebted here to the excellent work of Diana Raesner, who did a paper for our seminar at the Getty Research Institute in 2007 on the depiction of Java in *Religious Ceremonies of the World.* Cf. Ernst van den Boogart, *Civil and Corrupt Asia: Image and Text in the Itinerario and the Icones of Jan Huygen van Lins-*

choten (Chicago: University of Chicago Press, 2003); Michiel van Groesen, "A First Popularisation of Travel Literature: On the Methods and Intentions of the De Bry Travel Collection (1590–1634)," *Dutch Crossing* 25 (2001), 104–108; Romeyn de Hooghe, *Les Indes orientales et occidentales et autres lieux* (Amsterdam: Van Hoeve, 1979 [originally 1710]); CC, IV: 98–134.

47. The Confession of a Savoyard Vicar appears in Book IV of Rousseau's *Emile,* and it was the section of the book that attracted the alarm of authorities. Quotes from *Emile,* Book IV, at http://projects.ilt.columbia.edu/pedagogies/rousseau/, pp. 959 and 992.

10. Rehabilitating Islam

1. As described in Benjamin J. Kaplan, *Divided by Faith: Religious Conflict and the Practice of Toleration in Early Modern Europe* (Cambridge, MA: Harvard University Press, 2007), 304–305.

2. CC, VI: unnumbered "Avertissement."

3. CC, VII: footnotes on 1 and 71. Because his work was published in French, Dutch, and Latin, Reland's name is alternatively rendered as Adrian Reland, Adriaan Reelant, Andriaan Reeland, Hadriani Relandi, or Adrianus Relandus. Adriaan Reelant, *La religion des Mahometans, exposée par leurs propres Docteurs, avec des Eclaircissemens sur les Opinions . . . augmenté d'une Confession de Foi Mahometane Qui n'avoit point encore paru* (The Hague: Isaac Vaillant, 1721). Reland first published the book in Latin in 1705 but it was not illustrated. The 1717 Latin edition (like the first published in Utrecht) included some illustrations, among them the genealogy, but not the scene of Mecca. Since Picart contributed a vignette to the title page of the 1721 French translation, he may also have been involved in producing the unsigned genealogy of Muhammad and the engraving of Mecca, both of which appear in CC, VII, likewise without signature.

4. Frederick Quinn, *The Sum of All Heresies: The Image of Islam in Western Thought* (Oxford: Oxford University Press, 2008), quote p. 43.

5. We have been fortunate enough to consult David Brafman, "Picart, Bernard, Hermes, and Muhammad (not necessarily in that order)," and Kishwar Rizvi, "Persian Pictures: Art, Documentation, and Self-Reflection in Bernard and Picart's Representations of Islam," in Lynn Hunt, Margaret Jacob, and Wijnand Mijnhardt, eds., *Bernard Picart and the First Global Vision of Religion* (Los Angeles: Getty Publications, 2010).

6. Ahmad Gunny, *Images of Islam in Eighteenth-Century Writings* (London: Grey Seal, 1996), quote from Paris police official, p. 137. For the article on the Koran in Voltaire's *Philosophical Dictionary* see http://www.voltaire-integral.com/17/alcoran.htm (accessed June 22, 2008).

7. Rolando Minuti, *Orientalismo e idee di tolleranza nella cultura francese del primo '700* (Florence: Leo S. Olschki Editore, 2006). Of particular value is Minuti's essay on the French translation of Reland (note 3, above), "L'immagine dell'islam nel Settecento. Note sulla traduzione francese del *De religione Mohammedica* di Adriaan Reeland," *Studi settecenteschi* 25–26 (2005–2006): 23–45, esp. 37.

8. See John Toland, *Nazarenus: or, Jewish, gentile, and Mahometan Christianity. Containing the history of the antient Gospel of Barnabas, and the modern Gospel of the Mahometans, attributed to the same apostle: this last Gospel being now first made known among Christians. Also, the original plan of Christianity occasionally explain'd in the history of the Nazarens, whereby diverse controversies about this divine (but highly perverted) institution may be happily terminated. With the relation of an Irish manuscript of the four Gospels, as likewise a summary of the antient Irish Christianity, and the reality of the Keldees (an order of lay-religious) against the two last bishops of Worcester* (London: J. Brown et al., 1718). For a modern edition see Justin A. I. Champion, ed., *Nazarenus/John Toland* (Oxford: Voltaire Foundation, 1999).

9. Nabil Matar, "Islam in Britain, 1689–1750," *Journal of British Studies* 47 (April 2008): 284–300.

10. Humphrey Prideaux, *The True Nature of Imposture fully display'd in the Life of Mahomet. With a Discourse annex'd, for the Vindicating of Christianity from this Charge,* 4th ed. (London: Printed for W. Rogers, 1708), esp. pp. xvi, 141–142.

11. Edward Maunde Thompson, ed., *Letters of Humphrey Prideaux, sometime Dean of Norwich, to John Ellis, sometime Under-Secretary of State, 1674–1722* (London: Printed for the Camden Society, 1875). Alexandra Walsham, *Charitable Hatred: Tolerance and Intolerance in England, 1500–1700* (Manchester: Manchester University Press, 2006), 321.

12. CC, VII: 291.

13. CC, VII: 114–115.

14. CC, VII: 115. Barthélemy d'Herbelot de Molainville, *Bibliothèque orientale, ou Dictionnaire universel contenant généralement tout ce qui regarde la connaissance des peuples de l'Orient* (Paris: Compagnie des libraires, 1697), 296. In his footnote Bernard gives the exact page for this reference.

15. *Four treatises concerning the doctrine, discipline and worship of the Mahometans: viz. I. An abridgment of the Mahometan religion: . . . II. A defence of the Mahometans . . . III. A treatise of Bobovius . . . IV. Reflections on Mahometanism and Socinianism, . . . To which is prefix'd, the life and actions of Mahomet, . . .* (London: Printed by J. Darby for B. Lintott and E. Sanger, 1712), 6. *The Koran, commonly called the Alcoran of Mohammed, translated into English immediately from the original Arabic; with explanatory notes, . . . To which is prefixed a preliminary discourse. By George Sale, gent.* (London: Printed by C. Ackers, for J. Wilcox, 1734), second page of unpaginated dedication. The index of subjects for the seven volumes in CC follows the Islam

section in volume seven and makes these references to imposture on pp. 19, 23, and 73.

16. We were alerted to the importance of the Ferriol collection by Brafman, "Picart, Bernard, Hermes, and Muhammad (not necessarily in that order)." *Recueil de cent estampes representant differentes nations du Levant tirées sur les tableaux peints d'après nature en 1707 et 1708 par les ordres de M. De Ferriol ambassadeur du Roi a la Porte et gravées en 1712 et 1713 par les soins de Mr. Le Hay* (Paris: Le Hay and Duchange, 1714).

17. In 1715 the *Recueil de cent estampes* appears with two new plates (including the dancing dervishes) and a twenty-six-page *Explication des cent estampes qui representent differentes nations du Levant avec de nouvelles estampes de ceremonies turques qui ont aussi leurs explications* (Paris: Jacques Collombat, 1715). The caption to the dancing dervishes is on p. 26. CC, VII: 252. John Trusler, *The Habitable World Described, or the present state of the people in all parts of the globe, from north to south; shewing the situation, extent, climate, . . . including all the new discoveries: . . . With a great variety of maps and copper-plates,. . . ,* 20 vols. (London: Printed for the author, at the Literary-Press, no. 62, Wardour-Street, Soho; and sold by all booksellers, 1788–1797), XIII: 14.

18. On Postel and Picart, see Brafman, "Picart, Bernard, Hermes, and Muhammad (not necessarily in that order)." Bernier's letter, "Le Quiétisme des Indes," published in September 1688, can be found in Henri Basnage de Beauval, *Histoire des ouvrages des savans,* IV (Sept. 1688–Feb. 1689): 47–52 [in vol. 1 (Geneva: Slatkine Reprints, 1969), 447–448]. Bernier is describing the practices of what he calls fakirs or yogis (*joguis* in French). He had come across Sufi doctrines (especially the Mystic Rose Garden of Shabistari) in his travels to India in the 1660s. See François Bernier, *Travels in the Mogul Empire, 1656–1668,* trans. Irving Brock (London: Archibald Constable, 1891), 320. François Bernier, *Abrégé de la philosophie de Mr Gassendi,* 8 vols. (Paris: J. Langlois, 1674).

19. CC, VII: 252. The footnote to the article to Spinoza can be seen at http://artfl.uchicago.edu/cgi-bin/philologic/contextualize.pl?p.3.bayle.3428481. Bernard only cites Jean Chardin's definition of a "Soufy" as "a kind of *dévot* who knows how to spiritualize religion to the level of ecstasy" (VII: 260). On the different heresies among the Shiites, see VII: 275–276.

20. CC, VII: 33.

21. CC, VII: 148.

22. CC, VII: 162. The additions by Durand are highlighted in Minuti, "L'immagine dell'islam nel Settecento," esp. pp. 42–43. See David Durand, *La vie et les sentimens de Lucilio Vanini* (Rotterdam: Aux depens de Gaspar Fritsch, 1717).

23. For these purposes double folio-page engravings have been counted as one and partial-page engravings have been eliminated. Only numbered pages of text

are counted, not blanks. This is one of the few sections in the work that is numbered consecutively.

24. Kishwar Rizvi finds a more pronounced difference between the representation of debauched Turks and more civilized Persians than we do. Kishwar Rizvi, "Persian Pictures."

25. *Histoire générale des cérémonies, moeurs, et coutumes religieuses de tous les peuples du monde. Représentées en 243 Figures dessinées de la main de Bernard Picard* [sic]: *Avec des Explications Historiques, & curieuses; Par M. L'Abbé Banier, de l'Académie Royale des Inscriptions & Belles-Lettres, & par M. L'Abbé le Mascrier*, 7 vols. (Paris: Chez Rollin fils, 1741).

26. Claudine Cohen drew our attention to Le Mascrier's trouble with the inspector of the book trade. See also Robert Darnton, *The Great Cat Massacre and Other Episodes in French Cultural History* (New York: Basic Books, 1984), 158.

27. *Histoire générale des cérémonies*, V: 299, footnote g, and 191, footnote a. Bernard complained bitterly of the changes introduced by Banier and Le Mascrier, including to the Islam volume, in his unpaginated "Avis au lecteur" that precedes volume 8. His subtitle to this volume read "Tome VII, seconde partie: Qui contient plusieurs Dissertations de Mess. les Abbés Banier & Le Mascrier, sur des matiéres qui ont quelque raport aux Cérémonies Religieuses, &c."

28. CC, VII: "Dissertation sur la religion des Sabéens," esp. 5–6. On the link between Sabians and Rosicrucianism and Freemasonry, see Tobias Churton, *The Golden Builders: Alchemists, Rosicrucians and the First Freemasons* (Boston: Weiser Books, 2005). See also R. Swinburne Clymer, *Rosicrucians and Their Teachings* (1923; repr., Whitefish, MT: Kessinger Publishing, 2003).

11. Dissent, Deism, and Atheism

1. CC, VI: 334, 339.

2. CC, VI: 4.

3. CC, VI: 233. *Reflexions morales, satiriques et comiques . . .* 3rd edition, Amsterdam, 1716, where the key identifies the Anabaptists as references on p. 218, line 16.

4. CC, VI: Avertissement, unpaginated. On the repudiation of enthusiasm in general see Michael Heyd, *Be Sober and Reasonable: The Critique of Enthusiasm in the Seventeenth and Early Eighteenth Centuries* (Leiden: E. J. Brill, 1995).

5. CC, VI: 348. Richard L. Greaves, "'That Kind of People': Late Stuart Radicals and Their Manifestoes, a Functional Approach," in Glenn Burgess and Matthew Festenstein, eds., *English Radicalism, 1550–1850* (Cambridge: Cambridge University Press, 2007), 87–114; Michiel Wielema, *The March of the Libertines: Spinozists and the Dutch Reformed Church (1660–1750)* (Hilversum: Verloren, 2004), ch. 6 on Pontiaan van Hattem.

6. Nine of the nineteen plates (counting double plates as two) were drawn by Louis Fabricius Dubourg and five were both drawn and engraved by Jan van Schley.

7. For one such diary see Bibliotheca Philosophica Hermetica, Amsterdam, MS 36 dated 1733–1734, 3 vols., "Discours du frére Noel . . . de la soeur Marianne."

8. CC, VI: 156; *Reflexions morales, satiriques et comiques . . .* 3rd edition, Amsterdam, 1716, where the key identifies the leader of the Camisards, p. 67. In the edition of 1733 the phrase appears on p. 94.

9. CC, VI: 175; Margaret C. Jacob, "Newton and the French Prophets: New Evidence," *History of Science* 16 (1978), 134–142; Clarke Garrett, *Spirit Possession and Popular Religion: From the Camisards to the Shakers* (Baltimore, MD: Johns Hopkins University Press, 1987).

10. Anne Dunan-Page, ed., *The Religious Culture of the Huguenots, 1660–1750* (Aldershot, UK: Ashgate, 2006), 163–172. British Library, MSS. ADD 4281, ff. 74–79.

11. CC, VI: 285.

12. CC, VI: 165.

13. CC, VI: 251, note b.

14. On Rousset and freemasonry see Margaret C. Jacob, *The Radical Enlightenment: Pantheists, Freemasons and Republicans,* 2nd rev. ed. (Lafayette, LA: Cornerstone Books, 2006). And on Cappadoce see Jacob, *Strangers Nowhere in the World: The Origins of Early Modern Cosmopolitanism* (Philadelphia: University of Pennsylvania Press, 2006), 105.

15. We have benefited greatly from Jesse Sadler, "The Collegiants, a Small Presence in the Republic, a Large Metaphor for the Book," in Lynn Hunt, Margaret Jacob, and Wijnand Mijnhardt, eds., *Bernard Picart and the First Global Vision of Religion* (Los Angeles: Getty Publications, 2010). For the number of Collegiants see M. Quak, "De Collegianten te Amsterdam in de periode 1722–1775" (master's thesis, University of Utrecht, 1983), 35–42.

16. CC, VI: 310.

17. CC, VI: 310–311, 320-321.

18. CC, VI: 347 (italics in text).

19. CC, VI: 347–348. John Toland, "Adeisidaemon, 1709," a manuscript translation into English, pp. 4–5, from the transcription kindly supplied by Justin Champion; the original is in The John Rylands Library, Manchester, UK.

20. CC, VI: 348.

21. *The Ceremonies and Religious Customs of the Various Nations of the Known World* (London: Printed by William Jackson, for Claude Du Bosc, engraver at the Golden Head in Charles-Street, Covent Garden, 1733–1739), VI: 217 and 228 (the italics are ours); Jacques Carré, "Hogarth et la Superstition," in Bernard Dompnier, ed., *La Superstition à l'Âge des lumières* (Paris: Champion, 1998), 153–168.

22. We are indebted to the discussion of religion found in Jan N. Bremmer, "'Religion,' 'Ritual' and the Opposition 'Sacred vs. Profane,' Notes towards a Terminological Genealogy," in F. Graf, ed., *Ansichten griechischer Rituale: Festschrift für Walter Burkert* (Stuttgart: Teubner, 1998), 9–32, and citing J. Samuel Preus, *Explaining Religion: Criticism from Bodin to Freud* (New Haven: Yale University Press, 1987), 23–39, on Herbert of Cherbury.

23. CC, VI: 302. In CC, VI: 334–339, Bernard offers a detailed description of the beliefs of "Pontien de Hattem" and his follower Woutelar [Hendrik Woutelaars], whose sect had been condemned by the States, and he follows this with a carefully drawn life of Spinoza quoting directly from the Lucas volume; see our Introduction. On Spinoza as a fatalist see J. C. Morrison, "Christian Wolff's Criticisms of Spinoza," *Journal of the History of Philosophy* 31 (July 1993), 405–420. On the reputation of Hobbes and Spinoza see Noel Malcolm, *Aspects of Hobbes* (Oxford: Clarendon Press, 2002), 457–497. For a present-day attempt to reconstruct Hobbes's materialism see Samantha Frost, *Lessons from a Materialist Thinker: Hobbesian Reflections on Ethics and Politics* (Stanford, CA: Stanford University Press, 2008).

24. CC, VI: 339.

25. CC, VI: 347.

26. CC, VI: 339. W. Molesworth, ed., *The English Works of Thomas Hobbes of Malmesbury* (London: J. Bohn, 1839–1845), vol. 7: 350, cited in Malcolm, *Aspects of Hobbes*, 40.

27. The *locus classicus* of that atheist interpretation remains the work of the great Harry Wolfson, *The Philosophy of Spinoza: Unfolding the Latent Processes of His Reasoning* (Cambridge, MA: Harvard University Press, 1934), 2 vols. And see his *Spinoza and Religion* (New York: New School for Social Research, c. 1950). On Spinoza and the radical Enlightenment see Jonathan I. Israel, *Radical Enlightenment: Philosophy and the Making of Modernity, 1650–1750* (Oxford: Oxford University Press, 2002).

28. For a careful and nuanced reading of Spinoza on God see Steven B. Smith, *Spinoza's Book of Life: Freedom and Redemption in the "Ethics"* (New Haven: Yale University Press, 2003), 39–43, italics added by us. Richard Mason would agree with Smith's reading of Spinoza; see his book *The God of Spinoza: A Philosophical Study* (Cambridge: Cambridge University Press, 1997), 25–32. Benedict de Spinoza, *Ethics*, ed. and trans. Edwin Curley (London: Penguin, 1996), 1. For Rousset's letter see Leiden University, Marchand MS 2, f. 47, 28 February (no date but almost certainly 1752), "Savey vous que cela auroit été grand train vers le Panthéisme si ces Thèses eussent passé et en meme temps les 10 énormes vol. de L'Encyclopèdie." For Jewish sources and the rereading of Spinoza see Yitzhak Y. Melamed, "Salomon Maimon and the Rise of Spinozism in German Idealism," *Journal of the History of Philosophy* 42 (2004), 67–96. Most current scholarship has abandoned the simple notion that Spinoza was an atheist; see Kenneth Seeskin, "Recent Work on Spinoza," *Jewish*

Quarterly Review 98 (Fall 2008), 553–558. For Coleridge on Wordsworth see Duncan Wu, *William Hazlitt: The First Modern Man* (Oxford: Oxford University Press, 2008), 4, citing a letter from Coleridge to John Thelwall, 13 May 1796.

29. CC, IV: 102; CC, III: 13, 184.

30. Leiden University, Marchand MS 2, 24 May (no year, but from the late 1740s), f. 29.

31. CC, VI: 334, 345 (esp. note b). Wielema, *The March of the Libertines*, pp. 163–204.

32. CC, VI: 333. A similar treatment of the freethinking of Collins can be found in James Dybikowski, "Anthony Collins' Defense of Free-Thinking," in G. Paganini et al., eds., *Scepticism, Clandestinity and Free-Thinking* (Paris: Champion, 2002), 298–325.

33. CC, VI: 333.

34. CC, VI: 335, note a, 337–338.

35. CC, VI: 339–346.

36. CC, VI: 302.

37. CC, VI: 303, 332, 316.

Conclusion

1. For a complete list of all editions and translations see Appendix B. Bernard's letter is in *Nouvelle bibliothèque ou histoire littéraire* 3 (February 17, 1741): 282. In particular, volume three, devoted to the West Indies, was improved, as Bernard testified himself: "Cette nouvelle edition est corrigée en beaucoup d'endroits. Je ne me suis pas contenté de revoir les dissertations qui m'appartiennent de droit: j'y ai encore ajouté quelques nouvelles remarques. J. F. B." For the changes in the volume on the West Indies see CC, vol. 3, new edition (Amsterdam, 1735), Avertissement. For the sales catalogue of Bernard's shop after his death: Bernard Cat., p. 33.

2. For the number of copies in the Rollin edition see *Histoire des religions et des moeurs de tous les peuples du monde*, 6 vols. (Paris: A. Belin, 1816–1819), I, Avertissement du Libraire.

3. Hermann Spiess-Schaad, *David Herrliberger: Zürcher Kupferstecher und Verleger (1677–1777)* (Zürich: Rohr Verlag, 1983), 52–57, 127–136. For the number of copies sold, see Paola von Wyss Giacosa, "Ethnographische Bildquellen der frühen Aufklärung: Bernard Picarts Illustrationen in den *Cérémonies et coutumes religieuses de tous les peoples du monde*," in Philip Kaenel and Rolf Reichardt, eds., *Interkulturelle Kommunikation in der europäische Druckgrafik im 18. und 19. Jahrhundert* (Hildesheim: Georg Olms Verlag, 2007), 96.

4. Even on the secondhand market complete sets continued to fetch high prices throughout the century. In 1816 complete sets still sold for 1,200–1,500 French francs, as testified by the Paris publisher Antoine Belin in 1816 (see note 1 above).

5. Joseph Zizek, "'Plume de fer': Louis-Marie Prudhomme writes the French Revolution," *French Historical Studies* 26 (2003): 625–626.

6. See letter of Jan Jacobus de Geer to his son, Charles, in Thomas Anfält, "Buying Books by Mail Order: A Swedish Customer and Dutch Booksellers in the Eighteenth Century," in L. Hellinga, ed., *The Bookshop of the World: The Role of the Low Countries in the Book-Trade, 1473–1941* ('t Goy-Houten: Hes and De Graaf Publishers, 2001), 263–276, esp. 265; Bentinck, Letter 27 November 1762, in: *Archives du correspondance inédite de la Maison Orange-Nassau*, 4ᵉ serie, Th. Bussemaker, ed., deel IV (1759–1768) (Leiden: A. W. Sijthof, 1914), 471–472; Wijnand W. Mijnhardt, "Verlichtingsidealen," *De Gids* (2007), 818–820.

7. Adrian Johns, *The Nature of the Book: Print and Knowledge in the Making* (Chicago: University of Chicago Press, 1998), 6–28.

8. For the criticism of Banier and Le Mascrier see CC, 8 (labeled vol. VII, 2nd part), "Avis au Lecteur." Of course Bernard was a successful pirate and a plagiarist himself as well. His *Etat de l'homme dans le péché original* never made clear whether it was simply a translation or a liberal adaptation of Beverland's original text. For the Dupin case see Jonathan M. Elukin, "Jacques Basnage and the History of the Jews: Anti-Catholic Polemic and Historical Allegory in the Republic of Letters," *Journal of the History of Ideas* 53 (1992): 603–631.

9. See, for example, P. Dom Prosper Gueranger, *Institutions liturgiques*, 2nd ed., 4 vols. (Brussels: Société Générale de la Librairie Catholique, 1878), II, 484; for Le Mascrier's subversive activities see Alain Mothu, "L'édition de 1751 des Opinions Anciens," *La Lettre clandestine* 3 (1994): 357. Bernard published Mirabaud's treatise in 1740 in his *Dissertations mêlées, sur divers sujets importans et curieux*, 2 vols. (Amsterdam: Jean Frederic Bernard, 1740), I: 3–45.

10. Poncelin on Newton, see *Superstitions de tous les peuples du monde, ou tableau philosophique des erreurs et foiblesses dans lesquelles les Superstitions tant anciennes que modernes ont précipité les hommes de la plupart des nations de la terre* (Amsterdam [Paris]: Laporte, 1784), IV: 5. On Muslim culture see III: 97–128. [Jean-Charles Poncelin de la Roche Tilhac], *Superstitions orientales, ou tableau des erreurs et des superstitions des principaux peuples de l'Orient, de leurs moeurs, de leurs usages et de leur législation* (Paris: Le Roy, 1785).

11. Exactly the same work was published under the name of Robert Huish, a British hack famous for his work on bee cultivation. See W. C. Mackenzie, *Colonel Colin Mackenzie: First Surveyor-General of India* (Edinburgh: W. and R. Chambers, 1952). For Mackenzie's conception of history: Rama Mantena, "The Question of History in Pre-Colonial India," *History and Theory* 46 (2007): 396–413.

12. Charles A. Goodrich, *Religious Ceremonies and Customs, or The Forms of Worship Practiced by the Several Nations of the Known World, From the Earliest Records to the Present Time, on the Basis of the Celebrated and Splendid Work of Bernard Picart* (Hartford: Hutchinson and Dwier, 1834), 5. Possibly the last work in which Picart's

engravings were used is Frank Dobbins, *Error's Chains: How Forged and Broken—complete, graphic, and comparative history of the many strange beliefs, superstitious practices, domestic peculiarities, sacred writings, systems of philosophy, legends and traditions, customs and habits of mankind throughout the world, ancient and modern* (New York: Standard Publishing House, 1883). In the French-speaking world a similar undermining process was under way. In 1821 Poncelin produced the last version of sorts in French of *Religious Ceremonies of the World* in small octavo, capitalizing on its fame. The original text had been completely replaced, and it contained only fifty engravings: *Cérémonies religieuses de tous les peuples du monde* (Paris: E. Babeuf, 1821). The *Histoire pittoresque des religions, doctrines, cérémonies et coutumes religieuses de tous les peuples du monde anciens et modernes,* by François Clavel, 2 vols. (Paris: Pagnerre, 1844), completed the transformation.

13. Arnold van Gennep, "Nouvelles recherches sur l'histoire en France de la méthode ethnographique: Claude Guichard, Richard Simon, Claude Fleury," *Revue d'histoire des religions* 82 (1920): 139–162; Margaret T. Hodgen, *Early Anthropology in the Sixteenth and Seventeenth Centuries* (Philadelphia: University of Pennsylvania Press, 1964); Louis Henry Jordan, *Comparative Religion: Its Genesis and Growth* (1905; repr., Atlanta: Scholars Press, 1986), 509; Eric J. Sharpe, *Comparative Religion: A History* (1975; repr., London: Duckworth, 2006); David Pailin, *Attitudes to Other Religions: Comparative Religion in Seventeenth- and Eighteenth-Century England* (Manchester: Manchester University Press, 1984).

Appendix B

1. In the first volume Bernard Picart's name was wrongly spelled as Picard, which has resulted in many misspellings in the various subsequent editions.

2. In libraries the French editions of *Religious Ceremonies of the World* can have 7, 9, 11, and even 12 volumes. Typically sets are composed of the 7 volumes of the original Amsterdam edition, the 2 volumes of the *Suppléments* published by Bernard in 1743, the 2 volumes of the *Superstitions anciennes et modernes* that Jean Frederic Bernard published between 1733 and 1736, and the volume *Superstitions de tous les peuples du monde* that Poncelin de la Roche Tilhac published separately in 1784. The 12-volume edition published by Prudhomme consisted of the 11 volumes first mentioned plus an extra volume on later eighteenth-century religions.

3. The many reprints of the English knockoffs have been omitted.

Acknowledgments

W E WOULD never have been able to write this book in the way we have without the time and support granted us as Getty Scholars in 2006–2007. We gained much more than the usual time away from university obligations or even the exceptional opportunity of collaborating in person rather than by email across the Atlantic. Charles Salas and Gail Feigenbaum of the Getty Research Institute (GRI) encouraged us to set up the year-long seminar in which scholars from around the world came and presented papers or spoke to us in video conferences about "Picart" (the shorthand used for *Cérémonies et coutumes religieuses de tous les peuples du monde* since its publication). David Brafman, curator of Rare Books at the GRI, provided invaluable advice and assistance at every step along the way, and it is with heartfelt gratitude that we dedicate this book to him. Marcia Reed, the head of Collection Development, and Susan Allen, head of the GRI library, shared their knowledge of rare books on many occasions. With the encouragement of Thomas Crow, director of the GRI, Tom Moritz and his team in digital projects at the GRI prepared searchable PDF versions of the French original of Picart in time for us to use them for our research. They also prepared files of the English and Dutch translations owned by UCLA and the German translation in the collection of the Huntington Library. The Utrecht University Library provided vital financial assistance to the project. It is our hope that these files will be available to the public at the UCLA digital library as soon as they are made fully searchable. We are very grateful to Zoe Borovsky at Academic Technology Services of UCLA for helping us organize this aspect of the project.

From January to March 2007 Margaret Jacob and Lynn Hunt taught the Getty Consortium seminar for graduate students on Picart, or rather they presided over the seminar, which had ongoing input from Wijnand Mijnhardt, David Brafman, and Ann Adams of the University of California, Santa Barbara. Four of the students in the seminar then presented their papers, as did David, Ann, and Wijnand, in the conference on Picart held in December 2007. The conference was organized by Wijnand Mijnhardt and Margaret Jacob under the auspices generously provided by the Center for Seventeenth- and Eighteenth-Century Studies at UCLA and the GRI. We three prepared an edited volume of those papers that has been published by Getty Publications. Each of those papers and the others offered during the year-long seminar, including the student portion, provided invaluable perspectives from which we have benefited immeasurably. The collaboration among the three of us rests on a much broader network of collaboration, both personal and institutional, for which we are deeply grateful.

Finally, we express our deep appreciation to the two readers for Harvard University Press, who helped us to clarify and correct our arguments in many places, and to Kathleen McDermott and Christine Thorsteinsson for shepherding our book through the process of publication.

Index

Index

Religious Ceremonies of the World, significance of: for comparative religion, 1–2, 19, 308–310; for concept of religion, 1–2, 286–288; as overlooked, 3–4, 112, 308–309, 319n5; for religious toleration, 7–8, 17–18, 20–21

Religious Ceremonies of the World, sources for, 7, 10–11, 147–150, 157, 160, 176–177, 179–182, 241, 248–249, 254, 269, 278; travel literature, 5, 38–39, 109–110, 128, 141, 142, 143, 149–150, 153, 215, 221, 227, 236–237, 243, 247, 263–264, 320n9; Modena, 128, 179–182; Simon, 128, 180–181; Roman Pontifical, 142, 198, 199, 202, 206, 345n10, 351n4; Histoire des conclaves depuis Clement V, 143, 144; De Bry, 143, 146, 149–150, 153, 155, 156, 225; Chatelain's Atlas historique, 147, 149; Decker, 149–150, 153; Van Meurs, 150, 344n8; Basnage, 183; Dupin, 196, 207–208, 209, 352n16; Mastrozzi, 204, 352n11; La Hontan, 222, 223, 224, 354nn17,18; Bouchet, 227, 229–231, 232, 233, 234, 355nn25,27; Tavernier's Six Voyages, 228, 231, 355n26; Le Comte, 235–236, 237, 239, 356n34; Gagnier, 248, 249, 254, 261; Sale, 248, 254, 256, 261, 263; Boulainvilliers, 248, 261; Reland, 249, 254, 256, 261–264, 266, 268, 358n3; d'Herbelot's Bibliothèque orientale, 256, 261, 263–264; Vanmour, 257, 258, 259; "Rituel d'Alet," 352n10

Religious psychology: role of fear in, 21, 41, 42, 123, 214, 241, 245, 268, 272, 285–286; role of sexuality in, 39, 121–122, 123–124, 272

Religious toleration: in Dutch Republic, 5, 11, 14–15, 25–26, 30, 31, 33, 44, 67, 69–70, 71–72, 75–78, 79–80, 81–84, 124, 130–131, 132, 175, 177, 193, 263, 269, 282; and Bernard, 7–8, 10, 11, 15–18, 20–21, 124, 126, 130–134, 195, 213, 248, 255, 262–263, 266, 291, 302, 305; and Picart, 7–8, 10–11, 15, 20–21, 124, 126, 129–130, 130–132, 133–134, 291, 302; offered by Muslim rulers, 248, 252, 268; as natural principle, 255; Reland on, 262–264

Rembrandt van Rijn, 177, 179

Revelation 21:8, 211

Révolutions de Paris, 300

Rey, Marc Michel, 110–111, 133, 341n18

Ribaut, Jean, 143

"Rituel d'Alet," 352n10

Rizvi, Kishwar, 321n15, 358n5, 361n24

Robertson, William, 307

Roger, Abraham (Rogerius), 227

Rollin, Charles: De la manière d'étudier les belles lettres, 99

Rollin (publisher), 297, 305

Roman Inquisition, 19, 195, 233, 255

Roman Pontifical, 7, 142, 198, 199, 202, 206, 345n10, 351n4

Roman Processional, 142

Romanticism, 290

Rosa, Salvator, 336n22

Rosicrucians, 268, 276, 279, 287

Ross, Alexander: Pansebeia, 125, 126, 307

Rouille du Coudray, Dionysius, 329n13

Rousseau, Jean-Jacques, 3, 87, 110; Emile, 133, 245, 246, 253, 343n35, 358n47; on religion, 133, 245, 246, 343n35; on noble savage, 226; on Muhammad, 253; The Social Contract, 253

Rousset de Missy, Jean, 42, 43, 44, 82, 281, 282, 290, 291

Rubens, Peter Paul, 52, 54, 61–62, 63, 163

Russian Orthodox Church, 64, 200–201

Ruts, Nicolaas, 90, 93, 334n4

Rycaut, Paul, 263

Sabians, 268

Sadler, Jesse, 362n15

Sale, George, 248, 254, 256, 261, 263

Sandwich Islands, 307

Schudt, Johann Jacob, 350n23; Jüdische Merckwürdigkeiten, 178

Schuitpraatje, 87

Scientific Revolution vs. Enlightenment, 3–4, 128

Sexuality, 39, 121–122, 123–124, 264, 272

Sgard, Jean, 333n1, 336n22, 337nn26,28

S'Gravesande, Willem Jacob, 4

Shaftesbury, Anthony Ashley Cooper, 3rd earl of, 28, 36, 86

Shakers, 276

Sharpe, Eric: Comparative Religion, 308

Sheets, Elizabeth M., 333n1

Short, William Michael, 322n23

Siam, 232, 279

Sidney, Algernon, 28

Simon, Richard, 122, 266, 288; Critical History of the Old Testament, 31–32, 33, 75, 82, 180; commentary on Ceremonies and Customs Observed Today among the Jews, 128–129, 180–181

Smith, Adam, 3, 307

Socinians, 76, 254, 270–271, 272, 278, 282, 284, 287, 293, 294

Sodomites, 281

Solomon, 268

Sorbonne, 235

South American Indians, 216, 221